Eisenhower Center Studies on War and Peace

Architects of Intervention

Architects of Intervention

The United States,

the Third World,

and the Cold War,

1946-1962

Zachary Karabell

Louisiana State University Press *Baton Rouge*

Designer: Glynnis Weston
Typeface: Garamond Book with Modula display
Typesetter: Crane Composition, Inc.
Printer and binder: Edwards Brothers, Inc.

Library of Congress Cataloging-in-Publication Data:
Karabell, Zachary.
    Architects of intervention : the United States, the Third World,
and the Cold War, 1946-1962 / Zachary Karabell.
        p.   cm. — (Eisenhower Center studies on war and peace)
    Includes bibliographical references and index.
    ISBN 0-8071-2307-2 (cloth : alk. paper). — ISBN 0-8071-2341-2
(pbk. : alk. paper)
    1. United States—Foreign relations—1945-1953.   2. United States—
Foreign relations—1953-1961.   3. United States—Foreign relations—
Developing countries.   4. Developing countries—Foreign relations—
United States.   5. Cold War.   I. Title.   II. Series.
E813.K37   1999
327.73—dc21
                                                                        98-41366
                                                                        CIP

The paper in this book meets the guidelines for permanence and durability of the Committee
on Production Guidelines for Book Longevity of the Council on Library Resources. ♾

Contents

Acknowledgments

A large number of people contributed to this project, and a number of institutions provided me with financial support. I would like to thank the MacArthur Foundation, the Olin Institute of Strategic Studies at Harvard, the Eisenhower/Pappas Foundation, the Truman Library Institute, the Charles Warren Center, the Harvard History Department, the Center for Middle East Studies, the Center for International Affairs, and the John F. Kennedy Library for offering stipends, research money, and office space at various points during the research and writing.

The following people read all or parts of the work and shared their opinions with me. I thank them for making me think hard: Amy and Jiro Adachi, H. W. Brands, Douglas Brinkley, John Coatsworth, Tiffany Devitt, Jorge Dominguez, John Lewis Gaddis, Samuel Huntington, Martin Lee, Eric Olson, Roger Owen, Neal Rosendorf, John Rosenberg, Steve Schwartzberg, John Womack, and of course, Timothy Naftali. I also benefited from presenting the introduction at a conference hosted by the Carnegie Council on Ethics and International Affairs and its president Joel Rosenthal. Without the valuable insights and proddings of my advisers, Ernest May and Akira Iriye, this work could not have been completed. And finally, I thank Colby Devitt, who read and reread these pages and without whom they might never have been written.

Architects of Intervention

Introduction

O n the morning of September 16, 1973, the Shah of Iran, as he did each day, met with his oldest friend, court minister Asadollah Alam. The Shah was formal, as he always was, even though it was Sunday. He spoke softly, as he always did, and accepted the congratulations that Alam offered him. On this date thirty-three years earlier, the Shah had ascended to the Peacock Throne.

The Shah was respected throughout the world. In October of 1971, the rich and powerful assembled on his invitation at the ruins of ancient Persepolis. American vice president Spiro Agnew was there, as were the emperor of Japan, Haile Selassie, and the heads of state (or their representatives) of sixty-six other countries. The Shah was celebrating two and a half millennia of Iranian kings, stretching back to the Achaemenids and Cyrus the Great. Hundreds of millions of dollars were spent to provide the guests with hotels, tents, French food and wine, and assorted amenities. In front of the assembled dignitaries, the Shah strode to the tomb of his putative ancestors and proclaimed, "Sleep easily Cyrus, for we are awake."[1]

Two years later, on that September morning in 1973 when he met with Alam, the Shah enjoyed the knowledge that he was one of the pillars of American policy in the Middle East. He had the assurance of the Nixon administration that he could buy any non-nuclear weapons that he pleased, and his treasury was flush with revenue from oil. Yet, unlike Cyrus, the Shah did not sleep easily. Insecure and closeted, he feared always that his days were numbered and that conspiracies surrounded him. And on the thirty-third anniversary of his rule, he was obsessed with one man who had been dead for nearly six years: Mohammed Mosaddeq. "The worst years of my reign, indeed of my entire life, came when Mosaddeq was Prime Minister. The bastard was out for blood and every morning I awoke with the sensation that today might be my last on the throne."[2]

In 1973, it had been twenty years since Dr. Mohammed Mosaddeq had wielded any power in Iran, nearly twenty years to the day since the Shah conspired with the Eisenhower administration and the Central Intelligence Agency to remove his nemesis from power. Yet, though the Shah had won the contest with Mosaddeq, the old man still haunted him, even from the grave.

---

1. Asadollah Alam, *The Shah and I* (New York, 1991), 185; Roy Mottahedeh, *The Mantle of the Prophet* (New York, 1985), 326–27.

2. Quoted in Alam, *Shah and I,* 318.

If anything, the Shah's venom increased with time. In 1954, little more than a year after Mosaddeq's fall, the Shah visited the United States and spoke to the Washington press corps:

> In August of last year, Iran stood on the brink of catastrophe, but at the last minute of the eleventh hour, by the grace of God and the patriotic exertion of her people and their loyalty to the crown, Iran was delivered from a disastrous fate. And no wonder. Those who had hatched this diabolic plot paid no heed to the fact that between my people and me there is an unwritten alliance and unity of heart. Since bygone days, Iran has been ruled by kings. The glorious pages of her history for the last twenty-five centuries are resplendent with the heroic deeds of kings and the loyalty and love of their subjects.[3]

After Mosaddeq had been removed from power, he became an almost mythic figure for the Shah. On one side there was the abyss, represented by Mosaddeq and the forces of mob; on the other, order and progress represented by himself, the Shah an-Shah, King of Kings. The events of 1953 became the Shah's trial by fire, and he believed that the Mosaddeq interregnum had transformed him from a powerless ruler into a king. The removal of Mosaddeq enabled the Shah to rule Iran with an iron fist enclosed in a velvet glove and led to the stifling of anything remotely resembling democracy.

The Shah was a different man after 1953. Until then, he was judged by almost everyone as weak and indecisive. Some attributed these character traits to the dominating influence of his father, Reza Pahlavi Shah. An imposing figure with fierce eyes, the first Pahlavi Shah had cowed his eldest son.[4] After Reza Shah was forced to abdicate by the Allies during World War II, Mohammed Reza became ruler of Iran in name only. He was overshadowed by the ministers of Britain and the Soviet Union and by the Iranian Majlis, the Parliament. While he tried to fit into his father's autocratic role, he lacked both prestige and support.

When the war ended, the Shah's hold on the country was tentative at best. Over the next five years, he continued his efforts to consolidate his rule, first

---

3. Speech of December 14, 1954, in Record Group [hereinafter cited as RG] 84, 360.1 (Shah) in Lot 60 F 87, Box 5, Washington National Records Center, Suitland, Md. [hereinafter cited as WNRC].

4. See Ashraf Pahlavi, *Faces in a Mirror: Memoirs from Exile* (Englewood Cliffs, N.J., 1980), 11–27, for a vivid description of her father's influence on her brother. See also Marvin Zonis, *Majestic Failure* (Chicago, 1991), passim, for the psychological effect which Reza Shah had on his son.

over his own court, then over the army, and then slowly over the Majlis. The court and the army responded favorably to the Shah's efforts, but the Majlis was another matter. Mosaddeq's faction, the National Front, was a major obstacle.

In 1951, a long-simmering crisis between Iran and the Anglo-Iranian Oil Company (AIOC) came to a head. Mosaddeq led the drive for nationalization of the company and became prime minister. Charismatic and popular, Mosaddeq eclipsed the Shah, and the Shah resented it. To the monarchy, Mosaddeq was simultaneously a democratic and a demagogic threat. His radical reform programs jeopardized the hold of the traditional ruling groups, and his charismatic appeal to the Iranian people often allowed him to circumvent the opposition of both the Shah and the Majlis.

Mosaddeq's popularity placed the Shah in a precarious position. Without explicit guarantees from the British or the Americans, he could not risk dismissing the premier and alienating the people.[5] Mosaddeq became more stridently anti-British and more opposed to the monarchy with each passing day. Concerned for the future of his throne, the Shah began searching for ways to engineer Mosaddeq's removal. He asked his court minister Husayn Ala to see if the Americans would back the throne should Mosaddeq be dismissed.[6]

Until 1951, Britain was *the* great power in Iran. The United States had ceded Iran to the informal British sphere of influence, and the Truman administration was content to let Britain "call the shots" in Iran.[7] During the oil crisis, however, that changed. With the prospect of economic collapse and political upheaval in 1951, Iran suddenly seemed vulnerable. Slowly, the Truman administration became more involved. As British influence waned in the face of Mosaddeq's antagonism, the U.S. government stepped in to fill the gap. The Shah not only welcomed this development, he sought it.

The Shah was the invisible hand of August 1953, and he maintained until his death that the coup succeeded because "the people called" for him to return.[8] Though he overstated his role during August 1953, others have undoubt-

---

5. The Shah made these remarks in a bitter exchange with Ambassador Henderson. See Henderson to Department of State, September 30, 1951, Top Secret, *Foreign Relations of the United States* [hereinafter cited as *FRUS*], *1952-1954, Vol. X*, 185-88.

6. Tehran 4606 (Henderson to State), May 28, 1952, Secret, National Archives [hereinafter cited as NA] 788.00/5-2852; *FRUS, 1952-1954, Vol. X*, 384-86.

7. Bruce Kuniholm, *The Origins of the Cold War in the Near East* (Princeton, 1980), chap. 4; James Goode, *The United States and Iran, 1946-51* (London, 1989); Melvyn Leffler, *A Preponderance of Power* (Stanford, Calif., 1992); William Roger Louis, *The British Empire in the Middle East, 1945-1951* (Oxford, U.K., 1984).

8. Alam, *Shah and I*, 177; Mohammad Reza Pahlavi, *Answer to History* (Briarcliff Manor, N.Y., 1980), 90-91.

edly understated it.[9] While Mosaddeq was certainly at the forefront of the confrontation between Iran and AIOC, one thing is clear: without the active efforts of the Shah himself to remove Mosaddeq, Mosaddeq could not have been removed. The Central Intelligence Agency, the British government, the Iranian mob, the ayatollahs, none of these alone or in conjunction could have toppled Mosaddeq's government if the Shah had not wanted it. The Shah of Iran was not a pawn in his country's history. He shaped it, and the U.S. government helped him.

But the Shah could never escape the knowledge that without the aid of the United States, he might never have seen his thirty-third anniversary. He aspired to match the accomplishments of Cyrus; he intended to exceed the achievements of his father. He could do neither without help. The Shah was not the creation of the United States, but he required the assistance of successive U.S. administrations in order to create himself. He wished to be the sole architect of his destiny and that of his country; to his last moments, he bitterly resented the degree to which he needed the United States to realize his blueprint for modern Iran. He made a deal in 1953, and he kept making the same deal until the heirs of Dr. Mosaddeq overthrew him on a cold January day in 1979.

■

In the writing of cold-war history, the third world is often the forgotten player. As traditionally understood, the cold war is the story of the struggle between the United States and the Soviet Union. Possessing overwhelming power, these two countries embarked on an international struggle that revolved first around Europe and in time expanded to encompass much of the world.

This version of the cold war is what literary critics might call "the dominant narrative." One of the effects of this dominant narrative is that the writing of cold-war history has tended to suffer from a neglect of the periphery. The view from Washington pervades cold-war history, and the views from Moscow or the capitals of Western Europe have also received extensive attention.

The traditional interpretation has not gone unchallenged. For nearly five

9. For examples of authors who place primary responsibility for the coup on the Americans, see Kermit Roosevelt, *Countercoup: The Struggle for Control of Iran* (New York, 1979); Mark Gasiorowski, "The 1953 Coup D'Etat in Iran," *International Journal of Middle East Studies*, XXIX (August 1987), 261-86; and Donald Wilber, *Adventures in the Middle East* (Princeton, 1986), 188-91. (Wilber was part of the CIA team which executed Operation Ajax.) See also John Prados, *Presidents' Secret Wars: CIA and Pentagon Covert Operations since World War II* (New York, 1986), 91-98; William Corson, *The Armies of Ignorance: The Rise of the American Intelligence Empire* (New York, 1977), 351-53; and Nikki Keddie, *Roots of Revolution: An Interpretive History of Modern Iran* (New Haven, 1981), 138-41.

decades, Europeans have written their own versions of cold-war history, which not surprisingly stress the role of Europeans in determining the split between Eastern and Western Europe and in drawing the United States into European politics.[10] Furthermore, in the past two decades, a large number of studies have examined the cold war in the periphery, and many of these have demonstrated how local third-world actors played the superpowers off one another and attempted to carve out spheres of independent action in the midst of the nearly irresistible efforts of one power or the other to align them on one side or the other.[11]

And yet, despite multiple efforts, the story continues to be told most often from the vantage point of the metropolitan center and not often enough from the perspective of the periphery.[12] In American writings, the vantage point is usually Washington. Washington's importance in the cold war notwithstanding, an entire dimension of the cold war has been left in limbo, floating as a minor chord through traditional histories and commentaries.

Intervention was one of the most dramatic forms of interaction between the third world and the United States during the cold war. In retelling the story of several of the most significant of these early cold-war interventions, this work argues that both American and third-world actors designed an "architecture" for U.S. policy in their respective countries. The interventions discussed in these pages took the forms they did not just because of decisions made by U.S.

10. See, for example, Geir Lundestad, "Empire by Invitation? The United States and Western Europe, 1945-1952," in Charles Maier, ed., *The Cold War in Europe* (New York, 1991), 143-67.

11. Many works have examined the interaction between the United States and third-world nations. See, for example, Cole Blasier, *The Hovering Giant: U.S. Responses to Revolutionary Change in Latin America* (Pittsburgh, 1976); H. W. Brands, *The Specter of Neutralism* (New York, 1989); Michael Desch, *When the Third World Matters: Latin America and United States Grand Strategy* (Baltimore, 1993; Richard Feinberg, *The Intemperate Zone: The Third World Challenge to U.S. Foreign Policy* (New York, 1983); Melvin Gurtov, *The United States against the Third World* (New York, 1974); Walter LaFeber, *Inevitable Revolutions: The United States in Central America* (2d ed.; New York, 1993); Robert Mortimer, *The Third World Coalition in International Politics* (New York, 1980); Robert Packenham, *Liberal America and the Third World* (Princeton, 1973); Richard Rothstein, *The Weak in the World of the Strong* (New York, 1977); Mark Singer, *Weak States in a World of Powers: The Dynamics of International Relationships* (New York, 1972); Tony Smith, *America's Mission: The United States and the Worldwide Struggle for Democracy in the Twentieth Century* (Princeton, 1994). Of these, Brands is the most balanced in terms of addressing both the different third-world and American policy concerns. There have also been recent works such as Robert McMahon, *The Cold War on the Periphery: The United States, India, and Pakistan* (New York, 1994), that give equal weight to events in the periphery and their effect on Washington.

12. Note Arthur M. Schlesinger Jr.'s observation that one of the most overlooked aspects of cold-war history writing is the influence of client states on the superpowers. Schlesinger, "Some Lessons from the Cold War," *Diplomatic History,* XVI (Winter 1992), 47-53.

officials and agencies in Washington but also because of actions by Lebanese in the cafes of Beirut, by Cubans in the streets of Havana, by Iranians in the alleys of Tehran, by Guatemalans in the jungles of Guatemala. Contrary to the dominant narrative, this work suggests that cold-war interventions were the creation of multiple international actors.

Because the United States enjoyed what Melvyn Leffler has called "a preponderance of power" during the early cold war, the situation in any particular third-world country was often deemed of less importance than what was going on in Washington. That judgment was made by politicians, the media, and the informed public; it has also been made by historians and political scientists across the spectrum. Those who excoriate U.S. foreign policy have often treated the third world as a passive object that the United States used and abused.[13] Others have celebrated the beneficial influence that the United States exercised in the third world, at least until Vietnam.[14] Even those who synthesize the two positions have done little to alter the perception of third-world countries as decidedly less important actors in the cold-war drama.[15] As a result, cold-war history has tended to emphasize what decisions were made in Washington (or alternately Moscow) and what effect these had in the third world. The emphasis has not traditionally been on what types of policies were adopted by various third-world governments and concerned groups and what effect these had in the United States.

The greater attentiveness over the past decade to third-world histories and "area studies" has vastly expanded our knowledge of "peripheral" countries. Writers have drawn attention to ways in which Iranians manipulated Americans, the manner in which certain Cuban factions played on the fears of Washington, or the ways in which third-world neutrals such as Gamal Abdel Nasser used the bipolar conflict to their advantage. In looking at specific "bilateral relations" of the U.S. and such countries as the Philippines, Iran, Pakistan, and Korea, a

13. See William Appleman Williams, *The Tragedy of American Diplomacy: United States Foreign Policy, 1945-1980* (New York, 1959); and Gabriel Kolko, *Confronting the Third World* (New York, 1988). These are only two representatives of an extensive group of writers. Kolko, however, does far more to incorporate the role of third-world actors in his seminal study of Vietnam, *Anatomy of a War* (New York, 1985).

14. Arthur M. Schlesinger Jr., "The Origins of the Cold War," *Foreign Affairs* (Fall 1967), 22-52; Hans Morgenthau, *Politics among Nations: The Struggle for Power and Peace* (New York, 1949).

15. See Richard Ned Lebow and Janice Gross Stein, *We All Lost the Cold War* (Princeton, 1994); and Leffler, *Preponderance of Power*. Both of these books are excellent postrevisionist histories, but the focus remains the United States, the Soviet Union, and Europe. Like Bruce Kuniholm in *Origins of the Cold War in the Near East,* Leffler examines in considerable detail the cold war in the "Northern Tier" of Greece, Turkey, and Iran, but unlike Kuniholm, he does not analyze the internal politics of these countries, nor does he seem to believe that these were as important as what went on in Washington.

small group of scholars has demonstrated that U.S. policy was buffeted and influenced by the actions of third-world groups.[16]

Those works that highlight the role of the periphery in cold-war history, however, tend to be specialized. They develop the argument that the third world exerted influence on the United States in the context of a particular bilateral relationship. Building on these bilateral studies, this book attempts to generalize what has been *specific*. It emphasizes the roughly equal role of third-world nations as architects both of their own histories and of the international system of the cold war.

Though every book and each article need not reflect the perspective of the periphery, it is important to ensconce third-world architects in their rightful place in international history. As long as they are consigned to the background, we will continue to think of the third world as weak, passive, and subject to the whims of powers such as the United States. Historical analyses which echo that view will be translated in the present as being true, with unfortunate consequences for how we relate to the third world. For some time, African American scholars in this country have noted that the absence of African Americans as active participants in American history reinforced a political order in which African Americans were second-class citizens. In a related fashion, a view of the cold war in which third-world actors are buried beneath a history filled with Americans, Russians, and Europeans reifies an international system in which the third world is less important.[17]

Integrating the perspective of the periphery into the story is one major goal of this study. At the most basic level, that can be done simply by discussing what third-world officials were saying and doing. In the seven cases that make up this book, I have tried to juxtapose events in the periphery with events in Washington. The architecture theme is quite simple: an intervention, whether covert in Iran and Guatemala, or overt in Lebanon, or paramilitary in Cuba and Laos, has a specific shape that is the product of a large number of people and groups, both within the United States and in the periphery, both American and

16. See, for example, the excellent work of Bruce Cumings, *The Liberation and the Emergence of Separate Regimes, 1945-1947* (Princeton, 1981), Vol. I of Cumings, *The Origins of the Korean War;* Cumings, *The Roaring of the Cataract, 1947-1950* (Princeton, 1990), Vol. II of *Origins of the Korean War;* Nick Cullather, *Illusions of Influence: The Political Economy of United States-Philippines Relations, 1942-1960* (Stanford, 1994); Alexsandr Fursenko and Timothy Naftali, *"One Hell of a Gamble": Khrushchev, Castro, and Kennedy, 1958-1964* (New York, 1997); Mark Gasiorowski, *U.S. Foreign Policy and the Shah* (Ithaca, N.Y., 1991); Irene Gendzier, *Notes from the Minefield: United States Intervention in Lebanon and the Middle East, 1945-1958* (New York, 1997); Robert McMahon, *Colonialism and Cold War: The United States and the Struggle for Indonesian Independence, 1945-49* (Ithaca, N.Y., 1981); and McMahon, *Cold War on the Periphery.*

17. On the significance of this silence in literature, see Edward Said, *Culture and Imperialism* (New York, 1993).

non-American. Some have more influence than others, but all add something distinctive to the mix. All are architects.

But this juxtaposition naturally raises the question of influence. Who determined that the intervention would occur? Who conceived of the idea? Who executed the plan? This study suggests that third-world actors shaped U.S. policy.

This raises compelling questions about the nature of power and influence, but the idea that the third world determined what the United States government did or did not do is extraordinarily difficult to prove. It may be that the Shah of Iran, or Guatemala's Jacobo Arbenz, or exiled Cubans in Miami got the U.S. government to do something that it would not otherwise have done. But given the demands of historical scholarship, how can we demonstrate that? The paucity of evidence makes such proof difficult. In many third-world countries, official records from the late 1940s through the 1960s are either impossible to obtain or nonexistent. How can one prove the influence of the periphery without government documents and related primary sources from the periphery?[18]

In order to chart how third-world groups affected the development of U.S. policy, it would be nice to have evidence of direct influence—evidence, for example, that when the Shah of Iran requested U.S. aid against Mosaddeq, U.S. officials then decided to plan a coup. But American policy makers of the period were unlikely to think of themselves as acted on by the third world. Even if the arguments of the Shah helped persuade the Eisenhower administration to intervene, Eisenhower officials would not have written in their memoranda or diaries, "Decided to intervene as a result of pulls from Iran." Even if Iranian archives were accessible, they probably would not provide the microinformation necessary to chart the day-to-day interaction between U.S. officials and Iranian officials.

It may be that the key element in these interventions was not the goals of Washington officials but rather the actions of individuals and groups in the third world. It may be that—were it not for groups of landowners in Guatemala, or army officers in Iran, or royalists in Laos—U.S. intervention would never have happened or at the very least would never have gone beyond contingency planning. That question might be answered by counterfactual analysis, or by looking at some of the "dogs that didn't bark." In the end, however, the nature of the evidence in any one particular case makes it nearly impossible to prove how significant a role third-world actors played in shaping U.S. foreign policy.

That is the great value of examining a number of cases. In one episode, the presence of third-world actors in positions of power and influence within their countries agitating for U.S. interventions may be a factor in U.S. decision making, or their activities might be purely coincidental to U.S. policy. But seen in

18. For a thorough airing of these issues, see John Lewis Gaddis, "New Conceptual Approaches to the Study of American Foreign Relations," *Diplomatic History*, XIV (Summer 1990), 406–16, and the responses to Gaddis in *Diplomatic History*, XIV (Fall 1990).

case after case, the probability that their activities were central to U.S. policy increases. Even more, from the cases of Cuba and Laos, it would seem that when the groups urging Washington to act were not in a strong position, U.S. intervention failed. That implies that third-world actors were integral to the shape and success of the interventions.

Even though causality is difficult to establish, that should not preclude an exposition of U.S. interventions that draws attention to the possibility. That leads us back to juxtaposition. We can assemble parallel narratives, and from them we can speculate about the nature of influence. We can wonder to what degree an individual such as Castillo Armas in Guatemala was a "pawn" of the United States and how much he was an independent actor who successfully manipulated CIA officials to help realize his ambitions. We can weigh whether Camille Chamoun was an overbearing nuisance who made the U.S. intervention in Lebanon more problematic, or whether he was the one pulling the strings. In short, the juxtaposition of multiple perspectives raises a whole series of questions that usually aren't asked. In several hundred pages, I offer an interpretation of what happened and why.

In general, in the two decades after World War II and before Vietnam, the U.S. government acted in conjunction with a variety of third-world groups to maintain a particular system that was to their mutual benefit. Intervention was one of the means that Washington used to preserve that system, and it succeeded only when the interests of these two groups converged. The goal was to prevent dramatic changes in the status quo, the upsetting of which would potentially jeopardize both U.S. interests and those of conservative groups in the third world.

Intervention was principally aimed against those who threatened to disrupt the established order of their societies. U.S. officials granted the need for reform in much of the third world, particularly land reform, but they recoiled at the notion of revolution. Radical reform was also highly suspect, because it often loosened the bonds of traditional society and led to a period of disorder, even chaos. Almost to a man, U.S. officials believed that where there was chaos, there was an opportunity for Communism. Chaos would spell the end of the conservative economic order, the end of the status quo, and the inevitable ascendancy of the Soviet Union.

In the third world, traditional groups—landowners, clergy, the military—and their many supporters were both virulently anti-Communist and strongly against reform. Like the Shah in the early 1950s, they fought against the reformers and nationalists such as Mosaddeq. They fought for the privileges of land ownership and tax exemption and for the wealth which they had always enjoyed. And they were fortunate enough to find that their goals coincided nicely with the goals of U.S. policy makers in Washington. In country after country—in Greece, Italy, Iran, Guatemala, Lebanon, Laos, and Vietnam—reformers and would-be revolutionaries were defeated by these conservatives who had allied themselves with the United States. The status quo classes preserved their position with aid from the United States. And the U.S. government preserved an international system conducive to American business and U.S. strategic interests with the cooperation of these groups.

When the U.S. government tried to intervene when these local forces were not in place or had lost their influence, intervention did not succeed. There is no better example than the ill-fated intervention in Cuba at the Bay of Pigs. At the Bay of Pigs, the United States finally ran out of friends. It relied on exiles for the necessary help, and the planners of the operation convinced themselves that there were many supporters in Cuba itself when in fact there were few. The lesson of the Bay of Pigs was that intervention will fail in a country where there are no powerful entrenched groups willing to facilitate. That lesson was not learned. The planning of the operation was criticized, but the underlying assumption was that better planning and better execution would have yielded success. Few understood that, no matter how well designed, the operation was doomed to failure because conditions within Cuba were not favorable.

The argument that the periphery profoundly influences the center has been made by theorists of empire but rarely in relation to the United States during the height of the cold war.[19] One of the most compelling of these "peripheral" approaches was developed in the mid-1950s by two British scholars, Ronald Robinson and John Gallagher, in a 1953 article entitled "The Imperialism of Free Trade." Over the next twenty years, they further refined what is loosely known as the Robinson-Gallagher thesis.

Accounting for the surge in Britain's expansion into Africa after 1882, Robinson and Gallagher argued that "Europe became entangled in tropical Africa by two internal crises. Imbroglios with Egyptian proto-nationalists and thence with Islamic revivals across the whole of the Sudan drew the powers into an expansion . . . in East and West Africa. . . . Much of this imperialism was no more than an involuntary reaction of Europe to the various proto-nationalisms of Islam that were already rising in Africa against the encroaching thraldom of the white men."[20]

Until Robinson and Gallagher, almost all accounts of nineteenth-century European expansion explained the development in terms of tensions within European politics. Colonialism grew out of the rivalry between the European powers, and the burst of expansion in the late nineteenth century was presented

19. Lundestad, "Empire by Invitation?"; Michael Grow, *The Good Neighbor Policy and Authoritarianism in Paraguay: United States Economic Expansion and Great Power Rivalry in Latin America during World War II* (Lawrence, Kans., 1981). See also the Cornell University Press series positing different theories of empire: Michael Doyle, *Empires* (Ithaca, N.Y., 1986); Charles Kupchan, *Vulnerability of Empire* (Ithaca, N.Y., 1994); and Jack Snyder, *Myths of Empire: Domestic Politics and International Ambition* (Ithaca, N.Y., 1990).

20. Quoted in William Roger Louis, ed., *Imperialism: The Robinson and Gallagher Controversy* (New York, 1976), 75.

as a natural outgrowth of industrialism[21] and the rigid Bismarckian alliance system that prevented any significant change in Europe's boundaries. The scramble for Africa was discussed as a purely European phenomenon, even by critics such as Lenin. The tribes of Africa—the Egyptians, Moroccans, and Fulani, for example—appeared in these writings as compliant entities. Indeed, well after the middle of this century, writers who discussed European expansion consistently presented the conquest of Africa and Asia in terms of active and passive, superior and inferior, and male and female. One writer poked fun at the absurd sexism of imperial historiography, commenting, "To Europeans in the first half of the nineteenth century Africa was still a virgin continent. They had caressed her coasts but not yet penetrated her interior."[22]

In neither their book *Africa and the Victorians* nor in the article quoted above did Robinson and Gallagher fully break with the imagery of passive and active. However, they came close. They presented expansion as a function of more than what was decided in the capitals of Europe. They theorized that European imperialism was a result not just of "push" factors within Europe but of "pull" factors in the periphery. Many of the "pulls" Robinson and Gallagher identified were British businessmen who appealed to the British government to bail them out when their investments were threatened by local upheavals and those "proto-nationalist awakenings." Even so, the idea that Europe and Britain in particular were reluctant imperialists "lured" into colonial expansion was novel and, not surprisingly, controversial. Still, while acknowledging the impact of nationalist movements in Africa, Robinson and Gallagher saw Europeans in Africa as more influential in the capitals of Europe than the Africans themselves.

Writing alone in 1972, Robinson offered what he called a "sketch for the theory of collaboration." Here he went much farther toward examining the impact of the Africans on European colonial policy and came much closer to the approach adopted in these pages:

> Imperialism was as much a function of its victims' collaboration or non-collaboration—of their indigenous politics, as it was of European expansion. . . . Without indigenous collaboration . . . Europeans [could not] have conquered and ruled their non-European empires. . . . Although the white invaders could exert leverage on ruling elites they could not do without their mediation. Even if the bargains were unequal they had to recognize mutual interests and inter-dependence if they were

---

21. Of course, it is Lenin who is most famous for this equation; see his *Imperialism: The Highest Stage of Capitalism*. J. A. Hobson, an Englishman who wrote before Lenin, said much the same thing in *Imperialism* (London, 1902).

22. Bernard Porter, *The Lion's Share: A Short History of British Imperialism, 1850–1983* (London, 1984), 68.

to be kept. The main source of Afro-Asian collaborators was not in the export-import sector but among essentially non-commercial, ruling oligarchies and landholding elites.[23]

Robinson tackled one of the more perplexing questions of imperialism: how did a handful of European administrators and soldiers manage to dominate entire societies? Except for the 1857 Sepoy Mutiny, India was calm, as were Egypt after 1882 and Nigeria until the 1950s. They were all ruled with minimal effort for decades. That ended when the elites who had collaborated either ceased to cooperate or were no longer in a position to do so. Robinson explained the colonial system as a combination of imperial policies emanating from Europe and local politics on the periphery. As long as there were local collaborators, imperialism was possible. When these disappeared, the imperial system collapsed.

Like Robinson and Gallagher, I stress the role of local elites, as well as the interdependence between them and U.S. policy makers. In each case, the assumption is that the conditions for successful intervention lay within the particular country and were not purely a function of plans made in Washington. To repeat, the Bay of Pigs failed not because of faulty planning, but because the situation within Cuba in 1961 made its success impossible.

My position is less that successful intervention depended on collaboration than that it depended on the convergence of interests. Because of the use of the word during World War II, collaboration in political writing has come to suggest a perversion of how things ought to be. As far as the U.S. cold-war imperium is concerned, it was not just collaboration that made intervention possible; it was the neat fit between U.S. foreign policy and the domestic policy of a significant segment of the local population. Collaboration also suggests that those doing it altered their actions to suit the imperial power. The argument here is that local third-world actors were acting as they had always acted, long before the U.S. government appeared on the scene. Under this rubric, it would be equally accurate to say that U.S. foreign policy–makers "collaborated" with third-world elites. Robinson and Gallagher were interested in how Great Britain established and maintained its empire; they concentrated on the imperial power and how it interacted with the periphery. This work expands the story and applies a mode of thinking to the United States and the cold war that has traditionally been absent.

In the following pages, I do not make a rigorous distinction among different types of interventions. Some were paramilitary, others consisted primarily of massive military and economic assistance, and others were essentially uncontested invasions. But they were all results of a process that included the global aims of U.S. policy makers, the relative importance of a certain country in the overall framework of U.S. policy, the amount of effort policy makers were

23. Louis, ed., *Imperialism*, 129–39.

willing to expend in a particular country, *and* the situation within the country in question. Some elements of that process were determined wholly within the United States by American officials, but many others were not. Washington did not create the Shah, or Mosaddeq, or Shi'ism; nor did it create the opposition to the Arbenz government in Guatemala. Wherever it attempted to intervene, Washington confronted a series of local histories and local groups that defined the universe of possible actions as surely as the topography of these countries determined what types of military strategy were feasible and which were not.

In addition, the stories are familiar, and I make no claims to adding significantly to what is known. In some instances, I move to the foreground groups and individuals who have been in the background, and I have enriched the stories with bits and pieces from French, Spanish, and Arabic sources. In short, this book is an interpretive essay about the interaction between the United States and the third world during the early decades of the cold war.

To be fair, I should state that I approach this subject with my own biases. While some have applauded U.S. interventions in the third world as ultimately supportive of democracy,[24] my view is different. As a way of establishing or supporting conservative, anti-Communist, antirevolutionary regimes, cold-war interventions were usually antidemocratic. The subsequent histories of every country in which the U.S. intervened was typically brutal, with civil war, massive human-rights abuses, and ugly authoritarianism. While these developments may have occurred even if the United States had not intervened, the contention that intervention led to improved internal conditions is difficult to support.

Furthermore, though most of the U.S. interventions in this period were successful, it was a severely limited type of success. To begin with, success for whom? Success for planners in Washington, for the global cold-war interests of the United States, for the traditional oligarchy in various parts of the third world, for the military there as well, but certainly not success for the great mass of impoverished, uneducated people. In acting against indigenous nationalist movements, U.S. interventions helped keep the lid on a seething cauldron. When the pressures exploded in the 1960s and 1970s, they did so with a vengeance. Although they may have prevented chaos in the short term, these interventions may have helped intensify the chaos later on.

As the United States became more prone to intervene as the cold war progressed, it also began to lose the admiration of the third world. For much of the 1950s the countries emerging from European colonialism saw the United States as a bastion of freedom and justice. But as administration after administration intervened against nationalists trumpeting these very themes, the image of the United States became tarnished. By 1961, when the nonaligned nations met for their summit in Belgrade, the United States had replaced the Europeans as the number-one adversary. While the Soviet Union was hardly more accommo-

---

24. See Samuel Huntington, *The Third Wave: Democratization in the Late Twentieth Century* (Norman, Okla., 1991).

dating of genuine self-determination in the third world, it had intervened less and spoken more kindly about the aspirations of third-world nationalism. Thus, rather than creating a more secure sphere of influence, U.S. interventions instead generated antagonism against the United States. Finally, the seeming ease of using the CIA to topple an unfriendly government or briefly deploying the marines to support Washington allies helped generate in the U.S. government that false sense of omnipotence which ultimately led to Vietnam.

These biases undoubtedly color the analysis, but it is not my intent to present a polemic against U.S. interventions. Rather, it is to understand how they happened, why they happened, and what forces both within the United States and within the third world shaped them. I also hope that the story of the various interventions will be instructive to those tackling the question of intervention in the contemporary world. If anything, the cases examined show that, even at the height of the American Century, there were constraints on the power of the United States, and that the architects of the U.S. imperium were not only American and European, but Iranian, Guatemalan, Laotian, Cuban, and many others.

■

The seven cases covered receive somewhat uneven treatment. Underneath the overall interpretation, each particular episode has its subtheses, and I have not subjected them to some theoretical cookie-cutter that artificially forces them to look alike.

The book begins with a brief look at two non–third-world cases, Greece and Italy. The purpose of including these is that U.S. interventions in Greece and Italy established a template for U.S. intervention that was later used in Iran, Guatemala, Lebanon, Cuba, Laos, and elsewhere. They are the overture to the often dissonant symphony of U.S. intervention in the third world.

Greece and Italy put the world on notice that the United States would go to extraordinary lengths to preserve its sphere of interest against perceived threats. Just as these early interventions were primers for nascent American cold warriors, they conveyed a message to the Shah in Iran, to the bishops of the Catholic Church, to feudal lords in Lebanon, and their kin in other countries that the United States was a potential asset.

Although there were many countries where the United States "intervened" with moderate economic aid and diplomatic pressure to influence domestic politics, in only a few places did it use covert paramilitary or overt military force in a pointed effort to remove a government or stabilize one on the verge of collapsing. While the massive U.S. military deployment to Korea was certainly an intervention, it was also a war against other armies. As a military campaign, its dynamics were different from the interventions discussed here. Vietnam, as well, was clearly an intervention, but Vietnam is a history unto itself.

Iran, Guatemala, Lebanon, and Cuba are the core of the argument. Industrialization, modernization, urbanization, an efflorescence of nationalism, anticolonialism, these forces were present in each. And in each, a nationalist, reform-minded leader came to prominence and challenged the role of the traditional ruling groups. Arbenz in Guatemala, Castro in Cuba, Mosaddeq in Iran, and Nasser in the Middle East—these names made national-security bureaucrats in Washington grimace. Charismatic, strong-willed, often careless in what they said and did, these men were a far cry from the conservative, status-quo groups who had governed their countries for centuries. Coming into their own after World War II, they called for radical change, and in the paranoid climate of the cold war, that sounded alarms in the casinos of Havana, the archdiocese of Guatemala City, the mansions of Beirut, the palace in Tehran, and the corridors of power in Washington.

The story ends with the confused probes into the former French colony of Laos. With little state structure and even less national identity, Laos in 1960 was challenged not by industrialization but by the simple problem of creating a viable state. With no strong central government, Laos lacked the structures familiar to Washington. The U.S. intervention in Laos, born out of an intense American ambivalence about neutralism, was haphazard, chaotic, and ambiguous. It was a harbinger of Vietnam.

But first, Greece.

1

Greece

Laying the Foundation

Once a decision was made, I did not worry about it afterward.
— Harry S. Truman, *Memoirs of Harry S. Truman*

We had no money, we had no army, nothing. . . . We used mostly American help to have enough of an army so as to be capable to maintain Greece as a free country. When I went to America in December of 1946 . . . my aim was to work for the possibility of American aid, and I insisted as much as possible, sometimes in a very vigorous manner. . . . People complained of intervention, but it was not intervention; it was interest in common.
— Constantine Tsaldaris

The situation in Greece, bad at the end of December [1946], deteriorated rapidly during January and February 1947. . . . [There were] increasingly alarming reports of imminent collapse due to mounting guerrilla activity, supplied and directed from the outside, economic chaos, and Greek governmental inability to meet the crisis. . . . All signs pointed to an impending move by the Communists to take over the country.
— Dean Acheson, *Present at the Creation*

A s one Greek-American writer commented in the early 1950s, "If Greece were located at the tip of Patagonia, we would care little if it were democratic or authoritarian."[1] In 1945, however, Greece was seen as the key to the eastern Mediterranean. With the Suez Canal a vital supply line to Western Europe and the ever-increasing importance of Middle East oil passing through the canal, Greece was of critical importance to the Allies. Keeping the eastern Mediterranean and Suez within the Western

---

1. L. S. Stavrianos, *Greece: An American Dilemma and Opportunity* (Chicago, 1952), 3-4.

17

sphere was vital to the British and to the rest of America's European partners.[2]

In February of 1947, the British announced that they could no longer provide aid to the Greek government in its war against a Communist-led insurgency. After weeks of intensive discussion in Washington, Harry S. Truman—former farmer, failed haberdasher, Missouri pol, and foreign-policy neophyte—called on Congress to authorize the aid plan that became known as the Truman Doctrine. Reacting to what he claimed was an encroachment of the Soviet Union on the free world, Truman enunciated a doctrine of freedom versus tyranny, and of American responsibility to come to the aid of the former.[3]

But that is only part, albeit an important part, of the story of the Truman Doctrine and the subsequent American intervention in Greece. The other part is the Greek civil war and the ultimately successful attempts of both the British and certain groups in Greece to draw the Americans in as the British departed. Viewed from Washington, Greece suddenly appeared on the radar screen as a country threatened by a Communist insurgency. Viewed from Athens, Greece in 1947 was in the midst of the third and most severe phase of a civil war.

As Robinson and Gallagher might have noted, U.S. officials saw themselves as deciding to act in Greece. These decisions, however, closely parallel the pull of events on the periphery of the U.S. sphere. The Truman Doctrine was a triumph for American internationalists such as Dean Acheson, but it also represented the culmination of assiduous British and Greek efforts to get the Americans to assume Britain's place in the eastern Mediterranean. At every stage, Greek leaders campaigned for U.S. aid and intervention; in the end, they received most of what they asked for.

Greece became a model for future interventions. In particular, the manner in which the U.S. military assisted the Greek army in developing a counterinsurgency strategy led to a series of assumptions that would later influence U.S.

2. War Department memo, "U.S. Security Interests in Greece," sent to Loy Henderson (Director, Office of Near Eastern and African Affairs, State Department), September 6, 1946, Top Secret, NA 868.00/9-646; Lawrence Wittner, *American Intervention in Greece, 1943-1949* (New York, 1982), 54-57; Leffler, *Preponderance of Power,* 125-27; Kuniholm, *Origins of the Cold War in the Near East,* passim.

3. The popular versions of this argument can be found in Walter Isaacson and Evan Thomas, *The Wise Men: Six Friends and the World They Made* (New York, 1986); David Fromkin, *In the Time of the Americans* (New York, 1995); and David McCullough, *Truman* (New York, 1992). The American-centric focus is also endemic to scholarly accounts. See Walter LaFeber, *America, Russia, and the Cold War, 1945-1992* (New York, 1993); Robert Pollard, "The National Security State Reconsidered," in *The Truman Presidency,* ed. Michael Lacy (New York, 1989), 205-34; and Howard Jones, *"A New Kind of War": America's Global Strategy and the Truman Doctrine in Greece* (New York, 1989). Jones offers the most extensive coverage of Greek politics and its effect on U.S. policy.

policy toward Vietnam in the early 1960s. The lessons of Greece, therefore, shaped U.S. officials' future decisions about intervention.

■

Formed in 1820, modern Greece had never really been unified; on the eve of World War II, the country remained divided by ancient rivalries, blood feuds, and ethnic divisions between the north and the south, between Turkish Greeks and mainland Greeks. During the war, Greece was occupied by the Axis powers, and German and Italian troops garrisoned the country. But while the Axis armies controlled the cities and major towns, the countryside belonged to the Greek resistance. That resistance was not unified, however, and rival Greek guerrilla groups fought against both the Germans and each other.

By late 1944, nearly two million Greeks were actively allied with the guerrillas. The largest group was the National Liberation Front (EAM) and its National Popular Liberation Army (ELAS), which had been created by the Greek Communist Party (KKE) to fight the fascists.[4] The actual number of guerrilla fighters was fewer than 100,000. Still, they kept 300,000 Axis troops bogged down in Greece long after the Greek government had fled and the army had surrendered.[5]

While the vast majority of the EAM/ELAS were patriots who cared little for and knew little about Communism, the organization was ultimately answerable to the Greek Communist Party (KKE). Until the war, the party was a marginal force in Greek political life, led by Nikos Zachariadis. Born in Asia Minor (Turkey) in 1902 and schooled in Moscow, Zachariadis was a short man with piercing eyes; he was "a virtuoso in abstract discussion," known for his intelligence, his magnetic personality, and his loyalty to Stalin.[6] Imprisoned by the Greek government, he was handed over to the Germans in April 1941 and spent the next four years in a concentration camp.

4. Haris Vlavianos, *Greece, 1941-1949* (New York, 1992), 27; Wittner, *American Intervention in Greece*, 2-4; Edgar O'Ballance, *The Greek Civil War, 1944-1949* (New York, 1966), 55-63.

5. Kuniholm, *Origins of the Cold War in the Near East*, 92; John Hondros, "Greek Resistance, 1941-1944," in *Greece in the 1940s: A Nation in Crisis,* ed. John Iatrides (Hanover, N.H., 1981), 42-45.

6. William McNeill, *The Greek Dilemma* (Philadelphia, 1947), 70-71. Evangelos Averoff-Tossizza, *By Fire and Axe: The Communist Party and the Civil War in Greece, 1944-1949* (New Rochelle, N.Y., 1978), 16-17; Averoff-Tossizza was defense minister and foreign minister in various Greek governments after the war. C. M. Woodhouse, *The Struggle for Greece, 1941-1949* (New York, 1976), 13-14. Woodhouse was Britain's special operations executive (SOE) officer in Greece as liaison with the guerrillas. For a particularly negative portrait of Zachariadis and the KKE in general, see D. George Kousoulas, *Revolution and Defeat: The Story of the Greek Communist Party* (London, 1965), 35-37.

At the headquarters of the exiled Greek government in Cairo, former ministers, army officers, a rump Greek army under British command, and assorted
bigwigs jockeyed for position. Monarchists loyal to King George II were determined to avoid a victory for ELAS and seemed at times to prefer a continued
Axis occupation until the defeat of ELAS was assured. The Liberals under the
ancient but wily Themistocles Sophoulis[7] wanted a parliamentary democracy,
perhaps with a constitutional monarch but preferably without King George.
There were also independents, such as the formidable George Papandreou, and
a considerable right wing, with some of its leaders still in Athens and some
collaborating with the Germans.

When Athens was liberated by British troops in October 1944, the stage was
set for a confrontation. Like many countries at the end of World War II, Greece
was devastated. Nearly five hundred thousand civilians out of a population of
seven million had died of disease and hunger or been killed during the war.
One-quarter of all the buildings in Greece had been destroyed, and two-thirds
of the merchant marine, one of the bulwarks of the Greek economy, was beyond
repair.[8] With the liberation from the Axis in October 1944, the newly returned
government controlled little of Greece outside of Athens. The countryside was
the stronghold of the guerrillas.

In December, relations deteriorated between the government of Prime Minister Papandreou and the nearly ten thousand ELAS forces in Athens. Papandreou
appealed to the British for help, and Winston Churchill responded by ordering
the British commander to act as if he were "in a conquered city where a local
rebellion is in progress." Eventually, ELAS retreated from the city and headed
north. As they left, they took more than thirty thousand captives, suspected
monarchists, collaborators, and unlucky people who happened to be in the
way. Driven on a forced march north during winter, as many as four thousand
of them perished.[9]

Throughout 1945, both the Papandreou government and EAM/ELAS continued their undeclared war. Right-wing extremists loosely allied with Papandreou
waged a "White Terror" against ELAS and the left in general, while ELAS
prepared for eventual civil war by stashing away th ousands of weapons in caves
in the mountains.[10] Meanwhile, the British believed that King George should

---

7. Averoff-Tossizza, *By Fire and Axe,* 163.

8. John Hondros, "Greece and the German Occupation," in *The Greek Civil War, 1943-1950,*
ed. David Close (London, 1993), 46. The figures come from a British War Office study conducted
in 1945.

9. Winston Churchill, *The Second World War, Vol. VI* (London, 1952), 262; O'Ballance, *Greek
Civil War,* 95; Vlavianos, *Greece,* 50-53; John Iatrides, "Liberation, Civil War, and the Americans,"
and Alexander George, "Demobilization Crisis," in *Greece in the 1940s,* ed. Iatrides, 146-66; Lars
Baerentzen and David Close, "The British Defeat of EAM," in *Greek Civil War,* ed. Close, 72-96.

10. Heinz Richter, "Varkiza Agreement and Civil War," in *Greece in the 1940s,* ed. Iatrides,
167-80; Woodhouse, *Struggle for Greece,* 144-45; Kousoulas, *Revolution and Defeat,* 220-27.

return as soon as possible, and that ELAS should be forcibly disbanded. But with the end of the war in Europe in May, the British were facing severe financial difficulties. They gave the Greek government what aid they could, but they could barely keep it afloat. By early 1946, inflation in Greece was rampant and corruption in Athens was ubiquitous.

A tainted election in March 1946, which was boycotted by the increasingly popular KKE, resulted in a major victory for the right-wing Populist Party led by Constantine Tsaldaris, even though less than half the population had voted.[11] Under an emergency security law, Tsaldaris authorized the arrest of thousands of ELAS supporters.

The KKE responded to government extremism with their own. Sometime during the summer of 1946, Zachariadis authorized Markos Vafiades to assemble the remaining ELAS forces in the northern mountains into a new organization called the Democratic Army. In August, this force numbered four thousand; in December it had swelled to eight thousand. By the end of 1946, the Third Round of the civil war was well under way.[12]

The British were convinced that the Democratic Army, Markos, and Zachariadis were taking orders directly from Moscow. In fact, Stalin seems to have given the Greek Communists little; he later told Milovan Djilas that it was absurd to expect the British and the Americans just to throw up their hands and let Greece fall to Communism.[13] But neither Churchill nor his successor Clement Attlee believed that the Democratic Army or Zachariadis was acting alone. Attlee and foreign secretary Ernest Bevin conveyed their concerns about Greece to the United States,[14] and by mid-1946, with the cold war in full bloom, the Americans were disposed to view the situation as yet another example of Soviet aggression against the free world.

British attitudes on the crisis strongly influenced a Truman administration that had paid minimal attention to Greece. But the Churchill-Attlee thesis that strife in Greece was a product of Soviet aggression was contested by the long-serving American minister Lincoln MacVeagh. MacVeagh was a true hellenophile. Schooled at Groton and Harvard, he had studied classical

11. See "Report of the Allied Mission to Observe the Greek Elections," April 1946, Department of State Publication #2522, Harry S. Truman Papers [hereinafter cited as HST] — Official File, Box 779, Truman Library, Independence, Mo.

12. Iatrides, "Civil War," in *Greece in the 1940s*, 205-10; Wittner, *American Intervention in Greece*, 41-49; David Close and Thanos Vermis, "The Military Struggle, 1945-9," in *Greek Civil War*, ed. Close, 100-103.

13. Svetozar Vukmanovic (General Tempo), a leading Titoist in Yugoslavia, confirms Stalin's disinterest in Greece. Vukmanovic, *How and Why the People's Liberation Struggle of Greece Met With Defeat* (London, 1950), 1-5; Milovan Djilas, *Conversations with Stalin* (New York, 1962), 119.

14. For Bevin's views, see House of Commons statement, October 22, 1946, enclosed in London 2262, October 28, 1946, NA 868.00/10-2846.

Greek and, after a stint in publishing, spent much of the 1920s reading Homer and visiting Greece. Appointed ambassador in 1933 by his old friend Franklin Roosevelt, MacVeagh thought Churchill had done a masterful job of making the situation worse. In January 1945, he wrote to Roosevelt personally:

> This affair in Greece is not the simple black and white proposition which so many . . . represent it to be. . . . It is rather a bastard offshoot of the traditional line of Greek revolutions, composed of social as well as political elements and fathered by international communism on a country economically ruined and politically distraught. The British have only played a midwife in the affair. It was not their fault that the child was conceived, but they have certainly lent themselves with astonishing ineptitude to its delivery.[15]

Throughout 1945, MacVeagh criticized British policy; he was particularly dismayed at the continued Allied support for the monarchy. MacVeagh saw the primary problem as one of governmental corruption and inefficiency, combined with economic collapse. In his view the British were doing little to address these problems. They supported the Populists and their leader Tsaldaris, while MacVeagh believed a broad-based coalition was imperative.[16]

Though MacVeagh may have been able to discern shades of gray, the same cannot be said of Truman's secretary of state James Byrnes. Formerly a Supreme Court justice and a southern senator who had outranked Truman, Byrnes was an imperious man who intended to march to the beat of his personal drummer at the State Department. A policy paper prepared at his direction in mid-1946 stated that EAM was "not a friend or ally of the Soviet Union; it is an instrument of Soviet policy."[17]

In 1946, the Truman administration became convinced that the Soviet Union was bent on world domination. The outbreak of civil war in Greece was interpreted by Truman and his advisers as another sign, if any were necessary, that Stalin would violate his wartime pledges and pursue a crafty and dangerous campaign against the west. Truman claimed in his memoirs that the Soviets had become an adversary only because of Soviet actions in Iran, Greece, Germany, and elsewhere.[18] But even if the Soviets had accommodated U.S. interests

15. MacVeagh to Roosevelt, January 15, 1945, in *Ambassador MacVeagh Reports: Greece, 1933-1947,* ed. John Iatrides (Princeton, 1980), 667-71.

16. *Ambassador MacVeagh Reports,* 625-90.

17. July 15, 1946, from the Byrnes Papers, in Wittner, *American Intervention in Greece,* 53.

18. Harry S. Truman, *Year of Decisions* (Garden City, N.Y., 1955), 75-82, 550-52, Vol. I of Truman, *Memoirs of Harry S. Truman,* 2 vols.

worldwide, Soviet Communism was an economic system incompatible with American capitalism. Where it spread, American trade could not. In the late 1940s, the Soviet Union was also the only other power capable of challenging the United States militarily. And as a nation with an ideology explicitly opposed to that of the United States, it was a rival. In each of these ways, the United States also posed a threat to the Soviet Union.

Until late 1946, the Truman administration considered Greece a British responsibility and a British problem. According to a December 1946 memo, "the United States has not taken an active role in Greece's internal affairs since Greece is considered to be in the British sphere of influence."[19] While Britain took care of the eastern Mediterranean and the Middle East, the United States concentrated on Eastern Europe, Germany, and Japan. American policy makers saw it as their role to support the British, though not if that meant a reconstitution of the British empire.[20]

In the fall of 1946, however, the Truman administration realized that Greece was descending into civil war and that victory for the Communists was foreseeable. According to an October memorandum on Greece:

> Many signs indicate that Greece is becoming a focal point in strained international relations and that its fate during the next few months may be a deciding factor in the future orientation of the Near and Middle East. . . . If Greece were allowed to fall victim to Soviet aggression, which aggression would doubtless be delegated to Albania, Yugoslavia, Bulgaria and the Soviet-inspired Left movement in Greece, there could not fail to be the most unfavorable repercussions in all of those areas where political sympathies are balanced precariously in favor of the West and against Soviet communism.[21]

As long as Britain continued to aid the Greek government, the United States saw no need to intervene. Only when Washington learned in early 1947 that the British were preparing to pull out of Greece did Truman and his advisers adopt a more activist policy.

Seen from Washington, the change in American strategy was a response born out of careful study of the situation in Greece in light of overall U.S. strategy toward Europe and the Soviet Union. Yet, from the periphery, that change coincided with a concerted campaign by the British and by the Tsaldaris government to convince the Americans to act.

19. Overby to Snyder, State Office Memorandum, December 20, 1946, John Snyder Papers, Box 19, Truman Library. See also John Lewis Gaddis, *The Long Peace* (New York, 1987), 55–57.

20. Louis, *British Empire in the Middle East.*

21. Memorandum Regarding Greece, prepared by the Division of Near Eastern Affairs, October 21, 1946, Top Secret, NA 868.00/10-2146.

In the midst of an economic crisis, the British were at a crossroads: they could not provide the Greek government with increasingly high levels of aid and simultaneously attend to domestic problems in Britain. Nonetheless, Attlee was not willing to abandon the British empire in the eastern Mediterranean, and the Greek government led by Tsaldaris was not prepared to face the insurgency alone. These two governments led a two-pronged attack to pressure the Truman administration to assume Britain's role as upholder of the status quo in Greece.

Toward the end of 1946, Prime Minister Tsaldaris bombarded Washington with demands for billions of dollars in aid. Tsaldaris personally did not impress the Americans. The patrician undersecretary of state, Dean Acheson, described him as a "weak, pleasant, but silly man" obsessed with obtaining war reparations from the Germans and economic aid from the Americans.[22] Mark Etheridge, the State Department official who was Byrnes's point-man on the Balkans, was less flattering: "Tsaldaris was a stupid fool."[23]

While Tsaldaris as an individual may have underwhelmed the American State Department, he was prime minister of Greece, and his anti-Communist bona fides were beyond dispute. His request for aid was born out of undeniable need, and he was unflagging in his efforts to warn the Americans that Greece was on the brink. In an interview in Paris, he said, "Greece is surrounded by the occupying armies of communism and her internal and social structure cannot continue to exist without outside aid."[24] Acheson noted after the prime minister's December visit to Washington that "Tsaldaris' main purpose appeared to be to exact firm commitment that US would extend immediate financial assistance to Greece. . . . [He] emphasized his belief that US must offer . . . assistance to Greece if that country is to maintain its territorial and political integrity and not fall prey to anarchists."[25] Tsaldaris may not have been very likable, but in less than a month the Truman administration did exactly as he had urged. Acheson, Etheridge, and others may have dismissed the messenger, but they got the message.

Tsaldaris was not the only Greek politician lobbying the United States. Even his opponents in Athens agreed that U.S. aid was imperative if the government was to defeat the Democratic Army. Meeting with MacVeagh in December, George Papandreou and Sophocles Venizelos presaged what Tsaldaris would say in Washington. Papandreou "stressed the mortal danger confronting Greece at the present juncture. . . . The problem must be met, he continued, by political,

22. Dean Acheson, *Present at the Creation: My Years in the State Department* (New York, 1969), 199.

23. Mark Etheridge Oral History, 31, Truman Library.

24. Quoted in John Kofas, *Intervention and Underdevelopment: Greece during the Cold War* (University Park, Pa., 1986), 55.

25. State Department to Athens, January 3, 1947, Secret, NA 868.00/1-347.

moral, military and economic measures . . . [and] the Allies must give Greece the military and economic help she needs."[26]

The British then made sure the message got through. At the end of February 1947, the British ambassador in Washington, Lord Inverchapel, delivered two notes to the State Department. One dealt with Greece, the other with Turkey, and both announced the decision of the Attlee government to terminate aid within six weeks. In addition, the British called on the United States to assume responsibility for staving off a collapse of the Greek government.

> The United States Government are as well aware as His Majesty's Government that unless Greece can obtain help from outside there is certain to be widespread starvation and consequent political disturbances during the present year. . . . His Majesty's Government take the view that it is most urgent that the United States Government should be able to decide what economic help they will give to Greece and what form it will take. . . . In view of the extreme urgency, both on economic and military grounds, the Greek Government should know what financial help is going to be available in the present year.[27]

The note included a specific breakdown of Greece's financial and military needs and requested that the United States take responsibility for them as of April 1.

While Acheson later described the notes as "shockers,"[28] the concerned officials at State already suspected that such a decision was imminent. With its treasury reserves precariously low and unable to meet the needs of its own economy, Britain was rapidly retrenching, pulling out of Palestine, India, and now the eastern Mediterranean. General George Marshall had replaced Byrnes as secretary of state, and he deferred to the judgment of Acheson that the United States must fill the gap left by the British in Greece.

In developing what would become known as the Truman Doctrine, Acheson was in part acting on the recommendations of MacVeagh, Etheridge, Tsaldaris, the British, and the head of the U.S. economic mission to Greece, Paul Porter. Porter had gone to Athens in December 1946 and was regularly sending telegrams filled with dire predictions of what would happen should the United States fail to come to Greece's aid.[29] Acheson also had the reports of the Central

---

26. Memorandum of conversation, December 9, 1946, enclosure to Athens 3408, December 11, 1946, Confidential, NA 868.00/12-946.

27. Aide-Memoire from the British Embassy, February 21, 1947, Top Secret, NA 868.00/2-2147.

28. Acheson, *Present at the Creation,* 217.

29. See, for example, Porter to Clayton (undersecretary of state for economic affairs), February 17, 1947, Top Secret, *FRUS, 1947, Vol. V,* 17-22; Etheridge to State, February 17, 1947, Top Secret, ibid., 23-25.

Intelligence Group, the interim agency that replaced the OSS and preceded the CIA. In early February a CIG report stated:

> The strife in Greece today is the outgrowth of longstanding political differences, accentuated by Soviet-inspired interference and an internal economy severely disrupted by the war. So bitter have these become that for months past anti-government forces under Communist leadership have been conducting intensive guerrilla warfare. . . . The consistent failure of Tsaldaris to offer . . . [opposition]groups genuine and responsible participation in a united Greek government . . . has obstructed the recovery . . . of stability in Greece. . . . The Soviets will not openly pursue their objectives. . . . They will continue to work through their satellites (Albania, Yugoslavia, and Bulgaria) to intensify dissatisfaction and unrest. . . . [In order] to counter these tactics . . . they will need outside aid.[30]

On February 21, 1947, Acheson warned Marshall that unless immediate aid were given to Greece, it would fall to the Communist insurgency.[31]

After a dramatic meeting in which Acheson presented the issue in apocalyptic terms to Truman and the ranking Republican senators of the Foreign Relations Committee,[32] Truman formally announced the plan to a joint session of Congress on March 12. He declared that assistance to Greece was imperative. "The very existence of the Greek state," he continued, "is today threatened by the terrorist activities of several thousand armed men, led by Communists. . . . The Greek Government is unable to cope with the situation. The Greek army is small and poorly equipped. It needs supplies and equipment if it is to restore the authority of the government throughout Greece." Truman stated that it was the responsibility of the United States "to support free peoples who are resisting attempted subjugation by armed minorities or by outside pressure."[33] Truman asked for $400 million in Greco-Turkish aid, and after some debate, that is precisely what Congress gave him.

Even as he called on Congress to fund Greek aid, Truman criticized the unrepresentative and repressive nature of the Greek government. While admitting that excesses were understandable given the turmoil, Truman insisted that reform must be a component of the aid program. He also went on at great length about the dual nature of American help. While the primary concern was economic, that was inseparable from the military. This melding of economic

---

30. Central Intelligence Group ORE 6/1, "The Greek Situation," February 7, 1947, Top Secret, HST—President's Secretary File, Box 254, Truman Library.

31. Acheson to Marshall, February 21, 1947, Top Secret, *FRUS, 1947, Vol. V,* 29–31.

32. Acheson, *Present at the Creation,* 220–23.

33. Truman address to Congress, March 12, 1947, Clark Clifford Papers, Box 6, Truman Library.

with military would soon cause confusion at the headquarters of the aid mission in Athens. The doctrine represented an approach to the cold war as a socioeconomic problem with a military dimension. This framework was developed in Greece, but it was soon applied everywhere.

Truman justified the plan by stressing that it came in response to requests by the Greek government. This gets into tricky territory. Whenever the United States intervened in the third world during the cold war, whenever it had intervened in Latin America in the decades before, it always claimed that it was acting in response to a request for help. That allowed various administrations to deny that they were motivated by greed or imperial interests. And it was usually true that someone could be found in the country in question who would ask for U.S. intervention. There are at least two ways of interpreting this pattern: either the United States government intervened for its own self-determined reasons and covered its action behind a false front, or there was some genuine give-and-take between the government in Washington and local forces.

The second option is more suited to the situation in Greece. While the Truman Doctrine may well have been motivated by global American concerns that had little to do with Greece, there were many in Greece who had actively courted the United States with an eye to future funding. They included not just Tsaldaris, Papandreou, Sophoulis, and the leading members of the political center and right in Greece, but also businessmen, shipping magnates, military officers, and Archbishop Damaskinos of the Greek Orthodox Church—not to mention the British. The fact that these groups within Greece sought American intervention to defeat the Democratic Army should not be underemphasized. As MacVeagh knew, beneath the veneer of Communists versus the government, the strife in Greece had been going on for decades. Military officers such as General Alexander Papagos fought ELAS during World War II and fought against reformers in the 1930s. Politicians such as Papandreou and Sophoulis had been fighting the monarchists or the Communists long before the Americans appeared on the scene. And in villages throughout rural Greece, battles between right-wing militants and the Democratic Army mirrored the local rivalries of generations past and often had nothing to do with Communist or liberal or royalist and everything to do with blood feuds. At a particular juncture in late 1946, the strategic aims of the American foreign-policy establishment matched the domestic aims of numerous influential groups within Greece. Out of that convergence, the Truman administration committed thousands of administrators and military advisers, and billions of dollars in loans and credits, to help a disintegrating and largely corrupt Greek government win a civil war against forces loosely controlled by the Greek Communist Party.

The Greeks called their civil war "Symmontopelemo," a gangster or bandit war.[34] That made it nearly impervious to conventional military measures. When

34. Robert McClintock, *The Meaning of Limited War* (Boston, 1967), 21. McClintock served as the American ambassador in Lebanon during the 1958 crisis.

the Truman Doctrine was passed, generous estimates had the Greek government effectively in command of only a small portion of the country, primarily the cities and portions of the south.[35] The Democratic Army numbered as many as twenty-five thousand by the summer of 1947, with hangers-on and support staff in the area of one hundred thousand. Scattered throughout the country in small mobile bands, these forces would strike quickly, at targets of their own choosing. They usually caught the Greek army by surprise, and they would disperse after an attack. Army units might pursue, but they were likely to encounter an ambush. That made army commanders profoundly reluctant to go after the guerrillas. The army preferred regular engagements, preferably by day, and away from the mountains.[36]

In 1947, the Greek army was unable to shift the balance in the countryside to its favor. Though with approximately 150,000 soldiers it far outnumbered the Democratic Army, the nature of the war made it difficult for the army to translate that numeric superiority into battle victories.[37] However, with the massive influx of American aid, the army began to lay the groundwork for taking the fight to the guerrillas. American military advisers started arriving in force after the summer, and they helped the Greek officers retool their strategy in the direction of counterinsurgency. Rather than large, fixed army units, the Greek army would match the guerrillas' tactics. In addition, improved intelligence work made it easier for the army to anticipate attacks and even to surprise the guerrillas. The army also continued to benefit from the support of right-wing militants who were less inhibited by legal niceties and who could terrorize suspected Democratic Army sympathizers without having to answer to opposition groups in Athens or to an American public that didn't like the thought of American dollars being used to round up and execute civilians.

But while the Greek army was improving, so too was the Democratic Army. General Markos was by all accounts a brilliant, popular, inspiring leader and "a man of the people." Forty years old at the end of 1946, he combined charisma and effective public relations to construct a formidable guerrilla force. His courage and rough-hewn manner made him accessible to his men in a way that most regular army officers were not. Disgusted with the venality and corruption of Athens, villagers throughout Greece referred to Markos simply as "our general."[38]

---

35. See Etheridge Oral History, 31, and Acheson, *Present at the Creation*, 199, for a scathing critique of Tsaldaris, who proposed an ambitious revenue program at a time when the Greek government could barely hold Athens.

36. Kati Marton, *The Polk Conspiracy* (New York, 1990), 105-10; Wittner, *American Intervention in Greece*, 106-109; Woodhouse, 205-206.

37. Jones, *"New Kind of War,"* 65-72.

38. *Time*, January 5, 1948; Kevin Andrews, *The Flight of Ikaros: Travels in Greece during a Civil War* (London, 1984), 20-21; Averoff-Tossizza, *By Fire and Axe*, 177-79; Jones, *"New Kind of War,"* 10; Kousoulas, *Revolution and Defeat*, 290.

Markos was firmly committed to guerrilla warfare, using tactics similar to those of the Communist revolutionaries in China: small units, short engagements, and a solid base in the countryside. Castro later adopted the same strategy in Cuba, and the Vietcong practiced it in Vietnam. However, Markos also relied on terror as a weapon. Like insurgents before and after, he was willing to raze villages, expel the inhabitants, and conduct spot executions of government collaborators. While the Democratic Army championed many of the causes of the "people," by early 1948 the people began to be disenchanted with the Democratic Army.[39]

Until the end of 1947, the momentum clearly lay with Markos. That changed in 1948, and by the end of the year, the Greek government was in a position to inflict the final defeat on the Democratic Army, which came in August 1949. The collapse of the insurgency was interpreted by the Americans and their Greek allies as a victory for the Truman Doctrine and subsequent U.S. micromanagement of the counterinsurgency. But the defeat of the Democratic Army may have had more to do with miscalculations by Zachariadis and developments within the Eastern Bloc than with decisions made in Washington or Athens. The lesson that U.S officials took away was that intensive economic and military aid administered by U.S. officials in conjunction with local groups in the targeted country was an effective recipe for success. Yet, if the Democratic Army had pursued a pure guerrilla strategy rather than overreaching for the cities, and if Yugoslavia's Marshal Tito had continued to supply the Democratic Army, the outcome might have been quite different.

Markos had little interest in conventional frontal assaults. He also questioned the need to capture towns and cities. His philosophy was: consolidate the countryside and the cities will eventually strangle. Zachariadis disagreed. Toward the end of 1947, he pushed for a transformation of Markos' guerrillas into a force capable of engaging the regular Greek army.[40] Under pressure from Zachariadis, Markos launched a frontal assault on the town of Konitsa on Christmas Day, 1947. After a two-week siege, he was repulsed by government forces. The attack demonstrated that the Democratic Army was not capable of the kind of warfare that Zachariadis wanted it to wage. Rather than taking the blame for the failure at Konitsa, Zachariadis held his rival responsible.

The fighting in 1948 resulted in a stalemate. The resurgent Greek Army made headway but could not penetrate the guerrilla strongholds in the north. The Democratic Army continue to harass villages and towns throughout Greece but never developed into a concentrated fighting force. But while the Greek government was fighting with the bonus of American aid and advice, the Demo-

---

39. Central Intelligence Agency, "The Current Situation in Greece," ORE 51, October 17, 1947, Top Secret, HST—President's Secretary File, Box 254, Truman Library; Woodhouse, *Struggle for Greece,* 217-11; Vukmanovic, *How and Why,* 39-40.

40. Jones, *"New Kind of War,"* 75-76, 118-20; Marton, *Polk Conspiracy,* 107-108; Vlavianos, *Greece,* 240-46; Woodhouse, *Struggle for Greece,* 215-23.

cratic Army was also receiving outside help, not from the Soviet Union, but from Marshal Yosef Broz Tito and the Communist government of Yugoslavia.

Tito's support for the Greek insurgents was in stark contrast to the position of Stalin. Tito provided safe havens for the Democratic Army across the Greek-Yugoslav border, and he fed and armed the guerrillas. Stalin, however, refused material aid to the armed insurgency. In addition to skepticism that Britain or the United States would permit a Communist victory, Stalin may also have felt that Greece was simply outside the Soviet sphere. Traditional Russian pan-Slavism extended as far as Yugoslavia and the northern Balkans, but not to Greece proper. Tito's independent course on Greece foreshadowed the Tito-Stalin split in 1948, a split that would have major repercussions in Greece.

Tito's aid was not unconditional. Like Markos, the Yugoslav leader favored the insurgency strategy. That was how he had won against the Germans in Yugoslavia, and he thought it was the best prescription for the Communists in Greece.[41] When Zachariadis began pushing for frontal assaults, he ran afoul not only of Markos but of Tito as well, and Tito voiced his displeasure during Zachariadis' frequent visits to Belgrade.

Even more problematic for the Democratic Army, Tito pressed for concessions on Macedonia. Needing Yugoslav aid, both Zachariadis and Markos made public statements indicating their willingness to see Macedonia detached from Greece. But while that mollified Tito, it alienated many Greeks. As long as the Democratic Army could present itself as a true defender of the Greek nation, it was a viable contender for the hearts and minds of the people. With the legacy of its wartime efforts against the Germans, and with the corrupt behavior of the Athens government, the KKE was for a time very popular. But its concession on Macedonia and its own internal divisions weakened it.[42]

The insurgents received a further blow when Tito was charged with "discrediting the Soviet Union" and expelled from the Cominform on June 28, 1948. By cutting Tito out of the Cominform, Stalin froze Yugoslavia out of the emerging economic system of the eastern bloc. As a result, after the summer of 1948, Tito began to tilt toward the west and the United States. He could not do that and continue to fund the Democratic Army.[43]

The dramatic rupture within the eastern bloc was mimicked within the Greek Communist Party. Markos was identified with the Titoist faction within the KKE; Zachariadis was a Stalinist. The Tito-Stalin split reproduced itself in Greece as a Markos-Zachariadis split. In January 1949, Zachariadis led a purge of the non-Stalinist hierarchy of the KKE. Markos was removed. The Tito-Stalin split may simply have provided Zachariadis with a convenient excuse to get

41. Richard West, *Tito* (New York, 1995), 102–93.

42. Vukmanovic, *How and Why*, 102–106; Wittner, *American Intervention in Greece*, 264.

43. CIA, "Continuing Satellite Aid to the Greek Guerrillas," ORE 67-48, October 8, 1948, HST—President's Secretary File, Box 256; Clifford Matlock Oral History, 28–29. Both in Truman Library.

rid of his rival; for whatever reason, the purge was the culmination of the tension between the two men and between the two philosophies of how the war should be fought. While the Democratic Army continued to receive aid from Albania and Bulgaria, Tito closed the Yugoslav-Greek border in July 1949, denying the KKE its safe havens in Yugoslavia. A month later, the Greek army led by General Papagos stormed the last significant fortress of the Democratic Army in the Grammos. The guerrillas were defeated and most were forced to flee to Albania and Bulgaria.[44]

American aid to the Greek government was certainly a pivotal factor in this defeat. The Americans were to the government what Tito was to the Democratic Army. By 1949, however, the American mission in Greece had moved in directions somewhat different from those suggested in the Truman Doctrine. While in 1947 economic aid and military assistance were emphasized, the latter soon mushroomed while economic aid was used to sustain the war economy more than to assist in development.

If MacVeagh had had his way, the Truman Doctrine would have been used to eradicate corruption in the Greek government. Seeing the insurgency as a political protest against Athens, he thought that the war could only be won by making the government more representative. However, MacVeagh's authority was undercut by the aid administrator appointed by Truman. Dwight Griswold was one of Truman's World War I buddies and a former liberal Republican governor of Nebraska. Candid and aggressive, Griswold was described as "an unmitigated jerk" by New York *Times* correspondent George Polk.[45] Chosen as the chief of the American mission in Greece in the spring of 1947, Griswold had executive authority for the program, and his mission operated separately from the American Embassy in Greece. Griswold's powers naturally impinged on MacVeagh's domain, and even if the two men had viewed the situation similarly, there was bound to be friction. As it was, their visions could not have been farther apart.[46]

MacVeagh's position is captured in a message he sent to the State Department on July 21: "I believe our policy of careful non-interference in Greek internal affairs to be one of our strongest assets with the Greek people."[47] Griswold, however, urged such interference. In August, as the last British troops left the country, Griswold urged that American troops should take their place, and that the promise of these forces should be used as a carrot to force a change in

---

44. Ole Smith, "The Greek Communist Party, 1945-9," in *Greek Civil War*, ed. Close, 145-50; Jones, *"New Kind of War,"* 198-99; O'Ballance, *Greek Civil War*, 180-82; Vukmanovic, *How and Why*, 105-106; Wittner, *American Intervention in Greece*, 271-80; Woodhouse, *Struggle for Greece*, 230-55.

45. Marton, *Polk Conspiracy*, 106-107.

46. Marshall to Griswold, July 12, 1947, Confidential, *FRUS, 1947, Vol. V*, 226-31; *Ambassador MacVeagh Reports*, 701-34.

47. *Ambassador MacVeagh Reports*, 720.

the government. MacVeagh responded on August 5: "I feel that every non-interventional influence at our disposal should be used to secure greater political unity here."[48]

Griswold began to get annoyed. In mid-August, he wrote to George McGhee, the Washington coordinator for Greek-Turkish aid programs:

> [MacVeagh] seemingly is anxious as anyone to have certain changes made but he continues to use such words as "gradually" and "we of course must not interfere" to such an extent that I feel somewhat alarmed. Candidly, I am fearful that the present opportunity will not be grasped. . . . In my judgement we do not need to be affected by a fear that we will be accused of "interfering." That accusation will be made even if we do nothing.[49]

MacVeagh continued to hammer out his central point. On August 19, he answered Griswold, saying that he still believed that a policy of noninterference was sound and warning that "no government openly set up under foreign influence can succeed in this country."[50]

MacVeagh steadily lost support in Washington. A cultured man, he was seen as soft by Griswold, and George Marshall soon concluded that Macveagh had to go. He was recalled just before Thanksgiving, 1947, and reassigned to Portugal. He wept when Truman told him the news.[51]

Though Griswold himself was soon replaced, the removal of MacVeagh was part of an overall restructuring of the American military mission in Greece. Evaluating the situation, Admiral Sidney Souers of the National Security Council expressed grave concern about "the failure of the Greek armed forces to defeat the guerrillas during the summer months." The result was that aid previously allocated to economic projects was being diverted to assist the military.[52]

After a series of high-level discussions at the end of 1947, the Truman administration decided that the war must be won before economic development could take place. According to a State Department circular at the time, "reconstruction in Greece must take second priority to establishing military security and elimina-

---

48. Ibid., 721–23.

49. Griswold to McGhee, Athens [undated], Secret, *FRUS, 1947, Vol. V,* 294–97.

50. MacVeagh to Marshall (Secretary of State), August 19, 1947, Secret, *FRUS, 1947, Vol. V,* 299–301.

51. Wittner, *American Intervention,* 118–19; Jones, *"New Kind of War,"* 112–14; *Ambassador MacVeagh Reports,* 724–33.

52. Memorandum by Admiral Sidney Souers to the National Security Council, October 30, 1947, Top Secret, *FRUS, 1947, Vol. V,* 391–93.

tion of the guerrillas."[53] Marshall searched for a battle-hardened commander and found him in General James Van Fleet.

Van Fleet had made his mark in combat during World War II. General Dwight D. Eisenhower had described him as "definitely not the intellectual type, but direct and forceful."[54] As the head of the military mission in Greece, Van Fleet coordinated war strategy with the Greek government. He cared little if the Greek government was repressive, only that it was anti-Communist. He saw his task as molding the Greek army into a force capable of handling the insurgency, and he attended to that with a bull-headed determination.

Conceived as an economic-aid program for Greece and Turkey, the Truman Doctrine was, therefore, transformed by early 1948 into something quite different from the plan cooked up in the spring of 1947. The transformation of the doctrine from primarily an economic to primarily a military program becomes more understandable in light of the demands made by numerous factions in Athens for intensified U.S. military assistance. Many writers have explained deepening U.S. involvement in 1948 as a calculated response by Washington to a worsening situation. But in 1948 the insurgency was already on the retreat for reasons that had little to do with U.S. aid. Conservative groups in Athens tried hard to convince the Truman administration to increase aid at the very time when the military situation might have dictated a decrease.

Thus, while more than $200 million in economic aid was sent to Greece between the spring of 1947 and the end of 1949, more than $350 million in military aid was dispersed. This included hundreds of warplanes, more than four thousand artillery pieces, nearly ninety thousand bombs, several hundred thousand small arms weapons, and several hundred million pieces of ammunition.[55] While Van Fleet was strictly enjoined from allowing any American military advisers to participate in the fighting, he was instrumental in training the Greek army to meet the threat of insurgency. In many ways presaging the counterinsurgency doctrines that would be applied by Americans in Laos and Vietnam, Van Fleet and the Greek commanders designed a plan that would take the war to the guerrillas. According to the deputy chief of staff of the Greek army in 1948, the task was to "inspire [the guerrilla] with terror and with the feeling that there is no place where he may stay in safety by night or by day."[56]

By the summer of 1948, Van Fleet believed that the army was ready for a

---

53. Quoted in McClintock, *Meaning of Limited War,* 21; Michael Amen, *American Foreign Policy in Greece, 1944-1949* (Frankfurt, 1978), and Kofas, *Intervention and Underdevelopment,* both argue that economic, not military, concerns drove American policy in Greece.

54. Quoted in Wittner, *American Intervention in Greece,* 236.

55. Wittner, *American Intervention in Greece,* 253, cites figures from a U.S. Army Historical Division report.

56. Quoted in Jones, *"New Kind of War,"* 153; O'Ballance, *Greek Civil War,* 165ff.

major assault directed at the heart of the Democratic Army in the Grammos Mountains. In preparation for the attack, the Sophoulis government authorized a wave of arrests and executions.[57] Though the 1948 Grammos offensive was the largest operation of the civil war, its results were ambiguous. With the Greek government and the American military mission having expended so much effort and widely publicized the campaign, the failure to eradicate the Democratic Army and destroy their mountain refuge was a setback.

In the aftermath, there was a strong push within Greece for the resignation of Sophoulis and the appointment of a military strongman. There was also a strong push within the Truman administration for a greater American commitment, perhaps even combat troops. John Foster Dulles, future secretary of state and chief foreign-policy adviser to the Republican presidential candidate Thomas Dewey, was deeply opposed to tying American prestige any more closely to a potential morass in Greece.[58] American intelligence reports offered a pessimistic view of the situation:

> Unless the guerrillas are eliminated, there can be no real recovery in Greece. . . . The Kremlin has given no indication of abandoning its ultimate objective of bringing Greece under Communist control. . . . US funds and tactical advice have corrected many deficiencies in the army, but the army appears still unable to eliminate the guerrillas. . . . Meanwhile there is a widespread feeling that Greece is caught in the struggle between the West and the East, and that the Greeks are not merely fighting their own battle.[59]

Combined with this discontent was a rising tide in favor of a more authoritarian government and deep disenchantment with the economy because of massive inflation and the collapse of the drachma, partly brought on by the influx of American dollars. At the time, the United States was supplying approximately 20 percent of the entire Greek gross national product.[60]

The result was the rise of General Alexander Papagos. Appointed commander-in-chief of the Greek army by King Paul in January 1949, Papagos took the job on the condition that the Greek army be allowed to number 250,000 soldiers. That was a huge increase, and it siphoned off even greater amounts of aid. But

57. It was at this time that the body of New York *Times* correspondent George Polk was found floating in Thessaloniki's bay. Polk had been critical of the Sophoulis-Tsaldaris coalition. See Marton, *Polk Conspiracy.*

58. Dulles notes on meeting with Robert Lovett (Defense), August 28, 1948, John Foster Dulles Papers, Box 36, Seeley Mudd Library, Princeton University.

59. CIA, "Current Situation in Greece (October 1948)," ORE 28-48, November 17, 1948, Top Secret, HST—President's Secretary File, Intelligence File, Box 255.

60. Paul Porter Oral History, 58, Truman Library.

by this time, the Truman administration had accepted that military victory took priority, and Van Fleet was convinced that Papagos was the only hope. Averell Harriman, Truman's roving ambassador, reported that Greece needed "a semi-dictatorship under General Papagos."[61]

With more troops, Papagos was able to conduct sweeps throughout Greece, and by the summer of 1949 the guerrillas were confined to several pockets and their remaining demesnes in the Grammos and Vitsi Mountains. After careful planning and reconnaissance, Papagos launched the final offensive in August 1949. Named Operation Torch, the attack drove the weakened Democratic Army out of the mountains and forced them to flee to Albania. Short of supplies and with Yugoslavia closed to them, the guerrillas had little chance against the aerial attacks, napalm, and massive artillery that Papagos brought to bear. While nearly 10,000 guerrillas survived in Albania, Bulgaria, and in select pockets throughout Greece, Operation Torch destroyed the Democratic Army. All in all, the Third Round left at least 60,000 Greeks dead and made refugees out of another 800,000.[62]

By 1949, American aid had created a new bourgeoisie in Athens, comprising civil servants, merchants, shippers, and industrialists who capitalized on the burgeoning war industry. This class supported Papagos and harsh measures against the left in general. Combined with older conservatives such as Zervas and royalists such as Tsaldaris, these groups overwhelmed whatever nascent liberalism Sophoulis had managed to retain. Even the one-time conservative independent George Papandreou came to see the conflict in terms of a stark contrast between "Communist Pan-Slavism and Anglo-Saxon Liberalism." Communism, he said, "was the deadly enemy of freedom—the fascism of the Left."[63]

An entire class of the Athenian political leadership dealt every day with American diplomats, aid administerers, and military officers. Their world view, captured by Papandreou's denunciation of Communism, meshed with the world view of their American counterparts. It solidified the conviction of the Van Fleets and the Griswolds and undermined the more nuanced views of the MacVeaghs. The traditional ruling cliques in Athens (as well as the British) lobbied for U.S. aid in 1946–1947; these same groups nudged U.S. officials to emphasize the military rather than the economic and political aspects of the Truman Doctrine; and with the influx of U.S. dollars and goods, these groups expanded to become a new class of conservative anti-Communists in a Greece intimately bound to the Western alliance.

The appointment of Papagos marked the political victory of the new class,

61. Quoted in Jones, *"New Kind of War,"* 194.

62. Wittner and O'Ballance put the estimate at 160,000 killed, while Jones puts it at 60,000; Averoff-Tossizza says that at least 50,000 guerrillas died. Wittner, *American Intervention in Greece,* 253; O'Ballance, *Greek Civil War,* 202; Jones, *"New Kind of War,"* 220; Averoff-Tossizza, *By Fire and Axe,* 355.

63. George Papandreou, *The Third War* (Athens, 1948), 16, 55.

and the end of political reform for years to come. The conservatives had their victory, and they had won in part by defeating the reformist elements of the Truman Doctrine.[64] After his victory in 1949, Papagos summed up his philosophy that Communists everywhere must be defeated by "timely diagnosis and ruthless suppression." He referred to Communist strongholds as "infested areas" that required "cleansing."[65]

As one observer of these events remarked, after the defeat of the guerrillas, "Greece became a Cold War ally of the United States and a prototype for subsequent U.S. intervention in small, underdeveloped nations."[66] But the ally was a conservative Greek government, not the Greek people. This conservative clique continued to dominate Greek politics for much of the next twenty years and, when challenged in the late 1960s, helped bring to power the notorious "colonels government" that fell only after Greece's ignominious defeat in Cyprus in 1974. While this group and its supporters in the commercial classes had sought American aid, they subtly manipulated the aid program away from economic and political reform. Meanwhile, the Truman administration viewed Greece as its success story. To the degree that U.S. officials thought about the role of the Greeks, it was usually as either tools of international Communism or as "stupid fools" like Tsaldaris.

Greece introduced cold-war America to a "new kind of war," one it began waging with increasing frequency. But the foreign-policy establishment also began to employ a different weapon in these wars of intervention. The military and the State Department had designed the program in Greece, always under the direction of the White House. Soon, however, the president would come to rely more heavily on an agency that did not even exist when the Truman Doctrine was proposed, an agency that would first be used in Italy. The agency was the CIA.

---

64. Kotas Vergopoulos, "New Bourgeoisie, 1944-1952," in *Greece in the 1940s,* ed. Iatrides, 298-318; Marton, *Polk Conspiracy,* 148, 168; David Close, "The Reconstruction of a Right-Wing State," in *Greek Civil War,* ed. Close, 156-90.

65. Alexander Papagos, "Guerrilla Warfare," *Foreign Affairs* (January 1952), 215-30.

66. Wittner, *American Intervention in Greece,* x; Stavrianos, *Greece,* 228; also Andrews, *Flight of Ikaros,* passim.

2

Italy

A Secret Agency for an Open Election

It is of vital strategic importance to prevent Italy from falling under Communist control. Such a development would have demoralizing effect throughout Western Europe, the Mediterranean, and the Middle East. . . . Assuming that the present government survives the winter, the outcome of the April [1948] elections will depend not only on the results of interim aid, but also on the prospects for the success of the European recovery program.

—CIA Report, October 1947

During the First World War, we used to say that the situation in Germany was serious but not desperate, in Austria desperate but not serious, and in Italy desperate but normal. The Italian situation is always desperate but normal.

—Gaetano Salvemini

I n 1948, the Truman administration authorized the Central Intelligence Agency to assist the Italian Christian Democratic Party using "unvouchered funds." Millions of dollars of untraceable money flowed from the United States to select groups and individuals in Italy, and the Christian Democrats were victorious.

From this point forward, the CIA became the primary, though not the only, tool of U.S. covert intervention in foreign countries. Subsequent interventions in the third world were in most instances planned and executed by the CIA, on orders from the White House. Just as Greece established a framework for future U.S. counterinsurgency, Italy was a training ground for later U.S. interventions. As a result of its activities in Italy, the CIA was transformed from a bureau of intelligence and analysis into an architect of covert action.[1]

---

1. Rhodri Jeffreys-Jones, *The CIA and American Democracy* (New Haven, 1989), 42-52; Christopher Andrew, *For the President's Eyes Only* (New York, 1995), 70-75; John Ranelagh, *The Agency: The Rise and Decline of the CIA* (New York, 1986), 129-79; Corson, *Armies of Ignorance,*

In addition, the intervention in Italy witnessed many of the same dynamics of third-world interventions. Party leaders, government officials, and private individuals in Italy actively solicited U.S. assistance against the Italian Communist Party. They repeatedly warned of the danger of a leftist victory at the polls, and they played on American concerns of a Communist takeover of Italy. They themselves were hardly nonchalant about this possibility, and that in part explains the intensity with which they lobbied the United States for help. In addition, a powerful Italian community in the United States pushed the Truman administration to act, just as a vocal Cuban community in Florida would later push the Eisenhower and Kennedy administrations to do something about Fidel Castro.

When World War II ended, Truman thought that there was no longer a need for a large department charged with espionage, counterespionage, analysis, and covert operations. He ended the brief life of the Office of Strategic Services and reluctantly authorized the formation of a skeletal replacement called the Central Intelligence Group. It soon became clear that the toothless CIG was not enough. With the increasing tension between the United States and the Soviet Union, Truman listened to those of his foreign-policy team who warned that the Soviets with their behemoth intelligence-cum-internal security-cum-covert operations agency could take advantage of the lack of such organizations in Washington. Wary in 1945 of the idea of a peacetime spy agency, Truman needed little convincing in the tenser climate of 1947.[2]

In July of 1947, Truman signed the National Security Act, a bill that established the foundation of what has become known as the national-security state. In addition to creating the position of secretary of defense, the act's most important innovations were the CIA and the National Security Council. Along with the State Department, the triad of the NSC, the CIA, and the Defense Department determined, designed, and implemented much of the national-security policy during the cold war.

The 1947 bill gave the CIA the only explicit congressional authorization for espionage and paramilitary operations it would ever receive.[3] Under the act, the CIA was responsible for advising the NSC "in matters concerning such intelligence activities of the Government departments and agencies as relate to national security." In addition, the CIA was supposed "to correlate and

---

291-303; Thomas Powers, *The Man Who Kept the Secrets: Richard Helms and the CIA* (New York, 1979), 29-31.

2. Walter Pforzheimer, Memorandum for the Record, "Proposed Legislation for C.I.G.," January 28, 1947, Top Secret; National Intelligence Authority, "Minutes of the NIA's 9th Meeting," February 12, 1947, Top Secret, reprinted in Michael Warner, ed., *The CIA under Harry Truman* (Washington D.C., 1994); Ranelagh, *The Agency*, 104-29; Corson, *Armies of Ignorance*, chap. 5.

3. Not until 1949 was the CIA director given the authority to spend money for covert operations without congressional budgetary authorization. Central Intelligence Act of 1949, June 20, 1949, Warner, ed., *CIA under Harry Truman*, 287-94; Ranelagh, *The Agency*, 270.

evaluate intelligence relating to the national security, and provide for the appropriate dissemination of such intelligence within the Government." In deference to the FBI and its powerful director J. Edgar Hoover, the CIA was strictly enjoined from any domestic law-enforcement powers. In a final, vague clause, the CIA was instructed "to perform such other functions and duties related to intelligence affecting national security as the National Security Council may from time to time direct."[4] This clause is the basis of the CIA's legal authority to perform covert action, including paramilitary operations.

In 1949, Congress gave the director of central intelligence the power to allocate funds without specifying their use to congress. The CIA was thereby removed from congressional oversight, at least until the 1970s when the House and Senate intelligence committees were created. Under the 1947 act, Congress required the director of central intelligence to "protect intelligence sources and methods," which gave the director the legal right to withhold information from congressional—hence public—inquiries. The director could always respond to a question, "I can not reveal that information without jeopardizing a source or an intelligence collection method." Other than informal conferences with a select group of congressional leaders, the CIA was free to do its business in secret.

In 1947, no one in the Truman administration knew quite what to expect from the NSC or the CIA. At first, the NSC was truly an advisory group, convened to discuss issues without the president in attendance. It would then craft position papers recommending action or simply stating the consensus of its members about what U.S. policy should be in a particular area. However, after 1950 and particularly after 1953 when Eisenhower became president, the NSC gained substantial influence over national-security policy.[5]

Shortly after its creation, the CIA reviewed "the world situation" in general and Italy in particular. The CIA concluded, "The Italian economic situation is desperate and the political situation unstable." The CIA warned that in the event of an economic and political collapse, Italy could be taken over by the Communist Party.[6] With its coalition government and strong leftist parties, Italy seemed ripe for a revolution. It was the first problem for the fledgling NSC.

NSC policy paper 1/1 directed the CIA to help the Christian Democratic Italian government defeat the Italian Communist Party:

> The United States has security interests of primary importance
> in Italy and the measures to implement our current policies

4. National Security Act, July 16, 1947, Warner, ed., *CIA under Harry Truman*, 131–35.

5. John Prados, *Keepers of the Keys: A History of the National Security Council from Truman to Bush* (New York, 1991), 30–39; Corson, *Armies of Ignorance*, 285–95; Jeffreys-Jones, *CIA*, 35–45.

6. Central Intelligence Agency, "Review of the World Situation as It Relates to the Security of the United States," CIA 1, September 26, 1947, Secret, Warner, ed., *CIA under Harry Truman*, 139–48.

to safeguard those interests should be strengthened without delay. The United States should:

    a) give full support to the present Italian Government and to equally satisfactory governments by . . .

        1. Shipment of wheat and other essential commodities . . .

        2. Additional dollar credits.

        3. Further assistance to the Italian armed forces . . .

    b) Extend economic aid to Italy by mean of favorable US foreign trade policies. . . .

    e) Actively combat Communist propaganda in Italy by an effective US information program and by all other practicable means, including the use of unvouchered funds.[7]

From the start, NSC papers avoided explicit reference to CIA covert operations. That allowed the papers to be more widely disseminated throughout the national security bureaucracy without fear of compromising the secrecy of an ongoing operation. It also allowed the president to deny any specific knowledge of such operations if they became known. This principle would soon be referred to as "plausible deniability." Section "e" of NSC 1/1, with its reference to unvouchered funds, enabled the CIA to intervene covertly, and deniably.

Section "e" also represented the administration's commitment to psychological warfare. Psy-war was one of the most important and one of the least known activities of the national-security state. To carry out the more benign forms of open propaganda, the United States Information Agency (USIA) had been created. But while the USIA could be used to promote positive images of democracy, it did not have the capability to conduct covert psychological warfare. After some discussion, the NSC recommended that the CIA be given that responsibility. Truman approved, and NSC 4-A authorized the director of central intelligence, Admiral Roscoe Hillenkoetter, to undertake psychological operations, which would soon come to be known simply as "psy-ops." In response to what it saw as "the vicious psychological efforts of the USSR," the Truman administration authorized the CIA to conduct "covert psychological operations."[8]

Over the next few years, the CIA would develop a sophisticated psychological-warfare program. In part, psy-op specialists drew on the experience of the

7. NSC 1/1, "The Position of the United States with Respect to Italy," November 14, 1947, Top Secret, HST—President's Secretary File, NSC Files-Meetings, Box 203, Truman Library. See also *FRUS, 1947, Vol. III,* 724–26, in which, however, the last clause, "including the use of unvouchered funds," has been deleted.

8. Memorandum for the Director of Central Intelligence (Hillenkoetter), NSC 4-A, December 17, 1947, Top Secret, Warner, ed., *CIA under Harry Truman,* 173–76.

military during World War II. Many generals, especially Dwight Eisenhower, believed that propaganda and disinformation were vital tools of war. If one could spread rumors, create confusion, disrupt communications, or convince an enemy army or population that they could not win, then the battle was nearly won.[9] Psy-ops also drew on the experience of U.S. corporate advertising; selling the message of capitalism was not so different from selling its products.

Several months after NSC 4-A gave the CIA control of psy-war, central intelligence director Hillenkoetter, who was considered a nice man but not a particularly effective director,[10] described how the CIA would carry out psychological warfare. His memo stated that "covert psychological operations may include all measures of information and persuasion short of physical," and he gave the CIA's assistant director of special operations overall responsibility for coordinating psychological operations with other concerned agencies, such as the departments of state and defense, as well as with relevant individuals in the field, either American operatives or foreign contractors.[11]

Though there are few declassified documents detailing precisely what the CIA did in Italy, later reports on the nature and scope of psy-ops give some indication of what was done in Italy in 1947 and 1948. When the Psychological Strategy Board first met in 1951, it reviewed what had worked and what had not in the early years of the cold war:

> There is general agreement that the ideological aspects of the current conflict are extremely vital. . . . Thus far we have done little to defend against this ideological invasion [from the Soviet Union] or to attack it at its source. One cannot fight an ideological war without ideological tools. . . . Human activity follows this sequence: emotion, ideas, organization, and action. In our struggle against the Soviets we have organized and acted without developing a positive synthesis of our own ideas and without developing ideological shells to disrupt the basic concepts of the enemy. . . .
>
> The shattering effect of the Titoist propaganda line is a good illustration of Soviet vulnerability to ideological attack. What Tito has been doing is to throw the original book back into the Kremlin. . . . There is a good deal that can be learned from an analysis of Yugoslav propaganda. . . .
>
> Are we exploiting this ideological weapon? In fighting the cold war we have carefully examined every single possible, available tool for coping with the Soviets. We have tried agent

9. Corson, *Armies of Ignorance,* 200–201.

10. Jeffreys-Jones, *CIA,* 44–46; Ranelagh, *The Agency,* 113–14.

11. Hillenkoetter, Memorandum for Assistant Director of Special Operations, March 22, 1948, Top Secret, Warner, ed., *CIA under Harry Truman,* 191–95.

operations into the Soviet and satellite areas. We experimented tentatively with economic warfare and have done enough in this field so that we know the technique is difficult. The broad propaganda addressed to the mass of Russian people have so far made only a slight dent. . . .

Psychological warfare must always concern itself with concrete events and is therefore circumscribed by our lack of concrete intelligence and our media. We cannot, for example, promote friction between the factory foreman and one of his workers in some Russian city unless we know all the internal details of the particular plant operations and have some means of getting our message to the people in the plant. . . .

Every society ultimately rests on a moral foundation. If this can be undermined, the whole order will tumble. . . .

Against the Stalinists our ideological warfare should be entirely negative in aim, although not in character. . . . Two chief forces Soviet ideology has attempted to muzzle are (a) a belief in some sort of a Divine Being and hence a purposeful moral universe . . . and (b) the Soviets have tried to throttle the basic and instinctive desire of human beings to own property.[12]

Few documents better encapsulate the world view of American officials during the early cold war. While more clearly articulated than it was in 1948, the strategy discussed above was the same as the strategy employed in Italy. Using a combination of economic incentives and psychological, ideological covert operations, the Truman administration planned the defeat of the Italian Communist Party (PCI) at the polls.

The success of the covert campaign convinced American officials that covert operations were both practical and necessary to thwart Communism. But they never quite acknowledged that the PCI might have been defeated even without U.S. aid to the Christian Democrats. For the Americans, Italy was a victory for the United States covert operations; for the Italians, it was something else entirely.

The contours of U.S. involvement in Italy in 1947 and 1948 were determined by domestic Italian rivalries and opposing visions that had emerged from the cauldron of World War II. The intervention was not purely the product of a blueprint drawn up by bureaucrats in Washington, or by senior officials in the West Wing of the White House. Instead, the intervention was molded in response to various forces within Italy and in conjunction with various Italian officials who offered their own vision of how the United States could best ensure a non-Communist future for Italy.

12. "Ideological Warfare" (N.d. [probably late 1951]), Secret, HST—Psychological Strategy Board, Box 11, folder heading "Doctrinal Warfare," Truman Library.

The most significant of these were Alcide de Gasperi and the Christian Democratic Party (CD) that he led. Committed to parliamentary democracy and rigidly antifascist, de Gasperi was elected leader of the center-right CD soon after its founding in 1943. He saw it as "the party of law and order," and in 1945 he was an obvious choice for prime minister. An imposing, austere figure who had the blessing of the Catholic Church, the trust of industrialists and landowners, and a seeming willingness to compromise with elements of the left (much to the dismay of the Truman administration), de Gasperi led successive coalition governments in postwar Italy.[13]

The Socialists and the Communists (PCI) were de Gasperi's main competitors to the left. Led by Palmiro Togliatti, the PCI was a formidable presence in Italian electoral politics. He became leader of the party after the death of Antonio Gramsci in the early 1930s. Managing to survive Mussolini and spending much of the war in Moscow, Togliatti returned to Italy in 1944 and joined a coalition government. He impressed observers as "a man who had the manners and vocabulary of a professor of philosophy, and was such a gifted orator he could hold any Italian audience spellbound." Abjuring violence and seemingly dedicated to national unity and the defeat of fascism, he decided that elections would be the means of Communist ascent in Italy.[14] De Gasperi and many others doubted that the PCI would abide by elections; rather than risk Italy's future on the good faith of Togliatti and the PCI, de Gasperi sought to undermine them, and he tried to convince the Truman administration to assist in the PCI's downfall.

At the beginning of 1947, de Gasperi travelled to the United States and met with U.S. officials in Washington. Speaking with Secretary of State Byrnes, the Italian prime minister "said he hoped his visit would result in assistance to Italy as that country was now in the throes of an economic as well as a political crisis." He warned that the PCI could potentially "bring Italy within the orbit of Russian influence." For himself, de Gasperi swore that he would do everything in his power to combat the PCI, but he hinted that, without help, even his best efforts might not be sufficient.[15]

De Gasperi painted Italian politics as a struggle between two antithetical blocs, yet that hardly did justice to the political scene. Led by Pietro Nenni,

13. Elisa Carrillo, *Alcide de Gasperi* (Notre Dame, 1965), 133–37; H. Stuart Hughes, *The United States and Italy* (Cambridge, Mass., 1965), 141; Paul Ginsborg, *A History of Contemporary Italy: Society and Politics, 1943-1988* (New York, 1990), 42–48.

14. Robert Murphy, *Diplomat among Warriors* (Garden City, N.Y., 1964), 215; Lawrence Gray, "From Gramsci to Togliatti," in *The Italian Communist Party: Yesterday, Today, and Tomorrow*, ed. Simon Serfaty and Lawrence Gray (Westport, Conn., 1980), 25–29; Donald Blackmer, *Unity in Diversity: Italian Communism and the Communist World* (Cambridge, Mass., 1968), 12.

15. Memorandum of Conversation between Secretary Byrnes, Alcide de Gasperi (prime minister of Italy), Ambassador Tarchiani, and Ambassador Dunn, January 6, 1947, *FRUS, 1947, Vol. III*, 838–41.

the Italian Socialist Party lay somewhat to the right of the PCI and to the left of the Christian Democrats. Nenni was an expert at esoteric debate on the nature of socialism, but he lacked the dexterity of Togliatti or de Gasperi as a party leader. In the immediate postwar years, the socialists benefited from the widespread feeling among the working class that social reform was imperative but that the anti-Catholic Communist Party was not to be trusted.

Nenni faced stiff challenges to his leadership. Some of these came from within the party, but others lay across the Atlantic Ocean. U.S. involvement in Italy was in part propelled by the powerful Italian-American community within the United States. The links that Italian-American labor leaders established with conservative forces in Italy paved the way for subsequent CIA aid to those very same forces. And several of the most powerful Italian-Americans wanted nothing more than to see Pietro Nenni brought down.[16]

Until the mid-1940s, the center of Italian antifascism was New York City, home to luminaries such as the historian Gaetano Salvemini, Italian socialist and labor activist Serafino Romualdi, union leader Luigi Antonini and his assistant Vanni Montana, and exiles from Mussolini's regime, such as future Christian Democrat foreign minister Count Carlo Sforza. They intended to use their clout to shape postwar Italy.[17]

These men came from a European social-democratic tradition that was adamantly pro-reform and vehemently anti-Communist. Antonini in particular acted as a bridge between American labor unions and the Italian Socialist Party. Antonini was vice president of the International Ladies Garment Workers Union (ILGWU) and head of the New York Italian dressmakers union, which had some forty thousand members. Antonini believed in a socialist-right government in Italy, and he distrusted both de Gasperi and the Church. But most of all he distrusted Nenni, for reasons both personal and political.[18] In August 1946, Antonini traveled to Italy and conspired with other socialist leaders to diminish Nenni's influence. Calculating that the enemy of his enemy was a friend, Antonini softened his opposition to de Gasperi.[19]

Antonini channeled significant amounts of money from the United States to Italy. Through him, the American Federation of Labor gave more than $200,000 to anti-Communist groups in Italy in 1945 and early 1946. Antonini and the

16. Giuseppe Mammarella, *Italy after Fascism: A Political History, 1943-1965* (Notre Dame, Ind., 1966), 42, 117-18; James Edward Miller, *The U.S. and Italy: 1940-1950* (Chapel Hill, 1986), 156; Ronald Filippelli, *American Labor and Postwar Italy, 1943-1953* (Stanford, 1989), 21; Ginsborg, *History of Contemporary Italy,* 15-16, 85-87.

17. John Patrick Diggins, *Mussolini and Fascism: The View from America* (Princeton, 1972), 406ff.; Filippelli, *American Labor and Postwar Italy,* 11-36; Count Carlo Sforza, "Italy, the Marshall Plan, and the Third Force," *Foreign Affairs* (April 1948), 450-57.

18. Filippelli, *American Labor,* 22-42.

19. Ivan Lombardo Oral History, 10-12, Truman Library; Filippelli, *American Labor,* 86-94; Miller, *U.S. and Italy,* 217-18.

Italian American Labor Council spent $150,000 in late 1946 and early 1947 for the express purpose of bringing down the socialist leader. The money came from union dues and special funds collected from union members. While these sums were tiny compared to the $100 million loan that de Gasperi obtained from Washington in January 1947, they were more than ample to undercut Nenni.[20] With the cushion provided by American donations, Nenni's opponents within the socialist party were able to act more boldly and decisively than they might otherwise have. In January 1947, the socialists split into two camps. This split weakened the left as a whole and gave de Gasperi an excuse to expel the left from the government, which he promptly did in the spring of 1947.[21]

Until late 1947, the Truman administration seemed to have the best of both worlds: a weakened Italian left without direct action by Washington. Like any good politician, Truman wanted to seem responsive to the Italian-American community. It was a large voting bloc, particularly in New York and throughout the industrial northeast. Fiorello La Guardia, former New York mayor and head of the United Nations relief organization (UNRRA) in 1947, was an influential anti-Communist figure. The conservative Order of the Sons of Italy, which warily allied itself with Antonini, boasted five hundred thousand members, and it regularly flooded both Capitol Hill and the White House with mail warning of a Communist takeover in Italy if Truman did not do something.[22] Other organizations such as the Council for American-Italian Affairs, the Committee for Italian Democracy, and the Federation of the Italian-American Democratic Organizations did the same.[23] There were also a number of Italian-American members of Congress, and these individuals often wrote to the White House urging Truman to come to Italy's aid during the dire economic times after 1945.[24] Also important was the influence of the Catholic Church, which was strongly anti-Communist and pro–Christian Democrat.

20. Washington *Post,* January 5, 1947; J. L. Harper, *America and the Reconstruction of Italy, 1945-1948* (Cambridge, Mass., 1986), 108-16; Federico Romero, *The United States and the European Trade Union Movement, 1944-1951* (Chapel Hill, 1992), 90-100.

21. Sir Ashley Clarke Oral History, 22, Truman Library; Ginsborg, *History of Contemporary Italy,* 86, 104, 108; Hughes, *United States and Italy,* 145-146; Miller, *U.S. and Italy,* 226ff.

22. See Joseph Grew memo of June 1, 1965, referred to above. See also FBI report on the Order of the Sons of Italy, May 30, 1945; Truman letter to Felix Forte (supreme venerable of the order), March 20, 1946, HST—Official File, Box 838, Truman Library.

23. Letter to Truman from Jack Ingegnieros (president of the Federation of the Italian-American Democratic Organization), September 4, 1948, HST—President's Personal File, Box 586; Letter to Truman from the Committee for Italian Democracy [early 1948], HST—Official File, Box 838; Council for American-Italian Affairs Report, July 13, 1946, Philleo Nash Papers—White House Files. All in the Truman Library.

24. See letters to Truman from Congressman Vito Marcantonio, December 3, 1945, and from Congressman John Davis Lodge, March 11, 1948, HST—Official File, 233 Misc, Box 838, Truman Library.

In addition to being a region of deep concern to a large constituency in the United Sates, Italy was an integral part of Western Europe, and Truman officials believed that it had to be denied to the Communist bloc. In late 1947, therefore, when Washington realized that the Italian left was down but far from out,[25] Truman decided to aid de Gasperi directly.

Even though de Gasperi excluded both the socialists and the PCI from his coalition government in early 1947, the left still commanded immense popular support. In the spring, de Gasperi authorized an economic austerity program to combat inflation and restore some of the lira's value. While these measures pleased the business community and won the approbation of the Americans, unemployment shot up; workers, as well as the middle class in the north, were furious. The Christian Democrats began to lose support. Communist-inspired strikes racked northern factories and cities. Violence increased, and Togliatti found it harder and harder to adhere to the "new party" doctrine of peaceful competition for power. He was also faced with the challenge of the Marshall Plan, a multibillion-dollar economic-aid program designed to undermine support for Communism throughout Europe.[26]

The promise of massive economic aid was welcomed by de Gasperi and the center-right in Italy. Between June 1947 (when Marshall announced the plan at a Harvard commencement address) and congressional approval of the plan at the year's end, the economic situation in Italy deteriorated precipitously. As the PCI stepped up protest activities, Togliatti attacked the Marshall Plan and de Gasperi for embracing it.[27] Most Italians seem to have felt differently. Though the left viewed the plan as a trap to enslave Italy and Europe to American capitalism, the bulk of the Italian people were not so ready to reject money that Italy needed. De Gasperi's government may have been buffeted by protests and mass discontent, but because of the psychological boost of the Marshall Plan, Togliatti and the PCI had difficulty turning the CD's unpopularity into their gain.[28]

Oddly, the plight of the Communists in Italy gave the Truman administration more cause for alarm. The U.S. ambassador in Rome, James Dunn, reported in December that the

> Communists have been steadily losing ground politically throughout Italy and if free elections were to be held under

25. Filippelli, *American Labor,* 73, 97–98; Norman Kogan, *A Political History of Italy: The Postwar Years* (New York, 1983), 36.

26. Miller, *U.S. and Italy,* 236; Ginsborg, *History of Contemporary Italy,* 110–14; Lombardo Oral History, 4–6.

27. Miller, *U.S. and Italy,* 230–36; Lombardo Oral History, 12; Giuseppe Pella Oral History, 2–3, Truman Library.

28. Pella Oral History, 3–4; Leffler, *Preponderance of Power,* 185–86.

present circumstances or those foreseeable by March it will result in their defeat at the polls. It is the belief of the Italian intelligence services that as a result of this trend the Communists have abandoned hope of legitimate electoral victory and are now preparing for action by force. The series of strategically planned strikes and civil disturbances which they have already carried out and are expected to continue are the preliminary skirmishes leading to the attempt to overthrow the government.[29]

Guided by Dunn and NSC 1/1, the Truman administration prodded Congress to pass an emergency-aid bill of $600 million for Italy and France. And in line with NSC 4-A, more than $10 million of "unvouchered funds" was allocated by the CIA for anti-Communist propaganda and bribes to aid the CD.[30]

As several hundred million dollars of economic and military aid poured into Italy in the first months of 1948, the Italian ambassador in Washington, Alberto Tarchiani, maintained pressure on the Truman administration. Appointed soon after the armistice in 1943, Tarchiani was a prominent figure in Washington. As he wrote in his memoirs, he believed that Italy had no choice but to turn to the United States for aid against the PCI. It would be, he said, extremely difficult for Italy to remain "equidistant" from the cold-war superpowers, "because our economic condition will periodically compel us to turn to the United States as they [*sic*] are the only ones capable of helping us."[31] When the Truman administration undertook the covert actions of early 1948, it drew on the unflinching support of Tarchiani and his expertise in assessing Italian politics. Tarchiani's position was pragmatic: Italy needed the aid. To defeat the Communists, he would go far to satisfy the Americans, and de Gasperi listened to him.

In February 1948, the NSC issued NSC 1/2, which updated its policy on Italy. Many of the recommendations echoed those of the preceding November, and the document concluded that "the United States should make full use of its political, economic, and, if necessary, military power . . . to assist in preventing Italy from falling under the domination of the Soviet Union."[32] But a CIA report a few days later indicated that even with nearly $200 million in aid and the promise of the Marshall Plan, many Italians remained dissatisfied and

---

29. Dunn to Marshall, December 7, 1947, Top Secret, *FRUS, 1948, Vol. III,* 738-39.

30. James Miller, "Taking Off the Gloves: The United States and the Italian Elections of 1948," *Diplomatic History,* VII (Summer 1983), 34-55; Corson, *Armies of Ignorance,* 298-300; Leffler, *Preponderance of Power,* 190-98. For an example of how these funds were distributed, see Dunn to Marshall, January 29, 1948, *FRUS, 1948, Vol. III,* 824.

31. Alberto Tarchiani, *Dieci anni tra Roma a Washington* (Milan, 1955), 134-35.

32. NSC1/2, "The Position of the United States with Respect to Italy," February 10, 1948, Top Secret, *FRUS, 1948, Vol. III,* 765-69.

had to endure various privations. De Gasperi benefited from the close association with American aid and from the intimate support of the Vatican, but the outcome of the April elections was still in doubt. Though the report acknowledged that the left was unlikely to win an outright victory and picked the CD as the probable winner, it emphasized that many of de Gasperi's supporters were disenchanted with the huge deficits and austere anti-inflationary economics of the government.[33]

By March, the NSC offered an even gloomier appraisal. A Soviet-inspired coup in Czechoslovakia and the death of Jan Masaryk in February 1948 had removed the last vestiges of Czech democracy. The shock was felt throughout Europe, and Washington interpreted the events as a chilling warning of what might happen in Italy.[34] The NSC concluded that the bulk of the Italian people were anti-Communist and inclined toward the West, in part because they knew how vital was American aid. But sentiment notwithstanding, many Italians were being swayed as "the communists, forgoing armed insurrection for the time being . . . vigorously exploit legitimate economic grievances [and] social unrest."[35] Those sections of the document addressing the ongoing covert campaign are still classified, but the NSC recommended large amounts of aid and diplomatic support for the CD and other anti-Communist groups in Italy.

Much of the CIA money went to local organizations in Italy that worked to "get out the vote" for the CD. It also helped fund pamphlets and newspapers pushing a vigorously anti-Communist line. Specific districts and seats thought to be vulnerable were targeted. And while the specific pathways the covert aid took are impossible to ascertain given that the relevant documents are still classified, it would seem that the earlier links between Italian-American labor organizations and the OSS were utilized to good effect by the CIA in 1948.[36]

While these covert moneys smoothed the way to a Christian Democrat victory at the polls, the Truman administration took one final, decisive action before election day on April 18. Truman, Tarchiani, the Church, de Gasperi, and Dunn all believed that the Italian public associated a Christian Democrat victory with continued American aid. Given that no prominent Italian—not Nenni, not the Socialists, not even Togliatti and the PCI—questioned the critical importance of the hundreds of millions of dollars of aid, the link between continued money

33. CIA-ORE 47/1, "The Current Situation in Italy," February 16, 1948, HST—President's Secretary File, Intelligence File, Box 255, Truman Library.

34. Dunn to Marshall, March 16, 1948, Confidential, *FRUS, 1948, Vol. III,* 850–51; Charles Maier, "Alliance and Autonomy: European Identity and U.S. Foreign Policy in the Truman Years," in *Truman Presidency,* ed. Lacy, 284–86; Leffler, *Preponderance of Power,* 203–207.

35. NSC 1/3, "Position of the United States with Respect to Italy in the Light of the Possibility of Communist Participation in the Government by Legal Means," March 8, 1948, Top Secret, HST—President's Secretary File, NSC Files, Box 203. See also in *FRUS, 1948, Vol. III.*

36. Corson, *Armies of Ignorance,* 298; Romero, *United States and the European Trade Movement,* 94–96, 160–62.

and a CD victory was a potent weapon. On March 15, 1948, the Truman administration used it.

That day, the State Department issued a highly publicized press release announcing that economic aid to Italy would be terminated in the event of a Communist victory.[37] The reaction in Italy was immediate. The center and right lauded the bold move, while the Communist press decried the attempts of Marshall and Truman to blackmail the Italian people.[38] The charge was apt, but the strategy worked. When the Italians went to the polls in April, the Christian Democrats won 48.5 percent of the vote and an absolute majority of the seats in Parliament—305 out of 574. The PCI, in a Popular Front with former elements of the socialist party, obtained 31 percent, and actually increased their seat total from 106 to 140. The socialist remnant was badly defeated, and its representation in Parliament plummeted from 115 to 41.[39]

The Truman administration considered Italy a victory for its foreign policy. Believing that the election's outcome demonstrated the effectiveness of covert action, Truman became convinced that the CIA had a vital role to play in protecting the capitalist sphere. After April 1948, the attention of the administration turned elsewhere—to the pressing problems of a divided Germany and Berlin, to the question of NATO, and soon to the war in Korea. In considering Italy a model of policy formation and implementation, the Truman administration never looked beyond the statistics of the election to see what had actually been accomplished, and why it had worked the way it did.

The 1948 election was a victory for the Christian Democrats, but it boded ill for Italian democracy. De Gasperi's willingness to embrace American covert aid indicated a scorn for the democratic process, a scorn that would characterize the ruling Christian Democrat elite for years to come. The conservative northern Italian industrialists, businessmen, and politicians gladly took American money, paid lip service to democracy, and then used their informal networks to govern the country until the massive revelations of corruption disrupted the system in the early 1990s.

---

37. New York *Times,* March 16, 1948.
38. Dunn to Marshall, March 16 and 20, 1948, *FRUS, 1948, Vol. III,* 855–59.
39. Ginsborg, *History of Contemporary Italy,* 118.

3

Iran

Succeeding John Bull

Britain has suffered by Persian depredations losses which I am told may amount to 60 million pounds Sterling a yr.... We cannot I am sure go much further at this critical time in our struggle for solvency than proposals which you agreed were fair and just. It seems also to me, if I may say so, that it wld be hard prospect for Amer taxpayer to have to bribe Persians (and how many others?) not to become Commies. Once this process started it might go on long time in lot of places.

—Winston Churchill to Harry Truman

In August 1953, an American covert plan code-named Operation Ajax led to the ouster of the Iranian prime minister, Mohammed Mosaddeq. Just as de Gasperi and the Christian Democrats had carefully tried to lure the United States toward intervention in Italy, the Shah and his allies lobbied the Americans to intercede in Iran. In Iran as in Greece, the Americans were also pressured by the British. Long before the Americans, the British governments of Attlee and Churchill had plotted Mosaddeq's ouster, but not until late 1952 did the Americans come to agree with the British that Mosaddeq must be removed.

The Robinson-Gallagher framework offered an interpretation of the British empire in its heyday. In the period after World War II, the United States slowly began assuming Britain's place in world affairs. D. Cameron Watt referred to this process as "succeeding John Bull."[1] As it filled the gaps left by the British in Greece, Italy, Palestine, Southeast Asia, and Iran, the United States inherited not just an imperial mantle but also imperial liabilities. It became vulnerable to the same sorts of pressures on its periphery that Britain had felt a century before.

In fact, until Iran and Great Britain severed relations in October 1952, Washington was not swayed by the pull to intervene, a pull which came from both

---

1. D. C. Watt, *Succeeding John Bull: America in Britain's Place* (London, 1984).

Iran and Britain. Only when Britain was effectively removed from the scene did the U.S. government become vulnerable to the forces urging intervention. For it was only then that the United States "succeeded John Bull" in Iran.

The eclipse of the British in Iran had occurred several months before a change of administration in Washington. For that reason, perhaps, many people have assumed that the United States took action in 1953, but not in 1951 or 1952, because Truman did not share Eisenhower's enthusiasm for covert action and intervention. In both Iran in 1953 and Guatemala in 1954, Eisenhower took action where Truman had not. It is possible to explain this difference purely by reference to different individuals with different approaches in different administrations in the United States. Yet such an explanation elides the role of the periphery and the question of how changing circumstances and more aggressive tactics by groups in the periphery may have affected decisions in Washington.

■

The influence of the British was central to the outcome of the 1951–1953 oil crisis, but because of an earlier crisis, the U.S. government had already determined that a non-Communist Iran was a cold-war imperative. In conjunction with the Soviets and the British, the United States occupied Iran during World War II, and nearly thirty thousand noncombatant American troops served in Iran to manage supply routes to Russia. As the war drew to a close, the Roosevelt administration grew concerned about Soviet influence in Iranian Azerbeijan in the north.[2]

In 1946, in what some have identified as the first major confrontation of the cold war between the United States and the Soviet Union, Truman confronted Stalin and the Soviet foreign secretary, Vyacheslav Molotov, about their refusal to withdraw troops from Azerbeijan. Located in the northwest corner of Iran and spilling over into the Soviet Union, Azerbeijan had long resisted the efforts of Tehran to control it. When the province was occupied by Soviet troops in 1941, the nationalist movement in Azerbeijan was given a significant boost.[3]

---

2. There was, however, considerable friction between U.S. officials in Iran and the their British counterparts. The head of the U.S. legation in Tehran, Louis Dreyfuss, and the British ambassador, Sir Reader Bullard, disliked each other. Bullard, like many of his colleagues in Iran, was convinced that the Americans intended to supplant the British, while Dreyfuss was convinced that the British intended to use the Americans to reestablish the British empire in Persia. See Barry Rubin, *The Great Powers in the Middle East, 1941–1947* (London, 1980), 15–26; Howard Sachar, *Europe Leaves the Middle East, 1936–1954* (New York, 1972), 350ff.; Eduard Mark, "Allied Relations in Iran: The Origins of a Cold War Crisis," *Wisconsin Magazine of History,* LIX (Autumn 1975), 54–60.

3. Parviz Homayounpour, *L'Affaire d'Azarbaidjan* (Lausanne, 1966), 25–50; Goode, *United*

By 1945, the movement had coalesced around Jafar Pishevari, a former Comintern agent who had spent time in Moscow in the 1920s. In November 1945, Pishevari proclaimed Azerbaijan's independence and ousted the Shah's government from Tabriz.[4] He was able to do so, however, only because Soviet troops still occupied the province. The presence of these troops made it impossible for the Shah to order his army into Tabriz to squelch what amounted to a rebellion. Under the Tripartite Agreement of 1942, the British and the Soviets agreed to withdraw their forces from Iran within six months of the end of World War II. Given that the war did not end until August 1945, the Soviets were still within their rights to keep troops in Azerbaijan. But supporting an independence movement seemed to be violating the spirit if not the letter of the agreement. As good relations between the Soviets and the Western allies deteriorated in Eastern Europe and Germany, Truman officials had little difficulty interpreting events in Azerbaijan as a manifestation of Soviet expansionism. The U.S. consul in Tabriz linked Soviet actions in Iran with similar Soviet moves on Greece, Turkey, and Eastern Europe.[5]

Two tasks faced the Shah and his Western allies: getting Stalin to withdraw his troops and forcing Pishevari's collapse. The British played a secondary role to the United States during this crisis, although their interest in Iran was greater, their knowledge of the country deeper, and their stake in the outcome more significant. Perceived by Truman and Byrnes as a test of free-world willingness to stand up to "Soviet aggression," the Azerbaijan crisis occupied a top place on the national security agenda at the White House. As Byrnes expressed it, the United States was determined "to support Iran vigorously."[6]

As for Stalin, it seems that his reason for supporting Pishevari had less to do with Soviet territorial expansion than a desire for Persian oil. Stalin wanted the same concessions in northern Iran that Britain had in the south. Under the leadership of Prime Minister Ahmad Qavam—the only figure in Iran as respected, capable and experienced as Mosaddeq—the Iranian government agreed to give the Soviets an oil concession. But Qavam, a wealthy tea planter from the Caspian Sea area who was nothing if not innovative,[7] made the deal conditional on approval by the majlis. Having received his concession, Stalin ordered the evacuation of Soviet troops in May 1946.

States and Iran, chaps. 1–2; Louise L'Estrange Fawcett, *Iran and the Cold War* (Cambridge, U.K., 1992), 5–25; Keddie, *Roots of Revolution,* 83–85; Kuniholm, *Origins of the Cold War in the Near East,* 144–52.

4. Homayounpour, *L'Affaire d'Azarbaidjan,* 24–28, 64–67.

5. Richard Cottam, *Iran and the United States: A Cold War Case Study* (Pittsburgh, 1988), 69–71; James Bill, *The Eagle and the Lion: The Tragedy of American-Iranian Relations* (New Haven, 1988), 34–36; Kuniholm, *Origins of the Cold War in the Near East,* 308–12.

6. Robert Donovan, *Conflict and Crisis: The Presidency of Harry S. Truman, 1945–1948* (New York, 1977), 184–97; Louis, *British Empire in the Middle East,* 64ff.

7. George Allen, "Mission to Iran" (unpublished manuscript), 9, Allen Papers, Truman Library.

In later years, Truman pointed to the Soviet withdrawal as a triumph of hard diplomacy. During a press conference in 1952, Truman claimed that he had given Stalin an ultimatum in early March 1946 to remove his troops from Iran or face the consequences. The problem was, no evidence of this ultimatum could be found. Within hours of the president's assertion, a White House spokesman declared that "the President was using the term ultimatum in a nontechnical layman's sense."[8] After he left the White House, Truman said that he "decided that the Russian government ought to be informed on how we felt about this kind of conduct in internal relations. . . . I told Byrnes to send a blunt message to Premier Stalin."[9] Later, in an article in the New York *Times,* Truman stated:

> From my experience with the Russians, I learned that they are bound to move where we fail to make clear our intentions. For example, shortly after World War II, Stalin and Molotov brazenly refused to keep their agreement to withdraw from Iran. . . . The Soviet Union persisted in its occupation until I personally saw to it that Stalin was informed that I had given orders to our military chiefs to prepare for the movement of our ground, sea, and air forces. Stalin then did what I knew he would do. He moved his troops out.[10]

However, there is no evidence for any of this. Even in the official State Department publication, the foreign-relations volume published in 1969, the department's historical staff noted that no documentation of an ultimatum or of threats had been found.[11] The only official record is a March 6 note saying that the United States could not "remain indifferent" and urging the Soviets to honor their agreement.[12]

According to George Allen, who was ambassador to Iran from April 1946, no ultimatum was ever made. He believed—as did Harriman, Byrnes, and Allen Dulles—that Truman vastly overstated the American contribution to the resolution of the Azerbeijan crisis.[13] And Mozaffar Firouz, a prominent Iranian politician, journalist, and one of Mosaddeq's nephews, opined that even if there had been an ultimatum "it was a lot of talk. The Russians didn't care a damn about

8. James A. Thorpe, "Truman's Ultimatum to Stalin on the 1946 Azerbaijan Crisis: The Making of a Myth," *Journal of Politics,* IV (February 1978), 188–93; Rouhollah Ramazani, *Iran's Foreign Policy, 1941–1973* (Charlottesville, Va., 1975), 138–39.

9. Harry S. Truman, *Years of Trial and Hope* (Garden City, N.Y., 1956), 94–95, Vol. II of Truman, *Memoirs of Harry S. Truman,* 2 vols.

10. New York *Times,* August 25, 1957.

11. Thorpe, "Truman's Ultimatum," 192. The admission appears in *FRUS, 1946, Vol. VII.*

12. U.S. State Department, *Bulletin* (March 17, 1946).

13. George Allen to Alexander George, May 27, 1969, in Allen Papers, Truman Library.

the Truman ultimatum. It had absolutely no importance."[14] Although some have argued that enough signals were sent to Stalin to constitute an effective threat,[15] it seems clear that Truman either misremembered or willfully misrepresented his role in bringing about the Soviet withdrawal.

In the minicontroversy about what Truman did or did not say, it has also been forgotten that the Soviet pullout did not end the Azerbeijan crisis. Pishevari was still in power, and his party enjoyed wide support amongst Azeri speakers. The Soviets thought they had been given an oil concession by Qavam, but the majlis was in no mood to approve one. During the summer of 1946, after tense negotiations between Pishevari and Qavam in Tehran, Pishevari agreed to be reincorporated into Iran on the condition that Azerbeijani taxes be used in Azerbeijan, Azeri be used in the schools, and that Azerbeijan enjoy special semiautonomous status. In October, having lulled the Azerbeijanis into a false sense of security, Qavam abrogated the agreement with Pishevari. Finally, in December, the Shah ordered the Iranian army to retake Azerbeijan. Participating in the attack were the Iranian gendarmerie, who had been trained by Colonel Norman Schwarzkopf of the New Jersey police. (Colonel Schwarzkopf had helped solve the Lindbergh baby's kidnapping; years later, his son and namesake would lead the American forces in the Gulf War.) Resistance to the Shah's army was slight; the Soviets were peeved but did nothing. The final insult came a year later when the majlis voted 102-2 against granting the Soviets an oil concession.[16] As with the 1953 coup, the resolution of the Azerbeijan crisis owed less to great power machinations than to internal Iranian politics.

Nonetheless, the crisis set an important precedent for cold-war U.S. involvement in Iranian affairs. It also sent a signal to the Shah that the Americans would act if they believed Iran to be threatened by the Soviets. Whether he issued an ultimatum or not, Truman concluded from the experience that the Soviets must be treated forcefully or they would take advantage of the U.S. Along with Soviet pressure on Turkey that year, the crisis also convinced the Americans of the importance of the "Northern Tier," those Near Eastern countries along the southern border of the Soviet Union. As one intelligence report stated: "The strategic importance of Iran lies in: a) its geographical position in the Middle East bridge connecting Europe, Africa, and Asia; b) its consequent position with regard to lines of communications of other powers; c) its oil resources (Iran is the world's fourth largest producer). It is the center of the an arc formed by three independent states (Turkey, Iran, Afghanistan) which

14. Mozaffar Firouz Oral History, vol. 1, p. 9, Iran Oral History Collection, Houghton Library, Harvard University.

15. Kuross Samii, "Truman against Stalin: A Tale of Three Messages," *Middle East Studies* (January 1987), 95-107.

16. Cottam, *Iran and the United States,* 72-79; Fawcett, *Iran and the Cold War,* 63-65; Homayounpour, *L'Affaire d'Azarbaidjan,* 167.

border the Soviet Union.''[17] Although American oil interests were minimal, the British and Western Europe had a significant stake in Iranian oil, and the United States had a significant stake in Western Europe.

Until at least 1951, however, the United States deferred to Britain over Iran. But when the British refused to concede to Iranian nationalist demands for greater control over—and greater profits from—Iranian oil, American officials believed that Iran's stability was jeopardized. They therefore sought a resolution to the 1951 Anglo-Iranian oil crisis that would satisfy Iranian nationalism without encouraging Iranian radicalism.[18]

In 1951, the British were facing the stark reality that the empire was disintegrating. India was gone; Palestine and Greece were no longer in the British sphere. Latin American trade had long been lost to the Americans. The last vestige of British rule in Egypt, the garrison at Suez, was almost under siege and subject to the ire of the government in Cairo. But in Iraq, the Persian Gulf, and Iran, the British were still the preeminent power. The Anglo-Iranian Oil Company (with the British government a majority shareholder) and its oil refinery at Abadan provided vital revenue to a depleted British treasury. During World War II, the British had lost nearly Ł7 billion, or a quarter of their national wealth. Between 1945 and 1950, the AIOC returned to the British government more than Ł125 million in taxes. In addition, it paid approximately Ł50 million in royalties to the Iranian government. In 1950 alone, AIOC net profits were more than Ł100 million; both the taxes and the income were sorely needed in London.[19]

In the late 1940s, as Mohammed Reza Shah struggled for control with the nationalists in the majlis, many Iranians demanded that the British share a greater percentage of the profits with the Iranians. The British, however, could ill afford any diminution of oil revenue from the AIOC, which was the proverbial cash cow. The British met the demands with polite refusals and claimed that the sixty-year agreement negotiated with Reza Shah in 1933 was quite adequate. In short, the company did not intend to renegotiate until the 1933 accord came up for renewal in 1993.

As the British resisted, nationalist sentiment grew in the majlis. It was over

17. CIG SR-6, August 1, 1947, Top Secret, *CIA Research Reports-Middle East* (University Publications Microfilm), Reel 2, Harvard University Government Documents.

18. See, for example, Memo for Truman vis. Truman-Churchill meeting, Dec. 21, 1951, HST—President's Secretary File, General File, Box 116, Truman Library. See also see State Department memo of conversation between Acheson, Nitze, and Sir Oliver Franks, April 27, 1951, Truman Library, Acheson Papers, Memoranda of Conversations, Box 66. See also Henderson to State, Secret, Nov. 6, 1951, NA 888.253/11-651, *FRUS, 1952-1954, Vol. X,* 260-62.

19. Mostafa Elm, *Oil, Power, and Principle* (Syracuse, N.Y., 1992), 38, 98-99; Homa Katouzian, *The Political Economy of Modern Iran: Despotism and Pseudo-Modernism, 1926-1979* (New York, 1981), 182-83; Ronald Ferrier, ''The Anglo-Iranian Oil Dispute,'' in *Musaddiq, Iranian Nationalism, and Oil,* ed. James Bill and William Roger Louis (London, 1988), 164-92.

the issue of oil revenues that the National Front was formed in 1949, with Mosaddeq at its head. One of the front's stated goals was the nationalization of the AIOC. According to one of the front's leading members, Husayn Fatemi, the oil issue in 1949 was "as significant for Iran as was independence for Indonesia, India, Syria and Lebanon."[20] The front established oil as *the* issue for Iranian nationalists, and they cast their struggle as an anti-imperial one. Iranians were especially irritated that the British government obtained more than twice the tax income from the company than the Iranian government did.[21] The British saw the challenge as more than economic; they believed that if ground were yielded in Iran, then it would truly be the end of empire.[22]

The struggle between Iran and the company was further complicated by developments elsewhere in the Middle East. At the very end of 1950, the huge American oil consortium Aramco reached an agreement with Saudi Arabia. Under a new formula, the Saudis would receive 50 percent of the profits. The Venezuelans had recently obtained a fifty-fifty deal from Standard Oil of New Jersey (now Exxon) and Shell; the Saudis decided that they wanted the same, and they knew that Aramco could afford it. After two years of pressure and threats, the Saudis forced Aramco to concede, though the blow was eventually softened for the company when it was given a generous tax break by the U.S. government. This fifty-fifty profit sharing was a quantum leap from the traditional royalty payments which Western oil companies gave to the host countries. Not only was it a significant increase in revenue, but it was a symbolic recognition that the countries which housed the oil ultimately owned the oil.[23]

Once the fifty-fifty principle was accepted in Saudi Arabia, the other oil-producing countries demanded the same. While the Iranian prime minister General Razmara was inclined to compromise with the British, the National Front demanded that the Iranian government accept nothing less than a fifty-fifty agreement. Merchants in the bazaars and a number of the leading clerics joined the front. Two days after Razmara made a fateful speech in early March 1951 eschewing nationalization, he was assassinated by a member of the Fedayin i-Islam, a radical group owing rough allegiance to the Ayatollah Abol Qasem Kashani.

20. Fakhreddin Azimi, "The Political Career of Muhammad Musaddiq," in *Musaddiq, Iranian Nationalism, and Oil,* ed. Bill and Louis, 52–53; Ramazani, *Iran's Foreign Policy,* 192–95.

21. J. H. Bamberg, *The History of the British Petroleum Company: The Anglo-Iranian Years, 1928–1954* (Cambridge, U.K., 1994), 187.

22. Brian Lapping, *End of Empire* (New York, 1985), 204–26; Louis, *British Empire in the Middle East,* 632–46.

23. Daniel Yergin, *The Prize: The Epic Quest for Oil, Money, and Power* (New York, 1991), 433–46; Alan Ford, *The Anglo-Iranian Oil Dispute of 1951–1952* (Berkeley, 1954), 51ff.; Irvine Anderson, "The American Oil Industry and the Fifty-Fifty Agreement of 1950," in *Musaddiq, Iranian Nationalism, and Oil,* ed. Bill and Louis, 143–59.

The company's stubborn refusal to accede to the fifty-fifty principle was not universally supported in Britain. As an official in the Foreign Office commented:

> The Company still seemed to be thinking in terms of offering a little money here and another sop there, but all this . . . was entirely beside the point. What was required was a fresh start, on the basis of equal partnership. Unless the Company realised that, and were sincerely prepared to go forward in that direction, they might sooner or later find themselves without any installations in Persia: even if the Russians did not come in, nationalisation might expropriate the Company.[24]

This comment was eerily prescient. Within a month, an angry majlis under the leadership of the front had nationalized the AIOC.

The British were outraged. In newspapers, Parliament, and pubs throughout the country, the Iranians were denounced for what the British perceived to be an illegal action, and a humiliating one at that. Upon becoming premier in late April, Mosaddeq announced that the British government had no right to concern itself with the issue; the problem was between Iran and the company. The British government maintained that "on the contrary . . . HMG [Her Majesty's Government] have every right to intervene in defense of this great British interest in Persia, and, moreover have an important interest in the matter by reason of their majority holding in the company."[25] Prime Minister Attlee and Foreign Secretary Herbert Morrison (Bevin died in April 1951) were pressured by the opposition conservatives to reverse Iran's decision by force if necessary. The British workers at Abadan prepared for war.[26]

The British intended to take a firm line against anti-imperial Iranian nationalism. While the British during the crisis were not as blindly unreasonable as many have depicted them, they nonetheless refused to accept the inexorable reality of Iranian nationalism.[27] Reflecting official British attitudes, one former ambassador charged that the Iranians suffered from "a persecution mania."[28] The British position in 1951 was captured by Oliver Franks, a distinguished Oxford philosopher who was then Britain's ambassador in Washington. In

24. L. A. C. Frye (Eastern Department), February 6, 1951. Quoted in Louis, *British Empire in the Middle East,* 650.

25. London 6366, Report on Statement of Herbert Morrison in House of Commons, June 5, 1951, NA 888.2553/6-551.

26. Norman Kemp, *Abadan: A First-Hand Account of the Persian Oil Crisis* (London, 1953).

27. Louis, *British Empire in the Middle East,* 640–50, defends the British as having a more sophisticated grasp of developments in Iran, although he perhaps gives them too much benefit of the doubt.

28. Sir Reader Bullard, "Behind the Oil Dispute: A British View," *Foreign Affairs* (April 1953), 469.

discussions with Dean Acheson in April, Sir Oliver questioned the cohesiveness of the nationalist movement. In his view, "the fanatical religious element" was more attached to Islam than Iran; "the true nationalist element" consisted largely of university groups; "the landowning tribal and governmental groups" had little influence; and the Tudeh [Communist] party was looking to capitalize on the weakness of the other groups. And above all, Franks strongly implied that "the British were worried about U.S. appeasement in Iran."[29] That summer, as negotiations between Iran and Britain reached a stalemate, the Americans were drawn into the conflict.

American officials were disposed to accept the nationalization as a fait accompli, and they saw the British as acting out a Don Quixote fantasy by tilting at the wind-mills of nationalism. During a series of discussion between Franks and Acheson, the British ambassador conceded that the American position had some merits.

> [Franks] thought we [the Americans] were right in appreciating the seriousness of the nationalist feeling and that the British were wrong in underestimating it. . . . He thought that we were wrong and the British were more right in understanding who was using . . . nationalist feeling and for what purpose. He thought that small groups . . . were using it to turn the discontent of people against foreigners, chiefly British. He felt, therefore, that the answer to this nationalist feeling was not merely to give in to it.[30]

Acheson had little tolerance for foolishness, but it was not the illogic of the British position that disturbed him. It was that British intransigence would, in his view, lead to the loss of Iran from the Western sphere; and the only country that would benefit from that loss, according to Acheson and many in the Truman administration, was the Soviet Union. As he said, "our appraisal of the internal situation in Iran indicates nationalism is a real and potent factor in present situation. Hence we do not believe objectives in Iran can be achieved merely by setting ourselves up in opposition to it."[31] As for the Soviets, they would capitalize on nationalist discontent with Britain; the result would either be the capture of the nationalist movement by "indigenous fanaticism" or by Soviet "puppets."[32]

29. State Department Memorandum of Conversation among Franks, Acheson, and Paul Nitze, April 27, 1951, Top Secret, Acheson Papers, Memoranda of Conversations, Box 66, Truman Library.

30. State Department Memorandum of Conversation between Acheson and Franks, August 20, 1951, Top Secret, Acheson Papers, Memoranda of Conversations, Box 66.

31. Acheson, *Present at the Creation*, 505–506; Belgrade 206, Acheson to Harriman, August 24, 1951, Top Secret, NA 888.2553/8-2451.

32. NSC 107/2, "Iran," June 27, 1951, Top Secret, *FRUS, 1952–1954, Vol. X*, 71–73. See also State Department Memorandum of Conversation among McGhee, Franks, et al. April 18, 1951, Top Secret, NA 888.2553-AIOC/4-1851.

American attitudes mattered because both the British and Iranians of various stripes looked to the United States to mediate the dispute. In July, Truman sent his personal envoy, Averell Harriman, to Tehran.

Averell Harriman was born rich. The son of railroad magnate E. H. Harriman, a graduate of Groton and Yale, Averell was part of the loose East Coast elite known as the "Establishment."[33] A middling entrepreneur who had tried to do business in the Soviet Union in the interwar years, Harriman was one of the few magnates who actually supported the New Deal. Appointed U.S. ambassador to Russia in 1943, he had been George Kennan's boss during the formative period when relations between the wartime allies turned sour. After brief stints as commerce secretary and Marshall Plan administrator, he remained a Truman confidante and was often found at the president's card table during games of eight-handed poker. In 1951, he was sent to Iran and told to do what he could to mediate between the British and Mosaddeq.

The mission did not begin auspiciously. Pro-Tudeh demonstrators surrounded the American embassy and shouted "Death to Harriman."[34] Mosaddeq was glad to have Harriman in Tehran to help adjudicate,[35] but Harriman took an almost immediate dislike to the premier. When Mosaddeq warned Harriman about how evil the British were, Harriman, who had spent considerable time in England, was offended. He also had little respect for what he took to be Mosaddeq's ignorance about the technical details of the oil business.[36] While acknowledging that Mosaddeq was the most popular and powerful individual on the Iranian political scene, Harriman felt that the premier had "created an atmosphere which had made it possible for extreme elements, both right and Communist, to establish situation under which it is practically impossible to retreat. . . . Mosaddeq's rigidity thus results as much from practical political factors as it does from his emotionalism."[37]

Harriman believed that the only solution to the crisis was to get the British to accept the principle of nationalization. After that, the Iranians would be disposed to compromise on the specifics, and Britain would salvage its economic interests. He was critical of what he interpreted as a lack of realism on the part of British officials.[38] In August, after the World Court ruled that nationalization proceedings should halt pending negotiations, the Attlee gov-

---

33. For the best account of the links among these men, see Isaacson and Thomas, *Wise Men*. See also Rudy Abramson, *Spanning the Century: The Life of W. Averell Harriman, 1891–1986* (New York, 1992).

34. Abramson, *Spanning the Century,* 471.

35. Harriman to Department of State, July 17, 1951, Top Secret, *FRUS, 1952–1954, Vol. X,* 93.

36. Vernon Walters, *Silent Missions* (New York, 1978), 248.

37. Harriman to Department of State, July 19, 1951, Top Secret, *FRUS, 1952–1954, Vol. X,* 97–98.

38. Harriman to Department of State, July 20, 1951, Top Secret, *FRUS, 1952–1954, Vol. X,* 100–102.

ernment sent Richard Stokes to haggle with Mosaddeq. Harriman supervised these talks. In late August, Mosaddeq rejected the Stokes proposals which, while offering a more generous fifty-fifty profit sharing agreement, still held that nationalization was illegal and unacceptable. Harriman was thoroughly disenchanted with all parties, as he reported to Acheson and Truman. Stokes was inflexible; Mosaddeq emotional; and the Iranian oil minister, Husayn Makki, was "obsessed with [the] evils of [the] British and [the] oil company and has demagogic appeal to [the] people."[39] While he had not sided with the British, Harriman hardly lived up to Mosaddeq's expectations of a neutral third party mediator.[40]

The mission was not a success, nor did it end the pressure on the Truman administration to settle the crisis. Even more crucial, the British needed American support in order to proceed with plans to retake Abadan by force. During these months, the Attlee government seriously contemplated using British troops to annul the nationalization. While the British may have had the military means to undertake an invasion of Abadan, they were economically dependent on the United States and their military strategy in the Gulf region depended on close coordination with American forces. Without at least U.S. acquiescence, Britain would find itself diplomatically isolated and economically vulnerable. But there was strong sentiment in Britain for action. As Harold Macmillan, one of the leading lights of the Tory Party and future prime minister, put it, if the British evacuated Abadan without a fight, it would mean "the collapse of British power and prestige in the East."[41]

As early as May, the British press was reporting the mobilization of paratrooper units for possible use in southern Iran. The move toward force gathered steam during the summer. A British note to Mosaddeq warned of "most serious consequences" if the oil dispute was not resolved short of nationalization.[42] Morrison complained to the Americans that the Labor Party was being hammered in Parliament for seeming weak in the face of Mosaddeq's blustering.[43] The Americans met the suggestion that force should be used with stony refusals.

39. Harriman to Department of State, August 12, 1951, Top Secret, FRUS, 1952-1954, Vol. X, 132-33. Makki was a prominent member of the National Front and a staunch Mosaddeq supporter who would later turn against the premier.

40. William Langer of the Board of National Estimates prematurely reported that the Harriman mission appeared headed for success. See Langer memorandum for the DCI, "The Harriman Mission," August 3, 1951, Top Secret, HST—President's Secretary Files, Box 180.

41. Macmillan in House of Commons Speech, July 30, 1951, quoted in Louis, British Empire in the Middle East, 671.

42. Gifford (American ambassador in London) to State Department, May 16, 1951, Top Secret, FRUS, 1952-1954, Vol. X, 54-55.

43. Gifford to State Department, June 26, 1951, Top Secret, FRUS, 1952-1954, Vol. X, 69-71.

Send in troops, the leading Truman officials said, and Iran would be lost to extremism and Communism.[44]

After the collapse of the Harriman mission, Attlee made one final effort in the fall to convince the Americans to go along with a British invasion. Elections were coming up, and the Laborites were susceptible to Conservative charges of being "kicked around" by a fanatical Mosaddeq. U.S. officials maintained their previous position that there was to be no resolution of the oil dispute by force. On September 27, Attlee's cabinet decided not to authorize the use of force to keep British workers at Abadan.[45] A month later, Labor lost the election, and Winston Churchill, the lion himself, became prime minister.

Although the Americans refused to support an invasion, the foundations for an intervention laid by the British in 1951 were ultimately used by the Americans in 1953. The British not only contemplated the deployment of troops to Abadan, they also began to plan for the covert removal of Mosaddeq. On the initiative of two scholars at Oxford and the University of London, the British government began to build a network of anti-Mosaddeq forces in Iran in 1951. Christopher "Monty" Woodhouse, formerly a British operative in Greece, was sent to Tehran to organize the operation, along with Professor Robin Zaehner of Oxford.[46]

At first, the British government found no enthusiasm in Washington for Mosaddeq's removal, or at least no official enthusiasm. But when the Americans decided in late 1952 that Mosaddeq was a liability, they had more than two years of British arguments and planning to rely on. The CIA's 1953 Operation Ajax in many ways mirrored the earlier plans of British operatives. That suggests that the British were instrumental in the formation of American policy. They laid the foundation. In 1953, the Americans, the Shah, and the forces arranged against Mosaddeq finally did what the British had been advocating all along.

44. NSC 107/2, "Iran," June 27, 1951, Top Secret, *FRUS, 1952–1954, Vol. X*, 71–73; Acheson-Lovett phone conversation, September 25, 1951, Acheson Papers, Memoranda of Conversations, Box 66, Truman Library.

45. Harriman to State Department, August 28, 1951, Top Secret, British cabinet notes, September 27, 1951, *FRUS, 1952–1954, Vol. X*, 150–52, 173.

46. Christopher Woodhouse, *Something Ventured* (New York, 1982), 113–25; Gasiorowski, "1953 Coup D'Etat in Iran," 262–72.

4

Iran

Whose Coup?

*We may have done no more than mobilize forces that were already
there, but that was precisely what needed to be done, and it was
enough.*

—C. M. Woodhouse

*We were successful in this venture because our assessment of the
situation in Iran was correct. We believed ... that if people and the
armed forces were shown that they must choose, that Mossadegh
was forcing them to choose, between their monarch and a revolutionary figure backed by the Soviet Union, they could, and would,
make only one choice.... And most convincingly. The people and
the army came, overwhelmingly, to the support of the Shah.*

—Kermit "Kim" Roosevelt

*It is most obvious that the American government had no wish to
defend Iran's freedom and independence, but wanted to benefit
from our oil in the name of stopping Communism. That is just
what it did by exchanging a nation's freedom for 40 percent of the
shares of the oil consortium.*

—Mohammed Mosaddeq

The August 1953 coup was the culmination of a bitter rivalry
between the Shah and Mohammed Mosaddeq. The Shah's enmity
for Mosaddeq has already been noted,[1] but the premier's hostility toward the
Shah was equally pronounced. If one aspect of Operation Ajax was the replacement of the British in Iran by the Americans, another was the gradual fragmenta-
tion of Iran into two camps, one for the Shah and the other for Mosaddeq. The
Shah was the defender of privilege, tradition, and autocracy, and he allied
himself with the powers of the west. Mosaddeq came to represent reform,

---

1. See Introduction, pp. 1ff.

modernism, and democracy, though at the apex of his power in 1952 he began to exhibit signs of the very autocracy that he reviled in the Shah.

The enigmatic Mirza Mohammed Khan, Mosaddeq as-Sultaneh, later known as Dr. Mohammed Mosaddeq, was born in 1882, the child of aristocrats. He was educated in Switzerland before World War I, and his years of studying law imbued him with a knowledge of European liberalism. When he returned to Iran, he became one of the leading voices for parliamentary power and the rule of constitutional law. As Reza Shah eroded the power of the majlis during the 1920s, Mosaddeq denounced him at every turn as a dictator who would deprive Iranians of their freedom and pillage the country for his own benefit. But a majority of the merchants of Tehran, the mullahs in the mosques, and the landowners in the provinces preferred the dictatorship of Reza Shah to the anarchy that they believed to be the alternative. The great tribal confederations, the Bakhtiari in the west and the Qashqai in the south, surrounding the British oilfields, opposed Reza Shah's attempts to centralize power in Tehran; they were brutally suppressed. Eventually, Reza Shah cowed the majlis and exiled Mosaddeq.[2]

After Reza Shah was ousted by the Anglo-Soviet occupation in 1941, Mosaddeq again gravitated to the center of Iranian politics. As a member of the 14th Majlis (assembly) from 1944 to 1946, Mosaddeq spoke for Iranian independence from great-power influence. When the Soviets sought an oil concession similar to that which the British enjoyed in Abadan in the south, Mosaddeq sponsored a law outlawing further concessions to any foreign power.[3]

Excluded by his political opponents from the next assembly, he nonetheless became the leading figure of the National Front, a loose coalition of reformist aristocrats, intellectuals, and bazaar-connected politicians. The front included a significant religious element, led by the Ayatollah Kashani, and it advocated a program of constitutional democracy, social and economic reform, and neutrality in the emerging cold war.[4] And by 1950, because of its stance on the oil nationalization, it was the most important political movement in the country.

During the two years of his premiership, Mosaddeq garnered enormous attention in the British and American media. In 1951, as he faced off against the British over the AIOC, Mosaddeq was seemingly everywhere: in Tehran one moment, in The Hague the next, and then in New York to present Iran's

2. Muhammad Musaddiq, *Musaddiq's Memoirs*, ed. and trans. Homa Katouzian (London, 1988), 13–14, 88ff.; Homa Katouzian, *Musaddiq and the Struggle for Power in Iran* (New York, 1981), passim; Ervand Abrahamian, *Iran: Between Two Revolutions* (Princeton, 1982), 81–136; Fakhreddin Azimi, "The Political Career of Muhammad Musaddiq," in *Musaddiq, Iranian Nationalism, and Oil*, ed. Bill and Louis, 47–52.

3. Kuniholm, *Origins of the Cold War in the Near East*, 140–54; Farhad Diba, *Mohammad Mossadegh: A Political Biography* (London, 1986), 81–97; Abrahamian, *Iran*, 176–99.

4. Katouzian, *Musaddiq and the Struggle for Power in Iran*, 87–105; Abrahamian, *Iran*, 251–52.

case to the United Nations. Mosaddeq was a dramatic speaker whose histrionics attracted almost as much attention as his words. *Time*'s Man of the Year for 1951, he was described as "an appalling caricature of a statesman" more noted for his tendency to weep and faint when an argument wasn't going his way than for the logic of his positions.[5] And when discussing matters in private with American or British officials, he frequently conducted negotiations while lying in bed in his pajamas.

Yet for all the condescending epithets attached to Mosaddeq's name by the western media during these years—he was routinely referred to as "Old Mossy," and one *New York Times Magazine* article asked "Mossadegh: Prophet or Buffoon?"[6]—he was viewed with a certain grudging admiration by the Truman administration officials with whom he came into contact. Acheson remarked that in his years as secretary of state he "found compensation, indeed joy, in the qualities of friendly colleagues, of hostile combatants, and sometimes of neutral freebooters like Mossadeg."[7] In addition to liking the old man, McGhee commented wryly that Mosaddeq "never cried in my presence, perhaps because our meetings were not in the public eye and not worth the effort. . . . He was . . . an intelligent man and essentially a sincere Iranian patriot."[8] Vernon Walters, Truman's confidant and friend, translated Mosaddeq's French for American officials on a variety of occasions, and he formed the following impressions:

> Mossadegh in person was quite startling. I went with Mr. Harriman to his unpretentious home. After a brief wait, we were taken upstairs. . . . Dr. Mossadegh was lying in bed wearing a sort of mao jacket. . . . He was lying low in the bed with the palms of his hands crossed directly below his neck and he fluttered them gently up and down. . . . He appeared extremely pale and weak, and used this to great advantage. . . . Dr. Mossadegh had a most extraordinary nose. I have often commented that his nose was so large it made Jimmy Durante's seem like an amputee's. He was an extraordinarily friendly man. . . . One minute one had the impression that Mossadegh was really trying to find a solution for the oil problem, that an agreement was in sight. But the next conversation would take up on a note that made clear that any agreement was remote. He seemed to enjoy this. It was like dangling a fish on a line. . . . When the restoration of the Shah occurred, I devoutly hoped that nothing would happen to the old man. In fact, very little did.[9]

5. *Time,* January 7, 1952.

6. *New York Times Magazine,* September 28, 1952.

7. Acheson, *Present at the Creation,* 504.

8. George McGhee, *Envoy to the Middle World* (New York, 1983), 390.

9. Walters, *Silent Missions,* 243–63.

The American ambassador in Tehran in 1951 was Henry Grady, who had overseen the last two years of the American campaign in Greece. While Grady often
felt that Mosaddeq was "emotional" and at times "irrational,"[10] he believed
that Mosaddeq "is not to be discounted. He's a man of unusual ability, well
educated at European universities, and of great culture. He is a Persian gentleman."[11]

While favorably impressing a number of American officials, Mosaddeq was
almost universally disliked by the British. The British ambassador in Tehran, Sir
Francis Shepherd, described a visit to Mosaddeq in 1951: "He is both cunning
and slippery and completely unscrupulous. . . . He is rather tall but has short
bandy legs. . . . He looks rather like a cab horse and is slightly deaf. . . . He
conducts the conversation at a distance of about six inches at which range he
reeks of opium. . . . His remarks tend to prolixity and he gives the impression
of being impervious to argument." Shepherd believed that Mosaddeq's fainting
spells were simply histrionics that the prime minister employed to sway his
audience. All in all, according to Shepherd, Mosaddeq was a "lunatic."[12]

Other British officials were hardly more complimentary. Herbert Morrison,
the Labor foreign secretary until November 1951, called Mosaddeq "a naughty
boy."[13] These attitudes were typical of the British foreign-policy establishment,
and the change in Britain's government from Attlee (Labor) to Churchill (Conservative) in the fall of 1951 yielded no change at all in Britain's position toward
the Iranian prime minister.

To many westerners, Mosaddeq may have seemed a caricature more appropriate in a Broadway musical, but he was in fact shrewd, determined, and
dedicated to his country. He sought Iran's independence, and the struggle he
waged to extricate Iran from the dual orbit of Britain and the Soviet Union is
an archetype of third-world politics. As former British and French colonies
claimed their independence after 1945, nationalist leaders in many of them
adopted a distinctive philosophy of international relations. Jawaharlal Nehru in
India, Juan Perón in Argentina, and Mosaddeq in Iran were among the first to
advocate a policy of neutralism in the cold war. While countries such as Switzerland had long practiced neutralism, cold-war neutralism was sui generis. The
concept of cold-war neutralism was amorphous in the late 1940s and early
1950s, and it was not until the Bandung Conference in 1955 and the subsequent
nonaligned movement that it would be fully fleshed out.[14]

10. Tehran 3042, Grady to Secretary of State, May 30, 1951, Secret, NA 888.2555-A100/5-305.

11. *U.S. News and World Report,* October 19, 1951, quoted in Bill, *Eagle and the Lion,* 55.

12. Shepherd to Furlonge, May 6, 1951, Confidential, FO 371/91459/EP1015/201, quoted in
Louis, *British Empire in the Middle East,* 651–52.

13. U.S. Ambassador in the United Kingdom (Gifford) to Department of State, October 5, 1951,
Top Secret, *FRUS, 1952–1954, Vol. X,* 205–206.

14. Jawaharlal Nehru, *Jawaharlal Nehru's Speeches, 1946–1949* (New Delhi, 1961); Nehru,
Jawaharlal Nehru's Speeches, 1949–1953 (New Delhi, 1961); Joseph Page, *Perón: A Biography*

Nehru, Perón, and Mosaddeq enunciated the idea of a "Third Force" that rejected the either-or choice of the West or the Soviet Union. In fact, these leaders rejected the cold war as yet another method of great-power domination. Mosaddeq talked often of "negative equilibrium" or "positive neutrality." As he wrote in his memoirs:

> In countries like Iran, patriotic people have never tried to maintain their country's independence by resorting to a one-sided foreign policy, and turn their country into a protectorate by seeking refuge from one foreign power to another. On the contrary, they have been in favor of a complex foreign policy whereby they would be able to neutralise one foreign power by means of another, with the tactic of counter-balancing the demands of the one by those of the other.[15]

For Mosaddeq as for Nehru and others, it was the West that had defined the rules of international relations. Weaker countries such as Iran were forced to abide by the rules of great-power politics and seek a protector. Before World War II, that often meant incorporation into a European empire, as a colony or an informal protectorate. While Iran was never formally a colony, it confronted a strong legacy of European imperialism, and that legacy was a powerful force in Iranian politics in the 1940s and 1950s.

From Mosaddeq's perspective, Iran had been the unwilling pawn in a great-power game for more than 100 years. Throughout the nineteenth century, Iran was buffeted by the competing interests of imperial Britain and imperial Russia. As Russia expanded south and Britain stretched north from India and east from Suez, they collided in Iran, Afghanistan, and Central Asia. There the two empires played the "Great Game"; they fought, sometimes in battle, occasionally with plots and intrigue, often by proxy. Neither Afghanistan nor Iran was conquered, but their independence was tenuous at best. The Qajar Shahs of Iran survived by playing one side off against the other, ceding some territory here, some there. Iran also signed treaties with Britain and with the Russians, and in 1907, the two powers agreed to divide the spoils between them. Russia was granted a sphere in the north, while Britain was given the south. This imperial condominium preserved Iran's independence, but Iran's foreign affairs were determined in London and Moscow.[16]

In order to prevent the loss of what little autonomy Iran had, the government

---

(New York, 1983); Arthur Conte, *Bandoung: Tournant de l'histoire* (Paris, 1965); Mukhtâr Mazrâq, *Harakat adam al-inhiyâz fil alâqât al-dauliya* [*The Non-Aligned Movement in International Relations*] (Cairo, 1990), 23–30.

15. Musaddiq, *Musaddiq's Memoirs,* 430.

16. Peter Avery, *Modern Iran* (New York, 1965); Peter Hopkirk, *The Great Game* (New York, 1993); Keddie, *Roots of Revolution,* 1–78; Abrahamian, *Iran,* 1–109.

in Tehran intensified its efforts to use the competition between the powers to Iran's advantage. Politicians were judged based on the skill with which they threaded that needle. Mosaddeq remarked about one prime minister during World War I, "He was trying to use the rivalry between the allies i.e. France, Great Britain and Russia, and the central powers which consisted of Germany and Austria in such a way as to benefit Iran. He did not succeed and was therefore forced to proffer his resignation."[17]

It is ironic that two bitter enemies, Mohammed Reza Shah and Mosaddeq, had similar goals. Both were determined to rid their country of foreign domination. Iran was occupied by Britain and the Soviet Union during the war on the flimsy pretext that Reza Shah was planning to ally Iran with the Germans. With the Azerbeijan crisis as further proof, the Shah and Mosaddeq both concluded that until Iran was free from the overweening influence of the Russians and the British, it would never attain its rightful place in the world. With nearly identical nationalist aims, Mosaddeq and the Shah also agreed that it was necessary to involve a third power to break the grip of the traditional two. After the war, Germany was no longer a possibility, but the United States was. Just as the Shah sought to involve the Americans as a counterforce, so too did Mosaddeq.[18] And unlike Nehru, Perón, and other leaders in the third world, neither Mosaddeq nor the Shah saw the United States as a threat. While they were wary of the potential of the United States to assume Britain's imperial role in the Middle East, they preferred that risk to the devil they knew.

Throughout the summer and fall of 1951, the bulk of Mosaddeq's time was devoted to negotiations with the British over the nationalization of the AIOC, while the Americans acted as an intermediary. It may be that Mosaddeq tried to use the Americans to "neutralize" the British; it may also be that he thought that the Americans would "neutralize" the Soviets. It is certainly the case that he thought the Americans would not support the extreme British demands over oil, and in that he was certainly correct. As Acheson remarked, "the cardinal purpose of Brit[ish] policy is not to prevent Iran from going Commie; the cardinal point is to preserve what they believe to be the last remaining bulwark of Brit solvency." The United States, however, wanted mostly to prevent the domestic situation in Iran from deteriorating so much that Iran would become vulnerable to the Soviets and so be lost from the Western sphere.[19]

British intransigence over the AIOC was further proof in Mosaddeq's eyes that Britain was Iran's number-one enemy. While he distrusted Soviet Russia, Mosaddeq had a visceral antipathy for imperial Britain. He disliked the British as much as they disliked him. As George McGhee commented, "He didn't trust

---

17. Musaddiq, *Musaddiq's Memoirs*, 168-69.

18. Cottam, *Iran and the United States*, 62-69; Ramazani, *Iran's Foreign Policy, 1941-1973*, 80-138; Goode, *United States and Iran*, 5-58; Diba, *Mohammad Mossadegh*, 81-89.

19. Acheson-State, Top Secret, Nov. 10, 1951, NA 888.253/11-1051, *FRUS, 1952-1954, Vol. X*, 278-80.

the British at all."[20] Russia was a neighbor, and thus a more proximate danger. But because of the AIOC, Great Britain was far more involved in Iran's economy and domestic politics. British support for the Shah made the British even more suspect. While he was premier, Mosaddeq denounced the British countless times, but he hardly ever denounced the Russians.

Ambassador Henry Grady believed that Mosaddeq's anti-British campaign had made him an Iranian Gandhi, vastly popular and a champion of the people.[21] In talking with Grady, Mosaddeq explained why he pushed the AIOC nationalization bill through the majlis: "he regarded the oil company as a symbol of colonial, or semi-colonial attitude which led to interference . . . in the internal affairs" of Iran.[22] The nationalization plan was for Mosaddeq an arrow aimed at Britain. Before the bill was passed, he dreamed that a holy man appeared to him, urging him to "go and break the shackles from the feet of the nation."[23] And in a fervent conversation with McGhee and other American officials, he warned that the British government was a study in perversity. "You don't know how crafty they are," he told the Americans. "You don't know how evil they are. You don't know how they sully the things they touch."[24]

Mosaddeq's decades fighting Pahlavi autocracy were also spent fighting British imperialism, so much so that by 1952 the two had begun to blur. It is difficult to assess if he truly intended to let the Shah, whom he saw as an agent of the British by late 1952, remain in power. But given how vehemently anti-British Mosaddeq was and how closely he associated the Shah with the pro-British forces of reaction and dictatorship, the Shah had good reason to fear Mosaddeq.

Mosaddeq made no secret of his intention to curtail the powers of the monarch, or of his belief that the Shah should "reign not rule."[25] In the majlis during World War II, Mosaddeq directly challenged Pahlavi autocracy. In a speech in October 1944 he said, "If I am a Majlis deputy it is not for the sake of the shah but for that of the country. . . . According to the constitution the shah . . . has no right whatsoever to interfere in the country's affairs. . . . Therefore, the shah's position is ceremonial, that is the shah should assent to acts of parliament in a symbolic and ceremonial sense, for if you eliminate its ceremonial nature we would no longer have a constitutional government."[26]

Mosaddeq claimed that he was not a revolutionary; indeed, he defended his

20. McGhee was assistant secretary of state for Near Eastern affairs from 1949 to 1951. George McGhee Oral History, 48, Truman Library.

21. Grady to William Kiplinger, July 20, 1951, in Grady Papers, Box 1, Truman Library.

22. Tehran 2633, Grady to Secretary of State, May 1, 1951, Secret, NA 888.2553/5-151.

23. Mosaddeq speech to the majlis, May 13, 1951. Translated in Tehran 994, May 24, 1951, NA 788.13/5-2451.

24. Walters, *Silent Missions*, 247–52.

25. See Introduction. See also Musaddiq, *Musaddiq's Memoirs*, 460–61.

26. Quoted in Katouzian, *Musaddiq*, 54.

actions as being faithful to the "status quo."[27] Obviously, his definition of status quo was not accepted by many in Iran. For him, it was the Iranian constitutional system that existed on paper but that had never functioned in practice. Defending the written constitution and demanding that the government adhere to it was a radical position given the actual state of affairs in Iran in the 1940s and 1950s. While championing democracy, Mosaddeq was nonetheless a more profound threat to the status quo than he admitted.

The situation was more complex than the Shah versus Mosaddeq, but their rivalry defined the conflicts during the oil crisis. While they could not have been farther apart in their domestic visions for Iran—the Shah proclaiming that Iran was naturally suited to monarchy, Mosaddeq asserting that it must be a constitutional democracy—they were not as far apart on the basic foreign policy goal of freeing Iran from the great-power web.

As long as Mosaddeq symbolized Iran's fight against foreign domination, the Shah could not act against him. The Shah also could not turn to the British for help without appearing to be a British puppet. After the Harriman mission, the Shah complained that he was "helpless," and that Mosaddeq was too popular to be removed. He wished to take action, but he felt he could do nothing.[28]

In the fall of 1951, Mosaddeq traveled to the United States to present Iran's case to the United Nations. Britain had declared an embargo of all Iranian oil, and the rest of the world was honoring the embargo pending a resolution to the dispute. Mosaddeq used the UN appearances to gain the sympathy of world opinion, and of American opinion in particular. Ever the showman, he understood that there would be few subsequent opportunities to make a direct impression on the Truman administration.

While in New York, he talked frequently with Assistant Secretary of State George McGhee, and on a trip to Washington he met several times with Acheson and with Truman. The series of McGhee-Mosaddeq conversations is one of the most valuable sources for Mosaddeq's attitude toward the United States at this time, and for the attitude of U.S. officials toward him. He told McGhee that while "the British were always acting with the interest of their own pocket in mind . . . the United States was a disinterested party."[29] Although he appreciated the close ties between the Americans and the British, he nevertheless "felt that world peace should take priority over this feeling, and world peace was endangered by the situation in Iran."[30] McGhee gave no indication that Mosaddeq's sense of American priorities was mistaken. Indeed, McGhee, a thirty-

---

27. Musaddiq, *Musaddiq's Memoirs,* 296.

28. For the Shah's remarks, see Henderson to State, September 30, 1951, Top Secret, *FRUS, 1952-1954, Vol. X,* 185-88.

29. State memo of conversation by Vernon Walters, October 9, 1951, NA 888.253/10-951 *FRUS, 1952-1954, Vol. X,* 216-17.

30. State memo of conversation by Vernon Walters, November 9, 1951, NA 888.253/11-951, *FRUS, 1952-9154, Vol. X,* 269-71.

seven-year-old former oilman and Rhodes scholar considered an Anglophile, was violently attacked in the British Parliament for his seemingly unabashed partisanship for the Iranian premier.[31]

In addition to obtaining the support of the Truman administration in Iran's tortuous negotiations with the AIOC, Mosaddeq also wanted American economic aid. In meeting with American officials, he consistently exaggerated Iran's economic plight in order to squeeze money out of a reluctant administration.[32] Knowing how the State Department valued domestic Iranian stability, he emphasized the link between economic chaos and social unrest.[33] It was true that the Iranian government faced severe budget deficits because of the evaporation of oil revenues after the British oil boycott. But it is no less true that, at least in 1951, Iran's grave difficulties lay more in the future. Still, in meeting after meeting, Mosaddeq pushed for aid, and in meeting after meeting, U.S. officials admitted the need but made no promises.[34]

However, they continued to offer military assistance under the Mutual Security Act. Mosaddeq was extremely reluctant to accept it, in part because he was loath to strengthen an army whose loyalty was to the Shah and which might at some unspecified time act on the Shah's orders to depose him and terminate Iranian democracy. Mosaddeq also vehemently objected to the conditions attached to the military aid by the Mutual Security Act, which in effect required him to state Iran's alignment with the United States in the case of war with the Soviet Union. And he felt that the presence of military advisers impinged on Iran's sovereignty.[35]

In addition to his discomfort with the conditions attached to military aid, Mosaddeq was wary of even economic aid if there were strings attached. In early 1952, the CIA observed that Mosaddeq would continue "to oppose the development of closer military and political ties with the West." Even though U.S. aid would make it easier for him to stand firm in his negotiations

---

31. For a discussion of George Middleton's attacks, see McGhee, *Envoy to the Middle World,* passim.

32. State Department "Annual Economic Report—Iran," February 20, 1952, Unclassified, NA 888.00/2-2152. See also Katouzian, *Political Economy of Modern Iran,* 164–85. Katouzian calls the economic hardship extreme but notes that the Iranians often put up with severe economic limitations for the cause of national pride.

33. State Department Memo of Conversation among Mosaddeq, Truman, and Acheson, October 23, 1951, NA 888.253/10-2351, *FRUS, 1952–1954, Vol. X,* 241–44. See also Memorandum by Paul Borel, Office of National Estimates, on Mosaddeq's request for emergency aid, January 17, 1952, Top Secret, *FRUS, 1952–1954, Vol. X,* 328–30.

34. See, for example, Tehran 313 summarizing Mosaddeq-Grady conversation, September 4, 1951, NA 788.00/9-451.

35. NEA (Berry) to Acheson, "Application to Iran of Section 511(a), Mutual Security Act," January 8, 1952, Top Secret, NA 788.5-MSP/1-1852.

for an oil settlement, he refused to subject himself to American economic advice.[36]

Until the last days of his premiership in August 1953, Mosaddeq continued to press the United States for economic aid; but as early as 1952, he became concerned about drawing too close to the U.S. orbit. The policy of positive equilibrium may have led him to seek U.S. assistance to counterbalance the British, but it also precluded his moving Iran too far into the American sphere. It was a delicate balancing act that Mosaddeq attempted, hovering on the wire between Britain and Russia, Britain and the United States.

Despite Mosaddeq's qualms, throughout this period, the United States provided Iran with millions in military aid under the Mutual Security Act as well as technical assistance. The technical assistance amounted to $23 million in 1952 and 1953,[37] while military aid for the years 1950 through 1952 totaled $62 million.[38] This aid provided everything from tanks, rifles, and radios to irrigation works, x-ray units, and forty thousand eggs.[39] These goods and supplies were often desperately needed, and the military equipment enabled the Iranian army and gendarmerie to maintain internal order. But while aid for agricultural development and military aid to benefit the army were welcome to many in Iran, such aid did not help the government. It did not make it appreciably easier for Mosaddeq to supplement lost oil revenues, and that was what mattered at a political level.

In November 1951, the British went to the polls and turned out the Labor government in favor of Winston Churchill and the Conservatives. Accompanied by Foreign Secretary Anthony Eden, Churchill visited the United States in January 1952. In preparation for his visit, a number of briefing papers were drawn up for Truman. The papers reflect the division between U.S. policy and that of its closest ally. What is perhaps most revealing are the different attitudes toward colonialism and nationalism. As mentioned earlier, the Americans viewed nationalism as an inevitable force that had to be accommodated. The consequences for not accommodating it would be the loss of decolonizing, nationalist nations to the Soviet sphere, for the Soviets were adept at presenting themselves as friends of the oppressed.

According to one memo, unless the Truman administration distanced itself from British intransigence over the AIOC, the United States would be in danger

---

36. NIE-46, "Probable Developments in Iran in 1952 in the Absence of an Oil Settlement," February 4, 1952, HST—President's Secretary File, Intelligence File, Box 253, Truman Library.

37. State Department, "Iran Economic Survey," December 1954, Confidential, NA 788. 11/12-954.

38. Report to the Ambassador of the United States Military Mission in Iran, November 12, 1952, Secret, NA 788.5/11-1252.

39. Tehran 2341, April 24, 1952, NA 888.24224/4-2452; Tehran 1681, November 5, 1951, NA 888.00 TA/11-51; Tehran 1799, November 14, 1951, Secret, NA 888.00 TA/11-1451.

of "becoming tarred with the colonial brush."[40] Another document suggested that while Britain remained the "primary political and military" power in the Middle East, American political, military, and economic support were required to bolster the British position. U.S. objectives were to oppose colonialism, sustain British power, and at the same time counter "the growth of neutralism and deny communist penetration."[41] These were not necessarily compatible goals.

Just before Truman met with Churchill, his advisers prepared a concise statement of U.S. objectives in Iran:

> Our primary objective is the maintenance of Iran as an independent country aligned with the free world. A secondary objective is to assure access of the Western world to Iran's petroleum, and as a corollary to deny access to the Soviet bloc. In pursuance of our primary objective, it is the policy of the U.S. to extend to Iran, primarily through the Shah as the only present source of continuity of leadership, political support and military, economic, and technical assistance whenever this help will increase stability and internal security . . . and strengthen the leadership of the Shah . . . and demonstrate the intention of the U.S. to help preserve Iranian independence. The principal factor affecting the security of Iran and its alignment with the West is the oil controversy existing between Iran and Great Britain; thus it is the policy of the U.S. to bring its influence to bear in an effort to effect an early settlement of this dispute by agreement between the two parties.[42]

Truman's enthusiasm for brokering an agreement between Iran and Britain was not shared by Churchill. Over dinner at the British embassy in Washington, Churchill remarked that if he had been in office when the British were "kicked out of Abadan in a most humiliating way . . . it would not have occurred. There might have been a splutter of musquetry, but they would not have been kicked out of Iran." Churchill claimed that the reason for the Labor government's weakness in the face of Mosaddeq was Americans' refusal to support Attlee. He asked if perhaps the Truman administration would now agree to work with Britain and not at cross purposes with it. Acheson slyly threw the problem back in Churchill's lap, saying that of all the places where oil was exported, only

40. Memorandum for Truman on Churchill Talks, December 21, 1951, Secret, HST—President's Secretary File: General File, Box 116.

41. Steering Group on Preparations for Talks Between the President and Prime Minister Churchill: Negotiating Paper, December 31, 1951, Top Secret, HST—President's Secretary File: General File, Box 116.

42. Steering Group paper on Iran, January 5, 1952, Top Secret, ibid.

Iran was a problem, and in Acheson's view, it was a problem that transcended Mosaddeq.[43]

Several things stand out about the American position. One is that neither at this time nor at any time in the coming year did the Truman administration support a resolution of the crisis by force, either covert or overt. That did not signify support for Mosaddeq in Washington, but rather a sense that his removal would not solve the problem of oil and nationalism in Iran. Furthermore, the Truman administration accepted the principle of nationalization and acknowledged the right of sovereign nations to nationalize property provided that due compensation was forthcoming. The British did not agree, just as they would not agree over Suez in 1956 when the American government, this time led by Dwight Eisenhower, again refused to support the contention that nationalization was illegal.[44]

Finally, the Truman administration was ambivalent about neutralism in the decolonizing world. As one of the early proponents of neutralism, Mosaddeq posed a special challenge to a Washington increasingly accustomed to viewing the globe in terms of the "free world" versus "Communism." As an alternate approach, neutralism threatened the ability of the United States to create a solid free-world bloc. In the view of some State Department officials, neutralism represented "the greatest single obstacle to the achievement of . . . free world unity. . . . Neutralism is viciously undermining US and UN attempts to present a united front against Kremlin aggression."[45] Whereas Mosaddeq was a threat to the British because he undermined the empire, he disturbed the Americans because his neutralism undermined regional and global cold-war strategy.

The U.S. government was interested first and foremost in keeping Iran out of the Soviet sphere and keeping its oil accessible. That position made the United States vulnerable to manipulation from outside, from the Iranian "periphery" and from London, much as "protecting the route to India" had made the British government vulnerable to pulls from the periphery in the nineteenth century. The United States always maintained that if there was a danger of Iran being lost to the Western sphere, more aggressive steps might have to be taken.[46]

The task for the anti-Mosaddeq forces, then, was to convince the Americans that Mosaddeq would cause Iran to enter the Soviet orbit. As fate would have it, domestic events in Iran took a turn for the worse after the summer of 1952, and Mosaddeq was besieged by internal adversaries. This deterioration, in turn,

43. Acheson, Memorandum of Conversation, January 6, 1952, in Acheson Papers, Box 67.

44. All concerned American officials agreed. Harriman and McGhee both felt that Mosaddeq was impossible to deal with, but they also felt that, for Great Britain, there was no going back. See State Department Memorandum of Conversation among McGhee, Harriman, and the Heads of the Major U.S. Oil Companies, September 14, 1951, Secret, NA 788.00/9-1451.

45. NEA New Guidelines, April 26, 1951, Confidential, NA 888.2553/4-2751.

46. See NSC 107, March 14, 1951, Top Secret, *FRUS, 1952-1954, Vol. X*, 21-23.

coincided with the Truman-Eisenhower transition. The task for the anti-Mosaddeq forces thus became much easier.

The National Front dominated political life in Iran during this period. Along with Mosaddeq, other major figures either in or allied with the front were Mozaffar Baqai, an editor and a professor at Tehran University who had served in the majlis; Husayn Makki, who prior to the oil crisis was a well-known historian and friend of Mosaddeq; and Ayatollah Kashani, born in 1884, father of more than thirty children, and a long-time opponent of the British and speaker of the majlis after 1951.[47] The front was not, however, a unified political party. As a coalition of forces united by their commitment to oil nationalization, anti-British sentiment, and a belief in reform, the front gained strength from the adversarial relationship with the British. The presence of an external enemy was the glue that held the front together. Without the immediacy of an oil crisis, the various factions of the front would have been at odds, and in 1952, as the oil crisis hovered in limbo between acute emergency and settlement, the front began to break apart.

While there was no significant opposition in Iran to the front's stance on nationalization and expulsion of the British from Abadan, the issue of reform was far more controversial. The core of the front's support was the intelligentsia—some western-educated and most sharing a commitment to constitutionalism—and the merchants of the bazaar. Clothing manufacturers, coffee shop–keepers, bath house–owners, barbers, and the like supported Mosaddeq in significant numbers, and they had the backing of a significant section of the ulama (clergy).[48] These groups generally supported limitations on the Shah's power, smaller military expenditures, fairer elections, more equitable taxes, and land reform in the belief that Iran would be stronger, more stable, and more independent. They believed that land reform made economic sense. A more even distribution of wealth would mean a larger internal market for goods. But on this issue, the front came up against a wall of opposition.

Land reform was a major item on the political agenda of most developing countries in the 1950s. In Iran, the *principle* of land reform had the support of both the Shah and the National Front; unfortunately for those who might have benefited, they supported it for completely different reasons. At the beginning of 1951, the Shah ordered that a large portion of crown lands be sold to the peasants then occupying them. Although he claimed that his motives were based on a desire to see greater equity among the classes, the Shah may well have been motivated by less noble concerns. One of the unfinished campaigns initiated by his father was breaking the hold of the traditional landowning

47. Yann Richard, "Ayatollah Kashani: Precursor of the Islamic Republic?" in *Religion and Politics in Iran*, ed. Nikki Keddie (New Haven, 1983), 101–24; Mohsen Milani, *The Making of Iran's Islamic Revolution* (Boulder, Colo., 1988), 71–75.

48. Abrahamian, *Iran*, 371–75; Tehran 311 (airgram), "Evaluation of the Political Importance of the National Front," May 27, 1950, Confidential, NA 788.00/5-2750.

aristocracy. These individuals controlled vast fiefdoms. They were not dependent on the Pahlavi dynasty for their survival; in fact, they were competitors. In order to diminish the power of these landholders, who included among their numbers Mosaddeq and many of the front's leaders, the Shah needed to erode their base of support: their estates. The ulama also controlled large landholdings attached to mosques and seminaries. These estates provided income to maintain the clergy and allowed them to be independent of the throne. At best, the Shah's motives in redistributing land may have been both paternalist and Machiavellian. After Mosaddeq's fall, the Shah continued to pursue land reform in the White Revolution of the early 1960s. The result was a disruption of the countryside and a flood of immigrants to Tehran.[49]

Mosaddeq and the front also stood for land reform. For many in the front, land reform was a necessary step on the path toward weakening the power of the Shah and increasing popular participation in the economic and political life of the country. Until the peasants had land of their own, politics would be dominated by the conservative landholding elites. Even though Mosaddeq himself was of these traditional elites, his ambitions for Iran seem to have transcended his concerns as a landowner. While Mosaddeq's nationalization campaign had the support of many landowners, by early 1952, the landowners began to recoil from the populist, reformist rhetoric of the front. They feared that he meant to strip them of their wealth. At the same time, they listened as the Tudeh (Communist) Party touted a vehemently egalitarian line. With Mosaddeq pushing for land reform on populist grounds—reform which touched large individual estates more than clerical estates—it was easy enough for these landowning elites to turn against the front and align themselves somewhat unwillingly behind the Shah.[50]

The relationship of the Tudeh Party to the front was complex and ambivalent. With the Soviet Union just to the north, the Tudeh was largely under the thumb of Moscow, and it was outlawed after 1945. As of 1949, the Tudeh had perhaps twenty-five thousand members, but it could mobilize large crowds in Tehran and was capable of organizing strikes throughout the country. The party was popular among oil workers and factory workers, as well as parts of the middle class. There was in fact an overlap between the Tudeh bases of support and

49. Enclosure to Tehran 626, "The Question of Land Reform as It Seems to Be Developing in Iran," February 9, 1951, Secret, NA 788.00/2-951; Moojan Momen, *An Introduction to Shi'i Islam* (New Haven, 1985), 250–55; Barry Rubin, *Paved with Good Intentions: The American Experience and Iran* (New York, 1980), 90–122; Abrahamian, *Iran*, 264–65, 420–24; Keddie, ed., *Religion and Politics in Iran*, 152.

50. For a contemporary overview, see Tehran 1258 (airgram), "Study of the Landowners of Iran," by Mary Parrish, June 9, 1952, NA 888.16/6-952. See also Habib Ladjevardi, "Constitutional Government and Reform under Musaddiq," in *Musaddiq, Iranian Nationalism, and Oil*, ed. Bill and Louis, 80–85.

those of the National Front.[51] Not wishing to alienate the very middle classes that he relied on, Mosaddeq rarely enforced the ban on Tudeh during his premiership. It was a decision he probably regretted. Tudeh only halfheartedly supported the front, and for the most part fought it. And its capacity to mobilize crowds ultimately undermined Mosaddeq.

In general, Tudeh supported Mosaddeq on nationalization but was adamantly against any compromise with the AIOC. It excoriated American participation in the negotiations and charged Mosaddeq with succumbing to "British and American imperialism." In its newspaper *Mardom*, Tudeh celebrated when Mosaddeq was intransigent and denounced him as a traitor when he seemed to moderate his stance.[52] After July 1952, the party became more and more antagonistic toward Mosaddeq. It accused the premier of being a reactionary landlord who served the interests of his class.[53] In a double attack on monarchy and landlords, Tudeh circulated a poster on the Shah's birthday on October 26, 1952; it read "Death be to Shah and Royalty. Annihilation to the Son of Reza Khan. Long live our Democratic Party. Death be to the American aggressors. . . . Death to the blood-sucking landlords."[54]

Tudeh was particularly strong in Tehran and in Azerbeijan. Many of the American reports discussing the Tudeh threat originated with the consulate in Tabriz. These reports give the impression that Tudeh was entrenched throughout the country. In fact, outside of Azerbeijan and select pockets in Tehran, Isfahan, and other major urban centers, Tudeh had very little support. It attempted to infiltrate the army and had only limited success.[55] But it shouted loudly enough to be heard out of proportion to its actual strength. And because it supported the "anti-imperialist" aspects of the National Front, it was associated with the front in the eyes of Washington even though Tudeh was actually set against Mosaddeq. That association was cemented by the events of July 1952.

In May 1952, Mosaddeq accused the Shah of plotting with the British against him. The Shah denied the accusations and told court minister Husayn Ala that "steps must be taken in the near future to have Mosaddeq replaced." He asked Ala to sound out the Americans and see if they would support such a move.[56] There is no record of the American response. In early summer, Mosaddeq

51. CIA, "The Tudeh Party," ORE 23-49, July 18, 1949, Top Secret, *CIA Research Reports,* Reel 2; Tehran 588, November 3, 1951, Secret, NA 788.00/11-35.

52. Tehran 388 (airgram), "Communist Propaganda vis-a-vis the Mosadeq Government," September 20, 1951, NA 788.001/9-2051.

53. Abrahamian, *Iran,* 322-23.

54. Translated in Tabriz 23, NA 788.001/12-1252.

55. Osamu Miyata, "The Tudeh Military Network during the Oil Nationalization Period," *Middle East Studies,* XXIII (July 1987), 313-29.

56. Tehran 4606 (Henderson to State), May 28, 1952, Secret, NA 788.00/5-2852; *FRUS, 1952-1954, Vol. X,* 384-86.

demanded that he be made minister of war. As long as the Shah controlled the army, the monarchy could effectively curtail the front. The Shah balked. In a calculated move, Mosaddeq resigned on July 16, and the Shah appointed Ahmad Qavam to the premiership. Within hours, Qavam found himself feted by the American ambassador Loy Henderson.

A foreign-service officer who had cut his diplomatic teeth in Moscow in the 1930s, Henderson was a hard-line anti-Communist who called for action against the Soviets well before World War II ended. After helping shape American policy toward Greece, Henderson opposed the creation of Israel and ran afoul of prevailing opinion in Washington. Sent as ambassador to India, Henderson, a grim, humorless man, disliked Nehru, and the feeling was mutual. Given his distaste for the father of neutralism, he was an odd choice for the Iran embassy where dealing with the neutral Mosaddeq would be a daily requirement. But Henderson was deeply respected in the State Department.[57]

Henderson was disposed to support Qavam. In frequent meetings with court minister Ala, Henderson did not disguise his disapproval of Mosaddeq. At one point, he bluntly told the Shah that "Mosadeq's policies were leading Iran towards disaster." He emphasized that he thought Mosaddeq had to "retire," and he added that he could not have stated his views any more strongly "without openly and formally intervening."[58] Of course, even saying such things to the Shah, when Henderson was technically supposed to deal with the government (i.e., Mosaddeq) and not the head of state, stretched the bounds of diplomatic propriety. So when Mosaddeq resigned, Henderson did what he could to ensure the survival of his successor. Henderson promised Qavam that substantial American aid would likely be forthcoming. When he met with Qavam on July 19, Henderson said that:

> On several occasions, Mosadeq had asked for Amer financial aid and it had not been given him. Amer govt and public had been of opinion that kind of emergency which would justify budgetary aid did not exist when request from Mosadeq was recd. There was widespread belief in US that if Mosadeq had taken what US govt and public consider to be reasonable attitude resolution oil problem Iran wld have been able to overcome its budgetary difficulties without financial help from US. . . . It seemed to me personally that situation at present was somewhat different. It was my understanding that present govt was anxious solve oil problem on basis which wld be fair and reasonable to all concerned. . . . Yesterday, therefore, I had recommended to US Govt it consider request from Qavam

57. H. W. Brands, *Inside the Cold War: Loy Henderson and the Rise of the American Empire* (New York, 1991).

58. Tehran 162, July 13, 1952, Top Secret, NA 788.13/7-1252.

in somewhat different light from requests heretofore recd. . . .
I had, therefore, urged that US Govt give favorable consideration to extending financial aid to Iran sufficient to enable govt
to function until, say, Sept 20.[59]

Before Washington had a chance to decide on Henderson's suggestion,
Qavam was pushed out, and Mosaddeq resumed the premiership after crowds
in Tehran, including pro-Tudeh crowds, called for his return. When Mosaddeq
learned of the aid offer, he was livid. He accused the United States of showing
favoritism to Qavam. As far as he was concerned, the United States "had no
diplomacy . . . [and] was merely an agent of the British. . . . US had given billion
dollars aid to Turkey and yet when Iran was bankrupt and on verge Communism,
it had refused finan assistance." He warned that the results of the recent July
crisis had discredited the army and the old elites such as Qavam and had thereby
placed the Communists in a stronger position than ever.[60]

Within days, Mosaddeq was once again conciliatory, and he seemed to retreat
from his criticisms. Soon he was telling Henderson that "he was sure [Hender-
son] was friend of Iran. . . . Iran needed friendship of US."[61] In the meantime,
Henderson appealed to Washington for economic aid to Mosaddeq. Officials
in Washington and London concluded that the premier was now untouchable,
save by a military coup d'etat. Although General Fazlollah Zahedi was said to
be personally strong enough to carry out a coup, the political situation was
unfavorable, and the embassy recommended against backing any such plans.[62]
The meetings between Henderson and Qavam changed the dynamic of Mosaddeq's relationship with the United States. Until this point, Mosaddeq believed
that the United States would ultimately come to his aid. Henceforth, his relations
with the Americans would be more guarded.

In addition, having foiled the Shah's attempt to remove him, Mosaddeq took
steps to weaken the monarch, whom he viewed as little more than an ally of
the British against the forces of nationalism in Iran.[63] In late July, the majlis
granted Mosaddeq the authority to propose and enact legislation for six months
without prior parliamentary approval. To many in Iran, the award of these
"plenary" powers smacked of dictatorship.[64]

The primary impetus for granting emergency powers to the prime minister

59. Tehran 265, July 19, 1952, Secret, NA 788.13/7-1952.

60. Henderson to Department of State, July 28, 1952, Top Secret, *FRUS, 1952-1954, Vol. X,*
416-21. See also Tehran 514, August 3, 1952, NA 788.00/8-354.

61. Tehran 580, August 8, 1952, NA 788.13/8-852.

62. Henderson to Department of State, July 31, 1952, Top Secret, *FRUS, 1952-1954, Vol.
X,* 427.

63. Musaddiq, *Musaddiq's Memoirs,* 355, 451. See report by John Stutesman, second embassy
secretary, February 1952, NA 788.00/2-1652.

64. Fakhreddin Azimi, *Iran: The Crisis of Democracy, 1941-1953* (London, 1989), 200-20.

was the dire economic situation in Iran brought about by the oil embargo and the interruption of oil revenue. But Mosaddeq used his authority to erode the privileges enjoyed by the Shah. He decreed that many of the Shah's lands were to be transferred to the government and then distributed to the peasantry. He attempted to cut the military budget by nearly 40 percent. He cut the palace budget and used the savings for the health ministry. He forbade the Shah from dealing directly with foreign diplomats, and forced Princess Ashraf into temporary exile on the charge that she was intriguing against him. At the end of the six months, he managed to get the majlis to extend his powers for another six, during which time he went even further in the direction of land reform and curtailing the Shah's authority. In the process, he began to alienate his own supporters, who saw him becoming more like an autocrat than a democrat.[65]

Mosaddeq made gestures in August to suggest that he was about to settle with the British. In response, Henderson recommended that the only thing needed to push Mosaddeq over the top toward compromise was a ten to thirty million dollar grant.[66] But as Henderson's superiors considered his proposal, the talks between Iran and Britain broke down once again. It is unclear if Mosaddeq really intended to compromise or if he simply wanted the Americans to think that he might and so give him money.

By the fall, Mosaddeq was growing desperate for American aid and diplomatic support. In October, Iran severed diplomatic relations with the British. But until the end, as one Iranian official told Henderson, Mosaddeq expected the "US to prevent us from breaking relations by persuading British to understand our position and yield to our demands."[67] Henderson, no ardent supporter of Mosaddeq, got the message. He cabled Washington that if the United States was serious about preventing Iran "from drifting behind Iron Curtain," then it had to be prepared to make a decision "as difficult as that made in February 1947 regarding Greece and Turkey to come forward with economic aid on scale similar that given Greece and Turkey."[68] In spite of Henderson's warnings that Iran would likely become a Soviet stronghold without such aid, the outgoing Truman administration was more absorbed with the upcoming presidential elections than with radical changes in its Iran policy.[69]

65. Abrahamian, *Iran*, 272-73; Ashraf Pahlavi, *Faces in a Mirror*, 132-33; Sepehr Zabih, *The Mossadegh Era* (Chicago, 1982), 71-72.

66. See various telegrams of August 1952, *FRUS, 1952-1954, Vol. X*, 430ff.

67. Tehran 1220, Top Secret, September 20, 1952, NA 888.223/9-2052, *FRUS, 1952-1954, Vol. X*, 474-75.

68. Tehran 1301, September 27, 1952, Top Secret, NA 888.00 TA/9-2752.

69. Acheson did consider buying a limited amount of Iranian oil, but negotiations bogged down and no decision was made. Acheson, *Present at the Creation*, 680-85; Bamberg, *History of the British Petroleum Company*, 478-83. See also Acheson Aide-Memoire, [August 1952?], Acheson Memoranda of Conversations, Box 67a, Acheson Papers, Truman Library, and Acheson to Lovett, November 4, 1952, Top Secret, *FRUS, 1952-1954, Vol. X*, 510-12.

Until the fall of 1952, Mosaddeq was able to finance the government through ingenious and creative accounting, liquidation of nonessential expenses, and heavy debt in the form of government loans from the Iranian national bank. Without oil revenue, the government faced mounting expenses with a finite number of ways to meet them. For more than a year, Mosaddeq's popularity was unaffected by the economic problems, in part because of his successful appeal to Iranian patriotism. Suffering in the cause of Iranian independence from the British imperialists was a burden many were willing to bear, at least for a while. By late 1952, the National Front began to fray and the Iranian people began to complain in earnest.

According to the CIA, although economic problems alone were not sufficient to bring down the National Front, they aggravated tensions already present. In the estimation of the agency, the front was "united primarily by a common desire to rid the country of foreign influence and replace the traditional ruling groups."[70] Never a majority in the majlis, the National Front had the loyalty of about thirty of the seventy-nine deputies in the Seventeenth Majlis (1952-1953). The other deputies divided into several pro-British and/or royalist factions as well as several undecided blocs.[71] Even before the events of 30 Tir (July 21), observers noted the stresses in the majlis; newspapers from the different factions routinely fired off heated denunciations of each other. National Front papers called the royalists British stooges, while royalists warned that Mosaddeq was leading Iran down the garden path of Communist dictatorship.[72]

While Makki and Baqai were vital to Mosaddeq because they each commanded their own minifactions, Ayatollah Kashani was central to Mosaddeq's survival. A charismatic, fiery orator, Kashani had an independent power base in the religious sphere that made him nearly unassailable. The suspected connection between him and the Fedayin i-Islam terrorist group added a dangerous and somewhat sinister aura to the ayatollah. Furthermore, Kashani could mobilize the "streets." Even more than the Tudeh, Kashani was able to sway the Tehran masses through his own mosque-based network in both the bazaar and in working-class neighborhoods.[73] When Qavam briefly replaced Mosaddeq, it was Kashani who rallied the Tehran street masses (as well as crowds in several other urban centers), and when the army did not fire on the pro-Kashani, pro-Mosaddeq crowds, Qavam had to resign.

There is considerable debate on how pivotal Kashani was in restoring Mosad-

---

70. CIA-NIE 75/1, "Probable Developments in Iran Through 1953," January 9, 1953, Top Secret, HST—President's Secretary File: CIA Reports, Box 254. See also Tehran 873, "Iranian Political Trends," January 3, 1953, Secret, NA 788.00/4-2453.

71. Zabih, *Mossadegh Era,* 34-38; Abrahamian, *Iran,* 269.

72. See Tehran 1077, "The Iranian Political Situation," April 1, 1952, Secret, NA 788.00/4-1152.

73. Shahrough Akhavi, "The Role of the Clergy," in *Musaddiq, Iranian Nationalism, and Oil,* ed. Bill and Louis, 97-101; Abrahamian, *Iran,* 270-72.

deq to power. Some say that Mosaddeq would not have survived politically without Kashani's mobilization of the masses; others say that Mosaddeq was strong enough to come to his own rescue.[74] However, there is little doubt that Kashani did save Mosaddeq, whether or not Mosaddeq needed saving. As a result of his prominence during 30 Tir, Kashani was made president of the majlis, and he believed that Mosaddeq owed the premiership to him.[75] In the fall of 1952, Kashani continued to speak out against the British, the Shah, and the Americans. He accused the Americans of helping the British, though in an interview with *Time* magazine he hastened to add that he "did not mean that the American people are bad. They are a good and freedom-loving people" with an imperialist government. He was no friend of the Tudeh, because "Communism does not go with Islam." But as long as the Tudeh fought imperialism, he would not reject them as allies.[76]

In January 1945 the majlis extended Mosaddeq's powers for an additional six months. That was the final straw for Kashani. He declared that the extension conflicted with the constitution.[77] His motives were a mixture of ambition and a socially conservative rejection of the reforms. He opposed Mosaddeq's proposals to enfranchise women, claiming that the government's Islamic duty was to keep women at home rearing children.[78] By May, when asked about the premier, Kashani responded, "I reaffirm my support of Dr. Mossadegh's foreign policy. Unfortunately, however, Mossadegh has not taken a single positive step in the direction of internal reforms."[79] Meanwhile, Makki and Baqai also broke with the premier, with Baqai comparing Mosaddeq to Hitler. Each man had his own clique and his own public followers. After they denounced Mosaddeq, merchants, peddlers, workers, intelligentsia, and army officers also broke from the front. Businessmen who depended on international business for their livelihoods also abandoned the front. With the expulsion of the British, Iran was under an ever stricter international business boycott.[80] By the spring of 1953, therefore, Mosaddeq was left with a core of support in the National Front, strong popular appeal as an Iranian nationalist, the very ambivalent allegiance of the Tudeh whenever he confronted the British, and their enmity whenever

74. Akhavi thinks Mosaddeq would have been restored without Kashani's support. Abrahamian is more ambivalent. Yann Richard suggests that Kashani's role was central.

75. See Kashani interview with Henderson, Tehran 1774, November 12, 1951, Confidential, NA 788.00/1-1251.

76. Text of interview in Tehran 299, October 17, 1952, NA 788.00/10-1852.

77. Habib Ladjevardi, "The Origins of U.S. Support for an Autocratic Iran," *International Journal of Middle East Studies,* XV (May 1983), 78.

78. Abrahamian, *Iran,* 276.

79. Tehran 970, May 5, 1953, RG 84, Iran General records, 1953-1955: Lot 60 F 87, Box 5, 363 Kashani, WNRC.

80. Cottam, *Iran and the United States,* 101-103; Zabih, *Mossadegh Era,* 83-88; Abrahamian, *Iran,* 276-78; Henderson to State, November 5, 1952, Secret, *FRUS, 1952-1954, Vol. X,* 513-16.

he talked with the Americans. The majlis would not confront him directly, but most of its members were hostile. In February, he was almost overthrown.

The February coup attempt was precipitated by Mosaddeq's efforts to force the Shah to leave the country. Accusing the Shah of fomenting dissent in the majlis, discontent within the army, and general opposition to reform throughout the country, Mosaddeq suggested that the Shah travel abroad for a while. He claimed at the time, and for years afterward, that he had never insisted the Shah leave; he had simply suggested it.[81] Kashani appealed to the Shah to stay in the country, asserting that a constitutional monarchy depended on the monarch's actually being in the country.[82] Meanwhile, as Mosaddeq and the Shah were meeting to discuss the issue at the end of February, crowds assembled outside the palace and threatened Mosaddeq. The premier exited through a back door and sneaked back to his own house, which was quite near the palace.

Informed of the premier's movements, the crowd, several thousand strong and led by the giant wrestler Shaban Jafari "The Brainless," besieged the house. Shaban himself drove a jeep head-on into the gate in front of the mansion. Dressed in pajamas, Mosaddeq climbed over an adjoining wall and fled to the house next door, which happened to be the headquarters of an American Point IV aid mission. From there he proceeded to the Parliament, where he gave a speech denouncing "agents of our common enemy." With the support of the military, the rioters were dispersed.[83]

These riots were a dry run for the successful coup that came months later. While Kim Roosevelt and C. M. Woodhouse credit the CIA for causing the trouble, Mosaddeq interpreted the riots as a brainchild of the Shah and his supporters. While he knew of American and British attempts to destabilize his regime,[84] he believed that the crowds were assembled by the court and other "reactionary" groups doing the will of the British. This near miss was the final straw for Mosaddeq and the Shah, as well as for Mosaddeq and the majlis. Convinced that he was surrounded by enemies, Mosaddeq planned to dissolve Parliament.

Meanwhile, President Dwight D. Eisenhower was inaugurated, and U.S. policy shifted radically. After years of American refusal to cooperate with British covert plans against Mosaddeq, the United States had a president who was comfortable with covert warfare.

Eisenhower was known to all Americans as a war hero. Beyond that, his politics was largely a mystery. In his two terms as president, he would be seen as an affable if somewhat detached chief executive. In his news conferences,

81. Musaddiq, *Musaddiq's Memoirs,* 342-48; Henderson to State, February 28, 1953, Top Secret, *FRUS, 1952-1954, Vol. X,* 685-87.

82. Akhavi, "The Role of the Clergy," 108-109; Zabih, *Mossadegh Era,* 97-105.

83. Henderson to Department of State, February 28, 1953, Top Secret, *FRUS, 1952-1954, Vol. X,* 688; *Musaddiq's Memoirs,* 345-349; *Life,* July 1954.

84. Mark Gasiorowski makes a credible case that Mosaddeq was well informed about CIA efforts. Gasiorowski, "1953 Coup D'Etat in Iran," 261-86.

he was earnest but often incomprehensible, so badly did he mangle grammar and syntax. He often seemed to be golfing rather than governing, and many Americans believed that his aides actually ran the country. In particular, it was thought that Ike was led by his secretary of state, John Foster Dulles, and that Dulles was responsible for all major decisions concerning foreign policy. This image held up for decades after Eisenhower left office; but as records from his administration began to be declassified, it became clear that the image of a passive, disengaged Eisenhower was almost completely inaccurate.[85]

While Ike maintained an airy detachment in public, in private he was focused and involved. His principal advisers all claim that, in the Dulles-Eisenhower relationship, it was Ike who called the shots.[86] In foreign affairs, he set up the National Security Council to approximate the structure of an army staff. Specific tasks were assigned to specific individuals, and the chain of command was clearly delineated. Although the council debated issues and drew up policy papers which suggested courses of action, Eisenhower reserved the right to refuse the advice of the NSC. Ike's national-security advisers included Robert "Bobby" Cutler, formerly of the Old Colonial Trust Company in Boston; Dillon Anderson, a Pentagon official with roots in Texas politics; and Gordon Gray, chancellor of the University of North Carolina, who had specialized in developing psychological-warfare doctrines and had helped strip J. Robert Oppenheimer of security clearances in 1953. All were expert staff secretaries. They made sure that a problem was discussed and dissected, and they seem never to have made any decisions independent of the president. To borrow Truman's phrase, on national security the buck truly stopped with Eisenhower.[87]

During World War II, Eisenhower had been a staunch proponent of psychological warfare and covert paramilitary operations as a supplement to the grand strategy for defeating Germany.[88] As president, Ike intended to use the CIA as a weapon in America's cold-war arsenal—a weapon which, like nuclear weapons, could be deadly but, unlike nuclear weapons, was low-profile and cost-effective. The presence of Allen Dulles as head of the CIA was a sign of how close covert operations and intelligence were to Eisenhower's heart. Never before and never since have there been such close links between the White House, the State Department, and the CIA.

---

85. Stephen Ambrose, *Eisenhower: The President* (New York, 1984); Robert Divine, *Eisenhower and the Cold War* (New York, 1981); Fred Greenstein, *The Hidden-Hand Presidency: Eisenhower as Leader* (New York, 1982); Townsend Hoopes, *The Devil and John Foster Dulles* (Boston, 1973).

86. See oral-history interviews with Bob Bowie, Milton Eisenhower, Andrew Goodpaster, Gordon Gray, and John McCone, all in Eisenhower Library, Abilene, Kans.

87. Prados, *Keepers of the Keys,* 61-95; Gordon Gray and Dillon Anderson oral histories, Eisenhower Library.

88. Ambrose, *Eisenhower: The President,* 110-12; Blanch Wisen Cook, *The Declassified Eisenhower: A Divided Legacy of Peace and Political Warfare* (New York, 1981), 15ff.

The CIA and covert action were focal aspects of Eisenhower's "New Look" strategy for combating the Soviet Union and world Communism. The New Look was heralded by the Pentagon and Defense Secretary and former General Motors president Charles E. Wilson as offering more bang for the buck: fewer conventional forces, more nuclear weapons, greater overall efficiency.[89] That was in accord with Eisenhower's fiscal conservatism and his campaign pledge to balance the budget. In the privacy of White House meetings, the New Look also implied a greater reliance on covert policy. After all, what was cheaper than psy-ops and select teams of operatives along with their contract workers in the target country? It had cost the CIA scant millions to help the Christian Democrats in Italy. Compared to the billions needed for conventional warfare, and even compared to the billions needed for a nuclear arsenal, the CIA was cheap. It was also quiet, secret, and—in these early years—effective.[90]

A sharp distinction is often drawn between Eisenhower and Truman, but in many ways it is overdrawn. By the end of 1952, Truman was paying greater attention to psychological warfare, and his rhetoric about global cold war hardened. This was undoubtedly a product of the Korean War, which occupied the attention of the White House and of the American public.[91] Although Truman did not authorize the CIA to proceed with plans against Mosaddeq, he did allow coordination with the British at the very end of 1952.[92] And elsewhere in the world, he took a more uncompromising stance against supposed Soviet incursions in the "free world." In Iran, as in Guatemala, Truman came to the brink of covert intervention. The same pulls operated on his administration as on the Eisenhower administration in 1953. In 1952, under Truman, the United States government had not yet reached a point of no return in Iran, but there is good reason to think that if Truman had been president in 1953, he would have done as Eisenhower did. Truman officials were ill disposed toward Mosaddeq and increasingly disposed to an activist, interventionist American approach to the third world. There was no Truman intervention because the "push" from Washington had not yet converged with the "pull" from Tehran.

Thus while Eisenhower came to the White House undoubtedly more comfortable with covert action and more disposed to work against Mosaddeq, Truman

89. Ambrose, *Eisenhower: The President*, 171-73; McGeorge Bundy, *Danger and Survival* (New York, 1988), 244-55; John Lewis Gaddis, *Strategies of Containment* (New York, 1982), 148-60.

90. Robert Bowie and Richard Immerman, *Waging Peace: Eisenhower's Strategy for National Security* (New York, 1997).

91. See Walter Bedell Smith, "Memorandum for Members of Psychological Strategy Board," October 21, 1952, Top Secret, HST—Psychological Strategy Board, Box 13. See also Memorandum from Edward Lilly to Edmond Taylor, December 15, 1952, Secret, ibid., Box 11.

92. Moraya de Moraes Ruehsen, "Operation Ajax Revisited: Iran, 1953," *Middle Eastern Studies,* XXIX (July 1993), 474; Gasiorowski, "1953 Coup D'Etat in Iran," 270-74; Woodhouse, *Something Ventured,* 119-21.

might well have come to the same decision as his Republican successor had he remained in office. Differences notwithstanding, Eisenhower and Truman shared a similar sense of U.S. global interests. By the early 1950s, the Truman administration had already added to the arsenal of U.S. foreign policy by establishing agencies specifically committed to covert action and psychological operations. Truman pursued a less aggressive, less interventionist approach to Mosaddeq because, for a while, that seemed the best choice. As the political situation in Iran polarized, however, U.S. officials rethought their policy; and that rethinking coincided with a change in administration. The shift in U.S. policy toward Mosaddeq thus may have had less to do with the Truman-Eisenhower transition than with the deterioration of Mosaddeq's position and the increasing chaos in Iran in early 1953. As with Guatemala later on, the contrast between Truman and Eisenhower on Iran may have been the result of changed circumstances on the periphery rather than different attitudes in Washington.

Eisenhower was never particularly well disposed toward Mosaddeq. When his friend Swede Hazlett referred to Mosaddeq as "an emotional, psychopathic nationalist," Eisenhower did not disagree, but he lamented the "bungling" of Truman and Acheson and stated that it would be a tragedy to the western world if Iran with its 600,000 barrels of oil a day were lost just as China had been.[93] The first few months of Eisenhower's presidency were absorbed with the usual details of transition and the unusual crisis over ending the Korean War. But as early as March, the National Security Council began discussing Iran, and its members had few kind words for the premier.

According to John Foster Dulles, Iran was heading for a Mosaddeq dictatorship. While he did not feel that Tudeh was in a position to oust Mosaddeq, there was always the danger that if the premier fell, Tudeh and its sponsors in Moscow would be well placed to seize power. The council discussed a variety of measures, including the improbable one of buying out the Anglo-Iranian Oil Company and then settling with the Iranians. Secretary of Defense Charles Wilson added that, in his view, the United States still did not have an answer either to "the obvious collapse of colonialism" or to "Communism's new tactic in exploiting nationalism and colonialism for its own purposes." Wilson cautioned that "a dictatorship of the left" could easily slide into Communism, and it was up to the United States to figure out a way to prevent such a development in Iran.[94]

Although the NSC did not make any major policy shifts at this time, Wilson's observation is a key to understanding why the Eisenhower administration decided on Operation Ajax. First, officials shared the belief that the Soviets were becoming adept at utilizing the left in the third world. They interpreted Tudeh's support of Mosaddeq as part of Moscow's strategy to weaken all oppos-

---

93. From Eisenhower personal Papers, Box 51, Eisenhower Library.

94. Minutes of the 135th Meeting of the National Security Council, March 4, 1953, Top Secret, *FRUS, 1952-1954, Vol. X*, 692-99.

ing forces in Iran and, when only Mosaddeq remained, Tudeh and Moscow would pounce.

Mosaddeq's neutralism was a further irritant for Dulles. Eisenhower and Dulles objected to neutralism on moral grounds, but that did not preclude a pragmatic approach to neutral countries. Mosaddeq's refusal to choose sides in the cold war may have deeply disturbed the ideological secretary of state, but that in itself was no reason to institute a coup. In fact, as Eisenhower later wrote, a policy of neutralism was often the wisest course for third-world nations trying to fend off Communism.[95]

In the end, with negative reports streaming in from Henderson and from the British, Eisenhower officials believed that Mosaddeq was simply dangerous. Even though they conceded that Mosaddeq's ouster and hence a Communist takeover were unlikely, the chance that Iran might be "lost" with all the attendant humiliation for the new Republican administration was enough to make them decide in favor of a covert intervention. In the view of the administration, the costs of being wrong about Mosaddeq and seeing him and Iran fall were greater than the costs of a covert operation implemented for several million dollars, whose success or failure would never be known to the public. In the interests of preserving the status quo of an Iran in the Western sphere, Eisenhower decided to intervene against Mosaddeq.

At the same time, both the British and groups within Iran played upon the concerns of Washington. With its priorities clearly enunciated, the administration was vulnerable to external influence from the periphery. Having committed itself to maintaining a non-Communist third world, the administration became susceptible to cries for help from third-world elites who could make a prima facie case that they were threatened by Communism. And in Iran, as Tudeh and Mosaddeq were thrown more closely together in 1953, that case became easy to make.

After surviving the February scare, Mosaddeq pushed ahead with a far more extensive land-reform program. The premier virtually ignored the majlis, which was so set against him by spring that it was impossible to assemble a quorum. He scheduled a national referendum for August to determine if the majlis was to be dissolved and new elections held. Oddly, as the political crisis deepened the economy stabilized somewhat. Increased governmental efficiency in tax collections had improved revenue, and it was a good year for crops.[96] Thus, the economic situation was not central to the conflict in the spring and summer of 1953.

There has been a heated debate over the August coup. On one side, many claim that the United States overthrew a democratic government that would

95. Brands, *Specter of Neutralism*, 1–10, 306–308; Gaddis, *Strategies of Containment*, 104–105.

96. Tehran 1069, "Monthly Economic Survey, Iran, May 1953," June 11, 1953, NA 888.00/6-1153; Katouzian, *Political Economy of Modern Iran*, 170–85.

have transformed Iranian society and prevented the emergence of an authoritarian monarchy and thereby also prevented the subsequent rise to power of the Ayatollah Khomeini.[97] Others contend that Mosaddeq was overthrown primarily by internal opponents, the Shah in particular, and that even without American aid, he would have been ousted sooner rather than later.[98] At the time, in 1953, many in the Eisenhower administration believed that the coup was an American creation that saved Iran for the West and validated the CIA as the instrument of choice when dealing with fringe regimes.[99]

The events of August that led to Mosaddeq's fall were the result of both decisions made in Washington and the ongoing efforts of his Iranian opponents to undermine him. Without either of these components, Mosaddeq may have weathered 1953 and eventually reduced the Shah to a figurehead. The Eisenhower administration made its decisions while being beseeched by multiple voices in the periphery; those local forces looked to U.S. intervention because Mosaddeq had survived all previous attempts to get rid of him. The successful coup was thus a product of internal and external forces that complemented each other to perfection.

Eisenhower authorized Operation Ajax in June; shortly thereafter, Mosaddeq finally broke with the majlis and called for a referendum. The results showed Mosaddeq winning 99 percent of the vote. Given the improbability of ever achieving that total in a fair election, it is safe to assume that by August 1953, Mosaddeq was veering dangerously close to a dictatorship. It was not, however, a repressive regime, nor was it without extensive public support. Indeed, difficult though it is to gauge such things, it may have enjoyed the backing of a majority of the Iranian people. The CIA judged Mosaddeq's public position to be very strong in the spring of 1953. However, his political support diminished precipitously. By summer, his opponents included the court; Kashani and the religious establishment in the city of Qom; the landowners; businessmen; and some of the workers. In addition, the army was split, with its officers mostly loyal to the Shah and its soldiers divided; it was unclear if it would come to Mosaddeq's aid. Even more troublesome, Mosaddeq was backed by the Tudeh. Tudeh concluded that although he was an anti-Communist, he was fighting

---

97. Gasiorowski argues this in his article, although he makes the point about the 1979 revolution more explicitly in his *U.S. Foreign Policy and the Shah*. Cottam makes this point, 109, 259–68, as does James Bill, to a lesser degree, in *Eagle and the Lion*, passim. See also Farhang Rajaee, "Islam, Nationalism and Musaddiq's Era: Post-Revolutionary Historiography in Iran," in *Musaddiq, Iranian Nationalism, and Oil*, ed. Bill and Louis, 119–38, for the development of this interpretation within Iran itself.

98. Mark Lytle, *The Origins of the Iranian-American Alliance* (New York, 1987) pursues this line, as does Ruehsen in her article.

99. There are strains of this in Kermit Roosevelt's *Countercoup*, although his views are more subtle than has usually been acknowledged. See also Dwight D. Eisenhower, *Mandate for Change* (Garden City, N.Y., 1963), and Allen Dulles, *The Craft of Intelligence* (New York, 1963).

Communism's enemies. Thus, in an enemy-of-my-enemy-is-a-friend calculation, Tudeh threw its weight behind Mosaddeq.[100]

The actual story of the planning and implementation of Ajax has been frequently told, and what is offered here is only a cursory overview, partly because the coup owed its success less to specific operational details and more to the convergence of factors discussed above. The details of the coup are exciting and dramatic, as are those of most covert operations, carrying as they do the lure of the forbidden and the unknown.[101] But there is a problem with focusing on the few days in August during which crowds loyal to one faction or the other battled for control of the streets of Tehran, when the balance seemed at one moment to favor Mosaddeq but finally swung against him. Such a focus is misleading if one wishes to understand why Mosaddeq fell and why the United States intervened.

The coup began on August 16 when the Shah sent Colonel Nimatollah Nassiri to dismiss Mosaddeq; he planned to appoint General Zahedi as the new premier. Forewarned of the plot, Mosaddeq ignored the imperial order, and arrested the messenger. The Shah fled to Rome via Baghdad, and the initial coup was foiled. But Operation Ajax did not depend on Mosaddeq's willingly surrendering power to a junior army officer sent on the Shah's behalf. For months, Kermit Roosevelt of the CIA had been developing a network, made up partly of old contacts established by Woodhouse, Zaehner, and British intelligence in 1951 and 1952, and partly of new contacts made by Roosevelt. One new partner was Colonel Schwarzkopf, who appeared conspicuously in Tehran. There was also the Shah's twin sister Ashraf, known as "The Black Panther," who used her palace connections to solidify the pro-Shah forces.[102] Other conspirators were Shaban "The Brainless," and the Rashidian brothers, longtime opponents of Mosaddeq. And then there was General Zahedi himself.

Fazlollah Zahedi had made his career as Cossack lieutenant under Reza Shah, and in 1951 he was minister of the interior in Mosaddeq's cabinet. Arrested for his pro-German activities in 1943, Zahedi agreed with the nationalization and had little love for the British. Soon, however, he turned against the premier and became an outspoken critic. By late 1952, he was actively plotting against Mosaddeq, working with the British, and trying to convince the Shah to appoint him in Mosaddeq's place. After the abortive uprising in February and the murder of the chief of police in April, Zahedi took refuge in the majlis building to

100. NIE Memorandum for the President, March 1, 1953. Top Secret, *FRUS, 1952-1954, Vol. X,* 689; CIA Report, "Comment on the Iranian Situation," March 1, 1953, CIA Research Reports, Reel 2.

101. For two good accounts based on secondary sources, see Peter Grose, *Gentleman Spy: The Life of Allen Dulles* (New York, 1994), 363-68, and David Halberstam, *The Fifties* (New York, 1993), 359-69.

102. Ashraf Pahlavi, *Faces in a Mirror,* 133-47; Roosevelt, *Countercoup,* 52-53, 146.

escape arrest; his request for sanctuary was honored by the president of the majlis, the Ayatollah Kashani. By summer, he was the choice of Roosevelt and the CIA to succeed to the premiership. Although the Shah and Zahedi were not close, the choice was acceptable.[103]

When the Shah fled, Tudeh mobs flooded the streets of Tehran, denouncing the Pahlavis and the Americans. Roosevelt cleverly utilized this situation to his advantage; he paid agents to join the Tudeh crowds and attack statues of the Shah and deface mosques. The result was a wide revulsion among the religious Tehranis and a widespread belief that Mosaddeq meant to overthrow the monarchy. Fearing that he would be tarred with the brush of Communism, Mosaddeq ordered the gendarmerie to arrest Tudeh demonstrators. He met with Henderson to assure him that American lives would be protected and that he was against all lawlessness and Communism. Henderson gave no indication of American involvement in the disturbances and warned the premier that if order was not soon restored, all Americans would be instructed to leave Tehran. That would be a blow to Mosaddeq's prestige, perhaps a crippling one, and the premier promised to restore order.[104]

With Mosaddeq attacking his only active street supporters, Roosevelt then paid for and mobilized the pro-Shah mobs led by Shaban. On August 19, the two mobs fought in the streets. But the army remained loyal to the Shah, and Kashani remained aloof, refusing to order his supporters to aid Mosaddeq. The pro-Mosaddeq and pro-Tudeh crowds were overcome. Once again, Mosaddeq was forced to flee from his house in his pajamas, but this time his luck was not so good. His home was fired on by tanks and then ransacked by the mob, and Mosaddeq was apprehended and arrested. On August 22, the Shah returned triumphantly to Tehran, with his new premier Zahedi by his side. He thanked the people, God, and the United States for saving his throne.[105] Anthony Eden, recovering from an illness, wrote in his memoirs, "the news of Musaddiq's fall from power reached me during my convalescence, when my wife and I, with my son, were cruising the Mediterranean. . . . I slept happily that night."[106]

Zahedi had hardly begun his official duties when the Eisenhower administration offered him $45 million in emergency aid. It was hoped that the aid would be sufficient to tide Zahedi over for the next few months until a settlement was reached with the British. More aid was promised. In Tehran, the U.S. embassy pushed for a speedy trial of Mosaddeq as a signal that the days of anti-Western nationalism were past. In the United States, the press hailed Zahedi

103. Abrahamian, *Iran*, 278–80; Akhavi, "The Role of the Clergy," 110–11.

104. Henderson Oral History, 17, Columbia Oral History Project; Henderson to Department of State, August 18, 1953, Secret, *FRUS, 1952–1954, Vol. X*, 748–50; Cottam, *Iran and the United States*, 107–108; Yergin, *The Prize*, 466–72; Roosevelt, *Countercoup*, 183–97.

105. Roosevelt, *Countercoup*, 190–95.

106. Anthony Eden, *Full Circle*, 214, quoted in Musaddiq, *Musaddiq's Memoirs*, 280.

and the Shah; only the *Nation* offered a dissenting note, warning that Zahedi lent "an aura of Nazism" to Iranian politics.[107]

Mosaddeq was tried quickly by a military court and sentenced to three years' solitary confinement. At his trial, he defended his actions: "My only crime, and my great—even greater—crime, is that I nationalized the Iranian oil industry, and removed the network of colonialism. . . . My life, reputation, person and property . . . do not have the slightest value compared with the lives, the independence, the greatness and the pride of millions of Iranians."[108] Released at the end of his sentence, he lived out his years under house arrest just outside of Tehran; he died in 1967 at the age of eighty-five.

Zahedi agreed to settle the oil dispute with the British. But negotiations were still difficult; the Shah was worried that any settlement too generous to the British would lead to another Mosaddeq and plunge Iran into revolution. In September 1954, an agreement was finally reached. The National Iranian Oil Company would own Iran's oil and the Abadan refinery. However, the oil would be sold and essentially controlled by an international consortium. The British Anglo-Iranian company (soon to be renamed British Petroleum or BP) accounted for 40 percent of the consortium, Shell had 14 percent, the French were given 6 percent, and the major American oil companies split the remaining 40 percent. The nationalization was upheld and, as so many had predicted in 1951, the British never regained their position.[109]

The U.S. intervention in Iran in 1953 can be read in several ways. It can be seen as an Anglo-American coup against a third-world nationalist leader; it can be viewed as a plan hatched and implemented by the CIA in Washington. It can also be read as the culmination of assiduous efforts by Iranian groups opposed to Mosaddeq and opposed to the forces unleashed by his reforms; and it can be interpreted as the successful attempt of the Shah, his retinue, the army, landholders, and groups allied with clergymen such as Kashani to remove a formidable political competitor. Faced with a choice between becoming a client of the U.S. government or being swept away in a wave of nationalism unleashed by Mosaddeq, these Iranians chose American clientage. In Robinson-Gallagher's rubric, they collaborated with the imperialists. The Eisenhower administration, for its part, collaborated with the forces of royalism and reaction.

The Americans replaced Britain as the imperial power in Iran. Zahedi did not last long, and after a brief constitutional crisis in the early 1960s, the Shah established himself on the Peacock Throne. His monarchy was fully supported by the United States, and though the Shah promised that democratic reforms would eventually be instituted, they always seemed to lie in the distant future. Tudeh was ruthlessly eliminated, and the National Front struggled on as a fringe

107. *Nation,* September 1, 1953.

108. Musaddiq, *Musaddiq's Memoirs,* 74.

109. Yergin, *The Prize,* 476–78.

group of liberals who would briefly rise to prominence once again in 1978-1979 before being overthrown by Kashani's heirs.

Kim Roosevelt was awarded a medal by Eisenhower, although the reason remained an official secret. His warning that an operation such as Ajax required a perfect combination of domestic factors and a good reading of the internal situation would have been prophetic had it not been written in 1979, many years after all the lessons of Ajax were visible to twenty-twenty hindsight. Iran had gone so smoothly and cost such a paltry amount that Eisenhower and the Dulles brothers authorized another covert intervention almost immediately. This one would be on more familiar turf, in the traditional backyard of the United States. The operation was named PBSUCCESS, and its target was the president of Guatemala, Jacobo Arbenz.

5

Guatemala

Revolutionaries and Counterrevolutionaries

Arbenz was a bad president and a dangerous person.
— Miguel Ydígoras Fuentes

*[My three goals for Guatemala are]: To convert our country from
a dependent and economically semi-colonial nation into a country
economically independent; to convert Guatemala from a backward
country with an economy predominantly feudal, into a modern
capitalistic country; and, to see that this transformation takes place
in a manner which produces the greatest possible elevation of the
standard of living of the great mass of the people.*
— Jacobo Arbenz

The story of the U.S. intervention in Guatemala in 1954 is a staple of most books on the United States and the cold war. Most books tell a similar story. A reformist democratic government with a small amount of Communist support undertakes an ambitious land reform program. In the process, thousands of acres of land are taken from the American-owned United Fruit Company, at that time the largest landowner in Guatemala. Given the connections between the company and various high officials in the Eisenhower administration, the land reform leads to a confrontation between Guatemala and the "colossus of the north." The Guatemalan president, Jacobo Arbenz, is surrounded by Communist advisers and friends whose influence on him allows Washington to paint Guatemala as Communist-led. Eisenhower authorizes the CIA to remove the Guatemalan government. The CIA finds a suitable puppet and arms him. After a long campaign of psychological warfare and diplomatic pressure, the democratic government of Arbenz is overthrown by the CIA and its puppet Castillo Armas.[1]

---

1. Piero Gleijeses, *Shattered Hope: The Guatemalan Revolution and the United States, 1944-1954* (Princeton, 1991); Stephen Schlesinger and Stephen Kinzer, *Bitter Fruit: The Untold Story of the American Coup in Guatemala* (New York, 1982); Richard Immerman, *The CIA in*

This version of the 1954 events is not inaccurate, but it is incomplete. Seen from Washington or from the perspective of Arbenz, that is what happened. However, this explanation of the coup does not answer why it was relatively easy to topple Arbenz. There was remarkably little bloodshed, and the president quit his office before Castillo Armas even reached Guatemala City. Within a month, Guatemala was in the midst of a full-blown counterrevolution supported by large swaths of Guatemalan society, including the church, the army, the landowners, and segments of the urban intelligentsia.

Unlike Greece, Italy, and Iran, Guatemala had a long history of interaction with the United States, and Washington was accustomed to the role of great power and patron in Central America. When anti-Arbenz groups in Guatemala sought external help, their instinct was to turn to the United States because the U.S. had often intervened on behalf of similar groups in decades past.[2] Still, when the story of the 1954 Guatemalan coup is told, the question of how the reactionary forces within Guatemala finally succeeded in turning back the revolution is rarely addressed.

In the dominant narrative of cold-war history and of U.S.–Latin American history, Guatemala's small size and traditional status as a client of the United States has made it easy to underemphasize the degree to which various Guatemalan groups tried to "lure" (to borrow from Robinson and Gallagher) the Eisenhower administration to act against Arbenz. Traditional frameworks have also skirted the issue of how dependent the United States was on the "mediation" (Robinson again) of local groups in Guatemala to make such a covert intervention practical.

Furthermore, Colonel Castillo Armas is routinely described as a puppet. That characterization ignores the possibility that he was an architect of the intervention. When Castillo Armas invaded Guatemala from Honduras in June 1954, he started on the final leg of a long journey that had begun years before. He had been trying to overthrow the Guatemalan government for more than five years, and he was not alone in his efforts. In short, the revolution of 1944, which ended a dictatorship and led to the election of Juan José Arévalo, was

---

Guatemala: The Foreign Policy of Intervention (Austin, 1982). This story is not only the core of these major books on the coup but also the essence of most passing references to the coup in larger works. See Susanne Jonas, *The Battle for Guatemala* (Boulder, Colo., 1991); Prados, *Presidents' Secret Wars*, 98–107; David Wise and Thomas Ross, *The Invisible Government* (New York, 1964), 167–83; William Blum, *The CIA: A Forgotten History* (London, 1986), 77–89; Stephen Rabe, "The Clues Didn't Check Out: Commentary on 'The CIA and Castillo Armas' " *Diplomatic History,* XIV (Winter 1990), 87–95; John Coatsworth, *Central America and the United States* (New York, 1994), 67–74. Of the major books, Schlesinger and Kinzer are closest to the "Platonic ideal" of the traditional interpretation. Gleijeses provides by far the best-researched and most extensive coverage of the intervention and of Guatemalan politics, although he ultimately argues a modified version of the traditional thesis.

2. See LaFeber, *Inevitable Revolutions.*

opposed from the start by multiple segments of Guatemalan society. These groups, as surely as the Eisenhower administration, the CIA, and the United Fruit Company, enabled Castillo Armas to overthrow Arbenz. And it is this aspect of the intervention that has been largely neglected.

The 1954 coup fits nicely into various theories of dependency and underdevelopment. In general terms, dependency theory holds that economic relations between the United States and Latin America have been set up by the economically more powerful "norteamericanos" in such a way as to disadvantage Latin America. The result is chronic underdevelopment, widespread poverty, a fragile middle class, and a small number of extremely rich elites. These elites maintained their position with the help of the military and of the United States. The more strict Marxist school of dependency theory blames the capitalist system for the economic and social problems of Latin America. Others suggest that the capitalist system can be reformed so that the inequities are addressed.[3] However, the basic presumption is that economic systems drive relations between the United States and Latin America, and that the United States acts as an imperial power in the region.

Since the 1970s, dependency theory has been the primary paradigm for discussing U.S.–Latin American relations. But it is not a monolithic model. Some dependency theorists do claim that Washington is the main culprit, but many have a more subtle view of how dependency and underdevelopment work. All but a few writers agree that, except for a brief period at the turn of the twentieth century, the United States did not desire territorial domination. The American empire was economic, and although it was occasionally maintained by force, it was usually preserved and defended by local collaborators. As one writer put it, for those who sought to change the system, the immediate enemy was not the United States, but the local bourgeoisie.[4] It was the bourgeoisie in Latin America who collaborated with the Americans; it was they who oppressed the peasants and prevented development, selling out the raw materials of their countries to business interests in the United States.

Some writers have gone even farther. In his days as a social scientist, Fernando Henrique Cardoso (who was elected president of Brazil in 1994), wrote that dependency should be seen as "a relationship between external and internal forces . . . not based on mere external forms of exploitation and coercion, but [which are] rooted in the coincidence of interests between local dominant classes and international ones, and [which] are challenged by local dominated

3. For the classic Marxist view, see Andre Gunder Frank, *Latin America: Underdevelopment or Revolution?* (New York, 1969). For a survey of various theories, see Cristóbal Kay, *Latin American Theories of Development and Underdevelopment* (New York, 1989). See also John Sheahan, *Patterns of Development in Latin America* (Princeton, 1988).

4. Frank, *Latin America,* 272.

groups and classes."[5] Thus, there is a prominent branch of dependency theorists who believe that the policies of the U.S. government can only explain so much and that local forces within Guatemala bear at least equal responsibility for the post-1954 counterrevolution. While the system served the interests of an international power such as Great Britain or the United States, it was maintained on the ground by local forces whose interests were also served by underdevelopment.

Dependency theorists in Latin America have often been on the progressive or radical end of the political spectrum. American writers who have addressed U.S. policies in Latin America have tended to share these political predispositions. Oddly, while some Latin American dependency theorists have made a pointed effort to show how significant the "local dominant classes" were in resisting or subverting reform (and hence in luring the United States to intervene against domestic forces of reform or revolution), many writers in the United States have emphasized the "international ones," i.e., the United States, to the point where these local classes dwindle into insignificance. In addition, American books on the Guatemalan coup are often buttressed by the memoirs of the Arbenz apologists, many of them former members of his administration.[6] The result has been an American orthodoxy on the Guatemalan coup that borrows heavily from pro-Arbenz Guatemalans but that draws only selectively from dependency theory. This orthodoxy presents a Guatemala subverted not by local groups working with their patrons in Washington, but by Washington working with local puppets to destroy Guatemalan democracy. While that was certainly the effect of the 1954 coup, this picture does not do justice to the process that brought about the coup. It both exaggerates U.S. influence and ignores the complexities of Guatemalan society.

■

Until 1944, Guatemala was ruled by Jorge Ubico, a petty dictator undistinguished by anything except his skill at maintaining the status quo and his own regime. During his thirteen years in power, he kept the landed elite happy. The shock waves of the Bolshevik Revolution continued to buffet the Americas throughout the 1920s and 1930s, and Ubico was harshly anti-Communist. The landlords in their vast estates viewed the ideas emanating from the Soviet Union as a potential death sentence.

Ubico ruthlessly suppressed Guatemala's nascent labor movement, while the Good Neighbor policies of the Roosevelt administration precluded any

5. Fernando Henrique Cardoso and Enzo Faletto, *Dependency and Development in Latin America* (Berkeley, 1979), xvi.

6. These include books by Guillermo Toriello, Manuel Galich, Raul Osgueda, Juan José Arévalo, and Luis Cardoza y Aragon, all cited below.

interference by the United States. Besides, with American economic interests in Guatemala's two crops—coffee and bananas—few saw any problem with the Ubico regime. While the dictator's pro-German sympathies were an annoyance after 1940, he was solicitous to American business in Guatemala, particularly to the United Fruit Company (UFCO) and the American-owned International Railways of Central America. However, in 1944, Ubico was presented with demands for reform by university students. Instead of suppressing the protests, he resigned.[7]

The dictator's abrupt departure left a vacuum that was filled, surprisingly, by a democratic government. Returning from exile in Argentina, Juan José Arévalo was elected president of the new Guatemalan republic. A college professor with a reputation for moderation, Arévalo had the admiration of the young officers in the Guatemalan army, including Captain Jacobo Arbenz Guzmán. Arbenz was one of the interim leaders between Ubico's departure and Arévalo's election, and he admired the middle-aged professor. Arévalo appealed to the educated, urban middle class in Guatemala City, of which Arbenz was a member. The professor, who espoused spiritual socialism, enunciated his vision for the future soon after arriving in Guatemala in 1944: "Our socialism does not aim at ingenious distribution of material goods. . . . Our socialism aims to liberate men psychologically, to return to all the psychological and spiritual integrity that has been denied them by conservatism and liberalism."[8] He noted that "the 1944 Revolution was a rebellion against a political system installed in power in 1871. But this rebellion included all people, all classes and not a political party."[9] After years of dictatorship and corrupt elite politics under the guise of liberalism, Arévalo promised a democratic future and a new deal for the middle class.

During the six years of his presidency, Arévalo pursued a series of moderate reforms. A new constitution was written, with provisions for elected representatives and a strong presidency. A labor code drawn up in 1947 affirmed the right of workers to strike and unionize. And modest efforts were made to weaken the influence of America's powerful United Fruit Company. But on the whole, Arévalo's program was moderate. He did not attempt land reform in a country where more than three-quarters of the population were peasants and a few thousand landowners controlled almost all the land. His was essentially a middle-class, white-collar government, firmly supported by the young profes-

---

7. Manuel Galich, *Por qué lucha Guatemala: Arévalo y Arbenz* (Buenos Aires, 1956), 33–45; Gleijeses, *Shattered Hope*, 8–30; Jonas, *Battle for Guatemala*, 21–23; Ralph Lee Woodward, *Central America: A Nation Divided* (New York, 1985), 230–32. Galich was foreign minister of Guatemala in 1951–52.

8. Quoted in Woodward, *Central America*, 232.

9. Quoted in Galich, *Por qué lucha Guatemala*, 75 (my translation).

sionals, junior army officers, merchants, bankers, journalists, teachers, and students who flocked to the two major cities in Guatemala.[10]

The army in Guatemala was a key to the survival of the revolution. Although it comprised fewer than seven thousand men, the army was one of the few independent, cohesive institutions in Guatemalan society. While the 1944 coup against Ubico was supported by the officer corps, the Guatemalan army was by nature conservative. In this it differed hardly at all from other militaries in Latin America. Its role in post-Ubico society was defined in the 1949 constitution: "The national Army is instituted to defend the territorial integrity of the nation. . . . It is apolitical, essentially professional, obedient, and non-deliberative. . . . It is organized as an institution guaranteeing order and internal and external security."[11]

But as an organization dedicated to defending order and internal security, it was in fact quite political, and its relationship with the Arévalo regime was strained. While certain young officers such as Arbenz and Major Francisco Arana played leading roles in the Arévalo administration, many officers distrusted the direction that the revolution seemed to be taking.[12] Although Arévalo was rhetorically anti-Communist, he was avidly reformist, and he was supported by radicals in Congress. Segments of the officer corps feared that the future held decreased budgets for them and increased chaos in society. In Arévalo's six years in office, the army was responsible for nearly thirty coup attempts.[13]

There was resistance to Arévalo in other segments of society. The church and the elite landowners distrusted the New Deal clarion sounded by the one-time professor. But the army produced the two men who vied for control of Guatemala after Arévalo. Castillo Armas and Jacobo Arbenz were both leading officers in the Guatemalan army of the 1940s. Castillo Armas cooperated with the revolution as long as his patron Major Arana, the chief of armed forces, cooperated. Arana was killed in an ambush in July 1949, and it is possible that Arbenz was involved in the plot. Arana, described by the CIA as "a competent and persevering" officer, made no secret of his ambitions for the presidency; nor did Arbenz. Arana's death cleared the way for Arbenz to become president,

10. Jonas, *Battle for Guatemala*, 22–25; Gleijeses, *Shattered Hope*, 37–47; Jim Handy, *Revolution in the Countryside: Rural Conflict and Agrarian Reform in Guatemala, 1944-1954* (Chapel Hill, 1994), 23–35.

11. Article 149, quoted in Raul Osgueda, *Operación Guatemala $$OK$$* (Mexico City, 1955), 40.

12. Gleijeses, *Shattered Hope*, 50–68, 196; Frederick Marks, "The CIA and Castillo Armas in Guatemala, 1954: New Clues to an Old Puzzle," *Diplomatic History*, XIV (Winter 1990), 80–83; Richard Adams, *Crucifixion by Power: Essays on Guatemalan National Social Structure, 1944-1966* (Austin, 1970), 238ff.

13. Jesús García Añoveros, *Jacobo Arbenz* (Madrid, 1987), 31–33.

but it also made Castillo Armas into a mortal enemy of the revolution and of his erstwhile colleague.[14]

Born in 1914, an illegitimate child abandoned by his mother, Carlos Castillo Armas, like his rival Jacobo Arbenz, attended Guatemala's prestigious Military Polytechnic School and for a while attended classes at the U.S. army training center in Fort Leavenworth, Kansas. When it became clear by late October 1950 that Arbenz would win the presidential election, Castillo Armas led an attack of approximately one hundred men against an army base in Guatemala City. He had been planning the attack ever since Arana's murder, and he had even contacted the CIA in a futile plea for help.[15] Nineteen people were killed. Castillo Armas was shot twice in the leg and feigned death to avoid being killed. He was taken to a nearby hospital by his captors; the bullets were extracted; and he was then promptly moved to a prison cell. He remained there for less than seven months and escaped in June 1951, fleeing to Colombia.[16]

One prominent writer has remarked that Castillo Armas "would hardly deserve a footnote were it not that in 1953 he was selected by the CIA to lead the liberation of Guatemala."[17] Perhaps he would have languished in obscurity if not for the coincidence of his goals and those of the Eisenhower administration. Yet Castillo Armas had contested the 1944 revolution well before the CIA appeared on the Guatemalan scene. The power struggles within Guatemala's army existed independent of any meddling by the American government.

While Castillo Armas might have remained a lonely, unsuccessful conspirator without the CIA, he managed to assemble a hundred men in 1950 to challenge the government. Fidel Castro had fewer than that in the 1958, yet he eventually overthrew Fulgencio Batista in Cuba. Castillo Armas was representative of a prominent group within the army that challenged the Arévalo-Arbenz revolution. It is easy to discount him as a puppet of the Americans. It is more accurate to view him as a bona fide challenger to the reforms championed by Arévalo and Arbenz.

Opinions about Castillo Armas differ. After an interview in 1950, a CIA agent described him as "a quiet, soft-spoken officer who does not seem to be given to exaggeration."[18] Another portrait painted him as "short, slender, almost

14. Guatemala 582, Fisher (3rd Secretary) to Department of State, December 8, 1950, Restricted, NA 714.00/12-850; Immerman, *CIA in Guatemala,* 57–58; Gleijeses, *Shattered Hope,* 55; Handy, *Revolution in the Countryside,* 181–83; García Añoveros, *Arbenz,* 109.

15. CIA Report, January 19, 1950. Reprinted in CIA Research Reports (Microfilm Set), Latin America, Reel 5.

16. Guatemala 36, Kendon Steins (3rd Secretary) to Department of State, July 10, 1953, Confidential, NA 714.00/7-1051.

17. Gleijeses, *Shattered Hope,* 82.

18. Nicholas Cullather, *Operation PBSUCCESS: The United States and Guatemala, 1952-1954* (Washington, D.C., 1994), 5. This history was written under the auspices of the history staff of the Center for the Study of Intelligence, which is part of the Central Intelligence Agency. Until

petite. Always immaculate, he looked as though he had been packaged by Bloomingdale's. But he was personally brave. He had a dreamy air about him, almost mystical, or perhaps just plain dopey." A CIA officer familiar with him after 1952 said that Castillo Armas was "small, humble, thin guy" who "didn't know what he was doing and was in way over his head."[19] Guillermo Toriello, Guatemala's foreign minister in the last days of the Arbenz government, called Castillo Armas a "Judas" who sold Guatemala to the Americans for the latter-day equivalent of thirty pieces of silver.[20] E. Howard Hunt, later known as a Watergate bungler, and one of the CIA operatives involved in planning the 1954 coup, remarked on how Indian Castillo Armas looked.[21] Given that the Guatemalan people were mostly Indian and mixed-blood mestizo, Castillo Armas' ethnicity was significant, especially when compared with Arbenz who was very much of the white *ladino* elite.[22]

Whatever his personal merits or demerits, however, Castillo Armas was the proximate cause of the 1954 coup. He was the embodiment of the aspirations of the reactionary classes in Guatemala; he was a small man in all ways, but he would be more than a footnote even without the CIA.

Still, in 1950, it was clearly Arbenz who had the upper hand. Going into the November 1950 elections, he had every intention of riding Arévalo's coattails into the presidency. One campaign slogan was "Today Arévalo, Arbenz Tomorrow."[23] Arbenz was aided during the campaign by government officials and members of Congress, and their support gave him a substantial edge over his opponent Miguel Ydígoras Fuentes. Arbenz also had close ties to organized labor; he apparently promised the labor leader August Charnaud MacDonald that leaders of the workers' movement would be given three cabinet seats if he won.[24] Charnaud MacDonald was a left-leaning socialist, but Arbenz was also friendly with Víctor Manuel Gutiérrez, a self-professed Communist whose disdain for material goods earned him the nickname "the Franciscan."[25] There were few Guatemalan Communists in the 1940s. They were divided and had only tenuous links to Moscow. Nevertheless, the association of Arbenz with Gutiérrez was to have fateful consequences.

Arbenz's campaign rhetoric stressed the desperate need for economic reform

---

the summer of 1997, this history was classified because it was based in part on classified CIA records.

19. Quotations are from Schlesinger and Kinzer, *Bitter Fruit,* 122–23.

20. Guillermo Toriello, *La Batalla de Guatemala* (Mexico City, 1955), 73.

21. E. Howard Hunt, *Give Us This Day* (New Rochelle, N.Y., 1973), 117.

22. The CIA in particular regarded Castillo Armas' mestizo features as an advantage. See Cullather, *Operation PBSUCCESS,* 35.

23. Reported in Guatemala 304, September 20, 1950, Confidential, NA 714.00/9-2050.

24. Guatemala 87, Patterson (U.S. ambassador) to Department of State, March 15, 1950, Confidential, NA 714.00/3-1550.

25. Schlesinger and Kinzer, *Bitter Fruit,* 56.

in Guatemala, the necessity of continuing the process begun by Arévalo, and the danger of internal and external enemies who sought to undermine the revolution. In one speech early in the campaign, he defined the election as a contest between "two forces perfectly opposed." He was on one side, while on the other were individuals allied with the "old systems" that had stolen Guatemala's wealth and deprived the people of civil liberties.[26] Assessing candidate Arbenz, the American State Department reported that he was "realistic." The U.S. chargé in the Guatemala embassy also remarked that Arbenz's attitude toward United Fruit—the primary American business interest in Guatemala—was "devoid of prejudices."[27]

The other candidate, Ydígoras Fuentes, was supported by landowners; business interests associated with United Fruit and the American railway and shipping companies; the church; and a scattering of others throughout the society. A former general in Ubico's army, Ydígoras gravitated to the forefront of the conservative opposition after the death of Arana. Handsome, corrupt, and cruel, Ydígoras returned to Guatemala in the spring of 1950 from London where he had been passing his time as a Guatemala's representative on the International Olympic Committee. He harped on the Communist menace threatening Guatemala in the guise of Arbenz, and he spoke favorably of authoritarian government.[28] In one speech, he told voters to support him if they wished to save their "homes," "goods," and "enterprises from the Red attack which is threatening them."[29] He lost the election by nearly a three-to-one margin, receiving 73,000 votes to Arbenz's 266,000.[30] Implicated in Castillo Armas' attack on the army barracks in November, Ydígoras was in hiding on election day and fled the country after an Arbenz victory that he claimed was fraudulent.[31] It seemed that Arbenz had defeated the opponents of the revolution: Castillo Armas was in jail, Ydígoras in exile, and the United States government was only moderately critical of the new president. But it was not to last. Castillo Armas and Ydígoras would be back.

As for Arbenz, he was an elusive character. Born in 1913 to a *ladino* mother and a Swiss father, he attended the Polytechnic School and became an officer in the 1930s. In 1939, he met his future wife, María Vilanova. María was from

26. Reported in Guatemala 479, April 20, 1950, Confidential, NA 714.00/4-2050.

27. State Department Memo of Conversation: Milton Wells (chargé) and Arbenz, March 30, 1950, Confidential, NA 611.14/3-3150.

28. Immerman, *CIA in Guatemala*, 60–61; Miguel Ydígoras Fuentes, *My War with Communism* (Englewood Cliffs, N.J., 1963), 44–47; Gleijeses, *Shattered Hope*, 75–76, 82–84.

29. Reported in Guatemala 386, March 29, 1950, NA 714.00/3-2950.

30. Guatemala 575, December 7, 1950, NA 714.00/12-750.

31. According to Gleijeses, the election was as free as an election could be in Guatemala in 1950, given that women could not vote, while illiterate peasants were denied secret ballots and only allowed to make a public vote. Still, there was no evidence of systematic fraud. Gleijeses, *Shattered Hope*, 84.

a wealthy Salvadoran family of coffee-growers and had been educated at a college in California. They were both attractive and white, and while not economically of the upper class, they moved in elite circles. Many have commented on how deeply María Arbenz influenced her husband. Some have claimed that she was the more radical of the two and pushed him further left. She certainly had strong ideas about reform, and she was better educated than her husband, especially about Marxism. But while Jacobo may not have studied Marx, he played an active role in the revolution. In planning for the removal of Ubico, Arbenz insisted that the successor government be composed of civilians, and he was committed to a new constitutional era for Guatemala.[32]

The Truman administration was ambivalent about Arbenz, as it had been about Arévalo. After the election, the American embassy described Arbenz as "intelligent, unscrupulous, cynical, and ambitious." The report continued:

> Despite the mildness of Arbenz's own speeches and his assurances to the embassy, he was supported in the campaign by Leftists, was opposed by conservatives and moderates as a Leftist, and was elected a Leftist. This brings up a question as to whether his present Leftism is a matter of principle or a matter of convenience. . . . He is also known to have maintained relations with several Communists. . . . Despite Arbenz's considerable entanglement with the Leftist extremists, it is reasonable to suppose that his ambition is greater than his idealism, and therefore, he will seek to fashion his policies along what appear to him practical lines in choosing between the good-will of the United States and the domestic political support of the pro-Communists.[33]

This analysis echoed a CIA report written earlier that year. According to the CIA, Arbenz would be more conservative than Arévalo, more favorably disposed toward American business, and more repressive.[34] Both analyses proved to be wrong. Another report revealed that Arbenz had something of a drinking problem, and even speculated that he was a drug addict.[35]

The issue of Communism in Guatemala certainly concerned Truman and Acheson. Although they recognized that only a handful of Communists were

32. García Añoveros, *Arbenz,* 20ff.; Gleijeses, *Shattered Hope,* 136–41; Schlesinger and Kinzer, *Bitter Fruit,* 49–63; Immerman, *CIA in Guatemala,* 61–62. Also, Luis Cardoza y Aragon, interview by author, Mexico City, August 1991.

33. Andrew Wardlaw (2d secretary) to Department of State, December 21, 1950, Secret, NA 714.00/12-2150.

34. CIA SR-46, July 27, 1950, CIA Research Reports, Latin America, Reel 5.

35. Unnumbered telegram from U.S. Embassy–Guatemala, May 1952 [date unspecified], Guatemala Embassy records, 1949–1952, RG 84, Box 15, WNRC.

prominent in Guatemalan politics, American officials at the time often seemed to believe that a few were sufficient to create instability and strife.[36] According to a telegram bearing Acheson's signature, one aspect of U.S. policy was to make "moderate and reasonable elements" in the Guatemalan government see the danger of Communism by hinting that continued toleration of Communists would lead to a deterioration in U.S.-Guatemalan relations.[37] Guatemala was hardly a priority for the Truman administration, but in 1950, in the wake of Mao's victory in China and subsequent Republican attacks that Truman was weak on Communism, even a few Communists in a small Central American country were a sore point. Wary of Arbenz, Truman and Acheson nonetheless believed that there was no immediate danger of "losing" Guatemala.[38]

Officials at the CIA were not nearly as sanguine. In August of 1950, the CIA's Office of Policy Coordination, headed by Frank Wisner, suggested that the growth of Communist activity would transform the country into "a central point for the dissemination of anti-US propaganda." With that danger in mind, the OPC dispatched an agent to Guatemala City.[39]

When Arbenz gave his inaugural address in March 1951, the diehard conservatives in Guatemala were demoralized, and they were receiving little encouragement from a United States which had traditionally stood for their interests. Arbenz, however, did not trust that his victory would last. The landowners, the church, United Fruit, and the army were deeply entrenched in Guatemalan society, and coup plots were constantly being uncovered. In an October 1951 speech, Arbenz warned of individuals who strove to halt "the progress of our country. And it is not only internal enemies who hold the sword of Damocles, but foreign forces, illegitimately interested in destroying the revolutionary process in Guatemala."[40] The internal threats were the conservative groups; the external were a hodge-podge of conspirators such as Armas and Ydígoras; hostile neighboring governments in Nicaragua, Honduras, Cuba, and the Dominican Republic; and the ever-present "yanqui" in Washington.

Rather than bow to these pressures, Arbenz did precisely what the CIA and the State Department had predicted he would not do: he moved further left and became an advocate of more extensive reform. One member of Arbenz's government remarked that Jacobo had only one main goal, "the solution of the economic problem of the country, [which was] complicated by a feudal order

36. See Truman letter to Carlos Prio of Cuba, October 19, 1950, Confidential, NA 714.00/10-1950.

37. Acheson to Guatemala, May 5, 1950, Confidential, NA 611.14/5-550.

38. See Memorandum of Conversation among Ambassador Richard Patterson, Thomas Mann (State Department Director of Middle American Affairs), Ed Clark, and Mr. Cahn (Secretary to Senator Wiley), May 10, 1950, Confidential, NA 714.00/5-1050.

39. Cullather, *Operation PBSUCCESS*, 10.

40. Text of Arbenz speech, October 19, 1951, NA 714.00/10-2651.

and an imperial presence."[41] In 1952, he attacked the primary obstacle to social and economic development in Guatemala: the structure of land ownership.

Passed in June 1952, Decree 900 established the framework for agrarian reform. Land reform had been discussed by Arévalo, but he had not acted on the various proposals put forth during his presidency. When Arbenz undertook land reform, he embraced those worker and peasant organizations that had been most vocal in denouncing the inequities and calling for redistribution of land. These organizations—in particular the Confederación General de Trabajadores (CGTG) led by Víctor Manuel Gutiérrez, and the Confederación Nacional Campesina Guatemala (CNCG) led by Castillo Flores—were dominated by Communists, but they were not explicitly Communist organizations. With the exception of José Manual Fortuny and to a lesser degree Gutiérrez, most of the leading Guatemalan "Communists" were simply progressive leftists. Unlike their counterparts in Greece, Italy, and Iran, they were not directly answerable to the Soviet Union, nor did Moscow attempt to orchestrate their strategy. Indeed, many of those calling themselves Communists in Guatemala had scant knowledge of Lenin or Marx. They were intent on challenging the power of the traditional ruling groups, and they were strongly anti-imperialist and anti-American.[42] However, as seen from Washington, a Communist was a Communist was a Communist. Fortuny and Gutiérrez probably qualified under any definition, and they were close to Arbenz; they were also instrumental in designing Decree 900.

Until 1952, Castillo Armas, Ydígoras, and the forces they represented made little headway against a popular constitutional government. But once Decree 900 was implemented, the conservative groups no longer believed it was possible to wait out reform. They needed to act or face total, permanent defeat. They were fortunate that a change of administration in Washington brought to office a president more sympathetic to their perspective, but Truman might well have come to a similar decision.

As in Iran, the Truman administration had considered intervening in Guatemala.[43] It even began the preliminary stages of planning a covert action campaign against Arbenz in 1952, after the passage of Decree 900. Recently declassified CIA records show that this planning was extensive. The CIA contacted Guatemalan dissidents such as Castillo Armas, and agency officials met with Nicaragua's President Anastasio Somoza to discuss how best to proceed against Arbenz. The CIA chief of the Western Hemisphere Division, J. C. King, outlined an operation that would have supplied Castillo Armas with weapons and $225,000.

41. Galich, *Por qué lucha Guatemala*, 222 (my translation).

42. Juan José Arévalo, *Guatemala, la democracia, y el imperio* (Montevideo, 1954), 16-30; Gleijeses, *Shattered Hope*, 171ff.; Handy, *Revolution in the Countryside*, 63-85; Schlesinger and Kinzer, *Bitter Fruit*, 56-62.

43. Gleijeses, *Shattered Hope*, 123-48; Schlesinger and Kinzer, *Bitter Fruit*, 100-104; Immerman, *CIA in Guatemala*, 118-22.

The planned rebellion would also rely on assistance from Nicaragua, Honduras, and the Dominican Republic. Meeting with the CIA, State Department officials such as Thomas Mann and Edward Miller, assistant secretary for Inter-American Affairs, stated that they wanted Guatemala's government overthrown by force if necessary. In September 1952, the CIA received explicit authorization from Undersecretary of State David Bruce to proceed with the plans. However, less than a month later, in October 1952, Dean Acheson instructed the CIA to pull back. He was worried that the operation might be blown, and that the consequences of public failure outweighed the benefits of covert success. The agency kept Castillo Armas on a retainer and maintained what assets it could, but for the moment all plans were off.[44]

These declassified records leave little doubt that Truman and his advisers were willing to intervene and to do so covertly. The Truman administration decided not to proceed with an intervention against Arbenz in Guatemala, just as it had decided not to act on British suggestions to conspire against Mosaddeq in Iran. The administration was, however, *prepared* to intervene covertly in both situations. Given Truman's policies in Greece and Italy, there is no reason to suppose that the unwillingness to act derived from a discomfort with covert interventions in general. Having opted not to run for reelection, Truman in 1952 was a lame duck, not eager to undertake major operations. The situation in Korea remained unresolved, and Truman was naturally wary of further foreign-policy embarrassments.

Furthermore, in Guatemala as in Iran, Truman and his advisers had reason to suppose that problems would be resolved without recourse to intervention. Until all other avenues were exhausted, why risk a covert campaign against Arbenz? Although it would cost far less than a military campaign, a CIA intervention would demand money and time. In 1952, the Truman administration could reasonably hope that Arbenz would stop short of anti-American radicalism, and it was not convinced that Communism threatened Guatemala. If it had been convinced, it would have acted with the same alacrity that it had displayed in Greece and Italy. One reason why it was not convinced was that, until the land-reform bureaucracy undertook wide-reaching appropriations in late 1952 and early 1953, the internal Guatemalan opposition to Arbenz was disunited and unfocused.

As a result, the pull factors on Washington from Guatemala were not as strong in 1951 and 1952 as they would become in 1953. In Guatemala as in all the cases discussed here, intervention depended on a convergence of push factors and pull factors, of foreign policy in Washington and domestic policy in the periphery. During the Truman administration, these factors began to converge but not sufficiently to bring about an intervention.

Alternately, it is possible to explain the different decisions made by Truman and Eisenhower as purely the result of different cold-war beliefs. It is possible,

44. Cullather, *Operation PBSUCCESS*, 17–19.

therefore, to construct an explanation for the intervention that emphasizes the change of administrations in Washington, a new foreign-policy agenda, and a shift in philosophy. Such an American-centric explanation, however, overstates the foreign-policy differences between Truman and Eisenhower, and it does not fully answer the question of why American officials expended so much energy planning an intervention in 1952 only to abort it. But even more, an American-centric account overlooks the possibility that more intense pressure from the periphery after 1952 led to greater determination in Washington.

■

The agrarian-reform law spurred the counterrevolution in Guatemala. Decree 900 was partly written by Gutiérrez himself, although Fortuny's ideas were prominent. As editor of the newspaper *Octubre,* Fortuny had espoused the view that true revolution was impossible in Guatemala until the vast estates (latifundia) were broken up and the peasants given land.[45] According to Arbenz's ministry of propaganda, the reform law in no way contradicted the "profoundly capitalist" Guatemalan constitution. Guatemalan capitalism was supposed to benefit all citizens, not simply the privileged few.[46] Decree 900 announced that uncultivated land on estates greater than 224 acres was subject to expropriation. Landowners were to be compensated with long-term bonds for the land taken. According to a 1950 census, more than three-quarters of the land in Guatemala was owned by slightly more than 2 percent of all proprietors, while nearly three-quarters of all landowners owned less than 10 percent of arable land.[47] In a country of less than four million people with almost three million dependent on agriculture for income and sustenance, a total of twenty-two estates accounted for 13 percent of the arable land in the entire country. The proposed reform would affect at most 1,700 out of 341,000 private holdings.[48] These 1,700 were owned by the richest, most conservative groups in Guatemalan society, and by one American company—United Fruit, "La Frutera."

Numerous writers on Guatemala have seen United Fruit as the main reason for the American intervention in 1954. In fact, a standard interpretation of 1954 is that the Eisenhower administration decided to overthrow Arbenz as a direct result of the expropriation of United Fruit land under Decree 900. That analysis can be made to fit perfectly with a simplified dependency theory. If Latin America is in general kept underdeveloped by a capitalist system maintained

45. Handy, *Revolution in the Countryside,* 85.

46. May 1952, Ministry of Propaganda Publication, Guatemala Transcripts, Box 3, Library of Congress, Washington D.C. [hereinafter cited as LC].

47. Guatemala 286, March 2, 1952, NA 714.00/3-552.

48. Handy, *Revolution in the Countryside,* 82–83; Gleijeses, *Shattered Hope,* 152; Immerman, *CIA in Guatemala,* 65.

by business interests in the United States, then it makes sense to see UFCO as the driving force behind the anti-Arbenz movement within both Guatemala and the United States.[49] Without question, UFCO was a powerful force in Guatemala, and it enjoyed unusual leverage in the Eisenhower White House. The company was based in Boston and run by Samuel Zemurray, known as "Sam the Banana Man." The company had holdings throughout Central America. In Guatemala alone, it not only controlled more than half a million acres of land, but it was also a major shareholder in International Railways of Central America (IRCA). Between them, UFCO and IRCA employed nearly twenty thousand Guatemalan workers who were housed in company quarters. IRCA ran the only transportation to Guatemala's only Atlantic port at Puerto Barrios.[50] Edward Bernays, a Madison Avenue adman hired by United Fruit to manage its public relations campaign against Arbenz, later commented that "the native agricultural workers were treated as human machines rather than as human beings and without regard to their folkways or culture patterns."[51]

Arbenz authorized the implementation of Decree 900 against the company in 1953. At that time, the proposed expropriation totaled around two hundred thousand acres of unused UFCO land. By 1954, when a second round of expropriations was announced, the total was nearly four hundred thousand.[52] Considering that only 15 percent of UFCO acreage in Guatemala was under cultivation, the expropriations did not touch the actual production of the company. But almost immediately, there was a dispute over the value of the land taken under the reform law. The Arbenz administration used the figure which UFCO had declared as the value of its land on its tax returns: $1,185,000. UFCO, however, demanded nearly $16 million, and it denounced the expropriation as Communist robbery. In a letter to a high State Department official, John McClintock, vice president of UFCO, explained that in the company's view, the land expropriation was not an example of "a foreign state friendly to the United States engaging in a program of public utility or necessity and which finds itself indispensable to expropriate some private property to carry out its public purposes." No, said McClintock, this was a plan by Communists "to clear the country of all

49. See, for example, José Aybar de Soto, *Dependency and Intervention: The Case of Guatemala in 1954* (Boulder, Colo., 1978); Schlesinger and Kinzer, *Bitter Fruit;* Jonas, *Battle for Guatemala;* Coatsworth, *Central America and the United States;* Luis Cardoza y Aragon, *La Revolución Guatemalteca* (Mexico City, 1955); Toriello, *La Batalla de Guatemala;* Osgueda, *Operación Guatemala.*

50. Thomas McCann, *An American Company: The Tragedy of United Fruit* (New York, 1976), 45–60; Schlesinger and Kinzer, *Bitter Fruit,* 65–77; Gleijeses, *Shattered Hope,* 88–92.

51. Edward Bernays, *Biography of an Idea* (New York, 1965), 754.

52. McClintock (vice president of UFCO) to Thomas Mann (assistant secretary of state for Inter-American Affairs), February 25, 1954, NA 714.00/2-2554.

American enterprises." Once they achieved that goal, McClintock wrote, they would have uncontested control of Guatemala.[53]

These complaints were well received in the Eisenhower White House. Secretary of State John Foster Dulles and his brother Allen at the CIA had both worked for the New York law firm Sullivan and Cromwell, which numbered UFCO among its clients. The assistant secretary for Inter-American Affairs, Thomas Mann, was close to both McClintock and Thomas Corcoran, a powerful Washington lobbyist for United Fruit known as "Tommy the Cork." And Mann's successor, John Moors Cabot, was the brother of Thomas Cabot, the former president of UFCO.[54]

Still, for all the influence wielded by UFCO, its role in the intervention has been overstated. While Bernays, Corcoran, and the corporate brass certainly helped implement the operation that resulted in Arbenz's ouster, the intervention was not a result of the company's anti-Arbenz campaign. Indeed, at the very time that UFCO officials were pushing for action against Arbenz, the Justice Department was bringing an antitrust suit against the company. On the recommendation of the National Security Council, the suit was postponed in 1953 until affairs in Guatemala settled down.[55] But after Arbenz was removed, the reprieve ended; the Justice Department pursued its suit, and UFCO was broken up. UFCO was a convenient ally for the Eisenhower administration, as it was for the many elites who depended on its business in Guatemala. It was a factor in the overthrow of Arbenz, but it was one among many and less important than the local groups that plotted against Arbenz.

As shall be seen, the land reform resulted in power struggles throughout Guatemala. As the administrators of Decree 900 began to expropriate land, they often ignored local needs, and the agrarian reform was overseen by officials who sometimes used the law to pursue their own ambitions. As unrest over the reform spread, the groups that had been against the 1944 revolution from the start were reenergized. Opponents to Arbenz within Guatemala found support not just in Washington but in the neighboring countries of Honduras and Nicaragua. The story of the counterrevolution has rarely been told on its own terms. That counterrevolution needed the help of a supportive administration in Washington to achieve its goals, however, and found it in the Eisenhower White House.

53. McClintock to Mann, ibid.; Immerman, *CIA in Guatemala,* 81.

54. See letter from McClintock to Mann, October 13, 1952, NA 714.00/10-1052, confirming the weekend visit of Mann and his family to McClintock's home. Schlesinger and Kinzer, *Bitter Fruit,* 92–103.

55. Memorandum from Henry Holland (assistant secretary of state for Inter-American Affairs) to the undersecretary of state, October 14, 1954, Secret, NA 814.06/10-1454.

6

Guatemala

Ike and Armas

Our work with the friends from the North has ended in a complete triumph in our favor and, as I explained to you verbally on my last visit ... in a more active plan which will inevitably end in victory for all that we desire and for which we have been fighting for so long.

—Carlos Castillo Armas to Anastasio Somoza

Our basic national policies recognize the two threats to the maintenance of freedom, the fundamental values, and the institutions of the United States. One of these threats is *external:* it is the intention and action of Communist power to control and dominate the entire world. The other threat is *internal:* that the cost to the United States, as leader of the free world, of strengthening free world opposition to this external threat may seriously weaken the economy of the United States and thus destroy the very freedom, values, and institutions which we are seeking to maintain.

—Dwight D. Eisenhower, April 1953

As a market for our commercial exports, Latin America is as important to us as all of Europe and more important than Asia, Africa, and Oceania combined. . . . As a source of United States imports, the Latin American republics have even greater relative importance, standing well ahead of Europe or the other continents. . . . Almost 30 percent of all United States private, long-term foreign investment is in Latin America, this investment of some $6 billion is larger than the amount invested in any other part of the world except Canada. . . . One Latin American nation has succumbed to Communist infiltration. With this exception, however, the other Latin American nations share our desire for peace, freedom, and independence.

—Milton Eisenhower

T he implementation of land reform in Guatemala coincided with the transition from Truman to Eisenhower in Washington. The effect of Decree 900 was twofold: it provoked a counterrevolution in Guatemala, and it sounded alarms in the White House. On the face of it, the reform efforts of a middle-class, civilian, democratizing regime in Central America would seem to pose little danger to the United States. The association of several prominent Communists with the reforms disturbed Washington, but that in itself can not explain the eventual decision of Eisenhower to authorize and implement Operation PBSUCCESS. Ultimately, it was the refusal of Arbenz to bow to U.S. leadership in the Western Hemisphere, and the explicit rejection of U.S. cold-war policies that made Arbenz an anathema to the White House.

U.S. policy toward Guatemala was the product of an overall approach to the third world. While Europe was of course a high priority for Eisenhower, it was in the third world that the contest between ideologies was felt to be most fierce in the 1950s. By 1953, the lines in Europe had more or less solidified, with the exception of Berlin. In comparison with Truman, Eisenhower devoted far more time to the third world. In the early 1950s, the floodgates of decolonization burst open. Once Britain was forced to relinquish control of India, its empire—and those of the French, the Portuguese and the Belgians—began to fragment. The third world—encompassing Latin America and the decolonizing regions of Africa, Southeast Asia, and the Middle East—was in flux. In almost every third-world country in this period, one could find groups that claimed allegiance to Communism or the Soviet Union; to the United States or capitalism; to neutralism or socialism. One could also find groups that claimed to be both Communist and neutral, capitalist and anti-American, and other unconventional combinations. The allegiance of the third world was not yet decided, and the Eisenhower administration was determined to win it.

According to his aide Andrew Goodpaster, Ike's "idea concerning third-world nations was to work with them on development, to show them opportunities for self-government and tell the story of what the West had to offer."[1] It was a two-pronged strategy.

One prong was psychological; its task was to sell the United States model to the developing world. The Eisenhower administration placed increased emphasis on psychological warfare, and psy-ops were a central part of Operation PBSUCCESS against Arbenz. As one State Department paper stated, "the fundamental key to success in foreign policy is the extent to which [a] foreign government accepts the position" that the United States advocates. Psychological operations were one tool to persuade or coerce a foreign government to bring its policies into harmony with U.S. interests. Using Voice of America radio broadcasts, the United States Information Agency and its publications, and

1. Andrew Goodpaster Oral History, 10, Eisenhower Library.

"unofficial channels for influencing opinion abroad," the U.S. government tried to shape the policies of other governments to suit U.S. interests.[2]

The other prong was economic; to make the sale easier, the United States would provide the developing world with the means to buy the model, literally and figuratively. Aid programs would be designed to reinforce a positive image of the United States and make the American way more appealing than the Soviet. To prevent the third world from adopting "a communist way of life," Nelson Rockefeller, former coordinator of Latin American affairs in the Roosevelt White House, advised that U.S. aid be used to encourage the latent capitalism of the third world.[3]

The problem was that many in the third world did not seem to respond to these gestures. While few actively embraced Communism, many turned a cold shoulder to U.S. overtures and, like Mosaddeq, spoke of maintaining a neutral stance in the cold war. The doyen of third-world neutralism, India's Jawaharlal Nehru, developed the principles of *panchsheel,* five precepts of peaceful coexistence derived from Hindu teachings.[4] The idea of mutual respect and coexistence attracted those who resented the historic domination of the West over much of the developing world; it appealed to leaders and publics from the horn of Africa to the wilds of Patagonia to the jungles of Southeast Asia. At the Bandung Conference in April 1955, these principles were enshrined as the guiding philosophy of the developing world. Eisenhower wasn't impressed; neither was his secretary of state.

Soon after Bandung, Eisenhower mocked Nehru's belief in Mahatama Gandhi's teachings of nonviolence. "Let Nehru try it with the Russians," Eisenhower mused. "Let him try passive resistance with the Russians and see where he will get." As far as Eisenhower could tell, Nehru presented "a strange mixture, intellectually arrogant and of course at the same time suffering from an inferiority complex."[5] Eisenhower dismissed the substance of Nehru's policies, and he wrote off neutralism and the *panchsheel* as the immature ideas of an insecure man. These attitudes were typical of U.S. policy makers who confronted the resistance of third-world leaders such as Mosaddeq and Nehru.

But while relations with Nehru throughout the 1950s were often frosty, Eisenhower, and to a lesser degree Dulles, acknowledged that Nehru was nothing if not a strong-willed leader. Meeting with Nehru in Washington at the end of 1956, Eisenhower still found him difficult to understand, but he committed

2. Walter Radius, Department of State, "Psychological Operations in the Conduct of Foreign Policy," June 1953, WHC—Confidential Files, Box 61, Eisenhower Library.

3. Nelson Rockefeller memo for Eisenhower, "Action Program for Free World Strength," December 5, 1955, WHC—Confidential Files, Box 45.

4. Speech in the Lok Sabha, May 15, 1954, in Jawaharlal Nehru, *Jawaharlal Nehru's Speeches, 1953-1957* (New Delhi, 1958), 262.

5. Ann Whitman Diary, May 22, 1955, Whitman Diaries, Box 5, Eisenhower Library. Whitman was Eisenhower's personal secretary.

his administration to improved relations with India, and by his second term he had instituted significant aid programs.[6] Thus, while Eisenhower's ambivalence about neutralism remained constant throughout his presidency, that ambivalence did not preclude support for select neutral nations.

John Foster Dulles was even more stringent in his antineutral rhetoric. Writers at the time and historians since have depicted Dulles as a man driven by moralism. He was rarely pictured smiling, and he suffered from a muscular disorder that made one of his eyes tic uncontrollably. He was a successful lawyer, the son of a minister, the grandson of Benjamin Harrison's secretary of state John Foster, and the nephew of Wilson's secretary of state at the Paris peace conference Robert Lansing. As secretary of state, he combined foreign-policy expertise with rigid ideology. The paradox of Dulles, aptly described by George Allen, ambassador to Iran and later director of the USIA, was that while "he was a rational, reasoning type of individual, to some extent . . . in some matters he felt he had a pipeline on high, that is, a sort of mission to fulfill."[7]

Yet Dulles was more pragmatic than is usually believed.[8] On neutralism, he sounded every bit the dogmatist. Often quoted is his reference to the principle of neutrality as "an immoral and shortsighted conception." He spoke these words in 1956 and clearly had Nasser in mind. Though Eisenhower himself several days before had admitted that a country such as Switzerland might choose neutrality for perfectly moral and defensible reasons, Dulles meant what he said. Yet, as H. W. Brands has noted, the moral rhetoric of Dulles existed side by side with Dulles the realist secretary of state.[9] Dulles earnestly believed that neutralism in the face of Communism was immoral; that belief did not stop him from treating with neutrals any more than a belief in the inherent sinfulness of man might have stopped him from dealing with sinners.

In November 1953, Dulles addressed the Congress of Industrial Organizations (CIO) in Ohio. In a speech titled "The Moral Initiative," he said:

> On the free world front the colonial and dependent areas are the fields of most dramatic contest. Here the policies of the West and those of Soviet imperialism come into headlong collision. . . . The Soviet leaders, in mapping their strategy for world conquest, hit on nationalism as a device for absorbing the colonial peoples. . . . In the first phase the Communist agitators

6. Brands, *Specter of Neutralism*, 126–38.

7. George V. Allen Oral History, 22, John Foster Dulles Oral History Project, Mudd Library, Princeton University.

8. See Hoopes, *Devil and John Foster Dulles,* passim; see also the essays in Richard Immerman, ed., *John Foster Dulles and the Diplomacy of the Cold War* (Princeton, 1990).

9. Department of State, "Statement of John Foster Dulles at Iowa State College," June 8, 1956, Press Release #307; Hoopes, *Devil and John Foster Dulles,* 315ff.; Brands, *Specter of Neutralism,* 305–307.

are to whip up the nationalist aspirations of the people, so that they will rebel violently against the existing order. Then, before newly won independence can become consolidated and vigorous in its own right, Communists will take over the new government and use this power to "amalgamate" the people into the Soviet orbit.[10]

Dulles was not wrong about Soviet ambitions toward the third world. But he acted as if Stalin and the Kremlin had the capability to translate those ambitions into reality, as if there were Communist cadres world wide prepared to exploit new nationalist movements in order to destroy the independence of emerging states.

When Dulles turned his eyes south, to Central America, he saw a new nationalist government in Guatemala. He also saw Communists in Guatemala. Under the syllogism of the CIO speech, Communists planned to use nationalist fervor to destroy independence and bring countries into the Soviet orbit. In Guatemala, the nationalist government included some Communists. Thus it stood to reason that Guatemala was heading toward Communist dictatorship. The response of Dulles to the Arbenz administration was consistent with a rather simple and quite explicit world view that placed third-world nationalism on the same continuum as Communism.

Latin America in general and Central America in particular were often lumped with the decolonizing regions. When Dulles or Eisenhower spoke of the problems of nationalism or neutralism, they very much had Latin America in mind, along with the Middle East, Africa, and large parts of Asia. But unlike these other regions, Latin America was familiar to U.S. officials and had a legacy of relations with the United States, a legacy that was often quite bitter.

At the beginning of 1953, the NSC staff identified three basic problems that adversely affected relations between the United States and Latin America: "1) A wide-spread tendency toward immediate political change which produces political instability and demagoguery; 2) a great disparity in wealth and power between the United States and Latin America which, aided by old prejudices, keeps alive anti-Americanism and stimulates economic nationalism; 3) Communism."[11] The NSC believed that Latin America was "passing through a period of basic readjustment of classes." This was brought on by the charismatic leaders throughout the hemisphere, including Perón in Argentina, Vargas in Brazil, Cardenas in Mexico, Haya de la Torre in Peru, Figueres in Costa Rica, and Arévalo in Guatemala, most of whom had departed from the political scene by the early 1950s leaving in their wake heightened expectations. The most visible legacy of these leaders, at least to the NSC, was land reform: "Agrarian

10. John Foster Dulles, "The Moral Initiative," November 18, 1953, John Foster Dulles Papers, Box 75, Mudd Library, Princeton University.

11. Annex to NSC 144, March 6, 1953, Top Secret, OSANSA—NSC Policy Papers, Box 4, Eisenhower Library.

and similar reform laws designed to break the power of the oligarchs are applied with inadequate regard for compensating those whose property is taken." The anger of the masses was directed not only against "oligarchs" within Latin America, but at the "colonial" powers, particularly the United States. In the eyes of many in Latin America, "yankee imperialism" had deprived Latin Americans of their wealth and potential. Complicating it all was the infiltration of Communism throughout the hemisphere; Communists took advantage of resentment and political flux and stoked the fires of anti-Americanism.

The NSC saw three possible courses of action: compulsion, detachment, and cooperation. Compulsion would mean using overwhelming political and military force "to compel Latin American countries to act in accordance" with the wishes of the U.S. government. Detachment would mean "a policy of relative inaction, relying upon occasional favors, and the occasional display of military force in urgent circumstances." Cooperation would stress the interdependence of the Western Hemisphere and include significant U.S. assistance; that is what NSC 144 recommended. The NSC agreed with the principle of nonintervention in the internal political affairs of other American states as demanded by the Inter-American Rio Pact of 1947. However, the NSC noted that nonintervention precluded neither multilateral intervention nor unilateral U.S. intervention in the event that "overriding security interests of the United States" required it.[12] A year later, with the question of Guatemala very much on the mind of official Washington, the State Department recommended to the NSC that, faced with a country "in danger of control by anti-U.S. extremist factions, we should view the doctrine of nonintervention in pragmatic terms."[13]

The policy prescriptions adopted by the Eisenhower administration toward Latin America were guaranteed to aggravate the very forces that U.S. policy makers wished to deter. The easy endorsement of unilateral intervention was a throwback to the days of Teddy Roosevelt's "Big Stick," Taft's Dollar Diplomacy, and Wilsonianism when the United States intervened frequently in Central America and the Caribbean. But in a period of nationalist ferment, intervention would only add to the perception of the United States as an imperial power bent on keeping Latin America poor and subservient.

Until the massive outbursts of anti-American unrest throughout Latin America in 1958, Eisenhower pursued a policy not of cooperation, but of neglect combined with intervention. Military aid was provided, but the recommendations of Milton Eisenhower and Rockefeller for a large economic aid program were not acted on. Latin American nations interpreted the unilateral U.S. covert intervention against Arbenz as a sign that the days of the Good Neighbor were

12. Ibid. See also see text of NSC 144, March 4, 1953, in OSANSA, Box 4, Eisenhower Library. For a good discussion of NSC 144, see Stephen Rabe, *Eisenhower and Latin America: The Foreign Policy of Anticommunism* (Chapel Hill, 1988), 31–34.

13. State Department policy paper, "A Study of U.S. Problems and Policy," April 27, 1954, Secret, NSC Administration Series, Box 4.

over, and that the days of imperialism had returned.[14] That was not the message the Eisenhower administration intended to send, but it is the message most in Latin America received.

It was within this general framework that Ike's national-security establishment confronted Arbenz. However, without the development of anti-Arbenz and antirevolutionary forces within Guatemala and Central America, Eisenhower probably would not have acted against Arbenz. By the time the decision was made in late 1953 to undertake a covert operation, Arbenz was deeply enmeshed in controversies over land reform, and his enemies were working to cut short the brief life of Guatemalan democracy.

Until 1952, the forces opposed to the October 1944 revolution operated independently of each other. Factions within the army, the church, the business community in Guatemala City, and the major landowners of the coffee plantations resisted reform. They met in small groups to denounce Arévalo and Arbenz. They planned and plotted unsuccessful coups, and they tried to elect representatives to the assembly. On occasion, they met with U.S. embassy officials or with representatives of the Honduran, Nicaraguan, Cuban, and Dominican governments. At these meetings, they voiced their displeasure and appealed for support in undermining the Arbenz government, or at least slowing the pace of reform. Often, the issue was framed in terms of Communist influence in Guatemala, and the dangers of it. But until the land reform, these streams of opposition were distinct and uncoordinated.

Not that land reform *caused* the opposition to Arbenz. While it may have turned some who were undecided about the revolution against him, it was more a peg upon which the indigenous opposition could hang its hat. At first, it appeared that the agrarian reform would enjoy widespread popularity, with only a small elite minority opposed to it. The CIA predicted that agrarian reform would strengthen Arbenz, and that both Guatemalan landlords and the United Fruit Company would receive little sympathy from the public. According to a CIA report, "Redistribution of their land will be used to mobilize the hitherto inert mass of rural workers in support of the [Arbenz] Administration." More ominously in the CIA's view, the reform would "afford the Communists an opportunity to extend their influence by organizing the peasants as they have organized other workers."[15]

Soon after the passage of Decree 900, Arbenz set up a National Agrarian Department, which in turn oversaw hundreds of local committees (CALs or *comités agrarios locales*) that had direct authority over expropriations. A special agrarian bank was created in 1953 to fund the expropriations and compensate the owners. By 1954, more than one million acres had been expropriated

14. See Bryce Wood, *Dismantling of the Good Neighbor Policy* (Austin, 1985).

15. CIA National Intelligence Estimate, "Probable Developments in Guatemala," May 9, 1953, CIA Research Reports, Reel 5.

and distributed to as many as 100,000 families. One scholar estimates that perhaps 500,000 people directly benefited from the land reform.[16]

While there is no reason to doubt that the seizures were popular with the great rank and file of Guatemalans, the statistics do not convey the multitude of problems that confronted the CALs. The reform represented a social revolution in the countryside of a semifeudal country. At the local level, the expropriation decisions were made by the local committees and by individuals familiar with their particular region. The decisions were sometimes arbitrary or, worse, motivated by bribery or revenge.

Furthermore, Arbenz's government was anything but monolithic. Various revolutionary factions under the umbrella of the main revolutionary party, the Partido de la Revolución Guatemalteca (PRG), fought both with one another and with workers' federations. Among the latter was the Confederación Nacional Campesina de Guatemala (CNCG), cofounded and led by Leonardo Castillo Flores, and the Confederación Nacional de Trabajadores de Guatemala (CGTG), led by Gutiérrez. Land reform may have represented a social revolution, but it was also pork Guatemalan-style. Whoever controlled land reform stood a good chance to control the next government; peasants who are given land tend to remember fondly at election time those who gave it to them. For instance, the imperious Castillo Flores—a former teacher, labor organizer, and an avowed socialist who had urged land reform on Arbenz prior to 1952—complained frequently of the attempts of local agrarian committees to use the land reform to further the aims of Arbenz and the PRG.[17]

If the rivalry between revolutionary factions over land reform was intense, the struggle with those opposed to land reform was even more so. As Arbenz said in early 1953,

> The Agrarian Reform has come to revamp our economy. . . .
> And it has come to end old social traditions and old juridical
> concepts and has even caused an upheaval in conscience. . . .
> The question of agrarian reform has drawn the classic line in
> the sand: on one side those who are definitely with the revolution and on the other side those who are definitely against the
> revolution. There has been no place left for the middle ground
> as in all great historic decisions. There is no family, there is
> no class, there is no person now in our country, who has not
> felt . . . the impact of the commotions the agrarian question
> has caused in Guatemala.[18]

16. Handy, *Revolution in the Countryside*, 92; Gleijeses, *Shattered Hope*, 154–57.

17. Handy, *Revolution in the Countryside*, 41; Castillo Flores telegram, September 12, 1952, Guatemala Transcripts, Box 12, LC.

18. Arbenz annual report to the Guatemalan Congress, March 2, 1953, NA 714.21/3-353.

Arbenz may have overstated the impact of the reform as of early 1953, but he was not far off the mark in claiming that it was the defining issue of the revolution. Yet those uncomfortable with the reform were not all vastly wealthy owners of latifundial estates. Some were smaller landowners, army officers, and urban businessmen who viewed with particular concern one aspect of the land reform: unlawful seizures.

Most of the expropriations and redistributions were done with great care. Extraordinary efforts were made to take only surplus, uncultivated land from the major estates (*fincas* or *latifundia*), to ensure due compensation, and then to parcel out the land to those who had been working on it. However, there were also a number of highly publicized invasions of large estates by peasants. In some cases, these were preemptory acts by groups of mestizo or Indian peasants who had been told of the reform program and decided to act on their own without waiting for a decision by the CALs. At other times, the invasions were lawful occupations, sanctioned by the Agrarian Department but opposed by the landowners, who were in the process of petitioning the courts for an injunction against an expropriation.

The situation was further aggravated by racial politics. The peasants seizing the land were of Mayan origin while most of the estates they invaded were owned by ladinos (whites).[19] The Indians who seized land were understandably reluctant to surrender it. They viewed both the landowners and the Guatemalan government with grave mistrust; once ensconced on land that they believed rightly belonged to them, they perceived the efforts of the CALs to remove them as no different from the efforts of white landlords to evict them.[20]

Illegal seizures and overzealous applications of Decree 900 were problems that accompany most major reforms. However understandable, the violations were seized on by opponents of Arbenz and used as ammunition. In addition, the close involvement of Gutiérrez and the CGTG with the implementation resulted in widespread discomfort with the reforms. Gutiérrez was an admitted Communist, and although that did not mean that he was an agent of Moscow, it did mean that anti-Communist forces in Guatemala suspected Decree 900 was a Communist stratagem. That was certainly the position of the United States and the Truman administration.[21] But it was also true of a wide spectrum of anti-Communist opposition within Guatemala. Throughout Latin America, conservative institutions such as the church and the army, not to mention the business community, had a strong tradition of domestic anti-Communism, and

19. Handy, *Revolution in the Countryside*, 90-127; Gleijeses, *Shattered Hope*, 150-62; Adams, *Crucifixion by Power*, 398-401. See also Amy Elizabeth Jensen, *Guatemala* (New York, 1955), 182-88, for an extreme anti-Communist polemic.

20. The American embassy in Guatemala was prescient in predicting this difficulty. See Quarterly Labor Report, 2d quarter 1952, NA 814.06/7-2352.

21. State Department Office Memorandum, "Implications of the Guatemalan Agrarian Reform Law," May 22, 1952, Confidential, NA 714.34/5-2252.

Guatemala was no exception. The association between Gutiérrez and Decree 900 even made some Guatemalan liberals uncomfortable.[22]

As a member of Congress and head of the CGTG, Gutiérrez received countless telegrams and letters from peasant groups and CALs informing him of the progress of the expropriations. In the midst of the heated dispute with UFCO, a group from Santa Lucia wrote to Gutiérrez expressing solidarity: "The agricultural workers of this finca energetically protest the abusive memorandum of the Yankee imperialist Department of State. Solidarity with the Revolution. We defend our national sovereignty." Another telegram from Antigua declared that the peasants would not bow to the "great North American monopolies."[23] The rhetoric of many of the local committees was that of Marxist-Leninism, with emphasis on class struggle, colonialism, and imperialism. Although Communists accounted for less than 10 percent of the National Agrarian Department,[24] the high-profile association of Gutiérrez, Fortuny, and the Guatemalan Communist Party with the land-reform program, combined with the rhetoric of the non-Communists who were implementing it, alarmed significant pockets of Guatemalan society. In addition, Gutiérrez was a close friend of Arbenz, and at times he apparently acted as an intermediary between the president and various local officials responsible for land reform. Officials frequently complained about the failure to break up a particular estate, and Gutiérrez would pass these complaints along to Arbenz.[25]

There was never a numerical threat of Communist takeover in Guatemala, and most of the few thousand dedicated Communists in Guatemala are better understood as radical reformers than as Communists in the Leninist-Stalinist sense. Still, anti-Communism as an emotive, conservative movement, far from being limited to powerful elite groups, was popular in both rural and urban Guatemala. In major cities such as Antigua and Guatemala City, there were parties whose only platform was anti-Communism.[26] After the 1944 revolution, these parties had at times faced restrictions at the hands of the Arévalo and Arbenz administrations. Not only was the anti-Communist party of Ydígoras Fuentes harassed, but during the 1950 election campaign, the National Election Board canceled the registration of two of the major opposition coalitions on the pretext that, in calling for Arévalo's resignation, these parties had breached

22. José Balcarcel, interview by author, Mexico City, August 1991. Balcarcel was the head of a prominent law-student organization in Guatemala City in 1953–54. See also Ambassador Schoenfeld's discussion of the split within the liberal Partido Integridad Nacional over whether to support Decree 900 in light of its connection with Gutiérrez, Guatemala 1262, June 10, 1952, NA 714.00/6-1052.

23. Telegram to Gutiérrez of September 16, 1953, Guatemala Transcripts, Box 5, LC.

24. Schlesinger and Kinzer, *Bitter Fruit,* 58.

25. See the dozens of notes from local officials to Gutiérrez and from Gutiérrez to the president, Guatemala Transcripts, Box 18.

26. See the manifestos of these parties in NA 714.001/9-1451.

electoral laws.[27] While it is probably true that Arbenz thought "that the exercise of liberties should be restricted neither by citizens of Communist ideology nor by those holding an anti-Communist ideology,"[28] his government was obviously more comfortable with the expression of some ideologies than with others.

The tension between anti-Communist organizers and the Arbenz government was palpable, even before land reform. In July 1951, a series of protests erupted in Guatemala City. In its report, the U.S. embassy noted that the protests were "a spontaneous outburst of anger by the masses, particularly the women of the markets, against the Communists." Speeches called on the government to defend Catholicism, not atheistic Communism.[29] Guatemalan anti-Communism was strongly tinged with religion. In discussions with U.S. embassy officials, one prominent judge observed that "religious people of all classes" believed that Communism was a menace to the Catholic religion. Other anti-Communists based their opposition on "economic and political reasons." The judge felt that the former were genuinely scared of Communism, while the latter sought "to exploit the anti-Communist movement to gain their own political objectives. These people, who lump the Communists and the present Government together, come generally from the well-to-do classes of rural landholders and city capitalists and the real organizational leadership is in the hands of the followers of General Ydígoras Fuentes."[30]

While the opposition of the "well-to-do classes" to Arbenz was predictable, the presence of market women at the 1951 demonstrations was no aberration. These women, poor and devoutly Catholic, would make frequent appearances at demonstrations in the next few years, and they were indicative of how uneasy traditional Guatemala was with certain aspects of the Arbenz administration.

In March 1952, anti-Communists rallied in Guatemala City. Nearly 20,000 people from different classes and sectors of society attended the demonstration. Speakers emphasized their loyalty to the goals of the October 1944 revolution and endorsed the pursuit of social justice, economic reform, and constitutional government. It was because they endorsed the goals of Arbenz and the revolution, they said, that they were anti-Communist. Communism would mean the end of Guatemalan independence, the end of true reform, and subjugation to a foreign ideology.[31]

Soon after, two anti-Communist students were taken into custody by the authorities. Rumors spread that the students had been mistreated while in custody, and the U.S. embassy reported that "many women of the public market

27. Guatemala 168, August 14, 1950, NA 714.00/8-1450.

28. Galich, *Por qué lucha Guatemala,* 224 (my translation).

29. Guatemala 55, July 13, 1951, NA 714.00/7-1351.

30. Remarks of Judge José García Bauer to 1st Embassy Secretary William Krieg, September 21, 1951, NA 714.00/9-2751.

31. Text of speeches in Guatemala 968, March 23, 1952, NA 714.00/4-152. Estimate of attendance, NA 714.001/3-1852.

. . . became so indignant about the torture of the students that they began preparations for a strike in protest."[32] There followed a government crackdown on the market and a number of arrests. Subsequently, Arbenz made a speech in which he claimed that there was "a vast network of conspirators and saboteurs largely of students organized by anti-Communist groups."[33]

Much of the reporting on anti-Communist activities comes from U.S. embassy files, and it is fair to question whether these reports give an accurate picture of domestic developments in Guatemala. After all, since as early as 1950, the Americans had been accusing the Guatemalan government of dangerous pro-Communist leanings.[34] Given their ambivalence toward Arbenz prior to 1953, the Americans may have overemphasized the prevalence of anti-Communist sentiment. Yet Arbenz himself frequently denounced "conspirators," plotters, and "counter-revolutionaries." If these groups were indeed marginal, it is unlikely they would have been targeted by Arbenz as a force potentially capable of undermining his administration and the course of the October 1944 revolution.

The intensity of anti-Communism among market women is indicative of a general discomfort with the rhetoric of the revolution. Many anti-Communists had little to do with Ydígoras or Castillo Armas and, like the market women, were essentially apolitical people who endorsed the general aims of the revolution. A manifesto of the Anticommunist Party of Chiquimula stated that its members believed in democracy and wished only to "defend our dear country and not become victims of the exotic doctrine of Communism."[35] However, these sentiments were seized upon by groups of genuine conspirators, many allied with the now-exiled Ydígoras Fuentes and Castillo Armas. These groups were also encouraged by a powerful anti-Communist institution: the Catholic Church.

In the decades before the October revolution, the Guatemalan church had suffered severe repression. One of the side effects of Guatemalan democracy after 1944 was the reinvigoration of the Guatemalan church under Archbishop Mariano Rossell y Arellano. The Arévalo administration permitted more priests not of Guatemalan origin to enter the country. Free from the constraints of the Ubico dictatorship, Rossell encouraged the growth of Catholic educational organizations and allowed several Maryknoll priests to pursue their mission. In 1953, he invited Opus Dei to operate in Guatemala. Founded in the 1920s, Opus Dei was dedicated to increasing lay membership in the church. In Franco's

32. Amb. Schoenfeld to State Department, June 19, 1952, NA 714.52/6-1952. See also *New York Times,* February 24, 1953.

33. Text of speech in NA 714.52/6-2552.

34. See CIA-SR-46, Summary of Developments in Guatemala, July 27, 1950, Top Secret, CIA Research Reports, Reel 5. See also Spanish translation of a U.S. Intelligence Digest item, June 7, 1950, in which the author stated that "Guatemala is a center of Russian activity in a region of great strategic importance." Guatemala Transcripts, Box 70.

35. Manifesto (undated) in Guatemala Transcripts, Box 26.

Spain, Opus Dei was a powerful, secretive, and conservative organization. While its goal was to encourage spiritual values in everyday life, its introduction into Guatemala was part of a broader campaign by Archbishop Rossell to increase the power of the church in allegiance with the traditional, conservative social order. That made him an enemy of Arbenz, and he acted vigorously to undermine the revolution.[36]

Given the weak institutional structure of the Guatemala church, Archbishop Rossell's views defined the position of the church toward Arbenz. Rossell saw Communism as a manifestation of the devil; after Decree 900, he felt it was his mission to defeat what he believed to be the Communist government of Guatemala. In May 1952, he issued an episcopal statement in which he called on Guatemalans

> 1. To reject as completely Communist, atheistic, anti-Catholic and, therefore, anti-Guatemalan, all manifestations of the Communist, pseudo-Communist, philo-Communist and communizing organizations, such as the Alianza Feminina Guatemalteca. . . .
>
> 2. Not to be taken off guard when these pro-Communist organizations call for the holding of masses, organize religious meetings or distribute Catholic propaganda; but to realize that they are today just as they were yesterday, the eternal enemies of Jesus Christ and his Church, and like wolves in sheep's clothing, wish to gain entrance to the Catholic fold in order to destroy from within the faith of the unwary and sow schism and dissension.[37]

Rossell frequently condemned Arbenz in his sermons, and he successfully sought the support of both the Vatican and the Catholic hierarchy in the United States. Cardinal Francis Spellman was particularly receptive and helpful. Rossell's ire was given full expression in April 1954, while the coup was being planned with his knowledge. In a pastoral letter, he called for "a national crusade against Communism." He charged that Guatemala had been infiltrated by Communists, in the schools, in labor, in the press, and especially in the presidential palace. He called on Guatemala Catholics to use "all means" to free Guatemala of Communist influence; in essence, the archbishop gave his blessing to Castillo Armas and the counterrevolutionaries.[38]

The final and perhaps most important group that ultimately decided the fate of Arbenz was the army. The Guatemalan constitution designated the army as

36. Adams, *Crucifixion by Power*, 279-313.

37. Episcopal Statement of May 23, 1952, translated in Guatemala 1203, May 24, 1952, NA 714.00/5-2452.

38. Summary of Rossell y Arellano's letter, Guatemala 852, April 12, 1954, NA 814.413/4-1254.

the protector of the nation, and officers took that mandate seriously. That meant, however, that their loyalty was not necessarily to the Arbenz government. If they perceived that Arbenz was acting against the interests of the nation, they could rationalize acting against him by citing their responsibilities under the constitution. While Arbenz cultivated the younger officers and made sure that salaries were satisfactory, the relationship between Arbenz, Gutiérrez, and Fortuny combined with land reform made anti-Communist officers uncomfortable.[39]

Often, the army impeded the efforts of the CALs, and at times even prevented government representatives from carrying out expropriations. In April 1953, Castillo Flores wrote to Carlos Díaz, the head of Guatemala's armed forces, requesting that certain officers be disciplined for obstructing land reform and for other "anti-democratic activities." According to Flores, several officers urged local landowners in the department of Chiquimula "to take up their machetes and their pistols and defend their territory" against those who would seize it. That December, Castillo Flores complained that the military chief of Monjas refused to comply with the agrarian law and was actively plotting with "reactionary interests." In February 1954, Castillo Flores, Gutiérrez, and others close to Arbenz protested to Carlos Díaz that the army was thwarting Decree 900 and that the peasants now needed to be protected from the reprisals of local military units.[40]

In general, the military was concerned about the direction of the revolution and alarmed by the implications of the land reform. A small segment was unalterably opposed to Arbenz, and these worked with Castillo Armas, Ydígoras, and the United States to bring about a successful coup.[41] In April 1952, for example, Ambassador Schoenfeld met with the Comité Ejecutivo de la Liberación Nacional, which comprised colonels and former colonels who urged the U.S. embassy to take direct action against Arbenz. This group was apparently independent of Castillo Armas and Ydígoras. Like Arévalo, Arbenz was the target of plots and failed coups. Yet the military leadership was still guardedly pro-Arbenz and would remain so nearly until the end. For this reason, a major attempt to topple Arbenz failed in March 1953.

On March 29, more than one hundred rebels backed by the dictator of the Dominican Republic, Rafael Trujillo, attacked the town of Salamá.[42] They were quickly defeated and captured. They were, by and large, former army officers, and they were lauded by opponents of Arbenz. An anti-Communist manifesto stated, "The failed attempt of Salamá represents a gesture of desperation of the

39. R-18-53, Intelligence Report submitted by U.S. Army attaché, March 2, 1953, Secret, RG 84, Guatemala 350.21, WNRC; Adams, *Crucifixion by Power,* 254ff.; Handy, *Revolution in the Countryside,* 183–90; Cullather, *Operation PBSUCCESS,* 31–32.

40. Multiple telegrams and letters in Guatemala Transcripts, Box 1.

41. Guatemala 1075, April 25, 1952, Secret, NA 714.00/4-2552.

42. IR-49-53, Air Intelligence Report, April 9, 1953, Secret, RG 84, Guatemala 350. Some have claimed that Salamá was a failed CIA operation. See Ranelagh, *The Agency,* 265; Gleijeses, *Shattered Hope,* 220–21.

Guatemalan people, tired of the abuses and corruption of a regime as oppressive as the government of Arbenz, who acts in criminal complicity with the Army, the National Congress, the judiciary, and political lobbies and their leaders."[43]

Salamá exposed the longstanding enmity between Guatemala and its neighbors. While Mexico was largely uninvolved in Guatemala's affairs,[44] the governments of Nicaragua, El Salvador, Honduras, and the Dominican Republic were adamantly opposed to Arbenz. Nicaragua was ruled by Anastasio "Tacho" Somoza who, along with his sons, schemed to bring about Arbenz's downfall. An autocrat who enjoyed the support—financial and otherwise—of Washington, Somoza hoped to halt the winds of reform before they swept through Nicaragua. In Honduras, President Juan Manuel Gálvez gave succor to a hodge-podge of anti-Arbenz forces, including Castillo Armas himself. And in El Salvador, Major Oscar Osorio fulminated against the danger of Communist infiltration from Guatemala. Only Costa Rica under the neutral José "Pepe" Figueres abstained from anti-Arbenz propaganda.[45]

Each of these countries was governed by a conservative oligarchy—or, in the cases of Nicaragua and the Dominican Republic, dictators. Their antipathy to Arbenz, and to Arévalo before him, is understandable given their dependence on the traditional social and economic order. In Honduras, UFCO was powerful, and the Gálvez administration respected the interests of La Frutera. Land reform in Guatemala, and especially land reform against UFCO, would inevitably lead to similar demands in Honduras. In addition, there was a long tradition of rivalry among the Central American states. While there had been periods of cooperation, there were also deep traditions of antagonism. Plots fomented in one country against the leaders of another were nothing new.

The antagonism increased, however, after the passage of Decree 900. In a meeting with Arbenz in late 1952, El Salvador's Osorio declared that he was anti-Communist but not opposed either to Arbenz or to land reform.[46] These statements seem to have been diplomatic niceties rather than a true reflection of Osorio's attitude. Shortly before the meeting, Gutiérrez circulated an open letter in Guatemala accusing Osorio of waging an anti-Communist crusade in Central America in order to "strangle the liberty of the workers, peasants, and the people of Guatemala and to prevent the implementation of the Agrarian Reform."[47] Osorio also took his campaign to the Americans. He reported to the U.S. embassy that El Salvador was in danger "from provocative and aggressive

43. Manifesto in response to Salamá, undated. Guatemala Transcripts, Box 26 (my translation).

44. The exception was the Mexican labor movement. Under Vicente Lombardo Toledano and the Confederación de Trabajadores de América Latina, there were links with Gutiérrez and organized labor in Guatemala.

45. Woodward, *Nation Divided,* 240–60; Coatsworth, *Central America and the United States,* 72–77.

46. Schoenfeld report, September 25, 1952, NA 614.16/9-2552.

47. Open letter of September 2, 1952, Guatemala Transcripts, Box 5.

Guatemalan tendencies," and he warned of subversives infiltrating El Salvador from Guatemala. The Salvadoran press at the time was filled with reports of Guatemalan farmers fleeing their land after it had been seized by bands of "Communist-inspired" peasants.[48]

Guatemala's Central American neighbors were pivotal in convincing the Eisenhower administration that Arbenz was dangerous and had to be removed. Osorio, watching the break-up of Guatemalan estates on the Salvadoran border, began to coordinate plans with Ydígoras Fuentes. He met with the American ambassador in El Salvador and appealed for support. The ambassador was sympathetic. He said that while the United States was opposed to military intervention, it would not allow El Salvador to succumb to Communist aggression from Guatemala. The ambassador also urged the State Department to aid Osorio with arms and supplies.[49] Over the next year, Osorio repeatedly pressed for military assistance and urged Washington to act. Clearly, it was in his interest to emphasize the danger of Guatemalan Communism, especially if such warnings led to increased American aid.

Honduras was equally adamant. In conversation with the Boston Brahmin assistant secretary of state John Moors Cabot, Gálvez and his ministers repeatedly accused "Guatemalan Communists, backed by the Guatemalan government" of attempting to infiltrate Honduras, and "particularly the United Fruit plantations there."[50] While the American ambassador in Honduras expressed some doubts that there was any direct link between the Guatemalan government and Communist activity in Honduras, he acknowledged that "Hondurans entertain strong suspicions that Guatemala is operating under Soviet direction and intends to manoeuvre a pro-Communist movement in Honduras."[51]

Meanwhile, Nicaragua's Somoza was plotting with Castillo Armas. Given the close patron-client ties between Somoza and Washington, it has been easy for writers to dismiss Somoza's role in the coup as that of a handmaiden for Washington. Certainly, the Arbenz partisans who wrote in the aftermath of the coup, including Arévalo himself, described the actions of the neighboring governments as appendages to the U.S. covert campaign.[52] To support that interpretation, however, chronology and history must be distorted. Somoza and Trujillo, and Fulgencio Batista in Cuba, conspired against Guatemala well before any plans were made in Washington. While these autocrats served the interests of the U.S. government, they were not acting on instructions from Washington. Rather, they plotted on their own because the revolution in Guatemala was a direct threat to their conservative, repressive regimes. Their activities created a substantial pull on Washington to act.

48. San Salvador to State, February 16, 1953, Secret, NA 614.16/2-1653.
49. San Salvador 543, February 27, 1953, Secret, NA 614.16/2-2753.
50. Cabot to Amb. Erwin (Honduras), August 18, 1953, Secret, NA Lot 56 D 13.
51. Erwin to State Department, March 12, 1953, Secret, NA 714.001/3-1253.
52. Arévalo, *Guatemala,* 78–82.

Castillo Armas, meanwhile, had been scheming ever since the death of Arana. In 1951, the CIA reported that Castillo Armas was lobbying the United States for support in overthrowing Arbenz. He tried to convince the agents whom he met that the army was disillusioned with Arbenz.[53] Castillo Armas continued to contact the Americans, and they him, over the next few years. In October 1951, a member of his small movement met with U.S. embassy officials in Guatemala. His agent appealed to the United States to sponsor an uprising against Arbenz; he said that in the war against Communism, "the United States should drop some of its scruples [about nonintervention] if necessary to combat this unscrupulous adversary."[54] Castillo Armas himself met with U.S. officials in Panama in November 1951 to discuss his plans to stage an anti-Guatemalan riot in Honduras.[55] An unsigned report to the American army attaché in Tegucigalpa depicted Castillo Armas as confident that the Guatemalan military officers in the provinces would support a coup d'etat. The report also noted that Castillo Armas had recently "managed to get a hold of some money and to live in a better way." Still, Castillo Armas expressed dismay that "the anti-Government organization in Guatemala lacks heavy weapons, and he was not sure that sufficient small arms had yet been made available." Castillo Armas still had hopes that Somoza of Nicaragua, Batista of Cuba, and Trujillo of Santo Domingo would make good on their promised offers of arms, but he confessed that he had so far failed to conclude a deal with any of these leaders.[56]

While maintaining his pressure on the United States, Castillo Armas danced warily with his coconspirator and competitor Ydígoras. While Castillo Armas floated from country to country and eventually landed in Honduras, Ydígoras ended up in El Salvador after his defeat by Arbenz in 1950. Ydígoras claimed in his memoirs that he "was not inclined towards the conspiracies that sprang up against Arbenz from within and without Guatemala." Yet, he said, he eventually came to believe that "it would be necessary to resort to force of arms."[57] As early as March 1952, Ydígoras signed an agreement with Castillo Armas in San Salvador which bound the two men to coordinate their plans with one another. The agreement was reaffirmed more than a year later in Honduras in the infamous "Pacto de Caballeros," the Gentleman's Agreement.[58] Ydígoras

53. Report on Castillo Armas, August 2, 1951, Top Secret, CIA Research Reports, Reel 5.

54. Memorandum of conversation between William Krieg of U.S. Embassy in Guatemala and unnamed source on campaign by Armas to enlist U.S. support against Arbenz, October 22, 1951, Secret, NA 714.00/10-2251.

55. Memo of meeting between Armas and Murray Wise of U.S. Embassy in Panama, November 27, 1951, Confidential, NA 714.00/11-2751.

56. Unsigned report of October 27, 1952 to Colonel Francis Sawyer, Army Attaché, Tegucigalpa, Honduras, Guatemala 350, Box 15.

57. Ydígoras Fuentes, *My War with Communism*, 49.

58. The full correspondence between Ydígoras Fuentes and Castillo Armas was intercepted by the Guatemalan government and printed in a long pamphlet released by Arbenz's secretary of

was also involved in a variety of schemes against Arbenz. In Tegucigalpa, he met with the U.S. ambassador to Honduras, Michael McDermott, and asked that, when the time came, the United States "close its eyes and ears for a short time" while rebels invaded Guatemala from El Salvador and anti-Arbenz military officers revolted. The plan he presented is similar to PBSUCCESS, launched from Honduras in June 1954. During the conversation, he assured McDermott that he had already informed the CIA and the FBI.[59]

In his memoirs, Ydígoras claimed that during his exile he had been approached by two men introduced to him by Walter Turnbull, a retired executive of UFCO. According to Ydígoras, the men asked him to lead the revolt against Arbenz. In return for U.S. support, he would agree to establish a dictatorship and recompense UFCO for damages inflicted by Arbenz. Believing these conditions to be "unfavorable to Guatemala," he refused. As Richard Immerman has shown, this meeting may never have happened.[60] Ydígoras nonetheless used it to malign Castillo Armas.

Soon after the meeting, Ydígoras said, he learned that Castillo Armas "had been chosen as the person most fit to lead the military operation against Arbenz."[61] Ydígoras went on to characterize Castillo Armas as a man without a political following in Guatemala. He depicted the colonel as a tool of the CIA, a man "chosen" to play a part. Ydígoras had good reason to be resentful. Castillo Armas later reneged on the "gentleman's agreement." He became president and excluded Ydígoras from Guatemalan politics. The two men never ceased being rivals, and Ydígoras only became president of Guatemala after Castillo Armas was murdered in a coup in July 1957. Attempting to portray himself as the true savior of Guatemala from the supposed Communism of Arbenz and the demagoguery of Armas, Ydígoras cleverly maligned Armas by portraying him as nothing more than a paid CIA freebooter.

And that is precisely how Castillo Armas is remembered. The problem is that he was not simply "chosen." He chose, and he had been lobbying for support for years. Without question, he was an unappealing man who did his best to restore the glorious days of banana-republic dictatorship to Guatemala. He was an agent of counterrevolution who had no difficulty embracing the U.S. government, Somoza, Trujillo, and whoever else would pay him. And it is unlikely that his plans would have succeeded even without the CIA.

From one perspective, the U.S. government initiated the plan to remove Arbenz for its own reasons having to do with anti-Communism, UFCO, and Monroe Doctrine diplomacy. It then found instruments such as Castillo Armas.

---

propaganda in January 1954 under the title "Democracy Threatened: The Case of Guatemala." Guatemala Transcripts, Box 93.

59. Memorandum of conversation between Ydígoras Fuentes and Amb. McDermott, July 22, 1953, Secret, Guatemala 350.21.

60. Immerman, *CIA in Guatemala,* 131–32.

61. Ydígoras Fuentes, *My War with Communism,* 50.

Yet the evidence also indicates that Castillo Armas initiated his own plan and found instruments such as the United States. Washington was, after all, the logical place to look given its history of intervening in Central America and the uneasy relationship between official Washington and the Guatemalan revolution. In fact, it is reasonable to speculate that the decision to undertake PBSUCCESS owed more to Castillo Armas than is commonly thought. After all, he had been plotting for years; he knew the terrain and the Guatemalan military. Given the close correlation between Castillo Armas' earlier plans for a military coup and the eventual form of the CIA's intervention, it would seem that PBSUCCESS bore the imprint of the supposed stooge Castillo Armas.

For instance, by the time the Eisenhower administration initiated a covert operation to unseat Arbenz in the fall of 1953, Castillo Armas had already assembled a handful of troops and weapons. In July, Somoza had advised Castillo Armas to purchase weapons from a German firm in Hamburg called H. F. Cordes and Company, and there is a record of dozens of purchase orders of guns, napalm, and assorted armaments. Somoza also established training facilities, while Osorio in Honduras agreed to allow the rebels to use Honduran soil as a launching pad for the coup. These plans predate the decision of the Eisenhower administration to unleash the CIA on Arbenz.[62]

Eisenhower and Dulles both claimed that the reason for intervening was to stanch the flow of Guatemalan Communism.[63] Allen Dulles, the pipe-smoking director of the CIA, claimed that "communist stooges" had taken control in Guatemala, thereby necessitating an operation.[64] Richard Bissell, the former Yale professor who served as Allen Dulles' special assistant during the coup, explained that the operation was implemented only because Guatemala's government had been taken over by Communists.[65]

According to the CIA's own estimates, there were never more than one thousand members of the Guatemalan Communist Party.[66] And there was little question that they had sufficient power to overthrow the Arbenz government. The Eisenhower administration, however, viewed the close association among Arbenz, Fortuny, and Gutiérrez as proof that Arbenz was a proto-Communist. As the U.S. ambassador in Guatemala John Peurifoy remarked on first meeting with Arbenz in December 1953, "I am definitely convinced that if the President is not a Communist, he will certainly do until one comes along."[67] Piero Gleijeses,

---

62. See documents in Guatemala Transcripts, Box 93.

63. Eisenhower, *Mandate for Change*, 426–27.

64. Dulles, *Craft of Intelligence*, 205.

65. Bissell Oral History, 12, Columbia Oral History Project. Later, in his memoirs, Bissell expressed doubts that Arbenz was as big a threat as had been supposed. Richard Bissell, with Jonathan E. Lewis and Frances Pudlo, *Reflections of a Cold Warrior* (New Haven, 1996), 82.

66. CIA-NIE, "Probable Developments in Guatemala," May 9, 1953, Top Secret, CIA Research Reports, Reel 5.

67. Quoted in Immerman, *CIA in Guatemala*, 181.

no apologist for the American intervention, demonstrated after years of research and interviews that Arbenz, particularly by mid-1953, was indeed a closet Communist. In order to follow his convictions and enact land reform, he accepted the support of the only staunch allies available to him, Guatemalan Communists. Arbenz did not join the Communist Party until 1957, three years after the coup, when he was a broken man living in drunken exile; and his Communism was really a radical agrarian socialism. Still, the suspicions of the Eisenhower administration were more legitimate than has traditionally been assumed.[68]

But even if Arbenz was a Communist, so what? Tito was a Communist, and the United States supported him. Eisenhower and his advisers may have believed that the Guatemalan government was controlled by Communists, but they rarely suggested that Moscow was giving the marching orders. Indeed, reflecting bitterly on the coup, Arévalo wrote that if the State Department admitted that there were no more than thirty thousand hard-line Communists in all of Latin America, then it required willful fantasy to believe that this minority could lull the masses of Latin America to follow the Pied Piper of Communism.[69] The weakness of Communism in Guatemala has led many to conclude that it was only an excuse for an intervention undertaken for other reasons.

Communism was an excuse, but it was a necessary excuse, given the world view of U.S. policy makers and their specific concerns about the perils of Latin American nationalism opening the way for anti-American regimes. Without the Communist undertone of some of Arbenz's reforms, it would have been more difficult for the Eisenhower administration to justify (even to itself) the intervention against Guatemala. And without the links with United Fruit, the issue might not have risen so high on the national-security agenda. Following the logic of NSC 144 in the spring of 1953 and of Dulles' speech to the CIO in November 1953, the decision to intervene was made because the United States could neither tolerate nor risk a nationalist government in the Western Hemisphere that was well disposed toward the Soviet Union and ill disposed toward the United States. The concern about a possible Guatemalan "nationalist" domino effect was warranted; concerns about Moscow-directed Communism were not.

In coming to a decision, the Eisenhower administration was egged on by Castillo Armas, Ydígoras, discontented Guatemalan army officers, and Archbishop Rossell y Arellano. It is impossible to uncouple the decision to intervene from the presence of multiple pull forces within Guatemala and in Central America. Furthermore, without the strong internal Guatemalan opposition to Arbenz, Operation PBSUCCESS could not have worked. The decision, planning, and implementation of the covert operation depended on the active or passive cooperation of a large segment of the Guatemalan people, and the Eisenhower administration and the CIA could not have implemented such a plan had it not

68. Gleijeses, *Shattered Hope,* 377–81.
69. Arévalo, *Guatemala,* 29–32.

been for rivalries within Central America and conditions within Guatemala itself.

There is precious little documentation about the decision to initiate PBSUC-CESS, and it is impossible to pinpoint precisely when or why the decision was made. In the interest of "plausible deniability," the Eisenhower administration cast a veil of secrecy over the operation, and that veil continues to obscure the historical record. Like Truman, Eisenhower used the NSC as a shield from direct presidential involvement in covert action. His reasons for doing so were explained by Dillon Anderson:

> During the cold-war period there were CIA activities other than intelligence analysis, some of them in the field of gathering intelligence by what you might call unorthodox means, some of them in the field of what has later been identified as "operations," which were directed by Allen Dulles, the head of the CIA.

The president was not always advised about or conversant with the specifics of each and every one of such operations. Some of these details he preferred not to know.[70]

In March 1954, the president approved NSC 5412, which clarified the responsibilities of the CIA to carry out covert operations on the directive of the NSC for such purposes as discrediting "the prestige and ideology of International Communism"; countering "any threat or party or individuals directly or indirectly responsive to Communist control to achieve dominant power in a free world country"; and above all, fostering "underground resistance to facilitate covert and guerrilla operations" in countries "dominated or threatened by International Communism." Operations were to be designed in such a way "that if uncovered the U.S. government can plausibly disclaim any responsibility for them." In 1955, the 5412 committee (also known as the Special Group) was created. Composed of senior state and defense department officials along with the CIA and senior White House aides, the 5412 committee was responsible for overseeing subsequent covert operations.[71] Plausible deniability notwithstanding, it should not be supposed that Eisenhower was either unaware or uninformed. He may not have been briefed on all operational details, but the ultimate decisions were his.

By the fall of 1953, the Guatemala planning was fully underway. Frank Wisner, the CIA's deputy director of plans, was in charge of the operation. Wisner was a former OSS officer from Mississippi and a prominent Wall Street lawyer with strong connections to Allen Dulles and the rest of the early CIA elite collectively

70. Dillon Anderson Oral History, 110–12, Eisenhower Library.

71. NSC 5412, "Note by the Executive Secretary to the National Security Council on Covert Operations," March 15, 1954, Top Secret, Eisenhower Library.

known as the "old boys." He was also a master of psychological warfare and had worked extensively on developing propaganda operations in Europe. His deputy was Tracy Barnes of Groton and Yale, a former student of Bissell. Under Barnes was a host of operatives, including Howard Hunt and Albert Haney.[72]

In October 1953, John Peurifoy became ambassador to Guatemala. Originally from South Carolina, Peurifoy was an orphan who had worked his way into the State Department and up the career ladder. He had been ambassador to Greece shortly after the defeat of the Democratic Army. He was known as a tough, "pistol-packing" representative who was less a diplomat than an enforcer. He once remarked to a reporter, "I'm a Star Spangled Banner guy," and he often paraded around the embassy in a jumpsuit equipped with a shoulder holster. He also didn't mince words with Arbenz. When the latter complained that the United States was unfairly opposed to land reform, Peurifoy told him that the United States supported land reform in many countries, such as Greece and Bolivia. "The difference," said Peurifoy, "seemed to lie in the administration, not in the principle of assisting poor people to obtain land." After all, said the ambassador, land reform in Guatemala was in the charge of Fortuny and Gutiérrez.[73]

The key to the operation was the Guatemalan army. The CIA believed that the army was the sole force in Guatemala capable of resisting Communism and as yet uninfiltrated by Communism. It also believed that while the army was loyal to Arbenz, that loyalty was conditional. If it could be shown that Arbenz was a Communist who was also incapable of maintaining the strength of the military, then, the CIA believed, the army might well abandon Arbenz or even turn against him. In particular, if Arbenz was rendered incapable of supplying his officers with needed weapons and equipment, and if the officers began to doubt Arbenz's commitment to order, then they would fall back on their identity as the guardians of the Guatemala state and refuse to back the president.[74]

PBSUCCESS was designed, therefore, to target the army. By preventing Guatemala from importing arms and other materials, the United States would undermine Arbenz's efforts to keep his officers content. By undertaking a massive propaganda campaign, the CIA would encourage the suspicions of the naturally conservative military and at the same time alarm Guatemala's upper and middle classes. Using assets in Guatemala, the CIA distributed pamphlets stating that, as long as Arbenz and the Communists were in power, the army would be

72. Burton Hersh, *The Old Boys* (New York, 1992), passim; Evan Thomas, *The Very Best Men: Four Who Dared: The Early Years of the CIA* (New York, 1995), passim; Ranelagh, *The Agency,* 134-35.

73. December 18, 1953, Secret, NA 611.14/12-1754; Hersh, *Old Boys,* 345; Schlesinger and Kinzer, *Bitter Fruit,* 133-36.

74. CIA-NIE, "Probable Developments in Guatemala," May 9, 1953, Top Secret, CIA Research Reports, Reel 5; CIA Report, March 5, 1954, Top Secret, CIA Research Reports, Reel 5. See also Cook, *Declassified Eisenhower,* 240-42.

unable to purchase weapons. In the words of one pamphlet, any officer who believed that the Soviet Union would come to Guatemala's aid "required psychiatric help." Eventually, the United States would move against Arbenz, and if the army stood with him, it would be utterly defeated.[75]

The CIA was helped by Edward Bernays. Working for United Fruit, Bernays fed stories to the assistant managing editor of the New York *Times* describing the alleged training of Guatemalan Communists in Czechoslovakia. Bernays also met repeatedly with Peurifoy to discuss the best way to expose Guatemala in the U.S. press.[76] Building on the work done by Bernays and UFCO, Wisner developed his own propaganda apparatus. The result was multiple articles in the U.S. media trumpeting the Communist danger in Guatemala. On November 2, 1953, *Time* ran a story accusing the Guatemalan government of spending millions of dollars to counteract negative reports that were scaring off U.S. tourists. Peurifoy worked to publicize "Communist developments" and "to accelerate locally overt and covert anti-Communist propaganda."[77] The United States Information Agency adopted a policy of "maximum unattributed press and radio output" in Guatemala, i.e., black propaganda. Coordinating its activities with the State Department, the CIA, and Peurifoy, the USIA planted stories throughout Latin America, many of them emanating from press organizations in Mexico City.[78]

As the propaganda campaign intensified, Dulles went to the Inter-American Conference in Caracas in March 1954. Dulles planned to engineer a resolution denouncing Communism in Latin America as foreign intervention. He hoped to lay the groundwork for multilateral intervention by the Organization of American States against countries penetrated by Communism. Guatemala would not be named, although it was clearly the target.[79] While Dulles realized that most of the American states would be concerned about economics and aid rather than Communism, he planned to suggest that the two were connected. The implied message would be: support the United States against Guatemala, and the Eisenhower administration will be more willing to listen to your requests for aid.[80] The press campaign highlighting Communist penetration of Guatemala was designed to make Dulles' task at Caracas easier.

75. Cullather, *Operation PBSUCCESS*, 47–50.

76. Bernays, *Biography of an Idea*, 764; Michael McClintock, *Instruments of Statecraft: U.S. Guerrilla Warfare, Counterinsurgency, and Counterterrorism, 1940–1990* (New York, 1992), 139–42.

77. Peurifoy quoted in Cook, *Declassified Eisenhower*, 247.

78. Ibid., 252. See also Memorandum for the Operations Coordinating Board, "Report on Actions Taken by the U.S. Information Agency in the Guatemalan Situation," August 2, 1954, Secret, NA 714.00/8-254.

79. State Department Memorandum to assistant secretary of state John Moors Cabot, "Draft Memorandum on Handling of Guatemala at Caracas," February 10, 1953, Secret, NA 714.00/2-1054.

80. Dulles comments at Cabinet meeting, February 26, 1954, Whitman Files-Cabinet Series, Box 3, Eisenhower Library.

Witnessing the surge in anti-Guatemala publicity prior to Caracas and aware of Armas' activities, Arbenz and his foreign minister Guillermo Toriello assailed the Eisenhower administration.[81] At the conference, it was Toriello and not Dulles who won the hearts of the delegates. In a passionate speech, Toriello denounced the attempts of the U.S. government to set back Guatemalan democracy. He challenged the accusation that Guatemala "endangered continental solidarity." He stated that "the plan of national liberation which is being firmly enacted by my government has affected the privileges of the foreign businesses which had tried to halt the progress and economic development of the country." He charged the U.S. government with orchestrating a grand conspiracy that served the interests of United Fruit, and he implored the conference delegates not to succumb to the pressure emanating from Washington.[82]

Yet, while the delegates sympathized with Guatemala, the economics were such that Dulles could not be totally rejected. The conference passed a compromise resolution which declared that "international Communism, by its anti-democratic nature and its interventionist tendency, is incompatible with the concept of American freedom."[83] However, Dulles could not get the conference to endorse even the suggestion of intervention against countries imperiled by "international Communism." As the delegates knew, that would give the United States the international sanction to intervene; it would be tantamount to validating Big Stick diplomacy. And that the Latin American nations were unwilling to do.

The propaganda campaign and Caracas were having the desired effect on the Guatemalan army, however. As Arbenz became aware of the plans against him, he took pains to reassure the military of his intentions. In mid-November, he gathered one hundred of his most senior officers and explained that he understood their concerns about Communism in Guatemala and the resulting semipariah status of the country. He acknowledged that the government was having difficulty obtaining arms and equipment, largely because of the refusal of the United States to fill Guatemalan military orders. According to the U.S. embassy report, "An atmosphere of almost silent hostility prevailed at the meeting between the military and the president."[84]

Peurifoy was an enthusiastic proponent of targeting the army. In late December, he outlined the steps he felt necessary for a successful coup. While he believed that the army was uncomfortable with developments in Guatemala, he thought that the officers would only turn on Arbenz if they "believed the

81. Toriello, *La Batalla de Guatemala*, passim; speeches by Arbenz, Toriello, and former foreign minister Raul Osgueda in Gregorio Selser, *El Guatemalazo* (Buenos Aires, 1961), passim.

82. Quoted in Selser, *El Guatemalazo*, 58–62.

83. Resolution 93 of the Caracas Conference. Copy in OSANSA-NSC Policy Papers, Box 26, Eisenhower Library.

84. Guatemala 443, "President Arbenz Seeks to Reassure Army Officers," November 23, 1953, Confidential, NA 714.00/11-2353.

Communists were about to take over the Government lock, stock, and barrel." And they would only believe that if the United States government made the armed forces the focus of a concerted psychological campaign.[85] By February, as Caracas approached, U.S. embassy sources reported that the officer corps was getting more uncomfortable by the day, more skeptical of Arbenz, and less willing to stand by him in a confrontation with the United States.[86]

Still, by late spring of 1954, the coup planners were by no means certain what percentage of the officer corps would abandon Arbenz. Archbishop Rossell continued to denounce Arbenz, as did many of his priests, and they were aided by U.S. Catholic luminaries such as Cardinal Francis Spellman.[87] Directed by Barnes's deputy David Atlee Phillips, clandestine radio broadcasts blanketed Guatemala.[88] The propaganda apparatus churned out 100,000 copies of a pamphlet entitled "A Chronology of Communism in Guatemala," written in Washington, printed in Havana, and distributed throughout Latin America. The USIA also circulated more than 27,000 cartoons, posters, and anti-Arbenz broadsides. These were supplemented by some 200 articles, many in the Guatemalan press, trumpeting the dangers of Communism and Arbenz. However, anti-Arbenz press reports were limited within Guatemala proper because of tight censorship restrictions passed by the Arbenz government after Caracas. These restrictions indicate that the campaign was effective, or at least effective enough to alarm the Guatemalan government.[89] The campaign was so cleverly orchestrated that Arévalo characterized John Foster Dulles as a latter-day Joseph Goebbels, the infamous architect of Nazi propaganda.[90]

The coup moved into its final phase after the Swedish ship *Alfhelm* arrived in Puerto Barrios with a shipment of arms from Stettin. *Time* magazine described the episode as proof that the Soviets were planning to establish a stronghold in Guatemala.[91] John Foster Dulles announced at a press conference that the secrecy surrounding the arms shipment was proof of nefarious intent.[92] Eisenhower and Dulles used the arms shipment as an excuse for heightened pressure

85. See William Krieg (Counselor of Embassy) assessing Peurifoy's views in a letter to Peurifoy, January 27, 1954, Secret, RG 84, Guatemala 350.

86. Report of assistant air attaché, February 19, 1954, Confidential, NA 714.00/2-1954. See also remarks of Colonel Getalla in Peurifoy letter to Raymond Leddy (State officer in charge of Central America—ARA), January 5, 1954, RG 84, Guatemala 350.

87. Cullather, *Operation PBSUCCESS*, 50–51; Hunt, *Give Us This Day*, 99; Rossell, memo of conversation on the coup with Cardinal Spellman, December 22, 1953, in Guatemala Transcripts, Box 93.

88. Schlesinger and Kinzer, *Bitter Fruit*, 167–68; Hersh, *Old Boys*, 348–52.

89. "Report on Action Taken by the U.S. Information Agency in the Guatemala Situation," August 2, 1954.

90. Arévalo, *Guatemala*, 101.

91. *Time*, May 18, 1954.

92. Press Conference, May 25, 1954, Department of State Publication No. 279.

on Guatemala,[93] and Dulles agreed with his brother Allen and Frank Wisner at the CIA that the shipment was good propaganda for the coup.[94] No one mentioned that Arbenz had resorted to the *Alfhelm* because the U.S. embargo on arms to Guatemala was jeopardizing his control over the army. He also planned to arm the peasants in anticipation of the coming coup. Also not mentioned was the fact that the shipment consisted mostly of old, broken weapons as well as glassware and optical equipment.[95] Arbenz had been successfully cornered by the United States.

Meanwhile, Castillo Armas and the CIA had gathered a small rebel force in Honduras, with the full cooperation of the Honduran government. Shortly before the coup began, Allen Dulles prepared a memo for Eisenhower laying out the plans. These included the invasion of Armas' forces and an attack on the town of Zacapa, the bombing of Guatemala City by two antique planes operated by the rebels, and yet another round of propaganda and rumors designed to confuse the government and alarm the populace. John Foster Dulles refused to pass this memorandum on to Eisenhower, however, claiming that if the president were privy to the contents, it "would lead to charges that the President and this country were supporting revolutionary activities within Guatemala and would place the President in the dangerous position of appealing to citizens of a foreign country to revolt against their leaders."[96] The veneer of plausible deniability was maintained.

On June 18, Castillo Armas began the attack. Four contingents of between fifty and two hundred troops attacked at different points along the Guatemala-Honduras border. The small rebel air force also went into action. In Guatemala City, Arbenz was unable to get a precise measure of the rebels' strength, and radio reports and disinformation spread by the CIA made the invasion seem far more ominous than it actually was. Within nine days, the forces of Castillo Armas had advanced no farther than Chiquimula and Zacapa, still nearly one hundred miles from Guatemala City. The rebels lost two airplanes and were repeatedly defeated by the Guatemalan army, and the bombing did minimal damage to the presidential palace and other targets. Yet, although Castillo Armas was nowhere near a military victory, on June 27, 1954, Arbenz resigned and appealed to the Mexican embassy for asylum.[97]

In explaining the reasons for the coup's success, many have pointed to the June 20 decision by Eisenhower to supply Castillo Armas with additional air-

---

93. Memorandum of conversation between Dulles and Eisenhower, May 22, 1954, Top Secret, NA 714.56/5-2254.

94. Dulles telephone conversations with Wisner, May 18, 1954, and with Allen Dulles, May 18, 1954, in Dulles telephone records, Box 2, Eisenhower Library.

95. Gleijeses, *Shattered Hope,* 292–308.

96. Items from James Hagerty Diary, June 16, 1954, Hagerty Diaries, Eisenhower Library.

97. Cullather, *Operation PBSUCCESS,* 65–75; Schlesinger and Kinzer, *Bitter Fruit,* 173–204; Gleijeses, *Shattered Hope,* 336–50; Immerman, *CIA in Guatemala,* 164–68.

craft.[98] Yet, while further aerial raids were a psychological boon to the coup, the planes did remarkably little damage. Allen Dulles told Eisenhower that without more air support the rebels were doomed, but there is reason to doubt Dulles' assessment. Most who have pointed to the crucial importance of air cover in the Guatemalan coup wrote after the Bay of Pigs invasion, when some asserted that the refusal of Kennedy to authorize air strikes led to the defeat of the Cuban intervention. There may have been a tendency to stress the role of air cover in Guatemala in light of the failed operation in Cuba years later.[99]

In fact, as Nicholas Cullather demonstrated in his declassified history of the operation, PBSUCCESS nearly failed. The rebel troops were soundly defeated by the army, and the air raids were a military dud. Arbenz was not brought down by a well-planned paramilitary operation. He was, as Cullather describes, "deposed in a military coup."[100] That coup, of course, was in part the result of months of psychological warfare and propaganda designed to undermine the loyalty of the military to Arbenz. Yet the fact that it was the army that brought down Arbenz from within, rather than a rebel force armed and transported by the United States, highlights the importance of internal factors in determining the outcome of an intervention.

Arbenz resigned without a fight because the army deserted him, and the army deserted him because the church, the plantation owners, and the scared, disoriented populace of Guatemala City were convinced that Arbenz was driving Guatemala into a fatal embrace with Communism and a fatal conflict with the United States. That conviction was solidified by the propaganda that accompanied PBSUCCESS. In the days before Arbenz resigned, the chief of the armed forces, Carlos Díaz, informed him that the army would attack the presidential palace unless Arbenz stepped down. In later years, many bitterly attacked Arbenz for not fleeing to the countryside and there leading a guerrilla resistance to Castillo Armas. Yet Arbenz believed that the army would resist the rebellion once he resigned.[101] On that count, he was sadly mistaken. He spent his remaining years in Mexico, Prague, Moscow, Paris, and Uruguay. He even lived for a while in Castro's Cuba as a symbol of revolution. He died in Mexico in 1971.

As for Castillo Armas, he soon emerged as the power in Guatemala, especially after Peurifoy told Díaz in no uncertain terms that the United States intended to support Castillo Armas' bid for power. By late summer 1954, the counterrevolution was underway. The agrarian-reform program was abandoned, and land was returned to many of the landlords who had lost it. Castillo Armas created a strong centralized police state and left Ydígoras out in the cold. The elite

98. Cook, *Declassified Eisenhower*, 283; Schlesinger and Kinzer, *Bitter Fruit*, 176–78.

99. This is especially true of Bissell. See *Reflections of a Cold Warrior*, 85–89.

100. Cullather, *Operation PBSUCCESS*, 75.

101. Luis Cardoza y Aragon interview by author, Mexico City, August 1991. See also Cardoza y Aragon, *Revolución Guatemalteca*; Gleijeses, *Shattered Hope*, 347–51.

planters, industrialists, and businessmen who had supported the coup also found themselves locked out of a direct role in Armas' authoritarian government. They were pleased to see the status quo restored in the countryside, but they were not happy that the upstart colonel wielded so much power.[102] Eventually, a disgruntled army overthrew and murdered Castillo Armas in 1957.

The coup was a success for the Eisenhower administration and a victory for counterrevolutionary forces within Guatemala. (It was to have some negative consequences, however. Present in Guatemala City during the final months of Arbenz was a young Argentinean doctor named Ernesto Guevara. He watched as Arbenz crumbled without a fight, and he applied the lessons years later in Cuba. "Che" Guevara would not repeat what he believed were the mistakes of Arbenz.) In Washington, the coup enhanced the reputation of the CIA, and Bissell was promoted to deputy director of operations after Wisner departed in 1957. Bissell came to believe that as long as an operation was well planned, its success was likely.[103]

That belief was mistaken. Operation PBSUCCESS lived up to its name not because it was well planned but because the situation in Guatemala made it possible. Psychological warfare can only work when it taps into fears that are already present, and while the covert campaign against Arbenz was essential to Castillo Armas' victory, it would have fallen on deaf ears had it not been for general discontent with Arbenz in many quarters of society. The coup was a victory for a reactionary counterrevolution. It was a victory that owed a great debt to Washington, but it was not a victory manufactured solely in Washington. Neither the apologists for the Arbenz regime nor policy makers in Washington itself understood that, and nothing in the next few years upset their assumptions. Indeed, after Guatemala, the Eisenhower administration turned away from Latin America. The supposed threat from Guatemala had been eliminated, and the focus shifted to Asia, Europe, and the Middle East.

102. *Time*, September 13, 1954.

103. Schlesinger interview with Bissell (September 1979), in Schlesinger files, Hispanic Reading Room, LC.

7

Lebanon

From Cairo to Beirut

There is no room for choice. We are determined to live free and from this moment on, we will fight to the last man for this objective.
—Gamal Abdel Nasser

What happened in Egypt [with Nasser] proved one of the major arguments made by the adversaries of Nasserist politics in the countries which he wanted in his sphere of influence. The Arab peoples did not accept being manipulated by a young excitable, impetuous, inexperienced man, and even less by the ambitions of unscrupulous politicians. These people comprised a large, enfran- chised, religious, and conservative class which constituted a solid bloc [in the Arab world]. In addition, these hardly chose to bind their destiny to that of a destructive inglorious dictatorship which, instead of the freedoms promised, had instituted terror, and instead of affluence, had only increased misery.
—Camille Chamoun

In July of 1958, President Eisenhower sent fifteen thousand Marines to Lebanon to end a civil war. It was the largest military deployment conducted by the Eisenhower administration, and the most significant use of U.S. troops between the Korean War and Vietnam. The intervention was the culmination of the assiduous efforts of the various factions within Lebanon to draw the United States into the 1958 Lebanese civil war. This pull from Lebanon was met by a push from Washington, which was concerned about Nasser, oil, and regional stability. As Robinson and Gallagher might have argued, the intervention in Lebanon can be viewed as an example of how clients influence their patron. Knowing of U.S. sensitivity to Communism and Nasserism, Leba- nese leaders such as foreign minister Charles Malik and president Camille Cha- moun presented the Lebanese civil war as the apex of a regional struggle involving Nasser and the abyss of Communism on one side, and a pro-Western, market-driven, secular Middle East on the other. Holding themselves up as the natural allies of the United States in the Middle East, factions in Lebanon touched the right nerve in the Eisenhower administration. While the United States did not intervene to save Chamoun himself, it did intercede in order to shore up the system that Chamoun represented.

For an intervention so large, the episode has received only spotty discussion in the United States. The intervention has been used as a case study for presidential decision making in times of crisis, but the actual situation in Lebanon is given only cursory treatment in these accounts.[1] The intervention is also frequently discussed in passing as a footnote to U.S. policy in the Middle East as a whole during this period,[2] and a standard explanation holds that after the July 14, 1958, coup in Iraq, there was a brief moment of uncertainty and panic that the Middle East was about to fall to Nasser. That interpretation is satisfactory, albeit sketchy and incomplete. The dimension that is usually elided is that of Lebanese domestic politics.[3]

Seen from Washington, the U.S. intervention was an episode in the larger drama of containment, Middle East oil, and Nasserism. Seen from Beirut, however, it was a somewhat more significant but still small blip on the larger screen of long-standing Lebanese rivalries, competing individuals and factions, and intra-Arab struggles. Had it not been for the near-perfect convergence of domestic Lebanese politics and American foreign policy in 1958, the intervention could not have succeeded in restoring the status quo.

In Lebanon, the Eisenhower administration undertook what was essentially a nonadversarial intervention. That is not to say that all, or even most, Lebanese welcomed the presence of U.S. troops in their country. Rather, U.S. troops were not seen by most Lebanese as either a solution to their problems or a cause of their difficulties. While there was widespread condemnation of the

1. Alan Dowty, *Middle East Crisis: U.S. Decision Making in 1958, 1970, and 1973* (Berkeley, 1984); William Quandt, "Lebanon, 1958, and Jordan, 1970," in *Force without War*, ed. Barry Blechman and Stephen Kaplan (Washington, D.C., 1978); Herbert Tillema, *Appeal to Force* (New York, 1973).

2. For example, Thomas Paterson, *Meeting the Communist Threat* (New York, 1988), 159–89.

3. Of course, there are exceptions. Irene Gendzier has done by far the most significant work on both U.S. foreign policy and Lebanese politics. Irene Gendzier, *Notes from the Minefield: United States Intervention in Lebanon and the Middle East, 1945–1958* (New York, 1997); Gendzier, "The Declassified Lebanon 1948–1958: Elements of Continuity and Contrast in U.S. Policy toward Lebanon," in *Toward a Viable Lebanon,* ed. Halim Barakat (London: 1988), 187–207; Gendzier, "The United States, the USSR and the Arab World in NSC Reports of the 1950s," *American-Arab Affairs* (Spring 1989), 22–29; Douglas Little, "His Finest Hour? Eisenhower, Lebanon, and the 1958 Middle East Crisis," *Diplomatic History,* XX (Winter 1996), 27–55; Michael Bishka, "The 1958 American Intervention in Lebanon: A Historical Assessment," *American-Arab Affairs* (Winter 1987), 106–19; Agnes Korbani, *U.S. Intervention in Lebanon, 1958 and 1982* (New York, 1991); Erika Allin, *The United States and the 1958 Lebanon Crisis: American Intervention in the Middle East* (Lanham, Md., 1994).

intervention, it was condemnation less of the United States for intervening than of Chamoun and his allies for requesting help from the Americans. Examining the intervention from the perspective of Lebanese history, one is struck by how little significance the Lebanese attached to the actions of the United States, at least relative to the extraordinary weight which Iranians gave to the coup in Iran, which Guatemalans gave to Operation PBSUCCESS, and which Cubans gave to the Bay of Pigs.

Lebanese writings on the 1958 intervention focus not on the United States but on Lebanese politics. The most prominent Lebanese historian of these and later events, Kamal Salibi, interpreted 1958 as an internecine conflict; in his many writings, he has focused remarkably little on Eisenhower and the intervention.[4] One writer, less than a year after the events, spoke of the "two different Lebanons" which split asunder during a crucial time. In this telling, 1958 was a year of *thawrah,* or revolution. It was a popular movement of discontent and a rejection of Camille Chamoun's policies. While there was an "imperial conspiracy," it was a conspiracy not of the western imperial powers—Great Britain, France, the United States—but of the Arab monarchies in Iraq, Jordan, Saudi Arabia, and the Gulf. In this reading, U.S. policy and U.S. goals are hardly considered; the U.S. intervention was proof that Chamoun was willing to "tread on [Lebanese] independence. . . . He arranged with the greatest perfidy to send by telegraph to Eisenhower and Harold Macmillan an appeal for help."[5] Other commentators emphasized Chamoun's invitation as the pivotal action, not the actual dispatch of U.S. troops.[6]

Not all accounts, either at the time or later, take such a dim view of Chamoun. Some pass lightly over what he did or did not do and treat him as simply a manifestation of the major fault lines in Lebanese society. For most Lebanese writers, the 1958 crisis, involving not only the United States but the neighboring Arab countries, was a story of Lebanese domestic politics played out on an international stage.[7] One writer even viewed the 1957 Eisenhower Doctrine not as a policy emanating from Washington, but rather as one move in a game

---

4. Kamal Salibi, *A House of Many Mansions: The History of Lebanon Reconsidered* (London, 1988); Kamal Salibi, *The Modern History of Lebanon* (New York, 1965), 191ff.

5. Nadia Karami, *Waqi' al-thawrah al-Lubnaniyyah* [*The Facts of the Lebanese Revolution*] (Beirut, 1959), iv, 267–70 (my translations).

6. Ismail Musa al-Yusuf, *Thawrat al-ahrar fi Lubnan* [*Revolution of the Free in Lebanon*] (Beirut, 1965?), 157–59.

7. Halim Abu 'Izz al-Din, *Siyasat Lubnan al-kharijiyyah* [*The Foreign Relations of Lebanon*] (Beirut, 1966), 13–18; Muhammad Jamil Bayhum, *Lubnan: Baina al-mashraq w-al-maghrib, 1920–1969* [*Lebanon: Between East and West*] (Beirut, 1970), 129ff.; Fuad Ammun, *Siyasat Lubnan al-kharijiyyah* [*The Foreign Relations of Lebanon*] (Beirut, 1963), passim; Michel Asmar, *Ba'd al-mihna wa qabila* [*After the Ordeal and Before It*] (Beirut, 1959), 23ff.; Malcolm Kerr, "Lebanese Views on the 1958 Crisis," *Middle East Journal,* XV (Spring 1961), 211–17.

played by warring blocs of Arab states.[8] And those who saw Chamoun as more of an instrument of history than a maker of it also tended to view the outcome of the intervention in a more positive light. One commentator believed that the 1958 crisis and its resolution led to a more stable Lebanon and a more honest government.[9] That view was shared by many western writers in the 1960s. With Lebanon thriving, it was easy to believe that 1958 marked the end of violent factionalism and the birth of a unique, modern, heterogenous nation well on the way to full democracy.[10]

The Lebanese perspective that the United States was marginal to the events of 1958 may be as exaggerated as the American perspective of centrality. Yet those views should not and cannot be discounted. The 1958 U.S. intervention was a major undertaking that had a significant impact on Lebanon, but its architecture was not solely American. While Lebanese writers may have underemphasized the degree to which the 1958 crisis was influenced by the United States, they bring balance to an otherwise distorted sense of U.S. power and leverage. Seen from Washington, Eisenhower intervened to save a small, war-torn, and largely defenseless country from chaos, Nasser, and ultimately Communism. Seen from Beirut, Eisenhower did no such thing. Both of these perspectives are correct in their context. But the former reinforces the dominant narrative of the cold war, undermines the influence that local forces had on Washington, and does not allow for the Robinson-Gallagher notion of peripheral influences. When policy makers in Washington arrived at their decision in July 1958, Lebanese history, culture, and politics determined the range of options and, in subtle and not-so-subtle ways, enabled the U.S. government to act as it did.

■

In the Middle East of the 1950s, U.S. policy makers faced a more successful and charismatic nationalist leader and a more widespread nationalist movement than any that they had previously encountered. Gamal Abdel Nasser began his career as an army officer,[11] and he watched in horror as his unit and the entire Egyptian army were badly outmatched by the Israelis in the wars of 1948. Vowing to restore Egypt and the Arabs to glory, he organized the Free Officers who overthrew King Farouk in 1952. Nasser quickly emerged as their leader,

---

8. Bayhum, *Lubnan,* 129–30.

9. Asmar, *Ba'd al-mihna,* 23.

10. See, for example, the conference papers assembled in Leonard Binder, ed., *Politics in Lebanon* (New York, 1966); see also Jacques Nantet, *Histoire du Liban* (Paris, 1963), 14–15.

11. For a good biography of Nasser, see Jean Lacouture, *Nasser* (London, 1973). For Nasser's own motivations, see Gamal Abdel Nasser, *The Philosophy of the Revolution* (Cairo, 1954). See also Anwar Sadat, *Revolt on the Nile,* trans. Thomas Graham (London, 1957).

and as president of Egypt he instituted land reform and a new governing philosophy. The land reform was not as extensive as that proposed by Mosaddeq or undertaken by Arbenz, but it did reduce the power of large landholders in Egypt, and it was a symbol of egalitarianism. As for his ideology, Nasser saw Egypt paving the way for a united Arab Middle East, and he began broadcasting his vision throughout the Middle East via radio after 1953. The Voice of Cairo radio became one of Nasser's most potent weapons, and his words reached millions of Arabs in areas far from Egypt. Nasser's spin on Arab nationalism, combined with his charisma, formed the core of Nasserism. A loose set of ideals that had at its heart the union of all Arabic-speaking peoples into one Arab nation, Nasserism held great appeal in the Middle East. Interpreting Arab weakness in the face of the West as a function of divisions within the Arab world, Nasserism promised renewal and resurgence if unity was achieved.[12]

Nasser also refused to take sides in the cold war. He did his best to play off the Russians and the Americans, but he would join neither bloc. In late 1955, he concluded an arms deal with Czechoslovakia. In early 1956, he also managed to secure a promise of U.S. backing for a loan to fund the construction of the Aswan High Dam. The Czech arms deal created a climate of suspicion, and in July 1956, John Foster Dulles announced that the United States would not support the promised loan. Concluding that Nasser intended only to use the United States for revolutionary goals, Dulles opted out of the Aswan project, and he was bothered that Nasser believed he could manipulate the United States by dangling the threat of the Soviet Union.[13]

As a result of the loan cancellation, Nasser announced with great fanfare on July 26, 1956, that Egypt was nationalizing the Suez Canal. The subsequent Suez crisis saw the Eisenhower administration defending Egypt against a British-French-Israeli conspiracy to seize the canal. Yet, while distancing itself from the antediluvian imperialism of the European powers, the Eisenhower White House remained cool toward Nasser. As early as March 1956, Eisenhower had authorized the State Department to search for an alternative pan-Arab leader. Eisenhower's own choice for a rival to Nasser was King Saud of Saudi Arabia. By the fall of 1956, and in light of the Suez crisis, Eisenhower adopted what can only be called a containment strategy toward Nasser and Nasserism.[14]

In person, Nasser made a mixed impression on American diplomats. Raymond Hare, the U.S. ambassador in Cairo at the time of the Lebanese crisis, had a grudging admiration for Nasser's bravura. Believing that Egypt was the key to

12. Derek Hopwood, *Egypt: Politics and Society, 1945-1989* (2d ed.; London, 1991), chaps. 3-5; P. J. Vatikiotis, *Nasser* (London, 1978), 207-26.

13. William Roger Louis, "Dulles, Suez, and the British," in *John Foster Dulles and the Diplomacy of the Cold War*, ed. Immerman, 144-46.

14. See Eisenhower diary entry, March 28, 1956, Ann Whitman File, Eisenhower Diary Series, Box 9, Eisenhower Library. See also Peter Hahn, *The United States, Great Britain, and Egypt, 1945-1956* (Chapel Hill, 1991), 180ff.

U.S. strategy in the Middle East, Hare felt that there was no choice but to work with Nasser.[15] And Miles Copeland, the erstwhile CIA operations officer detailed to Cairo, had an unabashed admiration for Nasser's ability to squeeze what he wanted out of an international system designed to hobble nations such as his.[16] Dulles, however, came to view Nasser in much the same manner as had his former British counterpart Anthony Eden. In June 1958, Dulles remarked that he considered Nasser "an extremely dangerous person" and he compared "Nasser's characteristics to those of Hitler and Nasser's pan-Arab program to Hitler's pan-Germanism."[17] The ideology of Nasserism, more than the man himself, threatened Dulles and company. And this same ideology posed a threat to the myth of an independent Maronite-dominated Lebanon that was so cherished by Lebanese president Camille Chamoun.

Overall U.S. policy toward the Near East was defined in a series of NSC papers between 1953 and 1958. In order to block the Soviets from political or economic expansion in the region, the U.S. government sought to channel military equipment to the "Northern Tier" countries of Turkey, Iraq, Iran, and Pakistan. It encouraged the creation of regional-defense organizations such as the Baghdad Pact; it also undertook a variety of "cultural, economic and information programs," along with "covert activities in support of U.S. objectives." As British influence declined, the United States would take greater responsibility for the pro-Western orientation of the region. The greatest threat to that orientation was not, in the eyes of the NSC, a direct Soviet attack, or even Communist revolutions. It was, rather, "acute instability, anti-Western nationalism, and Arab-Israeli antagonism which could lead to disorder and might eventually open the way for an extension of Soviet control."[18]

The Eisenhower administration also struggled to come up with an effective response to Arab nationalism. Officials recognized that Arab nationalism was a force to be reckoned with in the region. Direct confrontation would only redound to the benefit of the Soviets. In January 1958 the National Security Council observed: "Many Arabs incline to the belief that their own interests are best served by a competition between the Free World and the Soviet bloc for Arab favor. The Arabs are confident of their ability to play such a game." Yet the White House was convinced that the Soviets would ultimately play such Arabs, and Nasser in particular, for dupes. In order to steer Arab states away from closer relations with the Soviet Union, the Eisenhower administration resolved "to accept the neutralist policies of states in the area, when necessary, even though such states maintain diplomatic, trade and cultural relations with

---

15. Cairo (Hare) 2968, May 15, 1958, Secret, NA 783A.00/5-1558.

16. Miles Copeland, *The Game of Nations* (London, 1969), passim.

17. State Department Memo of Conversation: Charles Malik, Amb. Dimechkié (Lebanon's UN representative), Dulles, Rountree, and others, June 13, 1958, Secret, NA 783A.00/6-1358.

18. NSC 155/1, proposed amendments of July 1954, Top Secret, OSANSA-NSC Policy Papers, Box 5, Eisenhower Library.

the Soviet Union." By appearing to support Arab nationalism, the United States could gently nudge Arab governments into the Western orbit.[19]

Unfortunately, the administration hardly spoke with one voice toward Nasser and the Middle East. At the same time that the NSC staff was recommending that Nasser and Arab nationalism be accommodated, John Foster Dulles described Nasser and his brand of Arab nationalism as dangerous to stability and inimical to U.S. interests:

> We fully agree . . . that Arab nationalism is constant factor in ME politics and that free world opposition to this nationalism, without good cause, can only advance position of Soviet as its fraudulent champion. We have always respected and supported constructive or "positive" nationalism. . . . On the other hand nationalism which appeals only to emotions and rejects moderate and reasonable approach to solution of problem is not force which can bring good to area. It is unfortunate this extreme brand of nationalism and Pan-Arabism which Nasser represents and which complicates not only free world efforts to reach understanding with him but also efforts to counter Soviet activity, Pan-Arabism of Nasser . . . can bring disaster upon ME.[20]

U.S. policy toward the region in the mid-1950s, therefore, can best be described as muddled. Many in the Eisenhower administration understood that, in order to achieve its goals, some accommodation with Nasser was imperative. Yet the leading policy maker, Eisenhower, and John Foster Dulles were not comfortable with the Egyptian leader. They believed in containing Nasser and searching for alternative champions of Arab nationalism, such as Nuri as-Said in Iraq or the Saudi royal family in Saudi Arabia. The result was neither overt confrontation nor genuine accommodation. And in 1958, Lebanese politicians took full advantage of Washington's uncertainties.[21]

The civil war that erupted in Lebanon in May 1958 was first and foremost a crisis in the domestic political system in Lebanon. The internal fissures in Lebanese society had developed over hundreds of years. Two of the main lines of division were religion and clan. Unlike most of the countries of the Middle East, Lebanon was and is multiconfessional. The primary religious cleavage was between Christians and Muslims; in 1958, Lebanon had a population of about 1.5 million with a very slight Christian majority. Furthermore, there were subdi-

19. NSC 5801/1, January 1, 1958, Top Secret, OSANSA-NSC Policy Papers, Box 23, Eisenhower Library.

20. State 2803 (Dulles) to Tokyo, June 27, 1958, Secret, NA 783A.00/6-2558.

21. For a detailed exposition of American interests in the Middle East in general and Lebanon in particular, see Gendzier, *Notes from the Minefield*, 21-42, 143-71.

visions within these two groups—and in terms of how individuals identified themselves, these subdivisions were far more important. The Christians were divided among Maronites (who numbered around 430,000), Greek Orthodox (approximately 150,000), Greek Catholics (90,000), Armenian Orthodox (60,000), and a smattering of Armenian Catholic, Syrian Catholic, and several others. The Muslims were also divided between Sunnis (290,000), Shi'is (250,000), and the Druze (90,000), who were hardly considered Muslim at all.[22] In Beirut, these groups lived side by side, but in the rest of the country, different groups tended to dominate different regions, with Maronites in the mountainous middle, Shi'is in the south, and Sunnis in the urban centers of the coast, particularly Tripoli to the north of Beirut.[23]

The loyalties of religious sects competed with the allegiance that individuals owed to their villages and, for lack of a better word, "clans." The structure of rural Lebanon is often called feudal, and although that term implies a western medieval system inapplicable to modern Lebanon, it holds insofar as it connotes loyalty to a local leader, known in Arabic as a *za'im*. Up until the 1980s, the political and economic life of Lebanon was controlled by a remarkably small number of people and an even smaller number of leading families. In the 52 years between 1920 and 1972, 425 deputies belonging to 245 families occupied a total of 965 seats in 16 assemblies. Between 1943 and 1982, a total of four families—the Solhs, the Karamis, the Yafis, and the Salems—controlled the premiership of 40 out of 53 cabinets.[24]

These *zu'ama* dominated not just politics but economics, and many of them owned large rural estates that facilitated their business dealings in Beirut and Europe. Many of them also maintained personal armies of bodyguards and retainers. At the time of the 1958 crisis, the opposition leader Sa'eb Salem remained in his Beirut mansion in the Basta district surrounded by armed retainers who temporarily camped out in an anteroom off the main garden. Sa'eb Salem has been called a "prototype" for big-city *za'im*. A powerful Sunni leader who aligned himself with Nasser and pan-Arabism in order to oppose Chamoun, Salem was a cigar-smoking multimillionaire nightclub owner with interests in the Lebanese oil and airplane industries. He outfitted his own private army in 1958 and frequently entertained the "spy of the century," Kim Philby, in his chateau. Like many of the *zu'ama,* Salem was an odd mix of personal ambition and noblesse oblige, and his adherence to a pan-Arab ideology was inseparable from his desire to humble the pro-Western Chamoun.[25]

22. John Entelis, *Pluralism and Party Transformation in Lebanon: Al-Kata'ib, 1936-1970* (Leiden, 1974), 26; Fahim Qubain, *Crisis in Lebanon* (Washington, D.C., 1961), 8-9.

23. Albert Hourani, "Ideologies of the Mountain and the City," in *Essays on the Crisis in Lebanon,* ed. Roger Owen (London, 1976), 34.

24. Samir Khalaf, *Lebanon's Predicament* (New York, 1987), 106-34.

25. Arnold Hottinger, *"Zu'ama* in Historical Perspective," in *Politics in Lebanon,* ed. Binder,

These *zu'ama* had fought for control of Lebanon for centuries, and many of the contenders in 1958 and also 1975 had rivalries that extended back a century or more. Although they had been known to make common cause, for instance against the French during World War II, their alliances were fleeting. The divisions sometimes followed confessional loyalties, and south of Beirut the Maronite leader Chamoun and the Druze lord Kamal Jumblatt competed for influence in the same area around the town of Deir al-Kamar. Sometimes, however, the rivalries superseded religious affiliation, and the Maronite *zu'ama* fought among themselves. In Lebanon as elsewhere, the personal was very often political.

Camille Chamoun, an upper-class Maronite Christian, was elected Lebanon's second president in 1952. Born in 1900, Chamoun quickly grew into his role as a patrician. An impeccable dresser, pompous, autocratic and aristocratic, Chamoun was an ardent francophile who believed that Lebanon's destiny was better served by Zurich and Washington than by Cairo and Damascus.[26] Chamoun had earlier resigned as Bishara Khoury's minister of the interior in protest over the latter's attempts to amend the constitution and serve a second term as president. In September 1952, Chamoun signed a document witnessed by, among others, Kamal Jumblatt, in which he pledged to uphold "the independence and integrity of Lebanon; nonalignment with any foreign government. . . . To abstain from using the influence and prestige of his office for personal monetary gain and self-aggrandizement. . . ."[27] Ironically, having established a reputation for fealty to the constitution, Chamoun attempted precisely what Khoury had. It was Chamoun's ambition to remain president for a second term that underlay the 1958 crisis.

Chamoun was passionately opposed to Gamal Abdel Nasser; he once compared Nasser's memoirs to Hitler's *Mein Kampf.*[28] Chamoun, like many leading figures in Lebanon, both Maronite and Sunni, was also explicitly anti-Communist. Communism faced particular difficulties in the Middle East. In a world where religious identity was still paramount, an antireligious ideology such as Communism was not widely welcomed. Chamoun's anti-Communism seems to have had less to do with religion and more to do with his Western orientation.

97; Desmond Stewart, *Turmoil in Beirut* (London, 1958), 35–37.

26. Camille Chamoun, *Crise au Moyen-Orient* (Paris, 1963). This memoir offers a vivid portrait of Chamoun in all his arrogance. See also the portraits of Chamoun in Wade Goria, *Sovereignty and Leadership in Lebanon, 1943–1976* (London, 1985), 35ff., and Sandra Mackey, *Lebanon: Death of a Nation* (New York, 1989), 47–48. One prominent contemporary of Chamoun claimed that until 1957, Chamoun embraced pan-Arab politics and was a supporter of Nasser. See Nadim Dimechkié, "The United States Intervened by Sending the Marines to Lebanon in 1958. Why Did This Happen?" (paper presented at conference on the 1958 intervention, University of Texas, Austin, 1991).

27. Quoted in Qubain, *Crisis in Lebanon,* 24.

28. Ibid., 337.

Forswearing both neutrality in the face of Communism and alliance with Nasser, Chamoun leaned to the powers of the West.[29] In doing so, he followed the example of Maronite lords of days past.

For centuries, Maronite nobles had turned to Europe for spiritual guidance, education, and protection against their Muslim and Druze neighbors. Maronite priests were trained in Rome, and in the nineteenth century, the French intervened several times to save the Maronites from Muslim reprisals. In 1860, after massacres of Maronites by the Druze, France sent troops to the Levant to bolster Ottoman forces and prevent further bloodshed. Over the next decades, Maronite Lebanon was administered separately from Beirut, Tripoli, and Sidon. The Maronites enjoyed privileged status, and with the reunification of Lebanon and the establishment of a League of Nations mandate administered by the French after World War I, the francophile Maronites retained their favored position.[30]

Effectively excluded from many positions of influence, the Sunnis in particular advocated pan-Arabism as the proper path for Lebanon.[31] During the Arab Revolt against the Ottomans during World War I, the nebulous streams of Arab nationalism coalesced. While the mandate system spelled the temporary defeat of Arab nationalism, the desire for independence from the Europeans remained strong. The Maronites' desire for independence, however, was tempered; they felt themselves to be a minority in the Arab world and therefore in need of the support of the West. For the Sunnis, on the other hand, strength lay in numbers—Arab Muslim numbers in Egypt, Syria, and throughout the Middle East.

In the early 1930s, a Greek Orthodox Lebanese named Antun Sa'adeh founded the Syrian Socialist Nationalist Party, also known as the *Parti Populaire Syrien* (PPS). Its platform called for Lebanese unity with Syria. This was a goal distinct from pan-Arabism. Sa'adeh believed that Syria and Lebanon were historically one, and during the 1958 civil war his party provided one of the few solid bases of support for Chamoun. It was an odd alliance, given that Sa'adeh himself had been arrested and executed by the Lebanese government in 1949, when Chamoun was minister of the interior. Yet the PPS had been organized in the 1930s with quasi-fascist overtones, one of which was stringent anti-Communism.[32] In 1958, confronted with a pan-Arab Nasserism that did not respect pan-Syrian ideology, the party joined ranks with Maronites who were also opposed to a Greater Syria but whose anti-Nasser and anti-Communist credentials were unimpeachable. Like many of the shifting alliances in Lebanese politics, this one was unpredictable, unstable, and fleeting.

Yet another vision of Lebanon was enunciated by Pierre Jumayyil and his

---

29. Chamoun Oral History, August 28, 1964, John Foster Dulles Oral History Collection, Mudd Library, Princeton University.

30. Meir Zamir, *The Formation of Modern Lebanon* (Ithaca, N.Y., 1985).

31. Zuwiyya Labib Yamak, *The Syrian Socialist Nationalist Party* (Cambridge, Mass., 1966), 41–43.

32. Ibid., 60–71; Goria, *Sovereignty and Leadership,* 32–35.

Phalange (al-Kata'ib) Party. The Maronite Jumayyil was a pharmacist by trade, and he ran a drugstore in the red-light district of Beirut. That earned him the nickname of "Pierre the Condom."[33] Hawk-faced and determined, he traveled to Europe in 1936 and attended the Berlin Olympics. He was impressed by Nazi discipline, and, on returning to Lebanon, co-founded the Phalange as a Christian youth organization similar to the fascist youth organizations in Europe.[34] The rigidly hierarchical Phalange was popular among the poorer Maronites who had immigrated from the mountains to Beirut in the 1930s and 1940s. Their motto was "God, Family, and Nation." With Lebanon still ruled by the French, the Phalange called for "a sovereign and independent state with alliance and friendship toward France."[35] After independence, Jumayyil advocated a "neither East nor West" identity for Lebanon, and he believed that the Lebanese could act as mediators between the competing factions in the Arab world.[36] When Chamoun was fast running out of allies in 1958, the Phalange stood by him; it brought not just rhetorical support but the backing of paramilitary groups.

These different movements might have fought each other had it not been for the unwelcome direct rule of the French. Independence from France was a shared goal,[37] and in 1943, rival sects and rival leaders sat down and agreed on a formula for governing Lebanon. The compromise was known as the National Pact, and it was an agreement between Bishara Khoury, a leading Maronite, and Riad al-Solh, a leading Sunni. Informal and unwritten, the pact was at best an imprecise arrangement, although in time it acquired a mythic sanctity quite at odds with its extraordinary vagueness. In line with the numerical superiority of the Maronites, it was agreed that the president of Lebanon would thereafter be Maronite; the premiership was reserved for Sunnis; and the speaker of the Chamber of Deputies would be a Shi'i. The chamber itself would be apportioned by sect, with a bare majority for the Christians to reflect their numerical superiority.

Equally important, the pact held that Lebanon was to be an independent state, looking neither westward to France and the Europeans nor eastward to Syria and the Arabs. It was based on the principle of friendship with the neighboring Arab states but independence from them.[38] As Khoury put it, the pact was "the fusion of two tendencies into one ideology; complete and final independence without resorting to the protection of the West or to a unity

33. Mackey, *Lebanon,* 50-52.

34. Entelis, *Pluralism and Party Transformation in Lebanon,* 45-47.

35. Phalange Basic Law, quoted in Michael Suleiman, *Political Parties in Lebanon* (Ithaca, N.Y., 1967), 232-35.

36. Press statement by Pierre Gemayel, translated in Beirut 548, March 22, 1955, NA 783A.00/3-2255.

37. Zamir, *Formation of Modern Lebanon,* passim.

38. Abu 'Izz al-Din, *Siyasat Lubnan,* 17-18.

or federation with the East."[39] This was quite a change for the Maronites, who in the nineteenth century had repeatedly sought European aid for protection against the Muslims and Druze. However, Khoury overstated the case. In essence, Solh and Khoury, Muslim and Christian, agreed to disagree. While committing themselves to an independent Lebanon in the short term, the Arab nationalists did not suddenly begin to think of Lebanon as a neutral country. The Christians still looked to Europe and viewed the surrounding Muslim world with anxiety; the Muslims still looked south and east to the Arab heartland.[40]

The reality of Lebanon as enshrined by the pact was sectarian, divided, and forever at odds. It was a mentality that not even Hobbes would have been proud of, for while Hobbes believed that the state existed to curb the antinomian tendencies of man, the Lebanese who framed the pact held that the state sanctified these divisions. Any weakening of the dividing lines could only come at the expense of one community and the profit of another. And while the National Pact succeeded in unifying the Lebanese elite, it underscored the fault lines within Lebanese society. As one scholar remarked, the pact demonstrated that "as a political culture, Lebanon is a collection of traditional communities bound by the mutual understanding that other communities cannot be trusted."[41] Thus, when Chamoun tried to swing Lebanon toward the West in 1957, a large portion of the ruling elite was deeply threatened. They believed that he had violated the pact, and they were determined to restore the status quo even if they had to destroy it first.

The pact was primarily an agreement between the two largest communities in Lebanon: the Maronite and the Sunni. The other Christian sects tended to side with the Maronites, and the interests of the Shi'i community were taken into consideration. The Druze, however, were largely left out of the pact. In the 1940s and 1950s, the two leading Druze lords were Majid Arslan and Kamal Jumblatt. Both were from old, powerful dynasties, but it was Jumblatt who occupied a pivotal position in the events of 1958.

Jumblatt was one of the most colorful characters to grace Lebanese politics. Born in 1917 and raised in his family demesne in the Shuf region, he rose to prominence in the 1940s. His modern house had been built on the ancient foundation of an old crusader castle, and Jumblatt combined elements of the old and new. On Sundays people came to his house to talk, complain, or ask for favors as many Lebanese did with their *zu'ama.*[42] They also came to hear

39. Quoted in Raghid Solh, "Lebanon and Arab Nationalism 1936-1945" (Ph.D. dissertation, St. Antony's College, Oxford, U.K., 1986), 289.

40. Hassan Saab, "The Rationalist School in Lebanese Politics," in *Politics in Lebanon,* ed. Binder, 276.

41. Michael Hudson, *The Precarious Republic* (New York, 1968), 34; David Gordon, *Lebanon: The Fragmented Nation* (London, 1980), passim.

42. Kamal Joumblatt, *I Speak for Lebanon,* trans. Michael Pallis (London, 1982), 31-32.

the news from their lord; as Jumblatt said, "in a way, I am their talking newspaper." He viewed the Druze faith as essentially unitarian: "The true Druze faith is the gnostic wisdom of Greece, Egypt, Persia and Islam all in one."[43] And as the heir to both a feudal and religious leadership role in the Druze community, Jumblatt understood his responsibilities. He commented, "I am often called 'the lord of Moukhtara,' sometimes a little ironically, as if there were some contradiction with my position as a progressive leader. I accept the epithet but not the intentions behind it: one must be a lord in the real sense of the term, lord of one's own life."[44] His family competed with the Chamouns and the Arslans for predominance in the Shuf, and Jumblatt's fight with Chamoun was in part a struggle over who would be lord of Deir al-Kamar.[45] Chamoun's dislike of Jumblatt, somewhat colored by the events of 1958, was expressed in his memoirs. He said that Jumblatt's father, on his deathbed, had confided in Chamoun that Kamal was "not normal" and asked Chamoun to treat the young man "with extreme patience."[46]

Jumblatt was a deputy in the chamber and head of the Progressive Socialist Party, which he had created in 1949. Although political parties in Lebanon were skeletal entities at best, Jumblatt developed a sophisticated platform. He was dedicated to a synthesis of east and west, with a bent toward socialism and pacifism. Gandhi was one of his heroes, and he accused Nasser of being a megalomaniac.[47] There was a mystical quality to his party's platform, which stated that the self-fulfillment of the individual was a primary goal in a world where industrialization had wrought incalculable spiritual harm. Jumblatt sought to reorient Lebanon away from confessionalism and toward a socialist Arab identity that would be distinctly Lebanese. He criticized the Maronites for valuing money above all else and valuing their Maronite identity before their Lebanese. That, he believed, was their great failing, and one that he feared would doom Lebanon.[48] In 1957–1958, he opposed Chamoun and the Maronite vision of Lebanon, for reasons personal, political, and ideological.[49]

Along with his progressive ideas for a socialist, independent Lebanon, he advocated a "third force" approach to international relations, a "neither East

43. Ibid., 37.

44. Ibid., 26.

45. Farid al-Khazen, "Kamal Jumblatt: The Uncrowned Druze Prince of the Left," *Middle East Studies,* XXIV (April 1988), 180; Kamal Jumblatt, *Haqiqat al-thawrah al-Lubnaniyya* [*The Truth about the Lebanese Revolution*] (Beirut, 1959).

46. Chamoun, *Crise au Moyen-Orient,* 392.

47. Suleiman, *Political Parties in Lebanon,* 219–21; Al-Khazen, "Kamal Jumblatt," 185; Mackey, *Lebanon,* 64.

48. Suleiman, *Political Parties in Lebanon,* 43–46, 219–24.

49. Jumblatt's opposition to Chamoun was evident to the United States as early as 1955. See Beirut 20, July 8, 1955, Confidential, NA 785A.00/7-855.

nor West" philosophy similar to that later espoused by Mosaddeq and then the nonaligned at Bandung. His thinking was in harmony with the National Pact, which had established Lebanon on the principle of nonalignment with the competing blocs within the Arab world. Under the pact, Lebanese foreign policy was supposed to ensure an independent Lebanon without serving the interests of one internal bloc over another.[50]

Until 1957, even Chamoun adhered to the "third force" principle. He refused to join the pro-Western Baghdad Pact, which united monarchical Iraq with Turkey and Pakistan. He also kept Lebanon outside of Nasser's pan-Arab orbit, much to the dismay of many Sunni and Shi'i leaders. His foreign minister, Dr. Charles Malik, the Harvard-educated former ambassador to Washington, was an international champion of nonalignment, and his keynote address at the Bandung Conference made almost as much of a splash as Nasser's.[51] Nonalignment, like the National Pact, seemed in the mid-1950s to be working. Then, abruptly, Chamoun shifted gears. He abandoned neutrality and endorsed the Eisenhower Doctrine. At almost the same time, Nasser began denouncing Maronite Lebanon. These were both fateful developments.

Although Nasser's attacks on Chamoun were a direct consequence of Chamoun's endorsement of the Eisenhower Doctrine in March 1957, Chamoun's acceptance of the doctrine was a direct consequence of his fear of Nasser and Nasserism. During the Suez crisis, Lebanon was one of the only Arab states not to break relations with Britain and France. For many of Nasser's supporters in the Middle East, that was interpreted as an active betrayal of Arab nationalism.[52] Several prominent members of Chamoun's cabinet resigned in protest, including Prime Minister Abdallah Yafi and Sa'eb Salam who would later be two of Chamoun's main opponents in the 1958 crisis. Replacing Yafi was Sami Solh, and Solh made Charles Malik foreign minister. The American embassy noted the change with some satisfaction:

> New Solh cabinet is strongest Lebanese Government in years and one most likely [to] respond [to] US policy. While Sami Solh perhaps not a strong man he has reputation for getting things done is still most popular leader among Sunni Moslems of Beirut and is known to be moderate and pro-West. Charles Malik needs no introduction. He is without doubt strongest

50. Abu 'Izz al-Din, *Siyasat Lubnan,* 24–25; Bayhum, *Lubnan,* 129.

51. Charles Malik, *The Problem of Coexistence* (Chicago, 1955). The speeches of Malik and Nasser are reprinted in *Afro-Asia Speaks from Bandung* (Jakarta, 1955). For the Arab perspective, see Mukhtâr Mazrâq, *Harakat adam al-inhiyâz fil alâqât il-dauliya* [*The Non-Aligned Movement in International Relations*] (Cairo, 1990).

52. Qubain, *Crisis in Lebanon,* 48; M. S. Agwani, ed., *The Lebanese Crisis* (New York, 1965), 2–4.

and most able man in Greek Orthodox community . . . [with]
well-known pro-Western sentiments.[53]

This pro-Western orientation of Chamoun not only angered Nasser, it alienated
competing factions within Lebanon. That orientation was made even clearer
when Chamoun's government accepted the Eisenhower Doctrine on March
16, 1957.[54] It was the only Arab country other than Iraq to do so. Leading
members of the anti-Chamoun opposition resigned from the Chamber of Deputies in disgust and formed a loose confederation known as the United Front.
Its platform: to restore Lebanon to its position as a neutral country.

Nasser reacted quickly. In an April 1957 broadcast of Radio Cairo, Chamoun
and his foreign minister, Charles Malik, were said to be "stooges of imperialism
. . . trying to stab the Arab people in the back in the heat of their gallant struggle
against imperialism. . . . Charles Malik and such are merely tools in the hands
of imperialism, carrying out its will and obeying its orders."[55] The war of words
between Nasser and Chamoun had begun.

The Eisenhower Doctrine initiated a series of events in the Middle East
and Lebanon that ultimately culminated in the 1958 civil war and the U.S.
intervention. Chamoun's reasons for adhering to the doctrine had to do with a
political calculation that the future of an independent Lebanon with a privileged
position for the Maronites could only be guaranteed by embracing Washington.
After Suez, Lebanon split into two loose but opposed camps. One, headed by
Chamoun and Malik, looked toward the West, not just politically but economically and culturally. The other—headed by individuals such as Yafi, Salem, the
Druze lord Kamal Jumblatt, and the Shi'i chief in Tripoli, Rashid Karami—
looked toward the Arab world, to the Arab nation, and to Nasser as their spiritual
leader.

53. Beirut 1277, re new Solh cabinet, November 19, 1956, Confidential, NA 783A.00/11-1956.

54. The text of the joint communique between Amb. Richards and the Government of Lebanon
is in Agwani, ed., *Lebanese Crisis,* 16–18.

55. Al-Sha'b Radio Cairo, June 15, 1957, in Qubain, *Crisis in Lebanon,* 53.

8

Lebanon

To the Shores of Tripoli

*People say Lebanon "adhered" to the Eisenhower Doctrine, or Leba-
non "joined" the Eisenhower Doctrine.... These statements have
no meaning at all. They are simply Communist propaganda. And
when they are made by scholars and professors in books, I pity the
scholarship that these people understand.... All that happened was
that the Americans acted, rightly or wrongly, without consulting
anybody in the world.... The unpardonable sin that some of us
committed, and we are very proud of it, and if this is a sin we are
sure to plead guilty eternally, the unpardonable sin was that we
took our independence seriously, and we decided that when Lebanon comes to a decision about its own destiny, its ultimate policy,
it consults nobody except itself.*

—Charles Malik

*The prospect of the spread of Nasserism into Lebanon, one of the
most pro-Western countries in the entire area, awoke lively reactions
in Washington.... By early June ... President Camille Chamoun,
who was rumored to have sent his wife's jewels and his grandson
out of the country, made urgent requests to the American Embassy
in Beirut ... for military equipment.... The Premier, Samy-as-Solh,
informed our Ambassador that the Lebanese people would welcome
assistance by American troops.*

—Robert Murphy

W hen the French, British, and Israelis tried to oust Nasser in October 1956 by invading Suez, Eisenhower refused to back them
because he could not support the reimposition of British and French colonial
control on the region. Having weakened the British and French, however,
Eisenhower realized that he had created a vacuum in the Middle East. Determined to fill that void with American, not Soviet, influence, Eisenhower presented an initiative to Congress on January 5, 1957. He asked that Congress
authorize the president to send military forces "to secure and protect the

territorial integrity and political independence of such nations, requesting such aid, against overt armed aggression from any nation controlled by International Communism."[1] In addition, Eisenhower wanted to supplement economic aid to the Middle East by $200 million above the amounts already appropriated. Appealing to the Senate to support the propose doctrine, Secretary of State John Foster Dulles said:

> We all, I know, recognize that the Middle East is a vital part of the free world. The people there have aspirations for liberty such as have always struck a responsive chord in the hearts of the American people. Much of the world's livelihood depends on the natural resources and avenues of trade of the Middle East. . . . It would be abhorrent and dangerous if that area were ruled by International Communism. Yet that is the present danger.[2]

After minimal debate, Congress voted to implement the Eisenhower Doctrine. Given, however, that international Communism was not a significant presence in any state in the Middle East (with the possible exception of Syria), Eisenhower clearly had another target in mind: Nasser and Arab nationalism.

In deliberations in the fall of 1956, the Eisenhower administration considered formally joining the Baghdad Pact.[3] As the brainchild of the conservative monarchical prime minister of Iraq, Nuri as-Said, the pact was the embodiment of status quo, anti-Nasser sentiment in the Middle East. While Iraq and Saudi Arabia championed a version of Arab nationalism, it was a far cry from the revolutionary, anti-imperialist, redistributive nationalism preached by Nasser. However, the United States decided that formally joining the pact would risk antagonizing those Arab states not in the pact.[4] Rather than becoming a member of the pact, the administration decided on the Eisenhower Doctrine. As the president explained to Jawaharlal Nehru, the United States refrained from the pact in part out of respect for the concerns of Nehru and the nonaligned. The Eisenhower Doctrine would allow the United States "to come

---

1. Quoted in Stephen Ambrose, *Eisenhower: The President,* 382. For the full text of Eisenhower's statement and of the resolution passed on March 9, see Agwani, ed., *Lebanese Crisis,* 4–16.

2. Department of State, Press Release, "Statement by the Honorable John Foster Dulles before a Joint Session of the Foreign Relations and Armed Services Committee of the Senate, January 14, 1957," In Box 8, Dulles/Herter Series, Eisenhower Library.

3. Memorandum of conversation with the president, November 21, 1956, Top Secret, DDE Diary, Box 19, Eisenhower Library.

4. George Lenczowski, *The Middle East in World Affairs* (Ithaca, N.Y., 1980), 283–87, 336–38; Fawaz Gerges, *The Superpowers and the Middle East: Regional and International Politics, 1955–1967* (Boulder, Colo., 1994), 25–30.

to the aid of those in the area who might want [U.S.] help if and when they should be attacked."[5]

Always lurking in the background was oil. Middle East oil reserves were not vital to the United States in the 1950s; domestic production of oil supplied American needs until the 1960s. Middle Eastern oil was, however, vital to Western Europe, which depended on petroleum from the Persian Gulf, Saudi Arabia, Iraq, and Iran. In addition, U.S. oil companies had vested interests in the Middle East, for they controlled the concessions in Saudi Arabia and were responsible for worldwide distribution. Lebanon figured into this picture because of Tapline, which transported Aramco (Arabian-American Oil Company) oil from Saudi Arabia through Syria and to the Mediterranean at the Lebanese port of Sidon.[6]

The betwixt-and-between policy of the administration toward Arab nationalism and Nasser was fully evident in the formation of the Eisenhower Doctrine. The refusal to support Britain, France, and Israel at Suez should have enhanced the image of the United States in the Middle East. Opposing the Suez invasion was both anti-imperialist and anti-Israel, and those were two of the lightning rods for Arab nationalism. Yet because the Eisenhower administration distrusted radical Arab nationalism and was ambivalent about continued British and French influence in the region, it did not consolidate the gains of Suez. Instead, Eisenhower put forth his proposal of January 1957. The results were predictable: the states already leaning toward the Western camp greeted the doctrine with enthusiasm, while Egypt, Syria, and significant minorities in Jordan and Lebanon denounced it.

Relative to Egypt or the Persian Gulf, Lebanon was a smaller piece in the puzzle of U.S. Middle East policy. Its army of seven thousand was no threat to anyone, and Communism had made negligible inroads. However, as Irene Gendzier has shown,[7] Beirut was the hub of U.S. intelligence activities in the Middle East, and the U.S. embassy in Beirut was an effective listening post and collator of espionage on regional developments. In addition, Beirut was a thriving commercial entrepôt that acted as conduit for trade between the Middle East and the West. Already by the late 1950s it was a commercial-banking center, and its cosmopolitan atmosphere made it a popular tourist destination for sun-worshippers throughout Europe and the United States. Known as the Paris of the eastern Mediterranean, it had a distinctly secular flavor. Lebanon was a potential ally, however small, and the U.S. government valued Middle Eastern

5. Eisenhower to Nehru, January 7, 1958, International Series, Box 27, Eisenhower Library; Patrick Seale, *The Struggle for Syria* (London, 1986), 286.

6. CIA-NIE 26, "Key Problems Affecting U.S. Efforts to Strengthen the Near East," April 25, 1951, Top Secret, CIA Research Reports, Mid-East, Reel 1. See also excerpts of NSC 120/1 (1952) quoted in Gendzier, "The Declassified Lebanon," in *Toward a Viable Lebanon,* ed. Barakat, 193-96; Gendzier, *Notes from the Minefield,* 160-71.

7. Gendzier, *Notes from the Minefield,* 160-71.

allies, no matter their size. Before Suez, the Eisenhower administration had provided Lebanon with moderate amounts of technical aid for roads and airports as well as nonlethal military equipment under the Mutual Security Act. The amount was less than $8 million for 1956.[8]

After Eisenhower announced his plan to Congress in January 1957, Lebanon became more important. As Chamoun began his tilt toward the West, the U.S. government began to search for Arab states willing to sign off on the proposed doctrine. While Charles Malik may have scoffed in later years at the notion that Lebanon adhered to the Eisenhower Doctrine,[9] that is precisely what it did. And the decision to do so paid off handsomely. It was understood by both Eisenhower and Chamoun that accession to the Eisenhower Doctrine came at the price of significantly increased U.S. aid to Lebanon. After Malik signaled support in January, the U.S. embassy in Beirut stated, "In recognition of this courageous support of United States and in light of our recent discussions with Chamoun and Solh on possible additional United States aid, we recommend immediate grant of $10 million fiscal year 1957 funds."[10] Charles Malik, who became foreign minister in Chamoun's post-Suez cabinet in late 1956, was the most effective Lebanese advocate of closer relations with the United States. Having lived in the United States for many years, Malik spoke fluent English and was more of an Americophone than the typical Lebanese Christian Francophone. Formerly the Lebanese ambassador in Washington, Malik also had close ties with none other than John Foster Dulles. When Eisenhower won the 1952 presidential election, Malik sent Dulles an official note of congratulations. Dulles responded within days and commented, "I greatly value what you say, especially since it comes from one for whom I have such high admiration."[11] Upon hearing of Dulles' appointment as secretary of state, Malik wrote another note, and Dulles responded, reiterating the sentiments expressed earlier.[12]

Of course, that correspondence demonstrates only that each official was properly schooled in diplomatic etiquette. Yet Malik and Dulles carried on a prolific and regular personal correspondence over the next several years, and its tone was unusually warm and friendly. In late 1953, Malik spoke to the American Political Science Association on the perils of Communism and the challenge to intellectuals. He sent a copy of the address to Dulles, and Dulles

8. Mutual Security Program—Outline of goals and spending for the Near East, FY 1958, WHC-Confidential Files, Box 42, Eisenhower Library. See also Beirut 319, January 30, 1956, Secret, NA 783A.5-MSP/1-3056; and Memorandum of Conversation, "Aid for Lebanon," June 21, 1956, Confidential, NA 783A.5-MSP/6-2156.

9. Charles Malik Oral History, John Foster Dulles Oral History Project, Mudd Library, Princeton University.

10. Beirut 1802, January 26, 1957, Confidential, NA 783A.5 MSP/1-2657.

11. Malik to Dulles, November 7, 1952; Dulles to Malik, November 10, 1952, John Foster Dulles Papers, Box 62, Mudd Library, Princeton University.

12. Malik to Dulles, December 15, 1952, Dulles to Malik, December 30, 1952, both ibid.

wrote a note endorsing Malik's views.[13] Later, Dulles asked Malik to entertain a young relative of the Dulles clan who was a Chase Manhattan Bank junior executive in Beirut. Malik complied, and Dulles sent a letter thanking him.[14]

These interchanges suggest a professional friendship. Malik was a man of some stature in Washington, and in the years before Dulles became secretary of state, he and Malik often gave speeches on similar topics with similar conclusions. In a 1952 *Foreign Affairs* article, Malik had written a critique of the feudal-agrarian structure of the Arab world, called for Arab unity, and suggested that Lebanon might be a mediating force between East and West.[15] Published by the Council on Foreign Relations, *Foreign Affairs* was the premier outlet for the views of the foreign-policy elite of the United States and allied countries. Malik was an intellectual and a diplomat who ensconced himself within the American establishment.

Malik's early enthusiasm for the nonaligned certainly distanced him from Dulles, but soon after Bandung, Malik began to have reservations about Nehru, Tito, and Nasser. He communicated these concerns to the U.S. government in conversations with Wilbur Eveland, a ranking CIA officer in the Middle East.[16] Furthermore, as an outspoken anti-Communist whose demeanor suggested refinement and culture, Malik was a powerful advocate of Lebanon in the United States, and his positive reputation in the eyes of Dulles[17] must have given Malik access and influence beyond that typically enjoyed by ambassadors from countries of Lebanon's size and significance. When the crisis of Lebanese politics accelerated in 1957 and erupted in 1958, Malik used this influence to full advantage.

The path was not easy, however. Having received the promise of $10 million in aid as a payoff for his public support of the Eisenhower Doctrine, Malik tried to negotiate that figure upward. The Eisenhower administration viewed Lebanon as an "important non-military base of US operations in the Arab world," and it was happy to extend "economic and technical assistance" in order to "maintain and, if possible, increase current Lebanese identification with US interests."[18] Malik, however, wanted more than "assistance"; he wanted direct aid or, to put it bluntly, cash. Claiming budget restraints,[19] the State Department was unwilling to increase aid to Lebanon as much as Malik wanted. Faced with this unexpected opposition, Malik heightened his rhetoric.

13. Malik enclosure to Dulles, September 10, 1953, John Foster Dulles Papers, Box 72.

14. Dulles to Malik, July 10, 1956, and Malik response, Dulles Papers, Box 105.

15. Charles Malik, "The Near East: The Search for Truth," *Foreign Affairs* (January 1952), 231–64.

16. Wilbur Crane Eveland, *Ropes of Sand* (New York, 1980), 113.

17. For further proof of this esteem, see Dulles' recommendation to Eisenhower that he meet with Malik in January 1957. Dulles memorandum for the president, January 14, 1957, Dulles/Herter Series, Box 8, Eisenhower Library.

18. Beirut 167, "Preliminary FY 1959 Program," October 1, 1957, Secret, NA 783A.5 MSP/10-157.

19. Beirut 1811, December 1, 1957, Confidential, NA 783A.5 MSP/12-157.

In conversations with the American embassy, Malik warned of the danger of Soviet influence in the region and especially in the UAR/Syria. At one meeting, Malik spoke of a "crisis of destiny which threatens to overwhelm Lebanon as a sovereign state. With each day that passes Communism gains fresh ground. . . . Then, too, the powers that be in both Egypt and Syria, together with their cohorts among the extreme Muslim nationalists in this country, are resolved by hook or crook to subjugate Lebanon."[20] Malik also made public pronouncements that the United States had promised levels of support which it clearly had not. In a speech to the Chamber of Deputies in November 1957, Malik expressed hope that the United States would soon provide Lebanon with ballistic missiles, and he reminded his audience that if the Lebanese government asked, the United States would oppose any aggression against Lebanon.[21] The Eisenhower Doctrine was hardly the open-ended commitment of this sort. It promised aid only in case of Communist aggression, but Malik attempted to stretch the security guarantee to cover any aggression, almost certainly with the threat of Nasser in mind.

The U.S. embassy was disconcerted by Malik's speech. Malik, however, told the ambassador that he had intended only to affirm close U.S.-Lebanese relations. The embassy secretary told Malik that the United States was sympathetic to increased aid for Lebanon, but that its capacity to advance such funds was limited. Malik responded that the U.S. government "could find funds if it sufficiently realized imminent danger of losing Lebanese and the Middle East." He stressed that the United States was faced with a choice of risking such a disaster or "giving concrete economic support now."[22]

Malik pressed his views on Robert McClintock, the U.S. ambassador after January 1958. McClintock recognized that the pro-Western government of Lebanon, and Malik in particular, had "staked its political life on being able to obtain substantial additional aid from the United States." As a result, McClintock informed the State Department, if the Eisenhower administration were "to state or otherwise demonstrate that it is not willing even to discuss positively additional aid with present Lebanese government, we would in effect almost certainly bring about its downfall."[23] While the ambassador did not believe that Lebanon needed the aid, he had succumbed to Malik's gambit. By creating an association between aid and the survival of the pro-Western Chamoun government, Malik made it increasingly difficult for the U.S. government to resist his entreaties. McClintock, a short, lean, mustachioed Irish-American with a sharp

20. Conversation between Malik and Alfred Haddad (Lebanese employee of the American Embassy) January 9, 1958 in Beirut 407, "Views of Foreign Minister Malik on Growth of Communist Influence," January 28, 1958. Secret. NA 783A.00/1-2858.

21. Quoted in Agwani, ed., *Lebanese Crisis*, 26–28.

22. Beirut 1811, December 1, 1957, Confidential, NA 785A.5 MSP/12-157.

23. Beirut 2236, January 2, 1958, Confidential, NA 783A.5 MSP/1-258.

temper, found both Malik and Chamoun exasperating,[24] and the State Department in Washington continued to vacillate on increased aid. The situation remained unresolved into the spring.

The urgency of Malik throughout 1957 and into 1958 regarding aid stemmed from shifts within Lebanon. Already upset with Chamoun's alignment with the West in late 1956 and early 1957, the opposition to Chamoun was further alienated by the elections of June 1957. In elections marred by violence, several prominent members of the opposition lost their parliamentary seats, including the Sunni leaders Abdallah Yafi and Sa'eb Salem, as well as the Druze lord Kamal Jumblatt.[25] Before the elections, Chamoun used his powers to create new parliamentary districts and change old ones. For example, Jumblatt now had to campaign in a district that was only partly Druze, the other portion being Maronite. The opposition deputy from Beirut, Sa'eb Salem, could no longer campaign in a purely Sunni district, and he, too, consequently lost.[26] The impetus toward redistricting may have been the creation of the United National Front (UNF) led by Salem, Abdullah Yafi, Rashid Karami, and rival Maronite leader and former foreign minister Hamid Franjieh. The manifesto of the UNF declared that the National Pact was inviolable and that Chamoun had violated the basic principles of Lebanese foreign policy when he embraced the Eisenhower Doctrine.[27] In the June elections, the UNF won only eight out of sixty-six seats and claimed fraud. Some prominent opponents of Chamoun were elected, including Rashid Karami of Tripoli, but many later commentators agreed that the vote was fraudulent.[28] Chamoun himself maintained until his death that the elections had been conducted fairly and accused the opposition of being nothing but mouthpieces for Nasser and his conspiracies.[29]

However, there is some indication of a conspiracy between Chamoun and the United States. In his memoirs, Wilbur Eveland claims that during the campaign he regularly traveled to the presidential palace with a suitcase full of money, which Chamoun and his advisers then distributed to their allies running for the chamber. Eveland claims that the CIA spent $50,000 alone on Charles Malik's victory.[30] Eveland's claims are difficult to corroborate, although his colleague and superior, Miles Copeland, said in *his* memoirs that the CIA regu-

---

24. Charles Thayer, *Diplomat* (New York, 1959), 2–3.

25. Beirut 697, "Anti-Americanism in Lebanon," June 5, 1958, Secret, NA 783A.00/6-558. On July 5, 1957, the opposition United National Front issued a manifesto detailing alleged voting frauds. For the text of the manifesto, see Agwani, ed., *Lebanese Crisis*, 35–36.

26. Arnold Hottinger, "Zu'ama and Parties in the Lebanese Crisis of 1958," *Middle East Journal*, 127–40.

27. Manifesto of April 1, 1957, in Agwani, ed., *Lebanese Crisis*, 29–32. The UNF platform is described in Bayhum, *Lubnan*, 131.

28. For example, Qubain, *Crisis in Lebanon*, 57; Al-Yusuf, *Thawrat al-ahrar*, 85.

29. Chamoun, *Crise au Moyen-Orient*, 383–85.

30. Eveland, *Ropes of Sand*, 252–57.

larly used money to influence elections not just in Lebanon, but in Syria as well.[31] Certainly, both the CIA and Chamoun had motivation for rigging the elections that would determine the chamber that would elect the new president in the summer of 1958. Under the Lebanese constitution, the president was limited to one term. The chamber, however, could amend the constitution, and Chamoun planned to run again.

The elections of 1957 were a political miscalculation by Chamoun.[32] As long as the leading *zu'ama* of the opposition were in Parliament, they could express their discontent through normal political channels. Commenting on the victory "for the pro-American policy of the Lebanese government," the U.S. ambassador remarked that the position of the Chamoun government might actually have been "more solid if a few influential Moslem leaders such as Abdullah Yafi . . . had been elected."[33] Excluded from the chamber, they had to find other outlets for their political ambitions.

The major crisis after the elections concerned Syria,[34] the problem child of the Middle East at the time. Its government was unstable; the country had seen multiple coups in the previous decade; and it was the weak link in the Northern Tier strategy of the United States. Nasser's influence in Syria was pronounced, and there was a strong Syrian movement working toward unification with Egypt. After the Syrian defense minister signed an economic-and-technical-aid pact with the Soviet Union in August 1957, the Eisenhower administration was convinced that Syria was fast becoming a Soviet satellite. On August 12, the Syrian government accused the United States of plotting against it. This accusation, apparently legitimate, led the Eisenhower administration to dispatch Loy Henderson, former architect of Greek aid and the Iran coup, to Turkey, Iraq, and Lebanon to coordinate anti-Syrian measures. Turkey's Adnan Menderes, Iraq's King Faysal, and Chamoun in Lebanon all urged action against Syria, but none was willing to be the first state to go out on a limb by publicly denouncing the Syrian government and asking the U.S. government for aid. In the end, despite an extensive campaign waged by the United States Information Agency, the Syrian crisis passed without any concrete action. In the process, the pro-Western Arab states lost ground to Nasser, who widely trumpeted the "conspiracy" of the "stooges of western imperialism" in the Middle East. Within six months, the Nasserite forces in Syria were victorious. In early 1958, Syria unified

31. Copeland, *Game of Nations,* passim.

32. Some commentators cite the elections as a direct cause of the civil war in 1958. See Leila Meo, *Lebanon: Improbable Nation* (Westport, Conn., 1965), 213–17.

33. Beirut 3073, June 17, 1957, Confidential, NA 783A.00/6-1757. See also Beirut 22 (Airgram), July 17, 1957, Confidential, NA 783A.00/7-1757.

34. The following discussion is drawn from Seale, *Struggle for Syria,* 286–300; David Lesch, *Syria and the United States: Eisenhower's Cold War in the Middle East* (Boulder, Colo., 1992), 141–50; and Gerges, *Superpowers and the Middle East,* 84–90.

with Egypt to form the United Arab Republic.[35] Although Syria was technically an equal partner in this union, in fact it was dominated by Nasser. It was also politically divided, with Arab nationalists fighting Communists, Communists fighting Syrian nationalists, and individuals loyal to the Hashemite monarchies of Iraq and Jordan trying to replace Nasser's UAR with a Hashemite-led pan-Arab state.

The events in Syria both drew Lebanon closer to the United States and enhanced Nasser's reputation at the expense of the Americans. During the crisis, Malik met with Henderson and warned of "the Communist thrust in Syria." He explained that the current problem was a "natural outgrowth of years of Communist preparations" and was in part an "answer to the Eisenhower Doctrine." Malik stressed that the "danger to Lebanon from subversion fomented and directed by a malignant Communism or neutralism or anti-Westernism in Syria is greater than danger of direct aggression from that country." Malik then took Henderson to meet with Chamoun. The Lebanese president told the U.S. envoy that "Communist subversion from Syria had already begun in Lebanon." There was, however, little evidence that Lebanon was in any danger of turning Communist, and both the United States and the Lebanese knew that.[36]

Chamoun and Malik's arguments are identical to those they made less than a year later when civil war erupted in Lebanon. The Syrian crisis of 1957 showed them that the Eisenhower administration was prepared to act in the region to counter radical regimes. They noted that the U.S. government did not require proof of Communist influence; it would act even if Communist aggression was "indirect." Given the U.S. attitude toward Nasser and radical Arab nationalism as serving the interests of the Soviet Union in the Middle East, indirect aggression could mean Nasserism. Malik made sure to cover all bases when he spoke of "Communism, neutralism or anti-Westernism." Communism was the catchword, but the other two forces were of equal concern to the United States. Chamoun and Malik must also have noted that the United States would only act if a regional ally fronted for them. Inaction over Syria was in part the result of the unwillingness of any state in the region to align publicly with a U.S.-backed intervention. In the summer of 1958, having inexorably committed himself to the United States, Chamoun would not have such misgivings.

Toward the end of 1957 and into 1958, there were widespread rumors that Chamoun intended to run for a second term. With the opposition members out of the chamber, Chamoun appeared to have enough votes to pass an amendment. As the furor erupted over these unconfirmed but ultimately accurate rumors, the union of Syria and Egypt into one United Arab Republic was announced on February 1, 1958. Many members of the opposition greeted the announcement with wild enthusiasm. Yafi proclaimed that the UAR would be

---

35. Malcolm Kerr, *The Arab Cold War, 1958-1964* (Oxford, U.K., 1965).

36. Beirut 563, August 28, 1957, Top Secret, Dulles/Herter Series, Box 9. Eisenhower Library.

the best guarantor of Lebanese security. Sa'eb Salem traveled to Damascus along with nearly 300,000 other Lebanese to salute the leadership of Nasser in the Arab world.[37] Rashid Karami met with Nasser on February 27 and declared, "We in the Lebanon believe that Lebanon is of the Arabs and for the Arabs. The Lebanese people, O President [Nasser], believe in your principles and mission, and are following your footsteps and example. . . . You can rest assured, O President, that when the hour strikes we will all leap up as one man to hoist the banner to which all the Arabs will rally—this is the banner which we wish to fly above us all. . . . If not we would rather all die for its sake."[38] Given the historic ties between Lebanon and Syria, some of the enthusiasm for joining the UAR may have had less to do with Nasser than with a tradition of Lebanese identity that saw Syria and Lebanon as one. However, the appeal of ascendent Nasserism was undeniable. Furthermore, Chamoun's opponents saw an opportunity to use Nasser to advance their campaign against Chamoun.

Meanwhile, Chamoun was preparing for a fight. The army was commanded by General Fuad Chehab, who would figure prominently in the summer crisis and ultimately succeed Chamoun. As early as mid-1957, Chehab let it be known that he would not allow Chamoun to use the army for his personal ambitions.[39] That precluded employing the military to undermine the opposition. As a result, Chamoun began to cultivate the Phalange, the PPS, the Lebanese gendarmerie, and his own private militia.[40] The opposition, meanwhile, gathered their own forces. Sa'eb Salem in the Basta district of Beirut, the Karamis in Tripoli, Jumblatt in the mountains east of Beirut, Shi'i notables in the south, these *zu'ama* commanded their own irregular militias. With the formation of the UAR, the situation in the countryside became increasingly tense, and Chamoun and Malik alleged that the opposition was being supplied by the Syrians, and ultimately by their master, Nasser.

In the spring of 1958, Malik began a renewed campaign for aid. He raised the stakes yet further and suggested that in the absence of further U.S. aid, Chamoun would fall and an anti-American government would come to power in Lebanon.[41] As of April, the State Department was sympathetic but still unresponsive. Dulles instructed the embassy to "inform Malik that in desire to be helpful . . . we have again reviewed Lebanese aid request at highest levels in Department. . . . We greatly regret that we have been unable to find funds to meet Malik's request."[42] This reluctance to acquiesce reflected State's growing ambivalence about the wisdom of Chamoun's seeking a second term.

37. Qubain, *Crisis in Lebanon*, 62–66.

38. Quoted in Agwani, ed., *Lebanese Crisis*, 44–45.

39. See Chehab conversation with U.S. Army attaché, May 30, 1957, Beirut 554, April 2, 1958, Secret, NA 783A.00/4-258. See also Beirut 2582, January 31, 1958, Secret, NA 783A.00/1-3158.

40. Beirut 637, September 5, 1957, Confidential, NA 783A.00/9-557.

41. Beirut 3431, April 15, 1958, Confidential, NA 783A.5 MSP/4-1558.

42. State 4106 sent to Beirut, April 29, 1958, Confidential, NA 783A.5 MSP/4-2858.

As tension mounted in the spring, the American ambassador in Beirut, Robert McClintock, declared that "it would be better for Lebanon, U.S. interests and the Arab world generally . . . if [Chamoun] stepped down at the end of his presidential term next September."[43] McClintock himself did not exactly see eye to eye with Eisenhower on Middle East policy. Throughout the crisis, he remained skeptical of the Chamoun-Malik chorus of impending doom. However, he seems to have diligently followed orders, whatever his personal views might have been.[44]

After months of armed tension, civil order disintegrated in May 1958. On May 8, the anti-Chamoun journalist Nasib Matni was gunned down in Beirut. The opposition immediately suspected that Chamoun was behind the assassination. That same day, forces loyal to the Karamis revolted in Tripoli. Violence spread to Beirut, where Sa'eb Salem and his militia seized control of the Basta district. Allied with the opposition United Front (UNF), Kamal Jumblatt attacked Chamoun's presidential palace at Bayt al-Din. Despite Chamoun's entreaties, General Chehab refused to intercede, and Chamoun called on the Phalange and the gendarmerie to combat the rebels. Charles Malik announced that the rebels were being aided by Syrian forces under the command of Nasser. The UNF countered that it was not they but Malik and Chamoun who were inviting foreign intervention by the United States and the Iraqis. In press releases of May 17 and 22, the United Front charged Chamoun with attempting to divert the focus away from the crisis of his presidency and Lebanese politics and onto an external scapegoat. In the eyes of the United Front, the insurrection stemmed from "the interference of the Western Powers and the Baghdad Past Powers." Having utterly failed as president, Chamoun and "his clique" were trying to shift the blame to the United Arab Republic. More ominously, this clique was attempting to "internationalize the domestic crisis and justify foreign intervention and the landing of foreign forces on Lebanese soil, thereby converting Lebanon into a base for a cold war in this region and subsequently a battlefield for a bloody and destructive war."[45]

The prescience of the opposition may in part have derived from information leaked to them from the Lebanese foreign ministry. On May 14, less than ten days before this press release, Ambassador McClintock informed Chamoun that the United States was "prepared upon appropriate request from President and GOL [Government of Lebanon] to send certain combat forces to Lebanon which would have dual mission of protecting American life and property and assisting GOL in its military program for preservation of independence and integrity of Lebanon which is vital to national interests of US and to world peace."[46] It may

43. Beirut 3310, April 3, 1958, Top Secret, *FRUS, 1958-1960, Vol. XI,* 20-21.

44. Thayer, *Diplomat,* 1-38.

45. Quoted in Agwani, ed., *Lebanese Crisis,* 76-77.

46. State 797/State 4253 to UN Ambassador and American Embassy, Paris, May 14, 1958, Top Secret, Eyes Only Lodge and Houghton, NA 783A.00/5-1458.

161

also be that the opposition had no direct knowledge of this communique, but they knew Chamoun and understood his goals. Their warning of what Chamoun intended was fully on target, although they were disingenuous in claiming that their insurrection was purely reactive and defensive in nature.

The two months between the outbreak of civil war and the U.S. intervention in July were filled with charges and countercharges by Chamoun and the opposition along the lines discussed above. Meanwhile, the Eisenhower administration was trapped between its pledge to support Lebanon's integrity and its desire not to use U.S. troops. Eisenhower and his advisers did not want to intervene. The costs and risks were high, and they feared that the presence of U.S. troops in the region could easily backfire to Nasser's advantage. At the same time, they were confronted with a relentless campaign waged by Malik and Chamoun to force an intervention. The White House had put off Lebanese demands for increased economic and military aid before May, but Malik had succeeded in sowing a seed of doubt that U.S. efforts were insufficient. When the civil war broke out in May, the Eisenhower administration was torn between its desire to shore up its allies and its resentment at what it perceived as Chamoun's attempts at "economic blackmail."[47]

During these two months, domestic Lebanese politics intersected with regional rivalries and U.S. foreign policy to produce an intervention. Chamoun's attempts to alter the political balance in Lebanon created a crisis. He and Malik chose to internationalize an internal dispute by enlisting the aid of the United States, Great Britain, and France. Their opponents attempted to enlist the aid of Nasser and Syria, and the two sides succeeded in turning the civil war into an international crisis. Chamoun and his allies presented the events after May 1958 as a function of Nasserite infiltration from Syria, while the opposition claimed that it was a function of western intervention on Chamoun's behalf. Each side developed its case in the press, over the airwaves, and in the chambers of the UN Security Council, and each side claimed that the other had violated the National Pact—Chamoun by aligning with the West, the opposition by aligning with Nasser and the Arab world.

With its predisposition to view Nasserism as a short step from Communism, the United States became more willing to intervene as it became more convinced that Chamoun's interpretation was correct. In assessing what it would do, the Eisenhower administration was animated by at least two considerations: what was the cause of the civil war, and would American interests in the region be hindered or helped by a military intervention? The United States government essentially agreed with Chamoun and Malik that the revolt was sustained by Nasser and the UAR. On May 15, Dulles instructed the American ambassador in Cairo, Raymond Hare, to tell Nasser that, in the view of the United States, "The legally constituted Government of Lebanon, a country which is friend of

47. Allen Dulles to the NSC, May 9, 1958, Minutes of the 365th Meeting of the National Security Council, DDE, Whitman File, NSC Records; *FRUS, 1958-1960, Vol. XI,* 35.

US, is . . . object of effort to destroy its authority and its overthrow by promotion of insurrection. We have received from source independent of GOL circumstantial evidence that those engaged in this subversive effort in Lebanon are being aided by elements and arms from UAR."[48] Dulles concluded with a veiled warning that the United States was committed to Lebanon's autonomy and that Nasser should think seriously about the effects of further UAR interference in Lebanon's domestic affairs.

However, while Malik maintained that the opposition was composed of "Communist, Nasserite, neutralist, anti-American, anti-Western, or other anti-Lebanese forces,"[49] the Americans did not believe that Communism was a factor in the dispute. In 1958, there were estimated to be fewer than eight thousand Communists in Lebanon,[50] and Ambassador McClintock, both at the time and in later writings, stated that he had never believed the UAR to be controlled by international Communism.[51] Ambassador Robert Murphy, formerly the invisible hand of the American high commissioner in postwar Germany who was sent to Lebanon in July, stated in his memoirs that "much of the conflict concerned personalities and rivalries of a domestic nature. . . . Communism was playing no direct or substantial part in the insurrection, although Communists no doubt hoped to profit from the disorders."[52] At the time, both McClintock and Dulles acknowledged that the absence of Communism as a significant factor would make it difficult to justify American intervention under the Eisenhower Doctrine.

As soon as the riots broke out on May 8, Chamoun mooted the possibility of American intervention. On May 11, Malik asked what the U.S. response might be to a request for a division of marines.[53] Two days later, Eisenhower and his advisers discussed the issue at the White House. Dulles "pointed out that he did not see how we could invoke the provisions of the Middle East [Eisenhower] Doctrine . . . since that would entail a finding that the United Arab Republic had attacked Lebanon and that the United Arab Republic was under the control of international Communism."[54]

But in spite of its reservations, the Eisenhower administration instructed McClintock to issue the assurance of May 14 quoted above. In addition to promising intervention as a last resort, McClintock stressed that U.S. troops

48. State 3117, May 15, 1958, Top Secret, *FRUS, 1958–1960, Vol. XI*, 54–55.

49. Letter of Malik to Dulles, May 11, 1958, NA 783A.00/5-1158.

50. Suleiman, *Political Parties in Lebanon*, 74.

51. Robert McClintock, *Meaning of Limited War*, 102–103.

52. Murphy, *Diplomat among Warriors*, 404.

53. Beirut 3779, May 11, 1958, Top Secret, NA 783A.00/5-1158, *FRUS, 1958–1960, Vol. XI*, 38–39.

54. Memorandum of Conversation, White House, May 13, 1958, DDE, Dulles Papers, reprinted in *FRUS, 1958–1960, Vol. XI*, 45–47. Dulles noted that under the provisions of the Mansfield Amendment to the Eisenhower Doctrine, U.S. troops could be deployed for the more general purpose of preserving the independence and integrity of Middle East nations.

would not be deployed to support the administration of Chamoun but only the "integrity" of Lebanon.[55] The United States demanded that before it took any action, Lebanon must submit its grievances to the Security Council. Dulles was asked at a press conference several days later whether the Eisenhower Doctrine could apply to the current situation in Lebanon. He answered that the United States did not believe that Lebanon was under armed attack from a country "under the control of international Communism." That didn't mean, however, that the United States could not take action. "There is," Dulles explained, "the provision of the Middle East resolution which says that the independence of these countries is vital to peace and the national interest of the United States. That is certainly a mandate to do something if we think that our peace and vital interests are endangered from any quarter." And of course, the secretary added, the U.S. government had "a duty" to protect "American life and property." Nonetheless, he assured the press that the administration was "not anxious to have a situation which would be in any sense a pretext for introducing American forces into the area."[56]

In private, administration officials as well as McClintock in Beirut were adamant that the goal of any intervention was not Chamoun's political survival. Chamoun, in fact, was to be "disabused of any thought that he has a blank check . . . with regard to military intervention."[57] Dulles also made sure that Chamoun understood the U.S. position: Chamoun was not to run again. Intervention would take place only to save Lebanon.[58] McClintock, however, doubted if Chamoun was capable of resisting the temptation to use the chaos and civil war to enhance his own power.[59]

Following the suggestion of the State Department, the Lebanese government took its case to the UN Security Council in June, alleging foreign interference from the UAR and calling on the UN to put a stop to it. Malik addressed the council with a laundry list of accusations. Included in his speech was a comprehensive array of press clippings demonstrating the UAR's antipathy to Chamoun and a series of accusations that arms and men were infiltrating Lebanon from the Syrian border, stirring up unrest.[60]

The UAR delegate countercharged that, far from intervening in Lebanon's internal affairs, it only wished to see Lebanon's integrity and independence

55. State to Lodge (UN), May 14, 1958, NA 783A.00/5-1458; State to Baghdad 2966, May 14, 1958, NA 783A.00/5-1458.

56. Statement of May 20, 1958, State Department press release PR 280, John Foster Dulles Papers, Box 128, Mudd Library, Princeton University.

57. Memorandum of a Conversation: Dulles meeting with the British ambassador and others, June 18, 1958, Top Secret, *FRUS, 1958-1960, Vol. XI,* 153-55.

58. State 5080, June 29, 1958, Top Secret, *FRUS, 1958-1960, Vol. XI,* 184.

59. Beirut 14, July 1, 1958, Top Secret, *FRUS, 1958-1960, Vol. XI,* 190-92.

60. The text of Malik's speech is reprinted in Agwani, ed., *Lebanese Crisis,* 122-59.

preserved from Chamoun's attempts to subject the Lebanese people to the will of the West and violate both the charter of the Arab League and Lebanon's own National Pact.[61] And within Lebanon, the opposition complained that Chamoun was relying on U.S. military aid to suppress the revolt. Jumblatt told U.S. embassy officials that by giving weapons to Chamoun's partisans, particularly the Phalange (Al-Kata'ib) party headed by Pierre Jumayyil, the United States was creating a vicious circle whereby Chamoun's opponents had to turn to the UAR.[62]

In mid-June 1958, the Security Council decided to dispatch an observation group to monitor supposed infiltrations. This group, called UNOGIL (United Nations Observation Group in Lebanon), consisted of representatives from Ecuador, India, and Norway, and it numbered nearly one hundred officers by the end of June. Much to Chamoun's dismay, when UNOGIL made its first report on July 1, it declared that there was scant evidence of large-scale infiltration and equally slim proof that Lebanese rebels were receiving arms from the UAR. Of course, UNOGIL admitted that it functioned under certain handicaps, including an inability to conduct observations at night and the inaccessibility of all but 18 kilometers of the 324-kilometer-long border with Syria because that was all that Chamoun's government controlled.[63]

UNOGIL's preliminary conclusions did not wholly contradict those of the Americans. In June, McClintock wrote that although there "had been undoubted subversion and infiltration from UAR," it was less in the way of arms and men than in press and radio incitements against Chamoun. While debilitating for Chamoun, these hardly warranted American military intervention.[64] However, the presence of UNOGIL was not seen as a positive development by Washington. Knowing that the group would find little material evidence of outside interference, the CIA reported that "the sending of UN observers to Lebanon makes it more difficult . . . to justify an intervention on the ground of countering UAR penetrations."[65]

Neither policy makers in Washington nor Chamoun's government was sure if the introduction of American military forces would be for the best. Once it had been established that under no circumstances would the United States intervene simply to help Chamoun amend the constitution and remain in power, it became a question of whether the United States should intervene to deter Nasser and secure Lebanon's pro-Western orientation.

Many were concerned that sending in the marines might have just the opposite effect. The CIA discussed the likelihood of an anti-American backlash should

---

61. Ibid., 159–81.

62. Beirut 4414, June 3, 1958, Top Secret, NA 783A.00/6-358.

63. Extract of UNOGIL Report, July 1, 1958, in Agwani, ed., *Lebanese Crisis*, 211–14.

64. Beirut 4404, June 2, 1958, Top Secret, NA 783A.00/6-258.

65. Special National Intelligence Estimate (SNIE 36.4-1-58), "The Lebanese Crisis," June 14, 1958, Top Secret, Dept. of State INR-NIE Files, *FRUS, 1958–1960, Vol. XI*, 120–22.

U.S. troops be deployed, and Dulles, McClintock and others shared this concern.[66] For his part, Chamoun was content to be an ally of the West but he preferred if possible to win his fight with minimal assistance.[67] He also realized by early July that he would be unable to remain president for a second term. It then became a question of ensuring that the next president was not an ally of his opponents.

The Eisenhower administration drew up plans for a landing code-named Operation Blue Bat, and it consulted with the British and the French.[68] McClintock, meanwhile, worked with Chamoun, Malik and opposition leaders to engineer a political settlement. The focus of these efforts was the Lebanese chief of staff Fuad Chehab. Many believed that if Chamoun would agree not to run again and hand over the presidency to Chehab, the crisis could be resolved. By all accounts, Chehab was an honest, upright man with no political ambitions. He had little tolerance for Communism and extreme Arab nationalism and little regard for what he saw as Chamoun's craven capitulation to the West.[69] By keeping the army neutral and refusing to suppress the fighting on Chamoun's behalf, Chehab made it known that he considered the revolt an internal matter of traditional Lebanese politics.

Throughout June and July, the situation was in flux. At one moment, it seemed as if a political settlement would be reached; the next, the rhetoric heated up and opposing factions clashed in the streets. In a late June press conference, Chamoun described what he claimed was foreign intervention in Lebanon in the form of weapons and financial aid supplied to his opponents, not to mention a "long and venomous campaign by the Press and Radio characterized by hatred and an appeal to rise in revolt." He continued, "These campaigns have been pursued without interruption during the last three months, through a controlled Syrian and Egyptian press and through nationalized Radio broadcasts in these countries."[70]

By July, the "Chehab solution" seemed to offer the greatest hope that the conflict could be terminated, but Chamoun insisted on serving out his term until the end of September—and that was unacceptable to his opponents. Meanwhile, Eisenhower stationed the Sixth Fleet in the eastern Mediterranean off the coast of Lebanon. That is how things stood when news arrived from Baghdad on July 14 that King Faysal II; his uncle Abdul-Ilah; and the scion of pro-Western governments in the Middle East, Nuri as-Said, had been overthrown and murdered in a coup by an obscure army officer who was rumored to be

66. Ibid.

67. Chamoun, *Crise au Moyen-Orient,* passim.

68. State to London, July 1, 1958, Top Secret, NA 783A.00/6-2658.

69. Beirut 554, "Conversation Between General Fuad Chehab and Colonel Robert Works, U.S. Army Attaché," May 30, 1957, NA 783A.00/4-2558. See also Beirut 3580, April 27, 1958, Top Secret, NA 783A.00/4-2658. For a good portrait of Chehab, see Mackey, *Lebanon,* 132-36.

70. Excerpted in Agwani, ed., *Lebanese Crisis,* 90-92.

a follower of Nasser. Within forty-eight hours, Eisenhower had authorized the landing of U.S. Marines in Lebanon, on the urgent request of Camille Chamoun.

Chamoun's reaction to the events in Iraq was to say to Washington "I told you so." McClintock reported that on July 14 Chamoun summoned him and said that the American "government . . . consistently underestimated this warning of danger in the Middle East. . . . Now [Chamoun said] developments in Baghdad had proved him right and US wrong. . . . Chamoun said he did not wish any more inquiries or specifications or conditions re our intervention. He would interpret our intention by our deed. He wanted 6th Fleet here within 48 hours or else he would know where he stood re assurances of support from West."[71]

In Washington, Eisenhower and Dulles decided that the costs of inaction were unacceptable. Although they knew that an American intervention risked fanning the flames of anti-Americanism in the Middle East, they believed it would be far worse if Lebanon succumbed to revolution and was lost as an American asset.[72] Briefing congressional leaders on his decision to send troops, Eisenhower and Dulles listed the consequences of American inaction. "The first consequence of not going in would certainly be that non-Nasser governments in the Middle East and adjoining areas would quickly be overthrown. . . . Senator Knowland said that . . . throughout the world a failure on our part to act would be a tremendous victory for Nasser."[73]

When Eisenhower made a public announcement of the marine landings on July 15, he stressed that they were at the invitation of the Lebanese government and that their primary mission was to protect American lives and property and preserve Lebanese independence. American lives and property were never really in danger, but Lebanon's stability was.

After months of hesitancy about intervention, Eisenhower made the decision to intervene with surprising swiftness. The Iraqi coup undoubtedly took him and the world by surprise, and the sudden collapse of the conservative, pro-Western Iraqi monarchy was a jolt to U.S. strategy in the region. Eisenhower was, in his own words, "shocked" by the coup and feared the elimination of Western influence in the Middle East.[74] Briefing the president, Allen Dulles reported that "the coup action was taken by pro-Nasir elements led by young army officers and backed by the mob."[75] There seemed to be little time for

71. Beirut 358, July 14, 1958, Top Secret, NA 783A.00/7-1458; *FRUS, 1958-1960, Vol. XI*, 207-208.

72. Memo of Conference with the President, July 14, 1958, DDE, Whitman File, Eisenhower Diary Series, Eisenhower Library; *FRUS, 1958-1960, Vol. XI*, 211-15.

73. Ibid., 218-20.

74. Dowty, *Middle East Crisis*, 50; Tillema, *Appeal to Force*, 110; William Quandt, "Lebanon, 1958 and Jordan, 1970," in *Force without War*, ed. Blechman and Kaplan, 232-39.

75. Briefing Notes by Allen Dulles, July 14, 1958, 2:30 PM, Top Secret, CIA Research Reports, Mid-East, Reel 1.

deliberation, and Eisenhower used his power as commander-in-chief to send in the marines.

The level of anxiety was undoubtedly raised a notch by appeals from other states in the region, calling on the United States to act and warning that a number of other countries could succumb at any moment to the same forces that had murdered Faysal and Abdul-Ilah. King Saud of Saudi Arabia demanded intervention not just in Lebanon, but in Jordan and Iraq itself. He threatened that if the United States and Great Britain failed to do something, Saudi Arabia would be left with no choice but to cooperate with the UAR.[76] The Turkish government urged an immediate intervention in Jordan and Lebanon, and the Iranians echoed these sentiments.[77] The Pakistani and Iranian ambassadors to the United States suggested that the case be brought to the UN Security Council, but they said there was no time to wait for the UN to deliberate; U.S. troops must be dispatched first.[78]

The situation was complicated by another crisis breaking in Jordan. King Hussein was another favored target of Radio Cairo in 1957 and 1958. Jordan was a weak country whose army was until 1956 largely controlled by a British officer. Hussein was related to Faysal, and he drew closer to Iraq after the formation of the UAR. As a colonial creation with no history of autonomy, Jordan was more susceptible than Lebanon to the winds of pan-Arabism. Hussein was only twenty-three years old when the Iraqi coup occurred, and his position was precarious. Radio Cairo called for his ouster and the absorption of Jordan into the UAR. In April 1957, the United States had dispatched the Sixth Fleet to the eastern Mediterranean after a coup attempt in Amman rattled Hussein's regime. Shortly before the July 1958 coup, King Hussein uncovered a supposed plot by pro-Syrian Jordanian army officers. When news of the Iraqi coup broke on July 14, the British coordinated plans with the United States, and the U.S. intervention in Lebanon was matched by a British force of paratroopers in Jordan.[79]

But Eisenhower's desire to establish U.S. credibility in the region, the crisis atmosphere, pressure from regional allies, and the urging of the British and French[80] were not themselves sufficient to force a U.S. intervention. For more than a year, U.S. officials had been bombarded by Malik and Chamoun with pleas for aid. These requests were put in the context of the threat posed to Lebanon by Nasserism and Communism, and Malik in particular used the opening provided by the Eisenhower Doctrine as justification for his entreaties. In

---

76. Ibid.

77. Memorandum of Conference with the President, July 14, 1958, *FRUS, 1958-1960, Vol. XI,* 218-24.

78. Memorandum of a Conversation among the Turkish, Pakistani, and Iranian ambassadors and State Department officials, July 14, 1958, *FRUS, 1958-1960, Vol. XI,* 228-30.

79. Kamal Salibi, *The Modern History of Jordan* (New York, 1993), 191-203.

80. William Roger Louis, "Britain and Lebanon in the 1950s" (paper presented at conference on the U.S. intervention in Lebanon, University of Texas, Austin, 1991).

the months leading up to the outbreak of civil war in May, Malik renewed his campaign. While the State Department consistently refused the requests for more aid, the requests had an effect.[81] Before July 14, U.S. officials were inclined to ascribe personal and internecine political motives to the Lebanese government in pushing for aid. Yet, after witnessing the Iraqi coup, Eisenhower, Dulles, McClintock and the U.S. foreign policy establishment were able to use a set of justifications that had been developed for them by Malik, Chamoun, and the partisans of the Lebanese government. They were already disposed to believe the worst of Nasser. Although U.S. officials had given Nasser and the UAR the benefit of the doubt before July, after July 14 the Lebanese government's accusations seemed validated. In discussing the question of intervention with his top advisers on July 14, Eisenhower parroted arguments that might have come verbatim from Malik and Chamoun. This is not to say that U.S. officials had not arrived at a similar analysis of the situation on their own, but there was a striking similarity between the internal arguments for intervention in Washington and the arguments pressed on Washington by the Lebanese government in the months preceding. In addition to the regional aims of U.S. foreign policy that pushed Eisenhower to intervene, there was the pull of Lebanese warnings that had made a subtle imprint on official Washington even before those warnings were taken altogether seriously.

Malik, Chamoun, and regional allies such as the Turks, the Pakistanis, and the Iranians tailored what they said to suit U.S. strategic sensibilities. That may account for the careless brandishing of the word "Communism" when there was no clear Communist threat. Knowing of U.S. sensitivity about Communism, various individuals may have consciously or unconsciously dangled the threat of Communism as bait. The wooing of a powerful patron by weaker, peripheral clients often leads the client to internalize the world view of the patron. The suitor's task is made far easier when he speaks the same language as his intended target. Thus, while the real motivation for Lebanese requests for intervention may have been purely local and driven by confessional rivalries, they presented their case in terms of U.S. strategic concerns in the Middle East. While the real motivation of the Iranians, Saudis, and Jordanians may have been to defeat progressive forces within their own borders, they couched their demands for intervention in terms of the danger of Communism and Nasserism.

Eisenhower dispatched the first contingent of marines to Beirut on July 15. At the height of the deployment in August, there would be approximately fifteen thousand U.S. troops stationed in Lebanon, but the numbers were smaller at first. The marines made an amphibious landing from the ships of the Sixth Fleet. On a sunny July afternoon on the beaches of Beirut, fully armed and poorly briefed, they waded ashore. The American soldiers found themselves

81. For examples of aid requests and U.S. refusals, see Beirut 3431, April 15, 1958, Confidential, NA 783A.5 MSP/4-1558; State to Beirut [no number], April 29, 1958, Confidential, NA 783A.5-MSP/4-2858; and Beirut 3715, May 7, 1958, Secret, NA 783A.5 MSP/5-753.

amid surprised sunbathers, who had retreated to the seaside for a break from the heat and from the violence of the streets.

Although the intervention itself was technically complex and required intensive planning and coordination on the part of McClintock, Admiral James Holloway, and Fuad Chehab, its goals were political and not military. Within hours of their arrival, U.S. troops took up positions around the Beirut airport. Throughout their stay they had remarkably little contact with the Lebanese. Their presence, combined with the efforts of Eisenhower's special ambassador Robert Murphy, defused the crisis; but they were not used as fighting forces or as substitute police. They were used, and used effectively, as a symbol.

Much could have gone wrong after July 15—U.S. troops could have gotten drawn into the fighting, the opposition could have gained renewed strength, Nasser could have actively denounced the United States, Murphy could have complicated the negotiations. Nonetheless, very favorable conditions existed for a successful deployment. Eisenhower understood his goals: to send a signal of the determination of the United States to remain the primary power in the Middle East. This signal was directed at Nasser, but even more at the adherents of Nasserism who wished to decrease the influence and economic predominance of the West in the Middle East. To achieve that goal all that was necessary was a show of force and a peaceful resolution of the Lebanese crisis in which Chamoun's opponents were denied victory.

That, too, was the best that Chamoun and his predominantly Maronite allies could hope for by mid-July. By then, Chamoun knew that his presidency was over. His goal was to deny his opponents victory, but with the coup in Iraq, they received a boost that probably would have catapulted them to victory in the presidential elections. Chamoun had only one trump card left—U.S. intervention—and he played it. Although he did not win, neither did he lose. Late July saw the election of the neutral Chehab to the presidency, and the opposing sides agreed to the formula "No Victor, No Vanquished" as the leitmotif of the settlement. Jumblatt and company realized that they would have to settle for a draw; given that Chamoun would be removed from power, they felt they had extracted some measure of revenge. For his part, Chamoun would remain an active player in Lebanese politics as a parliamentary deputy and a leader of the conservative, pro-Western Maronite elite.

Although the preconditions were favorable, there was much to be done after July 14. Ambassador Murphy entered into intensive negotiations with all the warring factions and painstakingly helped piece together a compromise. In the meantime, the Egyptians protested against the introduction of U.S. troops in Lebanon and took their case before the UN Security Council. India's Nehru expressed his discomfort and called for a speedy pullout of U.S. forces.[82] Khrush-

---

82. See discussion of Nehru's message to Eisenhower in Memorandum of Conference with the President, July 20, 1958, Top Secret, DDE Diary, Box 35, Eisenhower Library.

chev wrote to Eisenhower that "the armed intervention started by the United States in Lebanon and subsequently by Britain in Jordan . . . may lead to extremely dangerous and unforeseen results." He denounced the military leaders of the Sixth Fleet as "irresponsible" and accused the United States of unlawfully interfering in the internal affairs of Lebanon.[83] Khrushchev called for an international summit to settle the crisis. The Eisenhower administration claimed that the United Nations was designed for such disputes and that a summit was therefore unnecessary. By the time of the UN debate in August, the crisis had passed. U.S. troops had restored order with the full cooperation of the Lebanese army and General Chehab, and the opposition to Chamoun had called off their forces once it was clear that the presidency of their nemesis was soon to end. By early fall, all U.S. troops were withdrawn, and after a minicrisis over the composition of Chehab's cabinet, Lebanon was once again calm. For the next seventeen years, Lebanon enjoyed economic prosperity and appeared to the world a model heterogenous society. In 1975, that image would be shattered, as Lebanon was plunged into a civil war that made the skirmishes of 1958 seem like halcyon days.

Yet, in the short term, the U.S. intervention in Lebanon was a qualified success. It was an intervention that accorded with the goals of Chamoun's faction and of the Maronites in general. It was also an intervention that led to the removal of the aggravating internal cause: Chamoun himself. The reasons articulated by Chamoun and his faction were embraced by the Eisenhower administration even though the messengers were ultimately sacrificed. The subsequent Chehab administration was in fact less slavishly pro-Western and more independent; but by July, U.S. officials concluded that such a government would in the long run better suit U.S. interests. One lesson of the Iraqi coup for Eisenhower was that Arab nationalism was an inexorable force that the United States could not and should not attempt to oppose. After July 1958, the United States relaxed its stance on Nasser and sought to channel both him and Arab nationalism in more moderate directions.[84]

In NSC policy papers written immediately after the crisis, Nasser was viewed as an evil that the United States government could live with, provided he did not cross the line drawn during the Lebanese crisis.[85] In August the NSC concluded: "Whether or not we regard Nasser as representing the best interests of Arab nationalism, he has become so clearly identified with its great successes that no rival is likely to challenge him unless he suffers a series of defeats. Thus if we wish to portray ourselves as friends of Arab nationalism, we cannot ignore

83. Text of Khrushchev letter to Eisenhower, July 19, 1958, John Foster Dulles Papers, Box 131.

84. Memorandum of Conference with the President, July 24, 1958, Top Secret, DDE Diary, Box 35, Eisenhower Library.

85. See NSC 5820/1 adopted October 30, 1958, Top Secret, OSANSA-NSC Policy Papers, Box 26, Eisenhower Library.

the fact that in the eyes of the great mass of Arabs the test of our sincerity will be whether we get along with Nasser or oppose him."[86]

In the long term, the U.S. intervention was a small ripple in U.S.-Egypt relations, and only a slightly larger wave in modern Lebanese history. Given how that history evolved after 1958, it cannot be judged favorably. The 1958 civil war was the first major crack in the confessional balance struck in the National Pact. Changing demographics as of 1958 had already made Maronite political predominance an anachronism, and the replacement of Chamoun by Chehab did nothing to alter that. Without outside help from the United States, it is unclear if the Maronite community could have maintained its privileged position after 1958. Although the factions in 1958 did not follow strictly confessional lines, confessional identity was a good predictor of whether one was for or against Chamoun. In the next decades, the Maronites thrived, mainly because of their close economic ties with the West. But in 1975, it became clear that the events of 1958 were a warning that had not been heard. The status quo antebellum was maintained with the help of the Eisenhower administration, but in the end, the opposition was correct. The 1958 crisis was internal, and the United States had done little more than shore up a crumbling foundation.

86. Memorandum for NSC from Planning Board re appraisal of NSC 5801, August 19, 1958, Secret, OSANSA-NSC Policy Papers, Box 23.

9

Cuba

Flying Solo

My impression is that a great deal of influence, whether it was on the CIA or on other agencies here in the United States that dealt with these matters, came from the Cuban exiles. And I think they persuaded a number of people that things were ready to blow and all that it would require was a little bit of a push to get it going. . . . I am inclined . . . to believe that Cuban exiles and refugees had a disproportionate amount of influence on the assessment the United States Government achieved in this situation.
— Robert Hurwitch, Special Assistant for Cuban Affairs

We continue to believe that Castro's position in Cuba is likely to grow stronger rather than weaker as time goes on. . . . In brief, our basic conclusion is that while Castro will probably continue to lose popular support, this loss is likely to be more than counterbalanced by the regime's increasingly effective control over daily life in Cuba and by the increasing effectiveness for maintaining control.
— Sherman Kent, CIA Memorandum, January 1961

I n March 1960, the CIA was instructed by the 5412 Committee to begin planning a covert operation that would result in the overthrow of Fidel Castro. In charge of the operation was the CIA's deputy director of operations, Dr. Richard Bissell. A tall, awkward man who wore heavy, black-rimmed glasses, Bissell had come to the CIA via the economics department at Yale, where he had been an instructor. Bissell was fresh from his success in creating the U-2 spy plane, and he was undaunted by the task of removing Castro. As far as he and most of the Eisenhower administration were concerned, Castro was a buffoon with a following.[1] He had come to power with deceptive ease, and few doubted that he could be made to disappear as easily and as quickly as he had materialized in Havana on New Year's Day 1959.

1. For a good sketch of Bissell, see Peter Wyden, *The Bay of Pigs* (New York, 1979), 10–17; Ranelagh, *The Agency,* 310–28; and Hersh, *Old Boys,* 428–36.

Fidel Castro has survived far longer than anyone imagined possible, but his ability to destroy a CIA-backed intervention at the Bay of Pigs was a clear sign of his charisma and composure. The story of the Bay of Pigs is a familiar one, and the very phrase evokes an image of government ineptitude ranking just below Vietnam. The Bay of Pigs was John F. Kennedy's first failure as president, and it came before he had any victories. But the operation (called in various incarnations Operation Pluto, Trinidad, and Zapata) was an Eisenhower initiative, and responsibility for the debacle lies on the shoulders of both administrations, as well as on those of the individuals who designed and executed it— Allen Dulles, Richard Bissell, and their team.

The operation called for the training of Cuban exiles in Florida and Guatemala. At the appointed time, these exiles would be transported to Cuba on Cuban merchant ships escorted by the U.S. Navy. The U.S. Air Force would provide limited support to the invasion force, but direct American involvement was to be avoided at all costs. Once ashore, the exile invaders would fade away to the Escambray Mountains and become a guerrilla force. American radio beamed from Florida would bombard the Cuban people with anti-Castro propaganda. Within days or weeks, these guerrillas would rally the Cuban populace to their side, and Cuba would rise up and overthrow the hated dictator Fidel Castro.

Prior to March 1960, Cuban exiles living in Miami plotted against Castro with aid and advice from the CIA. These exiles whispered to agents in Miami and lobbied in the corridors of Washington that Castro was alienating the Cuban people. They claimed that no more than a third of the populace supported him, and they boasted that the Cuban people would rise against Castro if they believed that the United States would come to their aid.[2]

That is exactly what the Bay of Pigs operation counted on, and that is exactly what it did not get. The Cuban people did not rise up in April 1961. Mechanically, the Bay of Pigs was one failure after another: failure to land near the mountains, instead choosing the mosquito-infested, barren, and isolated Bay of Pigs; failure to provide sufficient air coverage to the rebels because Kennedy feared that the American role would be exposed; failure to conceal U.S. involvement in the months before the invasion, so that by April 1961, the New York *Times* had all but printed the names of the exiles and provided coordinates of the landing site; and failure to gauge the strength of Castro's military, which was surprisingly tenacious and efficient.

But the greatest failure of all was misreading the domestic situation in Cuba. Unlike the interventions that preceded it, the Bay of Pigs relied on collaborators who were in no position to collaborate. The convergence of interests that had been present in Iran, Italy, Greece, Guatemala, and Lebanon did not exist in

2. Edward Ferrer, *Operation Puma: The Air Battle of the Bay of Pigs* (Miami, 1982), passim; Hugh Thomas, *The Cuban Revolution* (New York, 1977), 569–71; Arthur M. Schlesinger Jr. Memo for Tracy Barnes, "Free Cuba Manifesto," March 29, 1961, Confidential, National Security Files: Countries: Cuba, Box 35A, John F. Kennedy Library, Boston, Mass. [hereinafter cited as JFK Library].

Fidel's Cuba. It existed primarily with the Cubans in Florida, and as events would show they were in no position to oust the leaders of the Cuban Revolution.

In the interventions discussed so far, the focus has been on the capacity of peripheral forces to exert pulls on U.S. foreign policy. The outcomes of those interventions suggested that convergence between American foreign policy and the domestic politics of the particular country was vital to the success of the intervention. The outcome of the Bay of Pigs lends even more weight to that conclusion.

As with earlier interventions, pull factors existed, but those pulls did not come from within Cuba. Instead, they came from Cubans in exile in the United States. Interests converged, but not between American foreign policy and Cuban domestic policy. The intervention took place without Cuban actors in Cuba. There is no equivalent to Tsaldaris and the conservative politicians of Athens; there is no Cuban Shah, or Cuban Chamoun. In fact, the efforts of exiles in Florida notwithstanding, there was not even a Cuban Castillo Armas, because the brigade that was trained in Guatemala was cut off from the exiled political leaders in Miami. Castillo Armas was both a political and a military insurgent. In the Cuban-exile community in 1960–1961, no leader united those two functions.

As in other interventions discussed, the architects of the Bay of Pigs were both American and non-American. U.S. policy makers, CIA operatives, and exiled Cubans all contributed to the architecture of the Bay of Pigs. But the Cubans lacked a strong, entrenched position within Cuba, and that made them "collaborators" who really were in no position to collaborate. In fact, the Cubans who advocated for and helped implement the ill-fated intervention resembled Robinson's "collaborators" more than the Greek, Italian, Iranian, Guatemalan, and Lebanese groups who worked with the U.S. government.

The Bay of Pigs is, therefore, a story of divergence rather than convergence. Rather than allying with powerfully entrenched groups who stood for the status quo, the U.S. government worked with disenfranchised Cubans who had lost out to Castro. The operation was implemented with little reference to the local geography—both physical and political—of Cuba itself. As a result, the Bay of Pigs stands in stark contrast to the previous interventions, and it demonstrates the peril of U.S. policy makers' acting in the belief that local histories and local actors are nonessential.

In trying to explain the Bay of Pigs, many have focused on bad planning. The postmortem presidential inquiry headed by General Maxwell Taylor assessed the failure as a product of bad coordination between the various branches and misuse of the CIA. A large paramilitary operation, concluded the commission, could not be kept secret, and it required capabilities that the agency did not have.[3] Following the commission's conclusions (the actual report was classified, but the substance gradually became known outside the government), many

3. *Operation ZAPATA: The Ultrasensitive Report and Testimony of the Board of Inquiry on the Bay of Pigs* (Frederick, Md., 1981).

subsequent writers zeroed in on President Kennedy's refusal to authorize a second air strike on Castro's forces. In what may be called the "air-strike orthodoxy," writers saw the lack of air cover as a prime reason for the inability of the exiled invaders to establish a secure beachhead at the Bahia de Cochinos.[4] This view was widely shared within the U.S. government, and by Allen Dulles himself.[5] Many in Congress felt the same way. Senator Prescott Bush, father of future president George Bush, was convinced that the Bay of Pigs was a well-planned operation that floundered only because Kennedy refused to authorize sufficient air support to the invading brigade.[6]

There are ample reasons to criticize the planning of the intervention, and the reluctance of Kennedy to authorize a second round of air strikes certainly made the task of the invaders that much more difficult. Faulty intelligence on the depth of the waters at the Bay of Pigs, and a mistaken assumption that the invaders could fade away to the Escambray Mountains some seventy miles away also contributed to the debacle. Furthermore, the CIA was wrong about the isolation of the landing site. Although it was a swampy, uninhabited area, Castro had recently had it surveyed for possible development, and new paved, multilane roads had been built connecting the bay to the more populated regions to the north.[7]

Yet even had the blueprint for the Bay of Pigs been perfect, the operation would have foundered as thoroughly and as completely as it eventually did. Castro's forces might have been dealt a more severe blow, but the ultimate outcome of the exile brigade would have been the same. It is a comforting myth that, if only the operation had been better designed, it would have yielded the desired results for policy makers and operatives in Washington. The myth is a component of the overall belief in U.S. preponderance during the cold war.

4. "Bay of Pigs Revisited: Lessons from a Failure," *Time*, July 30, 1965. This article summarized the conclusions of Theodore Sorensen's articles in *Look* and Arthur M. Schlesinger Jr.'s account in his memoir of the Kennedy administration; Schlesinger, *A Thousand Days: John F. Kennedy in the White House* (New York, 1965). For other examples of the air-strike thesis, see Ranelagh, *The Agency*, 349-51; Prados, *Presidents' Secret Wars*, 171-207; Richard Reeves, *President Kennedy: Profile of Power* (New York, 1993), 80-100; Michael Beschloss, *The Crisis Years: Kennedy and Khrushchev, 1961-1963* (New York, 1991), 114-17. Piero Gleijeses' provocative article on the Bay of Pigs places the air strike in the context of a manipulative CIA that intended to maneuver Kennedy into authorizing an invasion. Gleijeses, "Ships in the Night: The CIA, the White House and the Bay of Pigs," *Journal of Latin American Studies*, XXVII (February 1995), 1-42. Bissell in his memoirs still emphasized the air-strike problem, but he retreated from his earlier belief that the lack of further air support doomed the operation. Bissell, *Reflections of a Cold Warrior*, 194-95.

5. Dulles manuscript of an unpublished article for Harper's magazine, "My Answer to the Bay of Pigs," July 1965, 10-11, in Allen Dulles Papers, Box 35, Mudd Library, Princeton University; Hunt, *Give Us This Day*, 164-65; David Atlee Phillips, *The Night Watch* (New York, 1972), 109-11.

6. Andrew, *For the President's Eyes Only*, 503.

7. Haynes Johnson, *The Bay of Pigs* (New York, 1964), 80-83; Wyden, *Bay of Pigs*, 106-107.

Cuba was so small, with a population barely more than six million and a land mass a fraction of that of the United States. Its tiny revolutionary army was still in disarray after the disintegration of Batista's army in 1959, and its air force was minuscule. U.S. officials at the time, and writers later on, looked at Cuba and thought that it could never have defeated the United States; only the United States could have defeated itself.

If the invasion had been an overt, military, conventional attack conducted by the armed forces of the United States, that calculus might have worked. But the Bay of Pigs was designed as a large covert paramilitary operation, and it depended on a political reaction within Cuba. Given the contours of the operation as designed by Bissell and the CIA, its success hinged very much on the Cubans, both the exiled invaders and the Cuban people within Cuba. It was the latter group that inflicted the defeat, a defeat made possible because policy makers in Washington never fully grasped how much U.S. power was limited by domestic conditions in a country Americans had long considered weak.

The planners for the invasion had two models in mind: Guatemala and Iran.[8] The blueprint of, and the assumptions behind, the Cuba intervention closely resembled those of the Guatemala intervention. That is not surprising, given that the key U.S. officials had all been involved in Operation PBSUCCESS, which resulted in the removal of Arbenz. These architects—particularly Dulles and Bissell, but also E. Howard Hunt, Tracy Barnes, David Atlee Phillips, Jake Engler, and others—had the Guatemalan model very much on their minds as they prepared to oust Castro.[9] But Cuba was not Guatemala, and the Cuban Revolution and its leader Fidel Castro were of a different order than the Guatemalan Revolution of 1944 and its leaders Arévalo and Arbenz. While the Eisenhower administration correctly read the signals in Guatemala, it almost entirely misread them in Cuba. Given the long legacy of close U.S. involvement in Cuban affairs, that misreading is somewhat surprising. Historically, Guatemala was less prominent on Washington's horizon, and U.S. policy makers were less familiar with it than with Cuba. The collapse of PBSUCCESS would have been easier to imagine than the utter disaster of the Bay of the Pigs.

As Bissell remarked in later years, he and others hinged their plans on the belief that Castro would react to an invasion much the same way Arbenz had. "The chance of toppling Castro," he said, "was predicated on the assumption that, faced with that kind of pressure, he would suffer the same loss of nerve."[10] It is hard to imagine two individuals more different in temperament than Castro and Arbenz. The Guatemalan president was cautious and serious. He was dedicated to revolutionary change, yet he moved slowly and attempted to build

8. Robert Amory (CIA deputy director of intelligence, 1957-1962) Oral History Interview, 119-21, JFK Library; Bissell, *Reflections of a Cold Warrior,* 153.

9. Dulles, "My Answer to the Bay of Pigs"; Hunt, *Give Us This Day,* 117-21; Phillips, *Night Watch,* 109-11.

10. Bissell Oral History, 25, Columbia Oral History Project.

consensus. His speeches were eloquent and intellectual. He drew support mainly from the military and the middle class. His appeal, like that of his predecessor Arévalo, was anything but demagogic.

Castro, however, was a charismatic, bombastic, bearded ex-guerrilla who had captured the romantic imagination of the Cuban people. He was a leader who had stormed Cuba with an exile force of fewer than one hundred men stuffed into a tiny boat in 1956 and fled to the mountains with fewer than a dozen. While still fighting Fulgencio Batista, he had convinced New York *Times* correspondent Herbert Matthews that he had far more men under his command than he actually did; he had his men change outfits and parade around Matthews several times,[11] much as the Soviets under Khrushchev were thought to have repeatedly flown the same squadron over Red Square to convince the West that their air force was larger than it really was. Fidel thrived on lousy odds. In his early career as a guerrilla, he took risks that should have ended in his death and that did end in the death of many of his compatriots. His swagger and bravado were part of his appeal to the Cuban people, and part of the secret of his power. A psychological profile of Fidel would have shown that he was not a prime candidate to "suffer from loss of nerve" when faced with a possible insurrection.

The other model for U.S. policy makers was the Iranian coup of 1953. In late 1959, Eisenhower administration officials began to discuss the possibility of taking steps to remove Castro. One of the overt measures mooted at an NSC meeting in December of that year was a reduction of the Cuban sugar quota. For years, the United States had purchased the bulk of the Cuban sugar crop at prices above world market. Threatening to cut the quota was the most drastic economic measure available to the United States and would effectively spell the end of relations between Washington and Fidel's Havana. The secretary of the treasury, Robert Anderson, commented that "when Mossadegh began to take action contrary to Western interests in Iran, the Western countries ceased to buy oil from Iran." Anderson believed that the United States should do the same with Cuban sugar if Fidel appeared to be veering toward Communism. Allen Dulles responded that he "doubted that the actions which solved the Mossadegh problem in Iran could be applied to Cuba, because there was not enough production of sugar world-wide to permit such a solution." Although the Cuban operation used different tactics than had been employed in Iran, as officials contemplated removing Fidel, Iran and Mosaddeq were never far from their minds. While the dual models of Guatemala and Iran gave officials the sense that an intractable third-world leader could, if necessary, be removed by the CIA, the specific conditions that made those operations possible seem to have been forgotten when the Bay of Pigs invasion was designed.[12]

11. Tad Szulc, *Fidel: A Critical Portrait* (New York, 1986), 409–10; Robert Quirk, *Fidel Castro* (New York, 1993), 131–34.

12. Memorandum of Discussion at the 426th Meeting of the National Security Council, Decem-

After the revolution swept into power on New Year's Day 1959, Castro was one of several prominent leaders, although it was clear from the start that he enjoyed an overwhelming advantage over his would-be competitors. Fidel was the son of a prosperous planter; he had attended law school in Havana and was active in anti-Batista politics from the late 1940s onward. Arrested after an attack on the Moncada barracks July 26, 1953, Castro served less than two years in jail before being released under a special amnesty in 1955. After a year in exile in Mexico, he and his paltry band of followers landed in Cuba in late 1956. Along with his brother, the dedicated Communist Raul Castro, and a passionate, rigid Argentine doctor named Ernesto "Che" Guevara, Castro fought a guerrilla campaign against Batista in the southeast province of Oriente. His exploits were celebrated, but his success was not military. Able to survive and garner publicity, Fidel became the embodiment of the Cuban myth of resistance to oppression and imperialism.[13] When Batista's regime crumbled, it was not because Fidel had achieved a military victory. Rather, he had undermined the flimsy veneer of support for Batista by becoming a hero to the Cuban people and making Batista look like the petty dictator he was. In the end, the Eisenhower administration withdrew support from Batista because Castro and the rebels effectively demonstrated that his rule was without legitimacy.[14]

For much of 1959, the Eisenhower administration "probed and tested to see what Castro would do."[15] For the first month, Castro was not even officially in the government. The president, Manuel Urrutia, and the premier, José Miró Cardona, existed in a bizarre limbo. While leading the official government and exchanging representatives with countries around the world, Urrutia and Miró Cardona were aware that the real center of power in Cuba was the Havana Hilton, where Castro and his coterie were comfortably settled. In February, Miró Cardona bowed to this reality and resigned. A prominent lawyer who had spent years in Miami opposing Batista, he later emerged as a leader of the anti-Castro exiles.

In April 1959, Fidel visited the United States and addressed large crowds

ber 1, 1959, Top Secret, *FRUS, 1958-1960, Vol. VI*, 683-85; Morris Morley, *Imperial State and Revolution: The United States and Cuba, 1952-1986* (New York, 1987), 111-14; Richard Welch, *Response to Revolution: The United States and the Cuban Revolution, 1959-1961* (Chapel Hill, 1985), 50-52.

13. Good accounts of Castro's life include Quirk, *Fidel Castro*; Szulc, *Fidel*; Luis Conte Agüero, *Fidel Castro: Psiquiatría y política* (Mexico City, 1968). For Castro's speeches, see Martin Kenner and James Petras, eds., *Fidel Castro Speaks* (New York, 1969).

14. The reasons for Batista's fall are still fiercely debated. Batista himself and the U.S. ambassador to Cuba in 1958 both contended that Castro's victory was the result of cowardice in Washington and the refusal of U.S. officials to support Batista. See Earl Smith, *The Fourth Floor* (New York, 1962); Fulgencio Batista, *Cuba Betrayed* (New York, 1962).

15. Roy Rubottom Oral History, 73-74, John Foster Dulles Oral History Project, Mudd Library, Princeton University.

throughout the northeast, particularly at universities such as Harvard and
Princeton. In Washington, he had an audience with Vice President Richard
Nixon. After the meeting, Nixon prophetically commented that Fidel possessed
"those indefinable qualities which make him a leader of men. Whatever we
may think of him, he is going to be a great factor in the development of Cuba
and very possibly in Latin American affairs generally. He seems to be sincere.
He is either incredibly naive about Communism or under Communist discipline—my guess is the former. . . . Because he has the power to lead . . . we
have no choice but at least to try to orient him the right direction."[16]

Nixon's appraisal seems to have been shared by many in the U.S. government.[17] While officials always viewed Castro with skepticism, for much of 1959
they were at least willing to give him some latitude, or "enough rope to hang
himself."[18] After his swing through the United States, Castro returned to Cuba
and announced a land-reform program. In May, he set up the National Institute
for Agrarian Reform (INRA), which was charged with implementing the reform
law. The aim, as with agrarian reform in Iran and Guatemala, was to make it
easier for landless peasants to become proprietors; an additional goal was to
break the hold of landlords on the political and economic life of the country,
as with Guatemala in 1953. However, as it was applied, the law worked more
often than not to dispossess landlords without redistributing the land to the
workers and peasants. The power of the state was increased, but not the
economic base of the landless masses.[19]

Agrarian reform also entailed agrarian development, such as paved roads
and electrification of villages.[20] Accompanying the land program, the Cuban
Revolution began to nationalize large companies, although at this stage U.S.
companies were left largely untouched. Landowners and businessmen were to
be compensated by long-term bonds. The reaction of U.S. landholders in Cuba
was predictably antagonistic, but the Eisenhower administration, consistent
with its attitude during the Iran oil crisis and the Suez crisis, defended the
principle of nationalization. As long as the Cuban government paid a fair price

16. Nixon notes of meeting, April 19, 1959, NA 711.12/4-2459; *FRUS, 1958-1960, Vol. VI,* 476.

17. See Herter's notes on Castro's visit, April 23, 1959, Confidential, In Dulles/Herter Series,
Box 11, Eisenhower Library.

18. The expression was used by Assistant Secretary of State Roy Rubottom. Rubottom Oral
History, Mudd Library, Princeton University.

19. For a trenchant if somewhat over-the-top critique of the land reform, see Rufo López-
Fresquet, *My Fourteen Months with Castro* (Cleveland, 1966), 113-16. López-Fresquet was minister
of the treasury from January 1959 to March 1960. Teresa Casuso, who befriended Fidel in Mexico,
also criticized the implementation of the land-reform program; Teresa Casuso, *Cuba and Castro*
(New York, 1961), 200. See also Marifeli Pérez-Stable, *The Cuban Revolution: Origins, Course,
and Legacy* (New York, 1993), 66-72.

20. Louis Pérez Jr., *Cuba: Between Reform and Revolution* (New York, 1988), 320-21.

for the properties it expropriated, the Eisenhower administration did not oppose the measures. The U.S. ambassador in Havana, Philip Bonsal, did his best to be conciliatory, and he reassured the Cuban government that the United States desired only close relations with Cuba.[21]

However, Bonsal also expressed concern at the anti-American tone of Castro and the revolution. And in private, many U.S. officials voiced suspicion that Castro, while not a Communist, was determined to destroy U.S. business interests in Cuba.[22] Cardinal Spellman, the prominent Chicago prelate, opined that Castro was both Communist and insane, and U.S. property-owners in Cuba petitioned the State Department to do something about the land-reform law.[23] While the official stance of the Eisenhower administration was cool but proper, there was always an undercurrent of distrust.[24] As Castro became more stringently anti-American in his speeches during the summer of 1959, the latent U.S. antagonism toward the revolution became less latent. A series of highly publicized defections from the revolution by the likes of Major Huber Matos and Major Pedro Díaz Lanz were widely reported in the United States, and Castro was increasingly perceived as a dictator.[25]

In the fall of 1959, the Eisenhower administration began to consider measures that would lead to Castro's replacement. Assistant secretaries of state Roy Rubottom and Thomas Mann believed that "the Castro government was so seriously adverse to the United States" that the Eisenhower administration should deny him the benefit of the sugar quota. Rubottom then told Allen Dulles and Undersecretary Robert Murphy that in his opinion, "the time had come when the United States should give some consideration to supporting the anti-Castro people, that this man was a clear cut threat to the United States." Rubottom's superiors at State agreed, but they felt that "the actual means of providing the support would be carried out by another agency, not by the State Department."[26]

Policy evolved essentially along those lines. In public, the U.S. government threatened to cut back on the sugar quota, and it eventually did so in the

21. Bonsal at first compared the agrarian reform with similar successful measures in Japan. Philip Bonsal, *Cuba, Castro, and the United States* (Pittsburgh, 1971), 66–73.

22. Jules Benjamin, *The United States and the Origins of the Cuban Revolution* (Princeton, 1990), 180–85; Bonsal to Rubottom, July 16, 1959, *FRUS, 1958–1960, Vol. VI*, 561–62.

23. Memorandum of Conversation, Department of State, June 24, 1959, *FRUS, 1958–1960, Vol. VI*, 539–41.

24. Thomas Paterson has argued that the Eisenhower administration went to great lengths to keep Castro from coming to power in 1957–58, and, having failed in that goal, continued to seek ways to prevent him from consolidating the revolution. See Paterson, *Contesting Castro*.

25. Díaz Lanz testified before the Senate on the alleged abuses of the Castro regime. Quirk, *Fidel Castro*, 248–50.

26. Rubottom Oral History, 75–76.

summer of 1960. In secret, the Central Intelligence Agency began to plan for the covert removal of Fidel.

On November 5, Secretary of State Christian Herter (John Foster Dulles had died in May) wrote to Eisenhower echoing Rubottom's conclusions. While he suggested that the United States "should avoid the impression of direct pressure or intervention against Castro," he believed that there was no longer any hope that Castro would adopt policies in line with U.S. interests in Cuba. He felt it was thus necessary to help build up a credible opposition to Castro within Cuba.[27] In January 1960, the CIA's Special Group (also known as the 5412 committee) set up a special task force to formulate plans to oust Castro; many of the members of this group were veterans of the Guatemala operation.[28] They were responsible for crafting the directive that Eisenhower signed in March.

Entitled "A Program for Covert Action Against the Castro Regime," the March 16, 1960, document established the template for what would later become Operation Zapata and the Bay of Pigs invasion. It stated in part:

> The purpose of the program outlined herein is to bring about the replacement of the Castro regime with one more devoted to the true interests of the Cuban people and more acceptable to the U.S. in such a manner as to avoid any appearance of U.S. intervention. Essentially the method of accomplishing this will be to induce, support, and so far as possible direct action, both inside and outside of Cuba, by selected groups of Cubans of a sort that they might be expected to and could undertake on their own initiative.

The plan was to have four major components: the creation of a "unified Cuban opposition to the Castro regime . . . in the shape of a council or junta"; the creation of a propaganda offensive via "short and long wave gray broadcasting" facilities; the establishment of "a covert intelligence and action organization within Cuba"; and the development of a paramilitary force outside of Cuba. CIA officials would search for an "ambitious, uncontentious" leader of the opposition forces. It was important that such a leader and his council be identified as "pro-revolution . . . and anti-Castro because of his failure to live up to the original . . . [revolutionary] platform and his apparent willingness to sell out to Communist domination and possible ultimate enslavement." The slogan for the anti-Castro forces was to be "Restore the Revolution."[29]

27. Memorandum from Herter to the President, November 5, 1959, Secret, *FRUS, 1958–1960, Vol. VI*, 656–658.

28. Benjamin, *United States and Origins of the Cuban Revolution*, 189; Prados, *Presidents' Secret Wars*, 175; Bissell, *Reflections of a Cold Warrior*, 153.

29. A portion of this document is found in *FRUS, 1958–1960, Vol. VI*, 850–51, but much of it is deleted. A more extensive, although still censored, version is available at the Eisenhower

In spite of the plan to incite anti-Communist energies against Castro, the CIA and the Eisenhower administration as a whole did not consider Castro a Communist at any time in 1960.[30] As a CIA Special National Intelligence Estimate commented a week after Eisenhower signed the covert action plan, "We believe that Fidel Castro and his government are not now demonstrably under the domination or control of the international Communist movement." The estimate further predicted that Castro would not soon be under such control. Nonetheless, the authors concluded, Castro's policies satisfied the aims of the Latin American Communist movement by undermining the influence and image of the United States in the region.[31]

As hinted by Herter in his November 5, 1959, memo to Eisenhower and as stated explicitly in the March 16, 1960, course of action, the covert plan depended on the presence of an indigenous Cuban opposition to Fidel, both within Cuba and abroad. Between March 1960 and the April 1961 invasion of the Bay of Pigs brigade, the plan would undergo significant changes, the most important of which was a vast increase in the scale of the operation. But one thing remained constant: success was always thought to hinge on a cohesive, focused *internal* Cuban opposition to Castro. It never materialized. However, at the beginning of 1960, there were signs that an opposition was emerging. U.S. officials were not completely off the mark in hoping for a Cuban opposition to Fidel.

Beginning in the middle of 1959 and continuing over the next year, there was a steady stream of prominent defectors from Castro's revolution. The first prime minister of the revolution, the lawyer Miró Cardona, left Cuba in disgust and soon surfaced as a prominent anti-Castro activist in Miami. In addition to Huber Matos, the treasury minister Rufo López-Fresquet quit the government, and Luis Conte Agüero, who had stood by Fidel in the dark days in Mexico, denounced the revolution's increasing flirtation with Communism. Angel Quevedo, an early leader in the anti-Batista revolutionary directorate, also spoke out and was denounced by Fidel as a result. Manuel Artime, a prominent official in the National Institute for Agrarian Reform in 1959, broke with Fidel and left for the United States. He would later be one of the leaders of the Bay of Pigs brigade.[32]

The initial wave of refugees to arrive in Miami were of the upper classes, from the ranks of pro-Batista businessmen and Havana merchants, who took what property they could and left the country. But as 1960 began, the next wave of exiles came from a more diverse background. Airline pilots such as

Library, White House Office Files, Office of Staff Secretary, International Series, Box 4.

30. Bissell, *Reflections of a Cold Warrior,* 152–53.

31. CIA-SNIE 85-60, "Communist Influence in Cuba," March 22, 1960, Secret, OSANSA-NSC Briefing Notes, Box 6, Eisenhower Library.

32. Johnson, *Bay of Pigs,* 26–27.

Eduardo Ferrer,[33] middle-class students from the University of Havana, teachers, lawyers, shopkeepers, and individuals from a broad stratum of the middle class fled the island.[34] More than sixty thousand left for the United States in 1960 alone. CIA informants in Cuba reported dissatisfaction with the revolution, particularly among the politically moderate middle class. By the spring of 1960, Castro's rhetoric became more sharply anti-American and anti-imperialistic, and more oriented toward workers and peasants. As governmental "interventions" against businesses increased, there was a tendency among the middle class to wonder what direction the revolution was taking. While few broke outright with Castro, there were reports that people were "jittery, demoralized and disillusioned" with the revolution. As in Guatemala and the rest of Latin America, there was a deep pool of native anti-Communism that needed no replenishing by the United States. When Castro's rhetoric veered in the direction of Soviet anti-imperialism, and as admitted Communists such as Raul Castro and Che Guevara grew in stature, anti-Communist angst came to the surface.[35]

Even Castro himself acknowledged the existence of some middle-class trepidation. "What is happening in the middle class is that it is vacillating; it is very confused," he said in late March 1960.[36] That confusion increased as Castro steered the revolution toward the peasants and workers and directly against the imperialist legacy of the United States. In early summer of 1960, the Eisenhower administration finally announced drastic cutbacks in the annual Cuban sugar quota. That resulted in a pact between Cuba and the Soviet Union in which the Soviets promised to buy the sugar that the United States had refused. In July, Eisenhower announced a complete suspension of the year's sugar quota. In response, Castro authorized "interventions" against U.S. businesses in Cuba in the fall of 1960. The vicious circle of declining U.S.-Cuban relations further alarmed an alarmed tentative Cuban middle class.

Certain sectors of Cuban society were wary of Castro, but that did not mean that they were potential counterrevolutionaries. By most assessments, few Cubans were prepared to act against Castro. As Columbia University professor C. Wright Mills observed, the counterrevolutionaries consisted mainly of the old Batista elite and defectors from the Castro regime in Miami, along with isolated pockets within Cuba itself. "Every revolution has naturally left in its wake defection, resentment, and counterrevolutionary sentiment." Mills listed large landowners, real-estate magnates, gambling interests in Havana, and businessmen who formerly depended on export-import with the United States. Many

33. Ferrer, *Operation Puma.*

34. File marked "350–Political Refugees," in Lot 60 F 102, RG 84, WNRC. See also Theodore Draper, *Castroism: Theory and Practice* (New York, 1965), 122–25; Pérez, *Cuba,* 335.

35. CIA report, "The Cuban Situation," April 13, 1960, Secret, International Series, Box 8, Eisenhower Library. For the story of Guevara and the Bay of Pigs, see Jorge Castañeda, *Compañero: The Life and Death of Che Guevara* (New York, 1997), 196–202.

36. Quoted in Draper, *Castroism,* 125.

of them remained in Cuba, but they felt the revolution was going too far too fast. But Mills believed that there were "only a few counterrevolutionaries in Cuba, and they are certainly impotent to gather any elements around them." There was a good deal of discontent, but discontent, Mills concluded, did not necessarily translate into activity.[37]

Mills touched on the vital issue for U.S. officials contemplating Castro's overthrow: when does discontent become counterrevolution? The signs of disenchantment were everywhere, but as Mills implied, the expression of unease was perfectly natural in a revolution where the old order was collapsing, things were changing, and lives were being affected by each new revolutionary law. U.S. officials were faced with reports of unrest, and they based their plans on the assumption that such discontent could be the foundation of a genuine opposition. That assumption, however, was contradicted by both the CIA and by the experience of anti-Castro groups within Cuba itself.

In 1960, small, militant anti-Castro groups carried out acts of sabotage against the Cuban government. Targets included sugar mills and refineries, power stations, water mains, and public transportation. Two of the more prominent groups were the MRR (Revolutionary Recovery Movement) led by a number of disgruntled ex-Castro army officers, and the MRP (People's Revolutionary Movement), led by former interior minister Manuel Ray. Like ex-revolutionary officials Miró Cardona and Manuel Artime, Ray was later recruited by the CIA as a leader of the provisional government formed before the Bay of Pigs. The terrorist campaign of these and other groups polarized politics within Cuba even further. As the attacks increased, Castro intensified the already formidable powers of the state. Thousands were imprisoned without trial and held in cells formerly reserved for political opponents of Batista. At the same time, a large portion of the population recoiled against the violence and continued to support the goals of the revolution. Rather than creating massive defections from the revolution, these attacks seem to have reinforced people's loyalty to Castro. Forced to choose, they chose revolution.[38]

These cells of resistance to Castro were not entirely indigenous. Many included exiles who had been infiltrated into Cuba by the CIA. As part of the covert-action program, the CIA tried to construct a viable opposition network in Cuba that would both harass the regime and provide support to the eventual landing of the brigade. While the size of that landing was not specified at first, it was always understood in the CIA that guerrilla groups in Cuba were a vital component of any planned coup or uprising. To this end, the agency outfitted and aided small, armed infiltration groups.[39] By mid-1960s, the sabotage of sugar refineries was being orchestrated by the CIA task force; sabotage was in fact the covert component of the public termination of the U.S. sugar quota in the

37. C. Wright Mills, *Listen, Yankee: The Revolution in Cuba* (New York, 1960), 54.

38. Thomas, *Cuban Revolution*, 569–74.

39. Gordon Gray Oral History, 275–76, Columbia Oral History Project.

summer of 1960. Plans for refinery sabotage were accompanied by plans to arm successive waves of guerrilla infiltration groups made up of exiles.[40]

As of mid-1960, there was still some uncertainty within the CIA as to whether the eventual plan would involve a brigade-size invasion or simply multiple guerrilla cadres of twenty to thirty men each which would then combine with opposition groups already in Cuba. Bissell at first hoped that the infiltration teams would simply link up with the local opposition networks in Oriente province and the Escambray Mountains, and there wage a campaign similar to that waged by Castro against Batista in 1958.[41] Some of the guerrilla teams were trained at U.S. facilities in the Panama Canal Zone.

However, by the fall of 1960, the plan to create a viable Cuban guerrilla organization had failed.[42] Castro's militia kept intercepting weapons drops and the men who attempted to retrieve the weapons. The Cuban security forces worked with the army to track down the various groups and capture or kill the guerrillas. As Bissell later commented,

> There never was a command and control net, a true organized underground in Cuba. Because there was no underground, that is, no way in which a guerrilla band . . . could communicate its requirements with security, or receive instructions with security, either by radio or by runner, for these reasons it was unfeasible . . . to infiltrate either supplies or people who could join these groups and provide them with the means of communication with the outside. . . . There was a lot of resistance to Castro during that summer and autumn, but it was so poorly organized and security practices so poor that, except in the Escambray, the bands were rounded up fairly quickly. . . . It was therefore simply impossible to build up the basis of a resistance movement in the island.[43]

Even in the face of this seeming impossibility, the planners continued to rely on the eventual materialization of indigenous opposition. This willful refusal to accept the realities on the ground would ultimately cripple the intervention. Without abandoning the guerrilla option, the CIA in late summer 1960 started planning for a more sizable operation and began to focus on landing a brigade on Cuba. And for that, the agency had to work with Cuban exiles.

In an August meeting with Eisenhower, Allen Dulles asserted that a unified opposition had coalesced outside of Cuba. Composed of six prominent exiles,

40. Andrew Goodpaster Oral History, Eisenhower Library, 3.
41. Bissell, *Reflections of a Cold Warrior*, 154–55.
42. Hunt, *Give Us This Day*, 160; Bissell Oral History, June 5, 1967, 26–32, Columbia Oral History Project.
43. Bissell Oral History, 29–30.

the Revolutionary Democratic Front (FRD) had its headquarters in Mexico. In addition, the paramilitary training program of some five hundred Cubans by the CIA was proceeding as planned in the Canal Zone and in Guatemala, technically under the auspices of the FRD. The exiles made use of an air strip in Guatemala, built by the CIA on land provided by the president of Guatemala, Miguel Ydígoras Fuentes, who had finally acceded to the Guatemalan presidency after the assassination of his rival Castillo Armas. Bissell told the president that the CIA had identified "no less than eleven groups or alleged groups in Cuba with potential" to coordinate with the exiles in Guatemala. Eisenhower assured Bissell and Dulles that he would "go along" with the plan, provided that "the Joint Chiefs, Defense, State and the CIA" thought that there was "a good chance of being successful." As for cost, Eisenhower said that he "wouldn't much care" as long as it was successful.[44]

Concurrently, Bissell authorized an operation to assassinate Castro. According to a report prepared by the CIA inspector general in 1967,[45] planning for the assassination began in August of 1960. Before that point, there were several miscellaneous schemes devised by the CIA's technical-services division. These were much publicized in the mid-1970s when congressional committees under the chairmanship of Senator Frank Church and Congressman Otis Pike convened hearings on alleged assassination plots sanctioned by the U.S. government. One plan involved contaminating the air of Castro's radio studio with an aerosol spray that would act like LSD on those exposed to it. This was abandoned when the chemical was found to be unreliable. Another infamous idea that today is remarkable for its absurdity was to place depilatory powder in Fidel's cigars. Once his beard fell out, believed the CIA, his machismo image would be shattered and the revolution would be dealt a severe blow.

But Bissell's August 1960 program was more serious, and it resulted in an alliance between CIA operatives and members of the mafia who had formerly been major players in the Havana casino industry. Bissell, Dulles, and the agency's deputy director, General Pearré Cabell, were fully briefed on these developments, and Bissell committed at least $150,000 to the mafia project. Although these early plans came to naught, later efforts to use mafia members to harass or kill Fidel under the post–Bay of Pigs Operation Mongoose are believed by some to have intersected a conspiracy to assassinate John F. Kennedy. There is no doubt that the CIA engaged the services of certain mafia members in an ongoing effort to kill Castro. These efforts were operationally

44. Memorandum of meeting with the president, August 18, 1960, Top Secret, *FRUS, 1958–1960, Vol. VI,* 1057–60. Those present were Eisenhower, Bissell, Dulles, Gates (Defense), Anderson (Treasury), Dillon (undersecretary of state), Generals Persons, Lemnitzer, Goodpaster, and Gordon Gray.

45. CIA Memorandum for the record, "Report on Plots to Assassinate Fidel Castro," March 23, 1967, pp. 14–30, John F. Kennedy Collection of Assassination Records, NA, College Park, Md.

separate from the infiltration and paramilitary programs of 1960, but they were part of the overall effort to remove Castro from power.[46] As Bissell noted in his memoirs, while the misalliance with the mafia was not his idea, he endorsed it. "As I moved forward with plans for the brigade, I hoped the Mafia would achieve success. My philosophy during my last two or three years in the agency was very definitely that the end justified the means, and I was not going to be held back."[47] From the perspective of the agency, the best of all possible worlds would have been an assassination of Castro combined with the successful placement of guerrilla groups in Cuba. Once Castro was eliminated, those groups could assume control.

Yet, having failed to establish a viable guerrilla movement, the CIA still proceeded with both the assassination plots and the plans for an exile invasion, and CIA planners still assumed that, in either case, the Cuban people would react by rising against the revolution. In short, the CIA failed to draw the obvious lesson from the failure of the guerrilla groups: Castro and the revolution were popular.

Bissell, Hunt, and Allen Dulles did not learn that lesson, even though CIA intelligence reports on Cuba hinted at that very fact. Throughout 1960 and until the very eve of the Bay of Pigs landing, the CIA consistently reported that the opposition was weak and disorganized and that Castro remained firmly in control. Why these reports did not lead the planners of the invasion to question the chances for success has to do with the bifurcated structure of the CIA. The intelligence directorate, headed by Robert Amory, and the Board of National Estimates, headed by Sherman Kent, were separated from the directorate of plans (operations) by what amounted to a Chinese wall. While the CIA task force in charge of the operation (called WH/4) was fully aware of what the intelligence directorate was reporting, the intelligence officials were not aware of significant portions of the Bay of Pigs planning. Amory, at least, was furious when he discovered how much information he had not been privy to before April 1961. It was not that Amory and Kent were unaware of the operations, but they were not included in the day-to-day planning.[48]

In June 1960, the CIA National Intelligence Estimate on Cuba predicted that Fidel would remain in power for the remainder of the year unless he became severely incapacitated. While concluding that Castro was not a Communist, the NIE stated that he was deeply influenced by Communist rhetoric. And indeed, comparing the speeches of the head of the Cuban Communist Party, Blas Roca, with those of Castro, one finds similar themes of anti-imperialism, anti-Americanism, and anti-U.S. capitalism.[49] As for opposition to Fidel, the CIA believed that while it showed signs of growing, it continued to be "weak and

46. Ibid.
47. Bissell, *Reflections of a Cold Warrior,* 157; Thomas, *Very Best Men,* 226-36.
48. Amory Oral History, 123-25, JFK Library.
49. See Blas Roca's speeches in Blas Roca, *Cuban Revolution* (New York, 1961).

divided" and lacked "a dynamic leader."[50] In December, in a special NIE, the CIA Board of Estimates headed by Kent stated that even if the United States maintained pressure on Cuba at roughly the same level over the next six months, Fidel Castro's hold on the country would remain as firm as ever. "His overall popular support has declined since its high water mark of early 1959, but as a symbol of revolutionary change he retains widespread support among the poorer classes, particularly in the countryside. No other figure has emerged with the stature to challenge him." As for internal resistance to Castro, while it had grown over the last six months of 1960 and while there was a good deal of disillusionment over the failed promise of land reform, the CIA believed that Castro was effectively meeting any challenges. Through a combination of economic "carrots," stringent nationalist rhetoric, and highly effective security forces, he was able to contain local disturbances and break up most of the guerrilla bands operating throughout the country. And with each passing day, Castro's ability to meet the varied threats to his regime would increase.[51]

The general outline of the covert campaign depended from the start on the creation of a strong, cohesive opposition to Castro in Cuba. Yet in December, after nearly a year of planning that involved infiltration, propaganda, paramilitary training, and assassination plots, the CIA had not succeeded in creating that indigenous opposition. The CIA switched gears and started to focus on the "brigade concept" whereby a sizable group of Cuban exiles, trained by the United States and escorted to Cuba by a flotilla of U.S. Navy ships, would make an amphibious assault on Cuba. After months of intelligence reports to the contrary, CIA officers in the operations directorate still hoped that if the brigade could establish a beachhead, passive anti-Castro forces throughout Cuba would desert Fidel and rally to the brigade and the exiled government of the FRD.[52]

Although Bissell and Dulles claimed that the FRD was a viable external exile opposition group, it existed primarily because of the CIA. Its leaders—Miró Cardona, Manuel Artime, Justo Carillo, and Tony de Varona—were not creations of the CIA. Each had been pursuing anti-Castro activities independently. But the group would not have formed without CIA sponsorship, and its leaders hardly saw eye to eye. It was not, therefore, an opposition group that was independent of U.S. influence, nor was it seen as independent either by the U.S. government or by the U.S. and Latin American press. Furthermore, assurances by CIA officials that the FRD was credible were undermined by reports from the U.S. embassy in Havana. According to the embassy chargé d'affaires, not only was the FRD seen as a tool of the Eisenhower administration, but most Cubans and Americans who met with embassy officials believed that the front was

---

50. CIA-SNIE 85-2-60, "The Situation in Cuba," June 14, 1960, Secret, *FRUS, 1958-1960, Vol. VI*, 947-49.

51. CIA-SNIE 85-3-60, "Prospects for the Castro Regime," December 8, 1960, Secret, *FRUS, 1958-1960, Vol. VI*, 1168-74.

52. Bissell, *Reflections of a Cold Warrior*, 156-63.

"little more than a cockpit of jealousies, personal ambitions and frustrating inertia. . . . The fact that the Front is foreign based makes it an easy target for the Castro regime to brand as the vehicle of Yankee imperialism."[53] This was hardly the rosy picture provided by Bissell and Dulles.

In spite of embassy reports and CIA estimates that clearly stated that Castro was essentially unchallenged by a unified opposition, the CIA working group under Bissell's aegis continued to plan for a covert operation with the same set of assumptions and conditions that had been present from the start, and it persisted in believing that there would be a revolt in response to a paramilitary landing. The major change between March and December was an increase in the contemplated size of the landing. After the infiltration plan failed, Bissell realized that a landing of significant proportions was necessary, and the exile group in Guatemala was thus increased. As the number of exiles in training topped one thousand by December, their presence was no longer a secret. The covert operation was rapidly becoming an overt paramilitary one, with daily reports on the exiles in major U.S. newspapers. The only question mark that remained was the extent of CIA involvement.[54]

As one of its final acts, the Eisenhower administration terminated diplomatic relations with Cuba. For some months, Ambassador Bonsal had been in Washington, and the Havana embassy had been reduced to a skeleton staff. The final straw was a speech by Castro on January 2, 1961, describing the embassy as a center of counterrevolution, subversion, and espionage; he then demanded that embassy personnel be cut to eleven people.[55] After meeting to discuss the issue the following day, Eisenhower and his advisers decided that it was time to break off relations.

At the same meeting, these officials also assessed the current status of the exile group in Guatemala and the degree of support for Castro in Cuba. While Allen Dulles believed that "the white collar people were against Castro . . . the peasants and workers were still largely with him." However, while acknowledging that the Cuban militia and security forces were stronger than ever, Dulles claimed that "reliable reports indicated that the trend is against Castro." Dulles then informed the president that optimal timing for any movement of the exiles would be March. After that, the morale of the trainees would suffer. In addition, the Guatemalan government was becoming anxious about the increasing publicity; Ydígoras Fuentes did not feel he could continue to harbor the exiles for more than a few months. Their existence was being widely touted in newspapers throughout the hemisphere, and their presence was starting to be a liability for the Guatemalan government.[56] This "disposal" problem was a major factor

53. Havana 1280, December 6, 1960, *FRUS, 1958-1960, Vol. VI,* 1149-63.

54. Memorandum of meeting with the President (November 29, 1960), December 5, 1960, Top Secret, OSANSA—Special Assistant Series, Presidential Subseries, Box 5, Eisenhower Library.

55. Bonsal, *Cuba, Castro, and the United States,* 175.

56. Memorandum of meeting with the President (January 3, 1961), January 9, 1961, Top Secret,

in the deliberations within the new Kennedy administration that entered the White House later in January.

John Fitzgerald Kennedy was not only the first Catholic president but also the youngest to date. The Camelot mythology of his administration has presented the energetic president as an open-minded visionary. His speeches showed flashes of rhetorical brilliance, thanks to speechwriter Theodore Sorensen, one of the more diligent crafters of the Kennedy image.[57] As a presidential candidate and then as chief executive, Kennedy spoke in lofty, poetic terms of the potential of America to meet the challenge of a new age.

Yet beneath the breathtaking oratory Kennedy was as much an ideological cold warrior as his predecessors. He was determined to project an image of American strength. In a closely contested election with Richard Nixon, Kennedy sounded the alarm that the United States was falling behind in the cold war. In October, after the U.S. declared a near-total trade embargo against Cuba, Kennedy accused the Eisenhower White House of being lax on Castro. He proclaimed that the United States could not allow Castro to establish a base for the Soviet Union in the Western Hemisphere and he wanted to know why Eisenhower wasn't doing something more drastic about Cuba. Charging that the embargo was "too little, too late," Kennedy called for the United States to aid rebel forces in Cuba and to prepare to intervene. Nixon was furious. Kennedy had been briefed by Allen Dulles after securing the nomination, and Nixon thought that Dulles must have informed Kennedy of the covert plans against Castro. At the fourth presidential debate, Nixon lashed out at Kennedy for making such "dangerously irresponsible recommendations." Nixon was one of the strongest advocates in the White House for proceeding against Castro, yet in order to preserve the secrecy of the covert plans, he found himself in the awkward position of denouncing Kennedy for championing the same policy line in public.[58] The end result, however, was that Kennedy committed himself to a hard line against Castro during the election. He thus had limited options when he took the presidential oath on January 20, 1961.

Kennedy entered the White House acutely concerned about the third world. Even more than Eisenhower in 1953, Kennedy in 1961 viewed the third world as the primary battleground in the cold war. While Berlin remained unsettled, neither Khrushchev nor Kennedy had any immediate plans to undo the division between Eastern and Western Europe. The tense partition of Europe evolved into a status quo that neither superpower attempted to upset for the duration of the cold war. The third world, however, was fluid. New states were emerging from the wreckage of colonialism; as they entered the international arena, they were courted by the Americans and the Soviets. The task for the Kennedy

---

OSANSA—Special Assistant Series, Presidential Subseries, Box 5, Eisenhower Library.

57. Theodore Sorensen, *Kennedy* (New York, 1965).

58. Stephen Ambrose, *Nixon: The Education of a Politician, 1913-1962* (New York, 1987), 591-93.

administration was to convince the nations of the third world to pick the United States and its economic system over the Soviet Union and Communism. In the words of Walt Rostow, the MIT economics professor and senior adviser on the NSC, "the emerging less developed nations must be persuaded that their human and national aspirations will be better fulfilled within the compass of [the free] community than without."[59]

The sense of urgency over the third world was compounded by a speech delivered by Nikita Khrushchev in Moscow on January 6 and released to the Americans several days later. Not only did he ominously suggest that West Berlin was a weak point for the United States and NATO, but he pointed to the "national-liberation wars" breaking out around the globe. He declared that "the Marxist attitude to such uprisings . . . is most favorable. . . . The Communists support just wars of this kind whole-heartedly and without reservation."[60] The most pressing national-liberation war at that moment was in Laos, but Kennedy took the threat of Moscow-sponsored insurgencies as a global one. As he said to Congress in late March, "The free world's security can be endangered not only by nuclear attack, but also by being nibbled away at the periphery . . . by forces of subversion, infiltration, intimidation, indirect or non-overt aggression, internal revolution, diplomatic blackmail, guerrilla warfare or a series of limited wars."[61] That did not mean that the Kennedy White House interpreted all third-world nationalist movements and all civil wars in developing nations as Communist-inspired. In an address to the nation in June, Kennedy remarked that it was too easy "to dismiss as Communist-inspired every anti-government or anti-American riot, every overthrow of a corrupt regime, or every mass protest against misery and despair." As he later told Soviet journalist Alexei Adzhubei, "what we find objectionable and a threat to peace is when a system is imposed by a small militant group by subversion, infiltration, and all the rest."[62]

In order to swing the undecided nations of the third world into the American camp, the Kennedy administration adopted multiple strategies ranging from economic assistance to overt and covert propaganda to special-forces warfare and counterinsurgency. The reliance on a range of options was consistent with the overall Kennedy response to the Sino-Soviet threat. In nuclear policy, Kennedy adopted a policy of "flexible response." While this policy meant something quite specific in terms of nuclear strategy, it also describes Kennedy's approach to the third world. In each instance, the Kennedy team would select from a wide menu of options to stanch the spread of Communism and convince

---

59. Rostow speech June 1961, quoted in Gaddis, *Strategies of Containment,* 209.

60. Quoted in Reeves, *President Kennedy,* 40–41.

61. Quoted in Michael McClintock, *Instruments of Statecraft,* 164.

62. Radio address June 6, 1961; Kennedy-Adzhubei interview of November 25, 1961, quoted in Gaddis, *Strategies of Containment,* 209–10.

the peoples of the third world that their interests would be best served by placing themselves under the protective umbrella of Washington.

While the Kennedy administration viewed Latin America as part of the developing world where the contest between Moscow and the Washington would be acute, it also treated Latin America as a natural dependent of the United States. In dealing with Cuba, Kennedy officials, like their predecessors under Eisenhower, had a proprietary sense that was not present in Indochina, for example. The long legacy of the Monroe Doctrine and repeated U.S. interventions in Central America and the Caribbean meant that Camelot was not exactly laissez faire about anti-American riots or insurgencies. In spite of Kennedy's oft-stated belief that unrest in the developing world was frequently an expression of genuine unmet aspirations for better standards of living and more inclusive governments, when he turned to Cuba he saw a dangerous revolutionary government that would open the way to anti-American policies throughout the region and benefit the Soviet Union.

In order to win the hearts and minds of Latin America, Kennedy inaugurated an "Alliance for Progress" in the spring of 1961. Although the title was new, the program was an outgrowth of policy designed during the last years of the Eisenhower administration. The alliance promised a new era of cooperation and respect. Billed as a "Latin American Marshall Plan," the alliance would provide development aid to countries throughout the region. One White House aid wrote to Richard Goodwin advising against comparisons with the Marshall Plan on the grounds that "the problems of overcoming an ancient heritage of poverty, widespread illiteracy, and grave social, economic and geographical imbalances in the development process are fundamentally different from those engendering economic recovery in industrially advanced nations temporarily crippled by war."[63] Nonetheless, the basic premise of the alliance was that more aid would entice the wavering peoples of Latin America to resist the temptations of social revolution. In practice, the alliance was militarized, as the aid programs increasingly went to support the militaries of Latin America and their autocratic but anti-Communist governments rather than the development programs as initially envisioned.[64]

The alliance had a specific target in mind: Cuba. One of the many supposed advantages of the alliance from the standpoint of Kennedy was that it would deal a propaganda blow against Castro. There Fidel was, trumpeting his revolution with Che Guevara by his side, talking of copy-cat insurgencies throughout the Western Hemisphere. Kennedy hoped that the alliance, by outspending Castro, would show Cuban revolutionary promises to be hollow. Of course,

63. See Draft memorandum prepared for Richard Goodwin by Lincoln Gordon (Latin American Task Force, Department of State) vis Alliance for Progress, March 6, 1961, National Security Files—Subjects, Box 290A, JFK Library.

64. For a scathing critique of the alliance, see Coatsworth, *Central America and the United States,* 90.

the Kennedy White House did not intend to let the matter rest with the alliance and therefore proceeded with the CIA plans initiated by Eisenhower.

After the Bay of Pigs, Kennedy defenders claimed that Kennedy was rail-roaded by the CIA and presented with a fait accompli. He was told of the exiles in Guatemala and the plan to use them and assured that it would succeed.[65] Eisenhower defenders rejoined that there never was a plan for an invasion. There were, they said, only a series of options and possible courses of action that had been developed by the CIA in conjunction with the White House working group. Eisenhower reserved the right at any point to terminate one or all of the options, and he carefully monitored and vetted develop-ments.[66] He also organized his staff so that all points of view were aired, including dissent about the viability of the plans. And, said Allen Dulles, no assurance of success was ever given or ever would have been given by him and his officials at the CIA.[67] The failure, according to Eisenhower defenders, lay with the organization of Kennedy's White House and his inability to ask the right questions of the right people. He was too cowed by Bissell and Dulles, and he therefore did not discover the potential flaws and dangers as Eisenhower would have.[68]

In surveying the available documentation, it does not seem that Eisenhower elicited much in the way of dissent about the exile trainees or the plan to land them on Cuba. Nor does it appear that the only thing bequeathed to Kennedy was a set of options rather than an actual plan. At the January 3, 1960, meeting at the White House, Eisenhower and his advisers spoke very much as if there was a blueprint and a timetable. Certainly, Eisenhower might have called the operation off at the last minute, but there is little indication that he was leaning in that direction. However, almost three months elapsed between Eisenhower's departure and the launching of the invasion. In that time, the Kennedy adminis-tration assessed the options and decided to follow through. And the defense that Kennedy was presented with an all-or-nothing plan is untenable. Kennedy had a clear set of priorities, and he shaped the operation accordingly. In particu-lar, because of upcoming negotiations with Khrushchev over Berlin, he was determined to avoid the appearance of U.S. involvement in Cuba, and to that end, he both refused extensive U.S. air support and demanded that the landing site be changed, from Trinidad to the Bay of Pigs.

In January 1961, U.S. officials still believed that there was enough anti-Castro activity within Cuba to ensure the success of an exile landing. Both the

---

65. Sorensen, *Kennedy;* Schlesinger, *Thousand Days.* A more nuanced defense that apportions the blame between the administrations can be found in Chester Bowles Oral History, JFK Library.

66. Gordon Gray and Andrew Goodpaster oral histories.

67. Dulles "My Answer to the Bay of Pigs," 10-18.

68. Prados, *Keepers of the Keys,* 103-32.

Eisenhower and Kennedy administrations relied on a set of faulty observations to support that belief. The primary mistake was to trust evidence gathered from anti-Castro groups in Cuba as well as exiles in Miami.

The exiles who had fled to Miami, known pejoratively in Cuba as *los gusanos*—"the maggots"—made up the most cohesive contingent of anti-Castro forces. It was from them that the CIA recruited the paramilitary brigade that trained in Guatemala, and it was from them the U.S. government received some of its impressions about revolutionary Cuba. For example, Felix Rodriguez, who later helped capture Che Guevara in Bolivia, came to Miami in November 1959. He became a member of a group led by Pedro Díaz Lanz, which according to Rodriguez was composed of thirty to forty "young, idealistic Cubans." The objective of the group "was to commence military operations against Castro." At first, they had no place to train except the swamps outside of Miami, but by mid-1960, many of them had been recruited by the CIA to join the exile brigade. During the summer, the word on the streets of Little Havana in Miami was that some rich Cubans, with the support of the U.S. government, were paying to raise a force to contest Castro. These recruits reported to warehouses or other temporary headquarters. They were interviewed by CIA operatives. In addition to volunteering to fight Castro personally, they testified that among their friends and relatives, Castro was held in contempt.[69]

That, of course, was the same message the CIA was getting from the leaders of FRD. While these men tried to convince both the Eisenhower and Kennedy administrations that they had formed a united front, in truth, "all of the leaders wanted to be the next president of Cuba."[70] This was particularly true of Miró Cardona.

Miró Cardona struck many as an intelligent man and a savvy politician who could effectively weld the many disparate anti-Castro groups into a cohesive provisional post-Castro government.[71] As the former prime minister told Kennedy's special assistant Arthur Schlesinger, he was convinced that once the landings took place, "10,000 Cubans would immediately align themselves with the invading forces."[72] Miró Cardona believed that he was the most appropriate head of the FRD and that he should lead the provisional government that would be established when the brigade landed. He believed that the Cuban people supported many of the policies adopted by Castro, particularly insofar as these had redressed economic and social imbalances. He also thought that the activi-

69. Felix Rodriguez and John Weisman, *Shadow Warrior* (New York, 1989), 50–70. See also Dennis Kerbel, senior thesis, History Department, Harvard University, 1995.

70. Confidential source quoted ibid., 9.

71. Hunt, *Give Us This Day*, 154–56.

72. Schlesinger memorandum for the president, "Conversation with Dr. Miró Cardona," April 14, 1961, Secret, Schlesinger Papers—White House Files, Subject Files, Box WH 31, JFK Library.

ties of pro-Batista forces were hurting the FRD and the exile movement against Castro, and he took great pains to distance himself from them.[73]

While officials such as Schlesinger at the White House and Hunt at the CIA were impressed with Miró Cardona and other members of the FRD such as Manuel Ray, Castro was having a field day portraying them as pawns of the Americans. "Are those the men who will come to overthrow the armed people?" he asked sarcastically in a spring speech. "This mercenary government will not last twenty-four hours in Cuba."[74] After the invasion was defeated by Castro's military, the Cuban government published a four-volume history of the Bay of Pigs glorifying the victory. In it, Miró Cardona and the FRD are lampooned as hapless employees of the CIA and agents of "yanqui" imperialism.[75] The planners of the operation were not unaware of how the exiles were portrayed by the Castro regime, but they seem not to have understood the deep Cuban antipathy against U.S. intervention in Cuba's affairs. They thus underestimated how violently most Cubans would reject those associated with American intervention.

Many observers of Cuban history have noted that there was little coherence of class or social groups within Cuba in 1960. The upper classes and the sugar elite had been protected by Batista and by corrupt administrations before him, but those who had not fled to Miami after 1959 had become politically passive in Castro's Cuba. The middle sectors involved with trade or business in the cities had little class consciousness and no particular identity as a "bourgeoisie." And the rural and urban poor were united neither among themselves nor with each other.[76] Given the absence of communal solidarity before the revolution, regimes in Cuba tended not to be overthrown by a popular uprising. Castro's victory was the result not of a widespread revolt against Batista but of the inability of Batista to muster support. In spite of the assurances of the FRD and of the exile community that ten thousand people would immediately rise up to back the invasion, there was no reason, given Cuban history and society, to believe that such a spontaneous outburst would occur. Where were these thousands upon thousands of active, angry rebels going to come from? Had Eisenhower and Kennedy officials paid closer attention to Cuban history, they might have been less sanguine about the assurances of Miró Cardona and company.

To be fair, some CIA sources within Cuba reinforced such assurances. A report from the CIA station in Havana in late January 1961 stated that one informer told his CIA contact that "more and more men are taking to the hills

---

73. Memorandum of conversation among Miró Cardona, Adolf Berle, Arthur M. Schlesinger Jr., Philip Bonsal, April 5, 1961, Secret, Schlesinger Papers—White House Files—Subject Files, Box WH-31.

74. Quoted in Szulc, *Fidel*, 500.

75. Government of Cuba, *Playa Girón: Derrota del imperialismo* (4 vols.; Havana, 1961).

76. For an elaboration of these observations, see Ramón Eduardo Ruiz, *Cuba: The Making of a Revolution* (New York, 1968), 165–68.

to fight Castro." The same report said that a recent informal survey taken in Cuba revealed that less than 30 percent of the population was still with Fidel.[77] Also in January, Fidel made a speech warning that the United States was about to invade Cuba. It was common knowledge throughout the hemisphere that exiles were training in Guatemala, and Castro's informers apprised him of U.S. involvement. According to a CIA report, Castro made the speech because he "was afraid substantial numbers of his government officials and army would join the invaders and reinforce them. For this reason, he had to make a major crisis out of the [invasion] scare. He is now in the process of purging all suspects in the army and in the militia. . . . These moves by Castro have caused the people to laugh at him."[78]

Finally, shortly before the invasion, another CIA report stated that Castro was losing popularity, and that the Cuban people had begun to lose their fear of the government. "Cuban women have become leaders of the opposition activity and urge their husbands to undertake action to alleviate the present situation," said the report. Travelers to the interior of Cuba were said to have observed widespread disillusionment through all the provinces. Sources also indicated that the Cuban Army had been "penetrated by opposition groups and that it will not fight in the event of a showdown." The analysis concluded with an assessment of the source who provided these observations: "Although source is entirely reliable and is generally in a position to have access to the information on which he is reporting, his view of current conditions in Cuba may be somewhat influenced by his connections with opposition forces and his lack of close contact with pro-Castro Cubans."[79]

These reports may have been partly accurate. According to Carlos Franqui, editor and propagandist for the revolution before he defected, the Escambray Mountains in early 1961 "were full of rebels, at least a thousand. How was it possible? We knew who they were: peasants, workers, the common people. They weren't Batista supporters—those had all gone north. The middle class had also pretty much flown the coop. And it wasn't the CIA or any counterrevolutionary movement. They were too busy setting up an invasion brigade outside of Cuba." Rather, the rebels comprised people who felt they had been persecuted by the revolution. The Escambray Mountains in the Trinidad region had been forgotten by the revolution and exploited by the local commandante Felix Torres. Yet, says Franqui, rather than utilizing these guerrillas, the CIA instructed them to lie low until given the signal before the invasion. Inactive, they became careless, and Fidel moved against them, brutally. Franqui claims that after the

---

77. CIA Office of National Estimates, Report # 00-A3177796, "Increasing Opposition to Castro," February 1961, CIA Research Reports, Latin America, Reel II.

78. CIA Office of National Estimates, Report # CO-K 3,177,504, January 31, 1961, CIA Research Reports, Reel II.

79. CIA Report # CS 3/40,587, "Signs of Discontent among the Cuban Populace," April 6, 1961, CIA Research Reports, Reel II.

entire area had been sealed off, more than eight hundred guerrillas were rounded up before the Bay of Pigs landing.[80] Castro destroyed one potential ally of the U.S.-backed invasion before the exiles even embarked from Guatemala.

But the evidence of resistance was more than outweighed by evidence to the contrary. The chairman of the Office of National Estimates, Sherman Kent, never wavered from his assessment that Castro's regime was more entrenched than ever, and he reiterated that very point in a March 10 memo to Dulles: "We continue to hold to the view . . . that Castro remains firmly in control of Cuba and that his position is, if anything, likely to grow stronger rather than weaker as time goes on. . . . We see no signs . . . [of] any serious threat to the regime."[81]

Kent's warnings were not exactly ignored, but they were inconsistent with the operation being planned by Dulles, Bissell, Barnes, and their lieutenants. Even though the preponderance of reports from the directorate of intelligence stated bluntly that no uprising could be expected, no intelligence picture is unambiguous. The planners read what Kent and others were saying, but they also received intelligence that gave them hope. When they read reports from sources claiming that the island was disenchanted with Castro, they must have believed that things were unfolding according to plan. As for the NIE's and Kent's recommendations against proceeding with the invasion, Bissell's team simply dismissed those unwelcome conclusions or interpreted them so that they supported the plan.[82]

Bissell did a masterful job of making the square peg of the operations fit the round hole of the NIE's and Kent's reports. In a long memo prepared for JFK at the request of national-security adviser McGeorge Bundy, Bissell laid out his vision for the operation:

> About a year ago the Agency was directed to set in motion the organization of a broadly based opposition to the Castro regime . . . and trained paramilitary ground and air forces wherewith the opposition could overthrow the Cuban regime. . . . The Castro regime is steadily consolidating its control over Cuba. . . . There is no significant likelihood that the

80. Carlos Franqui, *Family Portrait with Fidel,* trans. Alfred MacAdam (New York, 1984), 111–15. While he was not always the most reliable witness, Franqui's account squares with that found in Wyden, *Bay of Pigs,* 108, and other descriptions of Castro's destruction of the Escambray rebels before the April invasion.

81. Memorandum for the director, "Is Time on Our Side in Cuba?" March 10, 1961, CIA Research Reports, Reel II.

82. Gleijeses says that they accepted the gloomy forecasts and therefore went ahead on the assumption that the failure of the landing would force Kennedy to authorize a U.S. invasion of Cuba. Gleijeses, "Ships in the Night," 35–42.

Castro regime will fall of its own weight. . . . Castro's position is daily getting stronger and will soon be consolidated to the point that his overthrow will only be possible by drastic, politically undesirable actions such as an all-out embargo or an overt use of force. . . . The Cuba paramilitary force, if used, has a good chance of overthrowing Castro or at the very least causing a damaging civil war. . . . Whatever embarrassment the alleged (although deniable) U.S. support may cause, it may well be considerably less than that resulting from the continuation of the Castro regime.[83]

Bissell read the estimates prepared by Kent and his staff. He knew that Castro's position was strong, yet he interpreted that information through a particular filter. He believed that there was still a small window of opportunity for the planned paramilitary invasion, and he warned the White House that there were only a few months left in which to act. After that, Castro would have consolidated his position beyond the capacity of a covert operation to remove him. In addition, the United States government would be left with the problem of what to do with more than one thousand Cubans in Guatemala. And Bissell warned that there would be irreparable damage to U.S. prestige if it appeared that Castro had intimidated the Americans to the point where they were scared to act.

There was no universal agreement among the agencies, and the Kennedy White House was aware of the disputes. The CIA was enthusiastic about the plan and its chances for success. The Defense Department and the chairman of the joint chiefs Lyman Lemnitzer expressed the opinion that "lacking a popular uprising . . . the Cuban army would eventually reduce the beachhead." Yet at meetings with the president throughout February, Lemnitzer and the Defense Department informed Kennedy that the plan "had a fair chance of success" and did not emphasize their misgivings.[84] The State Department was more pessimistic. Led by the taciturn Dean Rusk, State was concerned about the reaction of other Latin American countries. As the paramilitary operation went forward, State was concerned about the ramifications of the operation on the Alliance for Progress.[85] A secret, unilateral covert intervention in Cuba by the United States could easily torpedo the alliance unless the other Latin

---

83. Bissell memo on Cuba, February 17, 1961, enclosed with McGeorge Bundy memorandum for the president, February 18, 1961, Top Secret, National Security Files—Countries: Cuba, Box 35A, JFK Library.

84. Bissell, *Reflections of a Cold Warrior,* 164–66.

85. Edwin Martin, *Kennedy and Latin America* (New York, 1994), passim. Martin was assistant secretary of state for economic affairs (1960–61) and assistant secretary of state for Inter-American Affairs (1962).

American countries were consulted. Rusk and Adolf Berle both cautioned against precipitate action.[86]

Rusk was not, however, known for his assertiveness during meetings. Another prominent State Department official who thought that the CIA was going too far, too fast was the undersecretary of state, Chester Bowles. But Bowles was not included in these meetings and had few opportunities to air his objections.[87] The most vocal opponent of the CIA plan was Rusk's deputy, Thomas Mann, the assistant secretary for inter-American affairs. Mann had held the same position in the State Department during planning for the Guatemala intervention, but this time he dissented. As he remarked in a memo prepared two days before Bissell's February 17 exhortation,

> The military evaluation of this proposal is that "ultimate success will depend on political factors i.e. a sizeable popular uprising. . . . " It is unlikely that a popular uprising would promptly take place in Cuba of a scale and kind which would make it impossible for the Castro regime to oppose the brigade with superior numbers of well-armed troops. . . . The intelligence community . . . is unanimously of the opinion that time is running against us in Cuba in the sense that a declining curve of Castro's popularity is offset by a rising curve of Castro's control over the Cuban people. . . . I therefore conclude that it would not be in the national interest to proceed unilaterally to put this plan into execution.[88]

In his cover letter to both the Bissell and Mann memos, Bundy echoed Mann's conclusions and advised the president that "Castro's *internal* strength continues to grow."[89]

On March 11, Kennedy met with the task force, the secretaries of state and defense Rusk and Robert McNamara, and several of the joint chiefs of staff. Incredibly, even though the intelligence community had stated in no uncertain terms that Castro's internal position was strong, and even though Bundy had underlined (literally) that very point in a short memo to Kennedy, Kennedy remained committed to the operation. He had already been apprised of the opposing views of Bissell and Mann, as well as the general concerns of the

86. Memorandum of meeting with the president on Cuba, February 8, 1961, Top Secret, National Security Files—Cuba, Box 35A. See also Bundy memo for the president, February 8, 1961, ibid.

87. Chester Bowles Oral History, 28–30, JFK Library.

88. Mann to secretary of state, "The March 1960 Plan," February 15, 1961, Top Secret, National Security Files—Cuba, Box 35A.

89. Bundy Memorandum for the president, February 18, 1961, Top Secret, ibid.

State Department.[90] Dulles warned of the disposal problem if there was no action soon, and Bissell presented the proposed landing site at Trinidad on the southern-western coast near the Escambray Mountains. Limited air cover would be provided by Cuban-piloted B-26 aircraft untraceable to the United States.

Kennedy was uncomfortable with the plan, which called for a daylight invasion near a large town with no airstrip capable of handling B-26s. The covert fiction that there was no U.S. involvement demanded that the air cover could be attributed to Cuban air force pilots who had defected to support the brigade. Given the demands for air cover, the Trinidad plan would make U.S. involvement impossible to conceal. After the meeting, the task force revised the operation and recommended a new landing point: the Bay of Pigs.[91]

After the basic plan had been vetted at the White House on March 11, the task force designed a new operation, code-named Zapata. The principal assumptions remained the same, but the Bay of Pigs was far less suited to the proposed landing than Trinidad. More than eighty miles from the Escambray Mountains, the Bay of Pigs was too far away to allow the brigade to fade into the mountains and join the remnants of the indigenous opposition as guerrillas. The depth of the bay was not properly surveyed, nor were the swamps surrounding it. There were intelligence failures in misjudging the depth of the water and in overlooking the new roads that would allow Castro to quickly transport troops to the landing area. And there was the miscommunication about the amount of air support that the CIA anticipated would be available and the mistaken belief held by the planners that when confronted by difficulties, Kennedy would authorize whatever air cover was necessary to ensure the operation's success. As McGeorge Bundy said years later, "It never occurred to Bissell that if push came to shove, Kennedy wouldn't put in his stack. He never said, 'Do you really mean it? If we get the beachhead, will you back us up?' These worries were covered up. Once engaged, Bissell believed, Kennedy wouldn't allow it to fail."[92] Bissell rejoined that he was under the impression from Bundy's own memos during these weeks that the White House "understood the critical need for air superiority." However, he admitted that he never unequivocally told Kennedy that air cover was absolutely essential to the plan as conceived.[93]

Kennedy was unable to reconcile his desire to remove Castro with his concern that the invasion not be too "noisy." By "noise," Kennedy meant overt U.S. involvement. Even in early February, Kennedy had "pressed for an alternative to a full-fledged invasion, supported by U.S. planes, ships and sup-

90. Ibid. Gleijeses is particularly good on the Bissell-Mann dispute. He states that neither Mann nor Bissell saw the other's memo and that Mann's objections went nowhere. Gleijeses, "Ships in the Night," 22–28.

91. *Operation ZAPATA*, 11–17; Wyden, *Bay of Pigs*, 98–101.

92. Bundy interview with Evan Thomas in Thomas, *Very Best Men*, 247–48.

93. Bissell, *Reflections of a Cold Warrior*, 174–83.

plies." He wanted to explore the possibility of a gradual landing that could be done "quietly." As Alexsandr Fursenko and Timothy Naftali have shown, during the deliberations over Cuba, Kennedy was also considering Berlin and the possible impact of the Cuba intervention on relations with Khrushchev. He intended to meet soon with the Soviet premier in Vienna, and he had already decided to proceed with the summit before the Cuba invasion was launched. He had two aims: to demonstrate U.S. resolve on Cuba and to engineer a detente with the Soviets. These aims were not easily reconciled, but in an attempt to do so, Kennedy pared away what he thought were signs of overt U.S. involvement in Operation Zapata. However, given the scope of the operation, disguising U.S. involvement proved impossible; Bissell recognized that fact but neglected to impress it on the president.[94]

After a futile last-minute effort by Arthur Schlesinger to get the president to reconsider,[95] the invasion of the 1,400-man exile brigade began in the early morning of April 17. Several of the landing craft were hit by Castro's air force, to the surprise of the CIA and the U.S. Navy escort that had anticipated little resistance from Cuba's T-33 airplanes. By the morning of April 18, the brigade had established a beachhead. Castro moved his troops, complete with tanks and armored vehicles, to oppose the landings, and while his initial attack was rebuffed by the brigade, the exiles had to use most of their ammunition. Because no further air strikes were authorized by Kennedy, the CIA realized that the U.S. Navy escort could not safely resupply the brigade with ammunition. Already by the evening of April 18, the brigade was under heavy attack, and by the middle of April 19, approximately 1,200 men had been captured; another 100 were killed, and the rest escaped or had never even landed. They had killed as many as 2,000 of Castro's army.[96]

Kennedy met with the provisional government at the White House on April 19 to offer his apologies. Miró Cardona, Tony Varona, and Manuel Ray all demanded that the U.S. government continue its efforts to oust Castro. Kennedy assured them that he would never cease in his efforts to free Cuba from Castro. Given the subsequent implementation of Operation Mongoose and the multiple attempts to undermine Castro's regime and assassinate Castro himself, Kennedy was true to his word. At a press conference on April 21, Kennedy responded to a reporter who asked about rumors that Rusk and Bowles had opposed the invasion, "There's an old saying that victory has a hundred fathers and defeat is an orphan. . . . I am the responsible officer of this government."[97]

94. Fursenko and Naftali, *"One Hell of a Gamble"*; Memorandum of meeting with the president on Cuba, February 8, 1961, Top Secret, NSF—Cuba, Box 35A, JFK Library; Reeves, *President Kennedy*, 88–96; Bissell, *Reflections of a Cold Warrior*, 173.

95. Schlesinger memorandum for the president, "Cuba: Political, Diplomatic and Economic Problems," April 10, 1961, Secret, National Security Files—Cuba, Box 35A, JFK Library.

96. *Operation ZAPATA*, 25–35; Prados, *Presidents' Secret Wars*; Wyden, *Bay of Pigs*, 303.

97. Reeves, *President Kennedy*, 96–101.

This one-liner may have salvaged Kennedy's reputation and enhanced his public appeal, but responsibility for the failure hardly lay with Kennedy alone. The Taylor Committee concluded that errors had been made at each stage along the way, particularly by the CIA and the Defense Department. Yet the Committee's recommendations gave the lie to the prevalent belief in the administration that the fault lay with the architects in Washington. The committee suggested that in the future, the CIA not be allowed to oversee a paramilitary operation so large that it would more appropriately have been conducted as an overt military invasion. It recommended that the 5412 committee be abolished and a new group be set up to oversee covert operations. While the Taylor Report exempted no one from censure, its underlying presumption was that in the future, things could be done better by the U.S. government and that given a second chance, an operation such as Zapata could succeed.[98]

No one in the government stopped to ask whether *any* of the plans could have worked. No one seriously questioned the capacity of the United States to sponsor an invasion and overthrow a government considered inimical to U.S. interests. A number of individuals went on record as having opposed the Bay of Pigs. Bowles and Mann, for instance, understood that there would be no uprising of the Cuban people, and they criticized the plans for believing that there would be. Yet even these critics of the intervention did not seriously question the capacity of the U.S. government to overthrow Castro with a semicovert, Guatemala-style operation. They believed that Operation Zapata was a mistake, but they did not question whether the United States would be able to remove Castro by means short of an overt invasion.

It is true that there were signs of low-level opposition to Castro within Cuba, particularly in the Escambray Mountains. There were also indications of wide-scale middle-class disenchantment, and the CIA hoped to capitalize on those anti-Castro sentiments. However, the size of the operation made it possible for Castro's intelligence agents to anticipate what the United States was planning. Months before the invasion, he arrested any potential conspirators or sympathizers, thereby neutralizing what little active opposition there was to his regime. As for the vast majority of the Cuban people, they remained true to the revolution.

Furthermore, even though Castro did not know the details of what the United States was planning, he knew that they would eventually try something. He knew not just because of the countless failed infiltrations, and not just because of the abortive plots on his life in 1960. He knew with the certainty of a Cuban patriot that sooner or later the United States would act. That belief was central to the world view of any Cuban revolutionary.[99] From the moment he came to power, Castro started anticipating a U.S. invasion, and by 1960, that belief permeated Cuban society. Visiting the island that year, the venerable left-wing French existentialist Jean-Paul Sartre said of Cuba:

98. *Operation ZAPATA*, 30ff.
99. Benjamin, *United States and Origins of the Cuban Revolution*, passim.

Cuba is marching out in the open. For the timorous, the fate
of Guatemala becomes evidence. There is an order in the
New World which is elaborated in Washington and which is
imposed on the continent. . . . This order will not long allow
what it judges to be a small insular disorder. One day the armed
forces of the continent will come to make this protesting piece
of sugar see reason. But all the evidence of fatigue and fear
such as Guatemala have quite a different effect on the revolutionaries. They turn to rebellion. If the United States didn't
exist, the Cuban Revolution would perhaps invent it. It is the
United States which preserves Cuba's freshness and origi-
nality.[100]

Although undoubtedly biased in favor of Castro, Sartre identified a crucial
factor that the Kennedy administration seems to have missed: the Cubans
agitating for U.S. involvement were the fringe, not the Cubans supporting Castro
and the revolution. A repeat of the Arbenz coup simply wasn't possible in Cuba
because the internal conditions were not favorable. Unlike earlier, successful
interventions, the Bay of Pigs did not rely on a convergence of interests between
U.S. policy makers and entrenched groups within the country targeted for
intervention. Rather, it relied on a convergence between these policy makers
and exile groups. While there were numerous Cuban exiles willing to collaborate
with a U.S. intervention, they were in no position to collaborate. They were
in a position to plot, and they did that without the prompting of the CIA. But
without the presence of prominent, established, and significant groups within
Cuba whose domestic goals matched the foreign-policy goals of Washington,
the Bay of Pigs invasion never had a chance. Its failure was a foregone conclusion, long before the brigade set out for the swamps of Zapata one day in April
1961.

Neither the Eisenhower nor Kennedy administrations recognized that domestic conditions within Cuba, rather than air strikes or CIA blueprints, were central
to the outcome. U.S. officials were not conditioned to think in terms of the
domestic politics of third-world countries as having a primary effect on the
outcome of U.S. policy. While the Bay of Pigs exposed a number of weaknesses
in the CIA and in the national-security bureaucracy, the unlearned lesson was
that the domestic politics of the periphery can have a substantial effect on the
foreign policies of a great power.

The day after the collapse of the brigade, Kennedy spoke eloquently of the
challenges ahead. "The message of Cuba, of Laos, of the rising din of Communist
voices in Asia and Latin America—these messages are all the same," Kennedy
declared. "The complacent, the self-indulgent, the soft societies are about to
be swept away with the debris of history. Only the strong, only the industrious,

---

100. Jean-Paul Sartre, *Sartre on Cuba* (New York, 1961), 113.

only the determined, only the courageous, only the visionary who determines the real nature of our struggle can possibly survive." And Kennedy for one was determined that the American system would survive, "regardless of the cost and regardless of the peril."[101] Having failed to remove Castro, Kennedy turned again to another challenge a world away, in the Land of the Million Elephants: Laos.

101. Address to the American Society of Newspaper Editors, April 20, 1961, quoted in Reeves, *President Kennedy,* 98–99.

Laos

Into the Jungles

*My fellow Americans, Laos is far away from America, but the world
is small. Its two million peaceful people live in a country three times
the size of Austria. The security of all of Southeast Asia will be
endangered if Laos loses its neutral independence. Its own safety
runs with the safety of us all—in real neutrality observed by all.*
                                                —John F. Kennedy, March 1961

*Our unclear posture on neutralism is losing us friends, comforting
our enemy, and providing those in between with an opportunity
to play both sides for all they can get. . . . Neutralism, however, is
a fact of life. . . . The obvious good thing about neutralism is that
a genuine neutral is out of the contest. But can this be true in Asia?
If the Sino-Soviet bloc agrees to the neutralizing of Laos . . . is that
not a virtual victory for them? Neutrals are like manure, useful if
spread very thin but a nuisance in a heap.*
                                          —Kenneth Landon, National Security Council

B etween 1954 and 1961, the U.S. government thought that Laos
was the key to Southeast Asia, and it was over Laos and not Vietnam
that the early Kennedy administration struggled with the issue of third-world
neutralism and U.S. intervention. In January 1961, Eisenhower warned his young
successor that Laos was the most vital security issue confronting the United
States.[1] Laos was Vietnam before there was a Vietnam.

Yet, as one American writer acerbically observed, Laos was "neither a geographical nor an ethnic or social entity, but merely a political convenience."[2]

---

1. Roswell Gilpatric Oral History, 10, JFK Library. See also Marek Thee, *Notes of a Witness:
Laos and the Second Indochinese War* (New York, 1973), 13; Reeves, *President Kennedy,* 73-75;
Beschloss, *Crisis Years,* 84-86.

2. Bernard Fall, *Anatomy of a Crisis: The Laotian Crisis of 1960-1961* (Garden City, N.Y.,
1969), 23.

The country was divided into several competing factions, each headed by a royal prince or a ranking member of the traditional elite. One major faction described itself as pro-Western and cast its lot with the United States. Others championed Laotian neutralism, and fought over what that actually meant. The Pathet Lao allied itself with the North Vietnamese and the Communist bloc. When U.S. policy makers tried to find parallels for Laos, they made the mistake of treating it as an Indochinese Lebanon.

But Laos was unlike the countries in which the United States had previously intervened. Similarities to Lebanon notwithstanding, Laos was not a nation. It may have been a state, with a duly constituted government, borders, and an army, but as Bernard Fall astutely observed,[3] it lacked such traits as shared language and ethnicity, and it could call on no common history or geographic continuity with previous states or kingdoms. Laos comprised more than fifty distinct ethnic groups, and the Lao accounted for barely half the population. While the lowland Lao controlled the administration and much of the wealth of the country, they did not command the allegiance of numerous clans and tribes, such as the Hmong (Meo) tribespeople, who inhabited the mountain regions north of Vientiane.

Demonstrating the dearth of Laotian nationalism, a 1959 survey showed that less than 20 percent of Laotian villagers knew the name of the current king of Laos, who had been on the throne for more than fifty years. Only a slightly higher percentage of the people living in the main city, Vientiane, knew the name of the king, who lived north of Vientiane in Luang Prabang—"The City of the Golden Buddha." And of those surveyed, less than half knew that they lived in a country called Laos. One of the primary goals of the United States Information Agency's activities in Laos in the late 1950s was to acquaint the people of Laos with their own country.[4]

When officials in the Eisenhower and then the Kennedy administration considered the issue of Laos, they saw a small *nation* beleaguered by an external Communist threat. In contemplating intervention, therefore, they approached Laos much as they had approached Greece, Italy, Guatemala, Lebanon, Cuba, and the countries of Europe. They considered intervention a potential solution to the internecine conflict, a conflict the United States cared about primarily because of the strength of the Communist Pathet Lao and the close relationship between Laotian Communists and Ho Chi Minh in North Vietnam. But as Laos was not a nation, intervention on behalf of Laotian integrity was in fact impossible. There was no Laos to save.

The United States intervention leading up to the 1962 Geneva Accords stopped

3. Fall is not alone in this observation. See, for example, J. M. Halpern, *The Lao Elite: A Study of Tradition and Innovation* (Santa Monica, 1960).

4. Charles Stevenson, *The End of Nowhere: American Policy toward Laos since 1954* (Boston, 1972), 12–13; Oden Meeker, *The Little World of Laos* (New York, 1959), 106–107; Prados, *Presidents' Secret Wars*, 260ff.

short of a Lebanon-style military deployment. Contemplating such a course of action until April 1961, Kennedy after the Bay of Pigs was wary of another tragicomedy in Indochina. However, the massive amounts of U.S. aid until 1962 were so significant relative to the tiny Laotian economy that they constituted an intervention as formidable as landing a military division. In addition, the presence of several hundred military advisers and a smattering of CIA officers only muddied the already unclear political situation in Laos in the early 1960s.[5]

The story of U.S. involvement in Laos until 1962 is also inextricably bound to the later history of Laos as a secondary theater of the Vietnam War. For the rest of the 1960s, the U.S. government ostensibly held to a policy supportive of Laotian neutrality; but at the same time, the CIA armed and trained the Hmong tribes that lived on the Laotian border with North Vietnam. The Hmong were, in effect, American soldiers in the Vietnam War.[6] By the late 1960s, Laos was the target of the American air war against Vietcong supply routes that wove through northeastern Laos. As the conflict in Vietnam spilled over to Laos, the Pathet Lao became North Vietnamese auxiliaries. After the United States withdrew from Vietnam in 1973, Laos, like South Vietnam and Cambodia, was overtaken by Communist forces in 1975.

U.S. intervention in Laos until 1962 was neither a "success" such as Guatemala, Lebanon, Iran, Italy, and Greece, nor an explicit failure such as Cuba. Unlike these other areas, there was only minimal interaction between the U.S. foreign-policy establishment and entrenched domestic groups in Laos. Laos was different from previous interventions in that there was only a murky convergence of goals. With the Bay of Pigs, U.S. interests had converged precisely with those of the Cuban exile community (with dismal results), but in Laos as of the early 1960s, only General Phoumi Nousavan identified his interests firmly with the United States. Phoumi was able to sell himself as a U.S. client much as Castillo Armas had, and his army was substantial. But while Castillo Armas reflected the concerns of broad segments of Guatemalan society, Phoumi stood for himself. He commanded men and controlled territory in the south, but he simply did not have the personal prestige or the backing within Laos to be a viable executor of U.S. interests.

Because neither the Eisenhower nor the Kennedy administration undertook a full-blown military or paramilitary intervention, the stakes in Laos were relatively small. Nonetheless, the absence of convergence meant that U.S. policy toward Laos was bound to disrupt whatever internal balances had existed previously. Because U.S. policy was so purely a function of global cold-war strategy, and because Laos was primarily important to U.S. officials as a symbol of U.S. resolve, intervention in Laos never fit the domestic agenda of entrenched groups in

---

5. For a concise history of U.S. aid programs to Laos, see Timothy Castle, *At War in the Shadow of Vietnam: U.S. Military Aid to the Royal Lao Government, 1955–1975* (New York, 1993).

6. Jane Hamilton-Merritt, *Tragic Mountains: The Hmong, the Americans, and the Secret Wars for Laos, 1942–1992* (Bloomington, Ind., 1993).

Laos. The Bay of Pigs is an acute example of what happened in the absence of convergence with groups actually in the country; in Laos, where numerous domestic groups competed for influence, the faction advocating intervention was an ineffective partner.

From Washington's perspective, Laos was one of several threads of a complex Southeast Asian web. At the center of that web was Vietnam. In the spring of 1954, the Eisenhower administration gave serious thought to introducing U.S. troops to Vietnam in order to relieve French forces besieged by the Vietminh at Dien Bien Phu on the Vietnamese-Lao border. Unable to get the British to participate, Dulles and Eisenhower managed to avoid a commitment of American forces, a commitment that they were at once willing and loath to make. After the fall of Dien Bien Phu to the Vietminh in 1954, the Geneva Accords led to the de facto separation of North and South Vietnam as well as to a multilateral agreement that Laos would be neutral and demilitarized. Under the accords, both Vietnamese and French troops were to withdraw from Laos, and a portion of the Pathet Lao was to be integrated into the Royal Laotian Army.

While the Eisenhower administration accepted the Geneva settlement, it did not sign the agreement. U.S. officials did not want to leave themselves open to the charge that they had acquiesced in a partition that recognized a Communist North Vietnam. In August of 1954, the NSC resolved that the United States would "make every possible effort, not openly inconsistent with the U.S. government position as to the [Geneva] armistice agreements, to defeat Communist subversion and influence and to maintain and support friendly non-Communist governments" in Southeast Asia.[7] As a result, the Eisenhower administration initiated one of the most significant aid programs to any third-world country during the entire course of the cold war. In addition to tightening ties with the pro-Western regime of Thailand's Marshal Sarit, Washington opened the tap to the tune of nearly $50 million in aid per year to Laos. Of that figure, more than 90 percent was military aid. In a country of less than three million people, U.S. aid was more than five times the revenue at the disposal of the Laotian government in the 1950s.[8] It paid for the entire military budget of the 25,000-man Laotian army.

Between 1954 and 1960, the Eisenhower administration attempted to forge a Laos that would be firmly in the western camp. The military aid was designed to give the Laotian government the capacity to resist the Pathet Lao and its patron, North Vietnam. The aid was also designed as an incentive. Many Laotian elites in the capital city of Vientiane filled their purses with U.S. dollars. Corruption was widespread and widely known. Army officers enriched themselves, as did Laotian aid administrators. In the trickle-down world of kickbacks and nepotism, these officials then enriched others. A complex and multifaceted

---

7. NSC 5429/2 signed on August 20, 1954, in Castle, *War in the Shadow,* 12.

8. For figures, see Martin Goldstein, *American Policy toward Laos* (Rutherford, N.J., 1973), 130–38, 188. His numbers are taken directly from congressional reports on aid programs to Laos.

"aid" network developed, and it both supplemented and competed with the local economy. The army became the only source of skilled manpower in the largely agrarian economy, and U.S. aid became the predominant source of circulating currency. Rampant inflation was kept in check only by the equally rampant corruption.[9]

In its approach to Laos, the Eisenhower administration did not depart from its overall strategy toward the third world. As it demonstrated in Guatemala, Iran, and elsewhere, it viewed with deep suspicion any Communist participation in government. It believed that most third-world governments were inherently weak, and given their newness and the seething tensions in their respective countries, that view was not without merit. The self-declared neutralism of Laos was also a cause of concern to Eisenhower and Dulles. Laos was a participant in the Bandung conference and there affirmed its commitment to neutrality. In domestic politics, that meant embracing the disparate elements within Laos, and the Pathet Lao in particular. When the Laotian premier, Souvanna Phouma, proceeded in the late 1950s to honor the letter of the Geneva Accords and bring the Pathet Lao into the government, the Eisenhower administration turned against him.

In opposing the efforts of Souvanna to integrate the Pathet Lao into the government, Washington operated on the assumption that the Pathet Lao planned to use the cover of neutralism to subvert the government and seize control. The Eisenhower administration thought that the Pathet Lao army owed its existence to aid from both Ho Chi Minh and "international Communism." Claiming that true Laotian neutrality was impossible so long as the Communist bloc was endangering Laotian integrity, Eisenhower officials felt fully justified in funding anti-Pathet Lao forces.[10] But the basic premise was wrong. True, aid from North Vietnam helped the Pathet Lao. But while there was an ongoing contest in Laos between the Pathet Lao and the Royal Laotian government, it did not represent an insurgent challenge to a duly constituted government. It was an internecine struggle within the Laotian elite.

Not unlike Lebanon, Laos was controlled by a small circle of elites. Twenty or so major families dominated politics and owned much of the land. Most of the Lao elite were descendants of the royal families of Luang Prabang and Xieng Khouang in the north or Champassak in the south. Many carried the title of Tiao, or prince. Although French colonial administration in Laos had been slight, a large percentage of the elite had been educated in French schools and shared an affinity for French culture. The elite tended to be urban; unlike in Lebanon, ties between them and the peasantry were weak. Living far from their land,

9. Arthur Dommen, *Conflict in Laos* (London, 1964), 126–27; Jean Deuve, *Le Royaume de Laos, 1949–1965* (Paris, 1984), 86ff.; Goldstein, *American Policy toward Laos,* 130.

10. Eisenhower to Nehru, January 3, 1961, International Series, Box 27, Eisenhower Library. See also Hugh Toye, *Laos: Buffer State or Battleground* (New York, 1968), passim; Dommen, *Conflict in Laos,* 101ff.

the aristocracy did not have firm control over the peasants, and Laos was in any event not a rigidly hierarchical society.[11]

The most significant example of the interconnectedness of the Laotian ruling class was the relationship between Souvanna Phouma and Prince Souphanouvong. The two were half-brothers. Souvanna was the elder, born in 1901, and educated at the University of Paris. He worked as an engineer on various French projects in Indochina. During World War II, he joined the Lao Issara (Free Laos) movement, formed to resist the Japanese in Indochina. The leaders of postwar Laos, almost to a man, were veterans of Lao Issara, and the Pathet Lao drew heavily on its membership. Souvanna was described by Kennedy official Roger Hilsman as "plump, pipe-smoking, a lover of French culture, and a fiend at bridge." He was also quite wealthy.[12] As premier of Laos after 1954, Souvanna was a strong advocate of genuine Lao neutrality, a neutrality that would remove foreign influence in Laos internal affairs and allow the various factions to participate in the government. That meant an embrace of the Pathet Lao, an embrace made easier by the fact that his half-brother Souphanouvong was the leader of the Pathet Lao.

Known as the "Red Prince," Souphanouvong was more than a decade younger than Souvanna. Like his brother, he attended French schools and joined the Lao Issara. After the war, however, Souphanouvong had no interest in continuing to cooperate with the French. While Souvanna was a pragmatist who believed in the necessity of compromise to achieve his objectives,[13] Souphanouvong was more fiery and quick tempered. He married a Vietnamese woman, and when the French tried to reassert colonial control over Indochina after 1945, Souphanouvong assembled military cadres to combat French forces. These efforts culminated in 1950 with the founding of the Pathet Lao under the direct aegis of Ho Chi Minh.[14]

Until the late 1950s, Laotian politics were characterized by a constantly shifting pattern of governing coalitions. The fraternal bond between Souvanna and Souphanouvong is a fitting metaphor for the interconnectedness of the competing Lao factions. It was also a strong argument in favor of neutrality. No one faction was going to gain absolute predominance, and significant segments of the elite were willing to compromise and thereby preserve the status quo.

At the time of the 1954 Geneva Accords, the Pathet Lao and the Vietminh controlled more than three-quarters of Laos. But on becoming premier, Sou-

---

11. Stevenson, *End of Nowhere*, 14; Halpern, *Lao Elite*, 11ff.

12. Roger Hilsman, *To Move a Nation: The Politics of Foreign Policy in the Administration of John F. Kennedy* (Garden City, N.Y., 1967), 106; Thee, *Notes of a Witness*, 72–75; Dommen, *Conflict in Laos*, 20–21.

13. Sisouk Na Champassak, *Storm over Laos* (New York, 1961), 15. The author was a staunch anti-Communist politician who opposed Souvanna's attempts to deal with the Pathet Lao, yet he acknowledged Souvanna's realism even while disagreeing with it.

14. Joseph Zasloff, *The Pathet Lao* (Lexington, Mass., 1973); Castle, *War in the Shadow*, 7.

vanna refused to treat his younger sibling's followers as die-hard Communists. Given that the Pathet Lao were clearly being aided by Ho Chi Minh, Souvanna's stance disturbed the Eisenhower administration.[15] The Vietminh–Pathet Lao alliance also alienated many Laotians. There was no love lost between Laos and Vietnam. As one Lao official commented, "We detest the Vietnamese because they would like to sit on our heads."[16] Yet, the Pathet Lao were militarily strong and politically entrenched in the northeastern Lao hinterland. Adopting tactics similar to those of the Vietminh, though not nearly as brutal as Ho Chi Minh's cadres, the Pathet Lao fought for the allegiance of the peasants. As the United States pumped aid to the Royal Laotian Army, Souphanouvong took advantage of anticolonial sentiments and the general disenchantment with the corruption wrought by U.S. aid. The Pathet Lao excelled at guerrilla and ideological warfare and convinced many Laotians that the United States was simply reimposing colonial control in lieu of the French.[17] By 1957, the country was beset by chronic civil war, and Souvanna's efforts to integrate the Pathet Lao were torpedoed by an antagonistic Eisenhower administration and by Lao factions who sought to gain from allying with Washington.

Between 1957 and 1960, domestic politics seesawed between Souvanna and several explicitly pro-Western factions. In April 1960, Souvanna was ousted as premier and replaced by a coalition dominated by Phoumi Nousavan. Like Souvanna and Souphanouvong, Phoumi was a veteran of Lao Issara, but unlike them, he was not descended from the traditional aristocracy. Phoumi's rise was through the military. Tough, stubborn, with a talent for intrigue, Phoumi cultivated contacts with the CIA and spread the word that he fully supported a pro-Western Laos and fully rejected any accord with the Pathet Lao. His ties to the United States were enhanced by the fact that he was a distant cousin of Thailand's ardently pro-Western Marshal Sarit.[18]

Phoumi's attempt to place Laos securely in the Western sphere led to a counteraction. On August 9, 1960, a young paratrooper captain named Kong Le seized control of Vientiane, ousted Phoumi's coalition, and called for Souvanna's return. The coup surprised everyone, including Souvanna. Kong Le was an unknown quantity. He was not Lao but came from a Malay tribe in Laos. Twenty-six years old at the time of coup, he spoke fluent French and was a veteran of a U.S. Army ranger training program in the Philippines. A short, compact man who often dressed in crisp paratrooper fatigues, he saw himself as an anticolonial Lao nationalist, committed to neutralism and hence to Souvanna Phouma. He

15. Goldstein, *American Policy toward Laos,* 115.

16. Quoted in Halpern, *Lao Elite,* 54.

17. Deuve, *Le Royaume de Laos,* 43, 86; Fall, *Anatomy of a Crisis,* 110. For the Pathet Lao "party line," see Neo Lao Haksat, *12 Anneés d'intervention et d'agression de impérialistes américains* (N.p., 1966).

18. Dommen, *Conflict in Laos,* 77; Hilsman, *To Move a Nation,* 108; Deuve, *Le Royaume de Laos,* 358–59.

also decried the corruption generated by U.S. aid. In this too he echoed Souvanna, who had once called the aid program the equivalent of giving morphine to the Lao people.[19]

At Kong Le's invitation, Souvanna returned to Vientiane and resumed control of the government. Phoumi, meanwhile, rejected the Kong Le coup as pro-Pathet Lao and retreated to Savannakhet in the Laotian panhandle on the Lao-Thai border in the south. In October, on the recommendation of Ambassador J. Graham Parsons, the Eisenhower administration suspended aid to Souvanna's government and redirected the monies to Phoumi. Parsons, who had served in Laos for several years, had recently been appointed Eisenhower's assistant secretary of state for East Asia. He disliked Souvanna, and was a staunch Phoumi partisan. Picked by Eisenhower to negotiate with the competing factions in Laos in October 1960, Parsons, to no one's surprise, urged U.S. support for Phoumi. Eisenhower promptly acted on this advice.[20]

Bolstered by Washington's blessing and by its dollars, Phoumi advanced north and retook Vientiane at the end of December. He did so without in any way weakening Souvanna and Kong Le. Allied with Souphanouvong, Kong Le's forces made an orderly retreat north and settled in comfortably on the Plain of Jars. In December, the Soviets began airlifting supplies to the neutralist-Pathet Lao army. By January, Phoumi barely controlled Vientiane and select pockets throughout the Laotian panhandle and in the north. Together, Kong Le and Souphanouvong controlled nearly 70 percent of the country. That was the situation when Kennedy entered the White House.

As Kennedy and his advisers contemplated Laos, their outlook was influenced by the Eisenhower administration. Soon after New Year's Day 1961, Eisenhower explained the U.S. position on the crisis to India's Nehru:

> A new and tragic chapter in the brief history of Laos as nation
> has begun with the continuing air delivery of sizeable quantities
> of munitions and military supplies by the Soviet Union to the
> Pathet Lao rebel forces. . . . I am deeply troubled by the renewal
> of fratricidal warfare in this small and weak but strategically
> important Kingdom, whose only "offense" is geographical: it
> lies in the path of Communist expansionist intent in Asia, and
> is perhaps the most vulnerable spot on the entire periphery
> of the Communist-controlled Eurasian land mass. . . . We have
> no quarrel whatsoever with a neutral policy for Laos, so long
> as the Lao Government desires it. We do, however, have our
> own grave reservations as to the threat to Laos caused by

19. Deuve, *Le Royaume de Laos*, 102-104, 347; Fall, *Anatomy of a Crisis*, 184-85; Stevenson, *End of Nowhere*, 91; Goldstein, *American Policy toward Laos*, 204.

20. Fall, *Anatomy of a Crisis*, 170ff.; Dommen, *Conflict in Laos*, 158ff.; Goldstein, *American Policy toward Laos*, 213.

the bringing into the Government Communist-indoctrinated
elements having the support of, and very probably under the
guidance and direction of, outside Communist powers.

Eisenhower concluded by questioning Souvanna Phouma's policy of attempting
to integrate the Pathet Lao, and he asked Nehru to join the United States in
calling on Khrushchev to "withdraw USSR military assistance . . . to Communist-
directed forces in Laos." Nehru replied that he failed to see the vast difference
between Soviet and American aid in Laos. From his vantage, both powers were
interfering unduly.[21]

As Kennedy prepared to take over the government, the Eisenhower administration counseled that the United States should take any necessary measures
to assist Phoumi and keep Laos from falling to the Pathet Lao. According to
Eisenhower officials, the formation of the Phoumi-dominated anti-Communist
government with Prince Boun Oum as premier gave the United States "much
greater freedom of action than previously existed." In order to bolster
Phoumi's Vientiane regime, Eisenhower authorized a series of U.S. airlifts to
relieve the pressure being placed on Phoumi by Kong Le and the Pathet Lao
from the Plain of Jars.[22]

The president and his advisers even envisioned using U.S. troops to
strengthen the beleaguered Phoumi in Vientiane. The preliminary plan was to
fly troops to secure the two main cities, Vientiane and Luang Prabang. According
to the minutes of an early January 1961 meeting, Eisenhower said that "if we
ever resort to force, the thing to do is to clear up the problem completely. We
should not allow a running sore like the British had in Egypt or the U.S. had
in Korea."[23] This conviction that a U.S. intervention could "clear up the problem
completely" shows how little Eisenhower understood Laos. Although Eisenhower was convinced that he had so far preserved Laotian independence, his
administration had in fact been a disruptive force.

Until 1960, the Pathet Lao was rather muted in its demands, probably because
of the moderating influence of Souphanouvong. But by demanding the removal
of the Pathet Lao from the political scene, the Eisenhower administration forced
a polarization of the elite. Souphanouvong and Souvanna both lost support to
the more extreme factions to their left and right respectively. Younger Pathet
Lao cadres more susceptible to North Vietnamese influence rejected compro-

21. Eisenhower to Nehru, enclosed in State 1749 to New Delhi, January 3, 1961, Secret,
International Series—Nehru files, Box 27, Eisenhower Library. A summary of Nehru reply can be
found in the same file.

22. State 641 (to Vientiane), with report on recent conference between president and the JCS,
December 14, 1960, Top Secret, WHO, Staff Secretary, International Series, Box 9, Eisenhower
Library.

23. Memorandum of conference with the president, January 2, 1961, Top Secret, WHO, Staff
Secretary, International Series, Box 9.

mise with the "American imperialists" and their Laotian "puppets"; factions led by the likes of Phoumi and Boun Oum successfully portrayed neutralists such as Souvanna as Communists and so stripped them of U.S. aid.[24] At the end of 1960, Souvanna accepted aid from the Russians to compensate for the sudden termination of U.S. aid that Eisenhower had authorized.

On January 19, President-elect Kennedy met with President Eisenhower at the White House. Laos was high on the agenda. Going into the meeting, Kennedy was "anxious to get some commitment from the outgoing administration as to how they would deal with Laos which they were handing to us. [He] thought particularly it would be helpful to have some idea as to how prepared they were for military intervention." Meeting with Eisenhower and six cabinet members, Kennedy listened to Herter opine that "any proposal which would include Communists in the government would end up with the Communists in control of the government." Kennedy asked whether the United States should intervene if asked by its allies in the region. Herter said yes. "It was the cork in the bottle," he continued. "If Laos fell, then Thailand, the Philippines, and of course Chiang Kai-Shek [in Taiwan] would go." Kennedy left the meeting convinced that the Eisenhower team believed that intervention was "preferable to a Communist success in Laos."[25]

From the perspective of the Kennedy White House, the internal conflict in Laos mirrored the cold-war conflict between the Soviet Union and the United States. Each country had cultivated "proxy" factions in Laos, and various groups in Laos had opted for one superpower or the other to sponsor them. In a paper prepared just prior to the changeover in administration, an interagency task force on Laos concluded that an effective strategy in Laos depended on both political and military action. Given the current situation, the task force believed that pro-American groups in Laos were unlikely to achieve a military victory. "The present crisis in Laos," the report said, "can be viewed as being one of a number of focal points at which over-all U.S. policy is in confrontation with Soviet bloc policy. Many of the basic elements of that confrontation bear directly on the Laotian crisis and in turn will be affected by its outcome."[26]

Kennedy and his advisers accepted these basic assumptions. Laos was one of several arenas of the cold war, and as the most highly contested region in Southeast Asia, it was a "front-line" concern. By January 1961, it and not Vietnam was the first domino that U.S. officials feared would fall and thereby set off a chain reaction throughout Asia and beyond.[27] As a senior staff member of

24. Toye, *Laos,* 160–61; Fall, *Anatomy of a Crisis,* 190–92; Goldstein, *American Policy toward Laos;* 228–29; H. B. Fredman, *Laos in Strategic Perspective* (Santa Monica, 1961), 14–18.

25. Notes of conversation between Kennedy and Eisenhower, January 19, 1961, *FRUS, 1961–1963, Vol. XXIV,* 19–20.

26. Report Prepared by the Inter-Agency Task Force on Laos, January 1961, Top Secret, *FRUS, 1961–1963, Vol. XXIV,* 28–40.

27. Memorandum from McNamara to Kennedy concerning Eisenhower's statement that if Laos

Kennedy's NSC noted, "The stake . . . is not Laos but eventual control of the Indian Ocean Area. . . . The decision of our government regarding Laos cannot be decided on the merits of Laos and should be decided in the larger context."[28]

Seeing Laos as the linchpin, Kennedy officials did not depart significantly from the policy developed by Eisenhower. While the NSC churned out a paper titled "A New Look at Laos," it was in fact a restatement of the old looks at Laos: "The United States wants no war, no appeasement and no collapse in Laos. To prevent all this we need a different kind of commitment and a radically new sort of action."[29] Yet the actual recommendations for increased levels of aid and military assistance mirrored those of the Eisenhower administration.

Where the Kennedy administration did begin to depart was in its greater emphasis on rural warfare, on what would soon come to be known as counterinsurgency. The Pathet Lao frequently managed to gain the allegiance of villagers. Correctly assessing that insurgent, guerrilla warfare was the new mode of conflict in the third world, the Kennedy administration set up the Peace Corps and beefed up the Army Special Forces. But while Kennedy's NSC dressed up these programs as a radical departure from Eisenhower, they were really a continuation of Eisenhower's methods, albeit at an intensified level. In the fall of 1960, Eisenhower had authorized the dispatch of White Star teams, mobile special-forces training units. These helped train the Royal Laotian Army in counterinsurgency techniques, and while White Star numbers in Laos were increased by Kennedy, the strategy was essentially the same: entice and arm loyal villagers to fight Communist insurgents.[30]

As with the Alliance for Progress, therefore, the Kennedy administration improved on an Eisenhower tactic and effectively repackaged it. Astute packaging was part of the Camelot mystique. But while Kennedy officials may have convinced themselves and a good portion of the American people that its strategy toward Laos was a fundamental departure from a supposedly failed Eisenhower policy, it did not convince the factions in Laos. By March, the position of the Boun Oum–Phoumi government had not improved, and the neutralist–Pathet Lao forces were even more firmly in control of the Plain of Jars and the rest of the country. The Kennedy administration considered Souvanna

---

was "lost to the Free World," all of Southeast Asia would follow, January 24, 1961, *FRUS, 1961–1963, Vol. XXIV*, 41–42.

28. Memorandum for McGeorge Bundy from Kenneth Landon, February 3, 1961, Secret, NSF, Countries, Laos, Box 130, JFK Library.

29. "A New Look at Laos," February 3, 1961, prepared by Kenneth Landon, NSF, Countries, Laos, Box 130, JFK Library.

30. Stevenson, *End of Nowhere*, 174–84; Castle, *War in the Shadow*, 42–43. For an excellent survey of the Kennedy administration counterinsurgency doctrine, see Michael McClintock, *Instruments of Statecraft*, 100–203. For reference to special forces in Laos, see Memorandum of Conference with the president, February 23, 1961, Top Secret, NSF, Chester Clifton Files, Box 345, JFK Library.

unacceptable because he had "sought . . . to negotiate with the Pathet Lao as equals,"[31] and it held fast to its position that the Pathet Lao represented external Communist aggression.

The White House also planned for a possible military intervention, in spite of the reservations of some of the military chiefs. General Lyman Lemnitzer, chairman of the Joint Chiefs of Staff, did not support the introduction of U.S. combat troops into Laos. He thought that the deployment would have to be prohibitively large to ensure success, and he also feared that opponents would use the opportunity to denounce the United States as "trigger happy."[32] Other officers disagreed. Admiral Henry Felt, commander in chief of the Pacific, welcomed the opportunity to demonstrate U.S. mettle. Of course, as the officer with ultimate responsibility for the Seventh Fleet, Felt had certain parochial reasons for urging deployment of a marine contingent; success would reflect well on his command. However, the admiral hardly disregarded the dangers inherent in any large-scale operation, particularly if the North Vietnamese chose to respond in force.[33]

Although the administration was concerned about how the Soviets and the Chinese would react to U.S. intervention, it did not believe that either country regarded Laos as important enough to risk war with the United States. The CIA calculated that in the event of a U.S. deployment, the Communist bloc "would move to negotiate," although it did not rule out the possibility that the Soviets would urge either the Chinese or the North Vietnamese to intervene against the Americans.[34] The decision, then, revolved around two basic questions: were U.S. troops necessary to prevent a Pathet Lao victory, and could U.S. troops secure Laos for the Phoumi–Boun Oum government.

While these questions were asked repeatedly, it is unclear if they were ever answered definitively. Several commentators on this period have pointed to Kennedy's March 23 press conference as representing a turning point in U.S. policy toward Laos.[35] As dramatically described by Roger Hilsman, who was then head of INR in the State Department, Kennedy conducted the conference

31. Special Report prepared by L. D. Battle at request of General Clifton for the president, March 13, 1961, Secret, NSF, Countries, Laos, Box 130.

32. Memorandum of conference with the president, January 25, 1961, Top Secret, *FRUS, 1961-1963, Vol. XXIV*, 42–44.

33. Memorandum of conversation with the president, March 9, 1961, Top Secret, *FRUS, 1961-1963, Vol. XXIV*, 72–75; Fall, *Anatomy of a Crisis*, 155; Goldstein, *American Policy toward Laos*, 166; Dommen, *Conflict in Laos*, 188.

34. CIA-SNIE 58-61, "Possible Communist Reactions to Certain U.S. Courses of Action with Respect to Laos," February 21, 1961, Top Secret, *FRUS, 1961-1963, Vol. XXIV*, 59–62. See also Landon memorandum for Walt Rostow, "Choices in U.S. Policy toward Laos," March 7, 1961, Secret, NSF, Countries, Laos, Box 130, JFK Library.

35. Stevenson, *End of Nowhere*, 143–44; Goldstein, *American Policy toward Laos*, 236; Reeves, *President Kennedy*, 74–75.

with three easels behind him, each holding a map of Laos. The first showed the territory—colored red—controlled by the Pathet Lao in August 1960; the second showed the area controlled by the Pathet Lao and Kong Le's troops after December 1960; and the third displayed Pathet Lao advances into the Laotian panhandle in early 1961.[36] With each map, the red portion increased.

In his remarks, Kennedy tried to explain to the American public why Laos was important. After presenting a modified version of Eisenhower's domino theory, Kennedy stated that his administration "strongly and unreservedly support[ed] the goal of a neutral and independent Laos, tied to no outside power or group of powers, threatening no one, free from any domination." He further called for an immediate cease-fire and international negotiations to de-escalate the conflict. "All we want in Laos is peace, not war," he concluded, "a truly neutral government, not a cold war pawn."[37]

While this may have been the most explicit public statement committing the United States to Laotian neutrality, it was hardly a deviation from prior policy. After the 1954 Geneva Accords, U.S. officials had always defended the *principle* of Laotian neutrality, both in public and in private deliberations. However, the manner in which Eisenhower and Kennedy officials conceived of neutrality did not allow for genuine Laotian neutralism. Agreeing to a truly neutralized Laos meant accepting the Pathet Lao as a faction that would not soon disappear; it meant, in short, the very path that Souvanna and Kong Le were attempting to blaze. Yet, at the same time that President Kennedy was making a very public commitment to "a truly neutral government" in Laos, most U.S. officials were dismissing neutrality as unachievable.

The more the Kennedy administration discussed Laos, the less clear-cut it appeared. The country always had a "land of Oz" quality to it; George Ball, Kennedy's undersecretary of state, referred to Laotian politics as "a Kung Fu movie." John Kenneth Galbraith, the U.S. ambassador to India, remarked that as a military ally, "the entire Laos nation is clearly inferior to a battalion of conscientious objectors from World War I." The languid pace of life in Laos never ceased to bemuse U.S. officials there, and when they weren't fulminating about Communist influence, they often spoke in patronizing tones of the Lao people. On meeting Phoumi, Kennedy apparently remarked to his aides, "If this is our strongman, we're in trouble."[38]

While U.S. officials had a rather limited understanding of the complexities of Lao society, they did come to realize that Laos was indeed lacking the basic elements of a nation-state:

36. Hilsman, *To Move a Nation*, 91ff.; Roger Warner, *Backfire: The CIA's Secret War in Laos and Its Link to the War in Vietnam* (New York, 1995), 60–61.

37. Statement made on March 23, 1961. The text of Kennedy's speech is in Nina Adams and Alfred McCoy, eds., *Laos: War and Revolution* (New York, 1970), 393–97.

38. Thomas, *Very Best Men*, 278–81; Beschloss, *Crisis Years*, 161.

> The fundamental fact which has been at the core of all of our
> difficulties over Laos during the last five years is our failure to
> recognize that Laos is not a nation-state. We have continually
> applied to Laos policies appropriate in relations among nation-
> states, and as a consequence we have at best been made to
> look foolish and at worst we may be permitting a domestic
> Laotian controversy to become a genuine international crisis.

According to this sober memo prepared for Walt Rostow on the NSC and
forwarded to Bissell, if the U.S. objective was to neutralize Laos, "the only
effective policy is that of striving to build the country up to the point of being
a strong and effective political entity which can then follow a neutralist policy."
Laotian neutrality was impossible because Laos wasn't a state or a nation, and
only a state or a nation could achieve viable neutrality. Having miscalculated
in multiple ways, the United States could not back down because "having
worked ourselves into a confrontation with the Russians," U.S. prestige was at
stake.[39]

While Laos was certainly not a nation-state, that should not have disqualified
it from neutralism. Indeed, while this memo was a healthy dose of reality for
the Kennedy White House, it represents a misconception of neutralism. Of
course, the analysis was correct insofar as the presence of competing factions
without a unifying nation-state made Laos especially vulnerable to meddling
from outside. But what made Lao neutrality untenable was the willingness of
both the Soviet Union and the United States to sponsor competing factions.
Instead of helping an entrenched local group consolidate control over Laos,
U.S. intervention helped the Phoumi-Boun Oum government and the Hmong
tribespeople prevent a domestic solution to the crisis. Believing that it was
preserving the status quo, the Kennedy administration, like its predecessor,
was contributing to its destruction.

By April, the policy of the Kennedy administration was as follows: Laos was
weak; it lacked strong internal organization; the U.S. wanted a neutral Laos,
but Laos was not ready for neutrality; only after the United States aided Laos
in building strong state structures could it be viably neutral. Thus, until then,
Laos had to be shielded by the United States from the Pathet Lao, with economic
and military assistance if possible, and with the intervention of U.S. troops if
necessary.

As the neutralist-Pathet Lao forces gained at Phoumi's expense in March and
early April, the Kennedy administration agreed to an international conference
in Geneva to settle the issue. That accorded with the advice the ambassador
in Laos, Winthrop Brown, had given Kennedy in January. As Brown noted then,
a political solution to the crisis would only be tenable if it was negotiated

---

39. See memorandum from Rostow for Bissell, March 23, 1961, NSF, Countries, Laos, Box 130,
JFK Library.

internationally.[40] But in spite of the upcoming conference, the White House was anxious that gains by the Pathet Lao would reduce the leverage of the United States. Cease-fire negotiations were stalled, and Phoumi's position was eroding. Several civilian and military officials from the Defense Department, as well as the NSC, recommended that Kennedy seriously consider introducing U.S. troops, in conjunction with SEATO, in an "operation of a Lebanon type."[41]

Looking back on the spring of 1961, Kennedy remarked, "thank God the Bay of Pigs happened when it did. Otherwise, we'd be in Laos by now—and that would be a hundred times worse."[42] Among the many aftershocks of the failed intervention in Cuba, Kennedy lost faith in the CIA and the Pentagon. Believing that he had been misinformed about the probability of success in Cuba, the president became suddenly wary of such assurances about Laos.[43] And Kennedy was not alone. Defense Secretary Robert McNamara and his deputy Roswell Gilpatric began to doubt the credibility of their military advisers in the Pentagon. For several months, according to Gilpatric, McNamara refused to pass on the joint chiefs' recommendations to the president without having them checked by non-military staffers.[44] The Bay of Pigs substantially lessened the appetite of the Kennedy administration for intervening in Laos with U.S. troops.

A little more than a week after the brigade had been captured in Cuba, Kennedy and his advisers revisited plans to introduce U.S. troops into Laos. The consensus was that large-scale involvement in Laos was not a good idea, "even if the loss of Laos must be accepted."[45] Once he had decided that U.S. troops would not be going to Laos, Kennedy turned to the conundrum of how Laos was to be neutralized. In spite of skepticism about the viability of Laotian neutrality, after troops were ruled out, there was no other short-term option.

The administration did not put all its faith in a negotiated settlement. Just in case, the CIA increased its assistance to the Hmong and the emerging leader of the Hmong "irregulars," Vang Pao. In time, U.S. officials began to refer to Vang Pao as "the Wizard," after the Wizard of Oz. The Hmong was an independent, distinct ethnic group, and living on the border of Vietnam had given them a distinct distaste for the Vietnamese. Because the Pathet Lao accepted North Vietnamese aid, the Hmong hated the Pathet Lao, and Vang Pao established

40. Vientiane 1364, January 18, 1961, Secret, NSF, Countries: Laos, Box 130, JFK Library. See also Department of State Press Release, December 17, 1960 (No. 699).

41. Memorandum from Rostow to Kennedy, April 13, 1961, Secret, *FRUS, 1961-1963, Vol. XXIV*, 126.

42. Sorensen, *Kennedy*, 644.

43. Hilsman Oral History, JFK Library; Bohlen Oral History, ibid.; Goldstein, *American Policy toward Laos*, 241.

44. Gilpatric Oral History, JFK Library.

45. Memorandum of meeting on Laos, April 16, 1961, Top Secret, Presidential Office File—Countries, Box 121.

close ties with CIA officials and the White Star teams. By late 1961, he had more than nine thousand men; by 1963, more than thirty thousand.[46]

Although Robert McNamara recommended in early May that Kennedy send U.S. troops, Kennedy by then had decided that the future of Laos lay in Geneva. He appointed Averell Harriman to represent the United States during the negotiations, a job that lasted many months longer than Harriman first anticipated.[47] Harriman's position at the commencement of the Geneva talks in May was that "Laos should not be aligned with either side. . . . Laos should not be used for the advantage of either side. To this end the Laotian Government must be run by people who really believe in neutrality and not by people dedicated to Communist or U.S. interests."[48] As it turned out, the person who fit that description was none other than the much-maligned Souvanna Phouma.

On June 3, Kennedy met with Khrushchev in Vienna. At lunchtime, they took a walk through the gardens behind the American residence. Strolling through the Viennese afternoon, the two leaders discussed the world as it then stood, and the Soviet-American competition over it. Turning to Laos, Khrushchev accused the U.S. government of overthrowing Souvanna. He suggested that both he and Kennedy admit that they were supplying arms to competing factions, and he warned Kennedy that the Pathet Lao would win just as Mao won in China because Pathet philosophy appealed to the people. Kennedy accused Khrushchev of sponsoring a foreign intervention in Lao affairs by encouraging the Vietminh to assist Souphanouvong, while Khrushchev retorted that it was the United States that was sponsoring a foreign intervention through its ally Thailand. Both men did agree, however, to use their influence at Geneva to broker a truce among the warring factions. Both also agreed that "Laos was of no strategic importance and was not vital to either side." As a result, both could afford to see Laos truly neutral.[49]

It was a remarkable scene, these two world leaders discussing events in a tiny landlocked country in Indochina that neither had ever visited and that each dimly understood. They spoke of the factions in Laos as if they were pieces on a chessboard that they, the leaders of the two most powerful states, could move at will. They could even introduce other pieces, if that suited their interests. As far as the Laotians themselves, Kennedy and Khrushchev do not appear to have considered what role they might be playing in their own affairs. The relationship between U.S. policy and domestic factors within Laos was therefore quite tenuous. In the many debates in Washington over what to do in 1961, the vagaries of Laotian politics were decidedly in the foreground, and there

46. Warner, *Backfire,* passim; Hamilton-Merritt, *Tragic Mountains,* 94ff.; Castle, *War in the Shadow,* 38ff.; Thomas, *Very Best Men,* 284; Stevenson, *End of Nowhere,* 155ff.

47. Abramson, *Spanning the Century,* 582–88.

48. Paper prepared by Harriman at Geneva (n.d. [May?]), *FRUS, 1961–1963, Vol. XXIV,* 224–25.

49. Memorandum of conversation, June 3, 1961, Secret; Memorandum of conversation, June 4, 1961; *FRUS, 1961–1963, Vol. XXIV,* 225–31.

was little consideration of what the competing factions in Laos wanted and little regard for their capacity to settle their disputes among themselves. Rather than responding to pulls from the periphery, the United States grafted its global competition with the Soviet Union onto Laos, much as it then proceeded to do in Vietnam. However, while Kennedy and Khrushchev were playing God in Vienna, the competing groups within Laos were acting out their own drama, as they had been all along.

Throughout this period and after, the Laotians hardly lay supine while the great powers argued over them. Souvanna, Kong Le, Souphanouvong, Phoumi, the king, the Hmong tribespeople, and others pursued their own varied agendas. The effect of superpower rivalry was to intensify the stakes and deepen the divisions, but the superpowers did not create or define those divisions (although by the late 1960s, the Vietnam War did severely damage the ecosystem of internal Laotian politics). Often in spite of U.S. policy, these groups pursued their own agendas.

For example, in the face of White House efforts to undermine him, Souvanna continued to wage an extensive diplomatic and military campaign against Phoumi and against the Pathet Lao. The temporary alliance with the Pathet Lao after August 1960 was never more than that for Souvanna and Kong Le. Realizing that the White House was turning a deaf ear to his entreaties, Souvanna lobbied members of Congress for support. In a letter to Senator Mike Mansfield, he wrote the following:

> America wishes to preserve us from Communization, but those responsible for its policy have, ironically, done everything to the contrary and pushed the Kingdom back into an impasse, which, in the long run, is going to thrust it into the abyss of Communism. The Lao people are tired of insecurity, of fratricidal strife. . . . At the present time, great numbers [of soldiers] are joining the cause of the [Pathet Lao], as are the inhabitants of the countryside, not because they like this political party, but out of justified despair, out of resignation and of love of peace. You understand that . . . pacification by arms is an impossible solution in view of the topography and configuration of the country which lends itself to battles without end. . . . The moment has come for America to revise its Indochinese policy which is no longer adapted to events or to the development of the legitimate aspirations of the peoples of Southeast Asia.[50]

Over the next six months, while the national-security bureaucracy in Washington debated about what it should do in Laos, Souvanna steered toward a solution.

50. Souvanna Phouma to Mike Mansfield, January 7, 1961, enclosed in a letter from Mansfield to Kennedy, January 21, 1961. Mansfield echoed Souvanna's conclusions and called on Kennedy

He made overtures toward Phoumi and toward his half-brother Souphanouvong. In the spring of 1961, as the tide turned decisively in favor of the Pathet Lao and the neutralists in Laos, Phoumi and Boun Oum were forced to negotiate with Souvanna, even as they pocketed U.S. aid and schemed to defeat him and the neutralist–Pathet Lao coalition. While Kennedy and Khrushchev came to a tentative agreement in Vienna, Souvanna organized a summit of the "three princes"—Souphanouvong, Boun Oum, and himself—in Zurich. Their aim was to form a unified government.

A few days after Kennedy and Khrushchev took their walk, Souvanna met with Harriman in Geneva. He told Harriman that 80 percent of the Lao people were anti-Communist and that neutrality meant neutrality. He also contradicted the American perception that Souphanouvong was a Communist. He told Harriman that his half-brother was in fact a "Socialist" who would be more than content with neutral Laos free from great-power intervention. Souvanna pointedly impressed on Harriman that Phoumi was a "nothing," and that only he, Souvanna, could form a coalition government that would unite the disparate elements of Laotian society.[51]

At the end of June, however, Phoumi met with Harriman and the president in Washington. Phoumi continued to charge Souvanna with secretly working to advance the interests of the Communists, and he made a concerted effort to dissuade the Kennedy administration from working with Souvanna. But while Kennedy expressed appreciation for Phoumi's efforts in a difficult situation, he did not take up Phoumi's repeated attempts to denigrate Souvanna. While the White House had no intention of jettisoning Phoumi, Kennedy had obviously come to the conclusion that Phoumi's vision of a Laos firmly under the umbrella of the United States simply was not tenable.[52] And Souvanna's careful, deliberate manner as well as his casual charm had played no small role in altering how U.S. officials viewed Laos after June 1961. Although neither Harriman nor the White House was as sanguine about the Pathet Lao as Souvanna was, as the months went on, they were willing to give him some benefit of the doubt. At the same time, Kennedy did not alter his essential view of the Pathet Lao or Kong Le as Communist tools. CIA training of Vang Pao's Hmong army accelerated. In August, Kennedy authorized an increase in "mobile training teams in Laos to include advisers down to the company level, to a total strength of five hundred, together with an attempt to get Thai agreement to supply an equal amount of Thai for the same purpose. An immediate increase of two thousand in the number of Meos [Hmong] being supported to bring the total level to eleven thousand."[53] The plan was to use Vang Pao as a check not just upon Souphanouvong but on the North Vietnamese and Ho Chi Minh.

---

to reconsider any unilateral U.S. action. President's Office Files, Countries, Box 31, JFK Library.

51. Harriman to State, June 11, 1961, Secret, *FRUS, 1961-1963, Vol. XXIV,* 243-44.

52. Memorandum of conversation, June 30, 1961, *FRUS, 1961-1963, Vol. XXIV,* 283-86.

53. NSAM 80, August 29, 1961, quoted in Castle, *War in the Shadow,* 42-43.

After a year of intensive negotiations mediated and often complicated by the United States, the Soviet Union, France, and Britain, an agreement was brokered in Geneva in June 1962. It led to the formation of a national-unity government led by Souvanna, which included not just Phoumi but also Pathet Lao in the cabinet. In July, fourteen nations signed the Declaration and Protocol on the Neutrality of Laos that called for the withdrawal of U.S. and other foreign advisers. After many months during which prospects for a settlement seemed dim, negotiations had finally gone forward after a Pathet Lao offensive in northern Laos in May 1962. That attack ended the fragile cease-fire and exposed the deep weaknesses of the Royal Laotian Army. The State Department concluded that the attack had been provoked by Phoumi,[54] and it finally dawned on the White House that the Pathet Lao would have to be included in any coalition, whether or not Phoumi was amenable. Disgusted with the erstwhile client, Kennedy remarked, "Phoumi is a total shit."[55]

The 1962 agreement was in many ways a victory for Souvanna and his vision for Laos, but it was to be short lived. The coalition lasted less than two years before the Pathet Lao moved away from Souphanouvong's more moderate line and split permanently with the government and with Souvanna. After 1964, the Pathet Lao were determined to achieve for Laos what the Vietminh/Vietcong intended for Vietnam, and the continued black CIA operation to militarize the Hmong undermined from the start the Geneva settlement. In time, Souvanna gravitated closer and closer to the United States, and in time, Laos was drawn deeply into the Vietnam War. U.S. aid began flowing in even greater quantities after the Gulf of Tonkin resolution, and by the late 1960s, U.S. covert intervention in Laos had reached such massive proportions that it was covert to no one except the American public.

The Laos intervention was a cold-war graft that did not take. The models that Eisenhower and then Kennedy applied to Laos were remarkably unsuited to the domestic realities of that country; as a result, the outcome was unsatisfactory to all the architects. In the end, Laos set the stage for a far more problematic U.S. intervention in Vietnam. Having failed to act decisively in Laos, and therefore forced in 1962 to accept the neutral Souvanna, the Kennedy administration was determined to send a more forceful message in Vietnam. After recovering from the Bay of Pigs, Kennedy committed increasing numbers of military advisers and special forces to Vietnam in 1962. The precedent of Laos was never far from his or his advisers' thought. In Laos, the United States briefly considered a foray into the jungles. Within a few years, it would be in the jungles of Indochina. It was a decision most of the United States has come to regret, and a decision that wrought havoc on the Vietnamese, Cambodians, and Laotians.

54. State Department discussion paper for White House meeting, May 10, 1962, Top Secret, NSF—Countries/Laos, Box 131.

55. Kennedy's remark, made in mid-May 1962, is quoted in Reeves, *President Kennedy,* 309.

Conclusion

These seven interventions underscore the complexity of the cold-war system. Superpower bipolarity and the deterrent effect of nuclear weapons explain much; but regional, third-world architects drew their own blueprints and helped design the architecture for U.S. interventions. In fact, it may be inaccurate to characterize the cold war as bipolar at all if small, supposedly weak third-world countries exerted as much influence as this work proposes.

The history of early cold-war intervention offers some basic lessons for those contemplating intervention in the present.[1] Although the nature of the contemporary system is much disputed, one thing is evident: the reality of economic interdependence and several competing blocs means that, no matter how powerful it is, the United States will function within a community of weak and strong nations and that peripheral forces within that community will shape U.S. foreign policy. For the time being, the international scene is characterized by multiple centers of power and influence.

The primary lesson is that conditions in the country targeted for intervention are crucial to the success or failure of the intervention. For the period studied in these pages, internal conditions were essential determinants of how an intervention played out. No matter how well or how badly Washington planned for the 1953 coup in Iran or the 1961 landing at the Bay of Pigs, the outcome was conditioned by the political balance in Iran and in Cuba rather than by the wisdom of the CIA blueprint for the operation.

The second observation is that intervention is unlikely to work unless there is a significant convergence between the interests of entrenched local groups and those of the American foreign-policy establishment. Intervention was one method that the U.S. government employed to maintain its allies and eliminate its adversaries. At the same time, U.S. intervention in the cold war, like British intervention in Africa in the nineteenth century, was a tool used by third-world groups to preserve a domestic status quo that suited their domestic interests. The architects of intervention were to be found on both sides of the equation.

A third lesson is that success is usually limited to the short term. While the United States often managed to assist in removing a government, it did not and could not remake the various societies. At best, intervention benefited U.S.

---

1. Ernest May and Richard Neustadt, *Thinking in Time: The Uses of History for Decision Makers* (New York, 1986).

strategic interests and the interests of select local groups; but in time, the forces that intervention was supposed to contain erupted anyway and with renewed vigor. Guatemala descended into violent civil war in the 1960s, and the conflict satisfied neither the interests of Washington nor of many of the people who had supported or acquiesced in the Arbenz coup. The military prospered, and U.S. military programs in Guatemala prospered. The overall U.S. goal of harmonious relations with Latin America suffered. Iran, on the other hand, saw economic growth and authoritarian stability after the 1953 coup, but the Shah's failure to open the political system led to a new efflorescence of opposition in the late 1970s. Before Khomeini overwhelmed the Iranian revolution with his brand of radical Shi'ism, the successor to the Shah appeared to be none other than Mosaddeq's National Front. The 1953 coup had suppressed the reformist forces only temporarily. And of course, in Laos, intervention did not prevent the Communist takeover that Eisenhower so feared in 1960. It may have forestalled it for fifteen years, but it may also have backfired to such an extent that it helped cause that takeover. Short-term "neutralization" of Laos thus proved very short-term indeed, even by the standards of a U.S. foreign policy establishment that generally cannot plan five years ahead.

The final lesson speaks to the limitations of power and the power of the powerless. Even during the height of American power in the 1950s, the United States operated under certain constraints. Its military and economic force could overwhelm most countries. If Washington chose, it could mount an impressive campaign to destabilize governments in third-world countries. Yet in Guatemala, for example, Arbenz had alienated the landowners, the military, and the church. These groups wanted him gone, and they were willing to work with the United States to get rid of him. Without these entrenched forces working against him, Arbenz may well have resisted a purely external, American intervention. That the success of 1954 was in part due to domestic politics in Guatemala indicates the constraints on U.S. power in practice.

Similarly, the United States could have invaded Cuba in 1961. It most certainly would have defeated Castro's armed forces. But what then? Without groups to work with in establishing a new government, how would the intervention have had any permanence? Importing an exile government from Miami was not the solution, and the Kennedy administration knew it. Even with overwhelming force at its disposal, there were limits to what the United States could do, and there are even more limits today.

Unfortunately, the lesson that seems to have been learned from cold-war interventions, both from successes such as Iran and Guatemala, and failures such as Cuba and Indochina, is that when U.S. policy is sound, intervention is sound. As this work should have demonstrated, that lesson is faulty. It is based on a misreading of U.S. power during the cold war.[2]

---

2. For an analysis of mislearned lessons, see Yuen Foong Khong, *Analogies at War: Korea, Munich, Dien Bien Phu, and the Vietnam Decisions of 1965* (Princeton, 1992).

The early cold war ought to give would-be interventionists pause. The conditions under which intervention can succeed are particular and the nature of success fleeting. Even those advocating intervention for moral or humanitarian reasons should reflect on the legacy of limitations that characterizes cold-war realpolitik interventions. If it is difficult to force dramatic change in the government of a particular country, it is even more difficult to force a social-paradigm shift. If there is no entrenched legacy of human rights, of democracy, or community, U.S. intervention is not going to create one. Intervening may assuage the guilty moral conscience of a U.S. public or a U.S. government that cannot bear the thought of standing idly by while millions starve or thousands are killed. But beyond the brief period that U.S. troops are stationed or U.S. dollars are flowing, intervention is unlikely to be more than a stop-gap measure whose unintended consequences could leave the situation more precarious after the United States disengages than it was before the United States became involved.

If one believes in the endless capacity of the United States to shape the international arena, the stories told here are sobering and deflating. However, if one is seeking evidence of the viability of the third world in the international system,[3] then the story is actually encouraging. The capacity of small third-world states to influence a far stronger power indicates that they are not as powerless as they sometimes appear. The economic and military weakness of many countries on paper, their statistical inferiority, does not take into account the amount of unquantifiable power they can wield. The future may be grim for the third world, but if the cold war is any indication, those small, weaker states will fundamentally influence our foreign policy. Leaders of third-world countries will continue to exert a pull out of proportion to their size or putative strength.

Finally, there is the story itself, a story told too often from the perspective of the metropolitan center and not often enough from the vantage of the periphery. Perhaps this is a function of the old adage that history is written by the victors. There are no extant histories of the Punic Wars as told by the Carthaginians. Perhaps it is a product of the parochialism of the Americans of the United States. Perhaps it is the result of the charged ideological climate of the cold war, in which nuclear weapons and the ideological struggle between Communism and capitalism overshadowed the rich and complex international tapestry underneath. For whatever reason, a vital dimension of the cold war has traditionally been consigned to a secondary level of importance.

This work has inserted the third world into the main body of cold-war history. The edifice that U.S. officials and certain third-world groups constructed during the fifteen years examined was not particularly graceful or ennobling. It was a structure that stood against radical reform in societies that were deeply in need of radical reform. It was a structure that destroyed democracy in the name of

---

3. For a grim picture of third-world prospects, see Paul Kennedy, *Preparing for the Twenty-First Century* (New York, 1993).

resisting Communism. And it was a structure that denied basic freedoms to the many so that the few could enjoy theirs. However, it owed its basic contours to the vision of multiple forces within the third world. The ungainly nature of the building stemmed from the qualities of its architects, some of whom were U.S. officials, many of whom were not.

Establishing the central role of the third world in determining the international system neither glorifies martyrs such as Mosaddeq nor condemns conspirators such as Castillo Armas. It does lead to a sense of shared moral responsibility for the shape of the international system, and it acknowledges that third-world architects contributed much to their own structures. They will continue to do so, and the United States and other leading powers will continue to interact with them, influence them, and be influenced by them. We might hope that the builders of the future take note of the weaknesses of buildings past; but we can at least remember to give equal time where equal time is due, for the sake of historical accuracy and its power to inform the present.

Bibliography

Manuscript Sources

Acheson, Dean. Papers. Harry S. Truman Library, Independence, Mo.
Allen, George V. Papers. Truman Library.
CIA Research Reports. University Publications of America Microfilm, Frederick, Md.
Clifford, Clark. Papers. Truman Library.
Cutler, Robert. Papers. Dwight D. Eisenhower Library, Abilene, Kans.
Dulles, Allen. Papers. Seeley Mudd Library, Princeton University, Princeton, N.J.
Dulles, John Foster. Papers. Mudd Library.
Eisenhower, Dwight D. Papers and Diaries. Eisenhower Library.
Elsey, George M. Papers. Truman Library.
Grady, Henry. Papers. Truman Library.
Gray, Gordon. Papers. Eisenhower Library.
Guatemala Transcripts. Library of Congress, Washington, D.C.
Hagerty, James. Papers. Eisenhower Library.
Herter, Christian. Papers. Eisenhower Library.
Hoffman, Paul. Papers. Truman Library.
Jackson, C. D. Papers. Eisenhower Library.
Kennedy, John Fitzgerald. Papers. John F. Kennedy Library, Boston.
Kennedy, Robert. Papers. Kennedy Library.
Locke, Edwin. Papers. Truman Library.
Mann, Thomas. Papers. Eisenhower Library.
Nash, Philleo. Papers. Truman Library.
Schlesinger, Arthur M. Jr. Papers. Kennedy Library.
Schlesinger, Stephen. Papers. Hispanic Division, Library of Congress.
Sorensen, Theodore. Papers. Kennedy Library.
Souers, Sidney. Papers. Truman Library.
Snyder, John. Papers. Truman Library.
U.S. Department of State. Decimal Files, Lot Files, Consular Files. Diplomatic Branch, National Archives, Washington, D.C.

Oral History Collections

Columbia University Oral History Project. Butler Library, Columbia University, New York City.
John Foster Dulles Oral History Collection. Mudd Library.
Dwight D. Eisenhower Oral History Collection. Eisenhower Library.
Iranian Oral History Collection. Houghton Library, Harvard University, Cambridge, Mass.

John F. Kennedy Oral History Program. Kennedy Library.

Harry S. Truman Oral History Program. Truman Library.

Books and Articles

Abrahamian, Ervand. *Iran: Between Two Revolutions.* Princeton, 1982.

Abramson, Rudy. *Spanning the Century: The Life of W. Averell Harriman, 1891-1986.* New York, 1992.

Abu 'Izz al-Din, Halim. *Siyasat Lubnan al-kharijiyyah* [*The Foreign Relations of Lebanon*]. Beirut, 1966.

Acheson, Dean. *Present at the Creation: My Years in the State Department.* New York, 1969.

Adams, Nina, and Alfred McCoy, eds. *Laos: War and Revolution.* New York, 1970.

Adams, Richard. *Crucifixion by Power: Essays on Guatemalan National Social Structure, 1944-1966.* Austin, 1970.

Agüero, Luis Conte. *Fidel Castro: Psiquiatría y política.* Mexico City, 1968.

Agwani, M. S., ed. *The Lebanese Crisis.* New York, 1965.

Alam, Asadollah. *The Shah and I.* New York, 1991.

Alexander, Charles. *Holding the Line: The Eisenhower Era, 1952-1961.* Bloomington, 1975.

Allin, Erika. *The United States and the 1958 Lebanon Crisis: American Intervention in the Middle East.* Lanham, Md., 1994.

Ambrose, Stephen. *Eisenhower: Soldier, General of the Army, President-Elect.* New York, 1983.

————. *Eisenhower: The President.* New York, 1984.

————. *Nixon: The Education of a Politician, 1913-1962.* New York, 1987.

Amen, Michael. *American Foreign Policy in Greece, 1944-1949.* Frankfurt, 1978.

Ammun, Fuad. *Siyasat Lubnan al-kharijiyyah* [*The Foreign Relations of Lebanon*]. Beirut, 1963.

Andrew, Christopher. *For the President's Eyes Only.* New York, 1995.

Andrews, Kevin. *The Flight of Ikaros: Travels in Greece during a Civil War.* London, 1984.

Arévalo, Juan José. *Guatemala, la democracia, y el imperio.* Montevideo, 1954.

Aron, Raymond. *The Imperial Republic: The United States and the World, 1945-1973.* Englewood Cliffs, N.J., 1974.

Asmar, Michel. *Ba'd al-mihna wa qabila* [*After the Ordeal and Before It*]. Beirut, 1959.

Averoff-Tossizza, Evangelos. *By Fire and Axe: The Communist Party and the Civil War in Greece, 1944-1949.* New Rochelle, N.Y., 1978.

Avery, Peter. *Modern Iran.* New York, 1965.

Azimi, Fakhreddin. *Iran: The Crisis of Democracy, 1941-1953.* London, 1989.

Bamberg, J. H. *The History of the British Petroleum Company: The Anglo-Iranian Years, 1928-1954.* Cambridge, U.K., 1994.

Barakat, Halim, ed. *Toward a Viable Lebanon.* London, 1988.

Barnet, Richard. *Intervention and Revolution.* New York, 1968.

Batista, Fulgencio. *Cuba Betrayed.* New York, 1962.

Bayhum, Muhammad Jamil. *Lubnan: Baina al-mashraq w-al-maghrib, 1920-1969* [*Lebanon: Between East and West*]. Beirut, 1970.

Behbehani, Hashim. *The Soviet Union and Arab Nationalism, 1917-66.* New York, 1986.

Benjamin, Jules. *The United States and the Origins of the Cuban Revolution.* Princeton, 1990.

Bernays, Edward. *Biography of an Idea.* New York, 1965.

Beschloss, Michael. *The Crisis Years: Kennedy and Khrushchev, 1961-1963.* New York, 1991.

Betts, Robert Brenton. *The Druze.* New Haven, 1988.

Bill, James. *The Eagle and the Lion: The Tragedy of American-Iranian Relations.* New Haven, 1988.

Bill, James, and William Roger Louis, eds. *Musaddiq, Iranian Nationalism, and Oil.* London, 1988.

Binder, Leonard, ed. *Politics in Lebanon.* New York, 1966.

Bird, Kai. *The Chairman: John J. McCloy and the Making of the American Establishment.* New York, 1992.

Biska, Michael. "The 1958 American Intervention in Lebanon: A Historical Assessment." *American-Arab Affairs* (Winter 1987), 106-19.

Bissell, Richard, with Jonathan E. Lewis and Frances Pudlo. *Reflections of a Cold Warrior.* New Haven, 1996.

Blackmer, Donald. *Unity in Diversity: Italian Communism and the Communist World.* Cambridge, Mass., 1968.

Blasier, Cole. *The Hovering Giant: U.S. Responses to Revolutionary Change in Latin America.* Pittsburgh, 1976.

Blum, William. *The CIA: A Forgotten History.* London, 1986.

Bonachea, Ramón, and Marta San Martin. *The Cuban Insurrection, 1952-1959.* New Brunswick, N.J., 1974.

Bonsal, Philip. *Cuba, Castro, and the United States.* Pittsburgh, 1971.

Bowie, Robert, and Richard Immerman. *Waging Peace: Eisenhower's Strategy for National Security.* New York, 1997.

Brands, H. W. *Inside the Cold War: Loy Henderson and the Rise of the American Empire.* New York, 1991.

———. *The Specter of Neutralism.* New York, 1989.

———. "Decisions on American Armed Intervention: Lebanon, Dominican Republic, and Grenada." *Political Science Quarterly* (Winter 1987-88), 607-24.

Brown, L. Carl. *International Politics and the Middle East: Old Rules, Dangerous Game.* Princeton, 1984.

Bullock, Alan. *Hitler and Stalin.* New York, 1992.

Bundy, McGeorge. *Danger and Survival.* New York, 1988.

Cardoso, Fernando Henrique, and Enzo Faletto. *Dependency and Development in Latin America.* Berkeley, 1979.

Cardoza y Aragon, Luis. *La Revolución Guatemalteca.* Mexico City, 1955.

Carrillo, Elisa. *Alcide de Gasperi.* Notre Dame, Ind., 1965.

Casaus, Victor. *Girón en la memoria.* Havana, 1970.

Castañeda, Jorge. *Compañero: The Life and Death of Che Guevara.* New York, 1997.

Castle, Timothy. *At War in the Shadow of Vietnam: U.S. Military Aid to the Royal Lao Government, 1955-1975.* New York, 1993.

Casuso, Teresa. *Cuba and Castro.* Translated by Elmer Goldberg. New York, 1961.

Chamoun, Camille. *Crise au Moyen-Orient.* Paris, 1963.

Close, David, ed. *The Greek Civil War, 1943-1950.* London, 1993.

Coatsworth, John. *Central America and the United States.* New York, 1994.

Conte, Arthur. *Bandoung: Tournant de l'histoire.* Paris, 1965.

Cook, Blanche Wisen. *The Declassified Eisenhower: A Divided Legacy of Peace and Political Warfare.* New York, 1981.

Copeland, Miles. *The Game of Nations.* London, 1969.

Corn, David. *Blond Ghost: Ted Shackley and the CIA's Crusades.* New York, 1994.

Corson, William. *The Armies of Ignorance: The Rise of the American Intelligence Empire.* New York, 1977.

Cottam, Richard. *Iran and the United States: A Cold War Case Study.* Pittsburgh, 1988.

Cullather, Nick. *Illusions of Influence: The Political Economy of United States-Philippines Relations, 1942-1960.* Stanford, 1994.

————. *Operation PBSUCCESS: The United States and Guatemala, 1952-1954.* Washington, D.C., 1994.

Cumings, Bruce. *The Origins of the Korean War.* 2 vols. Princeton, 1981, 1990.

David, Stephen. "Explaining Third World Alignment." *World Politics,* XLIII (January 1991), 233-56.

Desch, Michael. *When the Third World Matters: Latin America and United States Grand Strategy.* Baltimore, 1993.

Deuve, Jean. *Le Royaume de Laos, 1949-1965.* Paris, 1984.

Diba, Farhad. *Mohammad Mossadegh: A Political Biography.* London, 1986.

Diederich, Bernard. *Trujillo: The Death of the Goat.* Boston, 1978.

Diggins, John Patrick. *Mussolini and Fascism: The View from America.* Princeton, 1972.

Divine, Robert A. *Eisenhower and the Cold War.* New York, 1981.

Djilas, Milovan. *Conversations with Stalin.* New York, 1962.

Doenecke, Justus. "Revisionists, Oil, and Cold War Diplomacy." *Iranian Studies,* III (Winter 1970), 23-33.

Dommen, Arthur. *Conflict in Laos: The Politics of Neutralization.* London, 1964.

Donovan, Robert. *Conflict and Crisis: The Presidency of Harry S. Truman, 1945-1948.* New York, 1977.

————. *Tumultuous Years: The Presidency of Harry S. Truman, 1949-1953.* New York, 1982.

Dorschner, John, and Roberto Fabricio. *The Winds of December.* New York, 1980.

Dowty, Alan. *Middle East Crisis: U.S. Decision Making in 1958, 1970, and 1973.* Berkeley, 1984.

Doyle, Michael. *Empires.* Ithaca, N.Y., 1986.

Draper, Theodore. *Castroism: Theory and Practice.* New York, 1965.

Dubois, Jules. *Fidel Castro: Rebel, Liberator, or Dictator.* New York, 1959.

Dulles, Allen. *The Craft of Intelligence.* New York, 1963.

Eisenhower, Dwight D. *Mandate for Change.* Garden City, N.Y., 1963.

————. *Waging Peace.* Garden City, N.Y., 1965.

Elm, Mostafa. *Oil, Power, and Principle.* Syracuse, N.Y., 1992.

Entelis, John. *Pluralism and Party Transformation in Lebanon: Al-Kata'ib, 1936-1970.* Leiden, 1974.

Eveland, Wilbur Crane. *Ropes of Sand.* New York, 1980.

Fall, Bernard. *Anatomy of a Crisis: The Laotian Crisis of 1960-1961.* Garden City, N.Y., 1969.

Farber, Samuel. *Revolution and Reaction in Cuba, 1933-1960.* Middletown, Conn., 1976.

Faris, Nabih, and Muhammad Tawfik Husayn. *The Crescent in Crisis.* Lawrence, Kans., 1955.

Fawcett, Louise L'Estrange. *Iran and the Cold War.* Cambridge, U.K., 1992.

Feinberg, Richard E. *The Intemperate Zone: The Third World Challenge to U.S. Foreign Policy.* New York, 1983.

Ferrer, Edward. *Operation Puma: The Air Battle of the Bay of Pigs.* Miami, 1982.

Filippelli, Ronald. *American Labor and Postwar Italy, 1943-1953.* Stanford, 1989.

Ford, Alan. *The Anglo-Iranian Oil Dispute of 1951-1952.* Berkeley, 1954.

Frank, Andre Gunder. *Latin America: Underdevelopment or Revolution?* New York, 1969.

Franqui, Carlos. *Family Portrait with Fidel.* Translated by Alfred MacAdam. New York, 1984.

Fredman, H. B. *Laos in Strategic Perspective.* Santa Monica, 1961.

Fried, Jonathan, et al., eds. *Guatemala in Rebellion.* New York, 1983.

Fromkin, David. *A Peace to End All Peace.* New York, 1989.

————. *In the Time of the Americans.* New York, 1995.

Fursenko, Alexsandr, and Timothy Naftali. *"One Hell of a Gamble": Khrushchev, Castro, and Kennedy, 1958-1964.* New York, 1997.

Gaddis, John Lewis. *The Long Peace.* New York, 1987.

————. *Russia, The Soviet Union and the United States.* New York, 1978.

————. *Strategies of Containment.* New York, 1982.

Galich, Manuel. *Por qué lucha Guatemala: Arévalo y Arbenz.* Buenos Aires, 1956.

García Añoveros, Jesús. *Jacobo Arbenz.* Madrid, 1987.

Gasiorowski, Mark. *U.S. Foreign Policy and the Shah.* Ithaca, N.Y., 1991.

————. "The 1953 Coup D'Etat in Iran." *International Journal of Middle East Studies,* XXIX (August 1987), 261-86.

Gendzier, Irene. *Notes from the Minefield: United States Intervention in Lebanon and the Middle East, 1945-1958.* New York, 1997.

————. "The United States, the USSR, and the Arab World in NSC Reports of the 1950s." *American-Arab Affairs* (Spring 1989), 22-29.

George, Alexander. *Bridging the Gap: Theory and Practice in Foreign Policy.* Washington, D.C., 1993.

Gerges, Fawaz. *The Superpowers and the Middle East: Regional and International Politics, 1955-1967.* Boulder, Colo., 1994.

Ginsborg, Paul. *A History of Contemporary Italy: Society and Politics, 1943-1988.* New York, 1990.

Girling, John. *America and the Third World.* London, 1980.

Gleijeses, Piero. *Shattered Hope: The Guatemalan Revolution and the United States, 1944-1954.* Princeton, 1991.

————. "Ships in the Night: The CIA, the White House, and the Bay of Pigs." *Journal of Latin American Studies,* XXVII (February 1995), 1-42.

Goldstein, Martin E. *American Policy toward Laos.* Rutherford, N.J., 1973.

Goode, James. *The United States and Iran, 1946-51.* London, 1989.

Gordon, David. *Lebanon: The Fragmented Nation.* London, 1980.

Goria, Wade. *Sovereignty and Leadership in Lebanon, 1943-1976.* London, 1985.

Government of Cuba. *Playa Girón: Derrota del imperialismo.* 4 vols. Havana, 1961.

Greenstein, Fred. *The Hidden-Hand Presidency: Eisenhower As Leader.* New York, 1982.

Grose, Peter. *Gentleman Spy: The Life of Allen Dulles.* New York, 1994.

Grow, Michael. *The Good Neighbor Policy and Authoritarianism in Paraguay: United States Economic Expansion and Great Power Rivalry in Latin America during World War II.* Lawrence, Kans., 1981.

Guillen, Pedro. *Guatemala: Prólogo y epílogo de una revolución.* Mexico City, 1964.

Gurtov, Melvin. *The United States against the Third World.* New York, 1974.

Haass, Richard. *Intervention.* Washington, D.C., 1994.

Hahn, Peter. *The United States, Great Britain, and Egypt, 1945-1956.* Chapel Hill, 1991.

Halberstam, David. *The Fifties.* New York, 1993.

Halpern, J. M. *The Lao Elite: A Study of Tradition and Innovation.* Santa Monica, 1960.

Hamilton-Merritt, Jane. *Tragic Mountains: The Hmong, the Americans, and the Secret Wars for Laos, 1942-1992.* Bloomington, Ind., 1993.

Handy, Jim. *Revolution in the Countryside: Rural Conflict and Agrarian Reform in Guatemala, 1944-1954.* Chapel Hill, 1994.

Harper, J. L. *America and the Reconstruction of Italy, 1945-1948.* Cambridge, Mass., 1986.

Hersh, Burton. *The Old Boys.* New York, 1992.

Hershberg, James. *James B. Conant.* New York, 1993.

Higgins, Trumbull. *The Perfect Failure: Kennedy, Eisenhower, and the CIA at the Bay of Pigs.* New York, 1987.

Hilsman, Roger. *To Move a Nation: The Politics of Foreign Policy in the Administration of John F. Kennedy.* Garden City, N.Y., 1967.

Homayounpour, Parviz. *L'Affaire d'Azarbaidjan.* Lausanne, 1966.

Hoopes, Townsend. *The Devil and John Foster Dulles.* Boston, 1973.

Hopkirk, Peter. *The Great Game.* New York, 1993.

Hopwood, Derek. *Egypt: Politics and Society, 1945-1989.* 2d ed. London, 1991.

Hottinger, Arnold. "Zu'ama and Parties in the Lebanese Crisis of 1958." *Middle East Journal,* XV (Spring 1961), 127-40.

Hudson, Michael. *The Precarious Republic.* New York, 1968.

Hughes, H. Stuart. *The United States and Italy.* Cambridge, Mass., 1965.

Hunt, E. Howard. *Give Us This Day.* New Rochelle, N.Y., 1973.

———. *Undercover: Memoirs of an American Secret Agent.* New York, 1974.

Hunt, Michael. *Ideology and U.S. Foreign Policy.* New Haven, 1987.

Huntington, Samuel. *The Third Wave: Democratization in the Late Twentieth Century.* Norman, Okla., 1991.

Iatrides, John O., ed. *Ambassador MacVeagh Reports: Greece, 1933-1947.* Princeton, 1980.

———. *Greece in the 1940s: A Nation in Crisis.* Hanover, N.H., 1981.

Immerman, Richard. *The CIA in Guatemala: The Foreign Policy of Intervention.* Austin, 1982.

————, ed. *John Foster Dulles and the Diplomacy of the Cold War*. Princeton, 1990.

Isaacson, Walter, and Evan Thomas. *The Wise Men: Six Friends and the World They Made*. New York, 1986.

Jeffreys-Jones, Rhodri. *The CIA and American Democracy*. New Haven, 1989.

Jensen, Amy Elizabeth. *Guatemala*. New York, 1955.

Johnson, Haynes. *The Bay of Pigs*. New York, 1964.

Johnson, Loch. *America's Secret Power: The CIA in a Democratic Society*. New York, 1989.

Jonas, Susanne. *The Battle for Guatemala*. Boulder, Colo., 1991.

Jones, Howard. *"A New Kind of War": America's Global Strategy and the Truman Doctrine in Greece*. New York, 1989.

Joumblatt, Kamal. *I Speak for Lebanon*. Translated by Michael Pallis. London, 1982.

————. *Haqiqat al-thawrah al-Lubnaniyyah [The Truth About the Lebanese Revolution]*. Beirut, 1959.

Kahin, George McTurner, and Audrey Kahin. *Subversion as Foreign Policy*. New York, 1995.

Kaplan, Robert. *The Arabists*. New York, 1993.

Karami, Nadia. *Waqi' al-thawrah al-Lubnaniyyah [The Facts of the Lebanese Revolution]*. Beirut, 1959.

Katouzian, Homa. *Musaddiq and the Struggle for Power in Iran*. New York, 1981.

————. *The Political Economy of Modern Iran: Despotism and Pseudo-Modernism, 1926-1979*. New York, 1981.

Kaufman, Burton. *Trade and Aid: Eisenhower's Foreign Economic Policy, 1953-1961*. Baltimore, 1982.

Kay, Cristóbal. *Latin American Theories of Development and Underdevelopment*. New York, 1989.

Keddie, Nikki. *Roots of Revolution: An Interpretive History of Modern Iran*. New Haven, 1981.

————, ed. *Religion and Politics in Iran*. New Haven, 1983.

Kemp, Norman. *Abadan: A First-Hand Account of the Persian Oil Crisis*. London, 1953.

Kennedy, Paul. *Preparing for the Twenty-First Century*. New York, 1993.

Kenner, Martin, and James Petras, eds. *Fidel Castro Speaks*. New York, 1969.

Kerr, Malcolm. *The Arab Cold War, 1958-1964*. Oxford, U.K., 1965.

————. "Lebanese Views on the 1958 Crisis." *Middle East Journal*, XV (Spring 1961), 211-17.

Khalaf, Samir. *Lebanon's Predicament*. New York, 1987.

al-Khazen, Farid. "Kamal Jumblatt: The Uncrowned Druze Prince of the Left." *Middle East Studies*, XXIV (April 1988), 178-205.

Khong, Yuen Foong. *Analogies at War: Korea, Munich, Dien Bien Phu, and the Vietnam Decisions of 1965*. Princeton, 1992.

Kofas, John. *Intervention and Underdevelopment: Greece during the Cold War*. University Park, Pa., 1986.

Kogan, Norman. *A Political History of Italy: The Postwar Years*. New York, 1983.

————. *The Politics of Italian Foreign Policy*. New York, 1963.

Kolko, Gabriel. *Confronting the Third World: United States Foreign Policy, 1945-1980*. New York, 1988.

Korbani, Agnes. *U.S. Intervention in Lebanon, 1958 and 1982.* New York, 1991.

Kousoulas, D. George. *Revolution and Defeat: The Story of the Greek Communist Party.* London, 1965.

Kuniholm, Bruce. *The Origins of the Cold War in the Near East.* Princeton, 1980.

Kupchan, Charles. *Vulnerability of Empire.* Ithaca, N.Y., 1994.

Lacouture, Jean. *Nasser.* London, 1973.

Lacy, Michael, ed. *The Truman Presidency.* New York, 1989.

Ladjevardi, Habib. "The Origins of U.S. Support for an Autocratic Iran." *International Journal of Middle East Studies,* XV (May 1983), 225-39.

LaFeber, Walter. *America, Russia, and the Cold War, 1945-1992.* New York, 1993.

———. *Inevitable Revolutions: The United States in Central America.* 2d ed. New York, 1993.

Lamb, Richard. *War in Italy, 1943-1945.* New York, 1994.

Lapping, Brian. *End of Empire.* New York, 1985.

Laqueur, Walter. *Europe in Our Time: A History, 1945-1992.* New York, 1992.

Lebow, Richard Ned, and Janice Gross Stein. *We All Lost the Cold War.* Princeton, 1994.

Leffler, Melvyn. *A Preponderance of Power.* Stanford, 1992.

Lesch, David. *Syria and the United States: Eisenhower's Cold War in the Middle East.* Boulder, Colo., 1992.

Little, Douglas. "His Finest Hour? Eisenhower, Lebanon, and the 1958 Middle East Crisis." *Diplomatic History,* XX (Winter 1996), 27-54.

Little, Tim. *Modern Egypt.* London, 1967.

López-Fresquet, Rufo. *My Fourteen Months with Castro.* Cleveland, 1966.

Louis, William Roger. *The British Empire in the Middle East, 1945-1951.* Oxford, U.K., 1984.

———, ed. *Imperialism: The Robinson and Gallagher Controversy.* New York, 1976.

Lytle, Mark. *The Origins of the Iranian-American Alliance.* New York, 1987.

McCann, Thomas. *An American Company: The Tragedy of United Fruit.* New York, 1976.

McClintock, Michael. *Instruments of Statecraft: U.S. Guerrilla Warfare, Counterinsurgency, and Counterterrorism, 1940-1990.* New York, 1992.

McClintock, Robert. *The Meaning of Limited War.* Boston, 1967.

McCullough, David. *Truman.* New York, 1992.

McGhee, George. *Envoy to the Middle World.* New York, 1983.

McMahon, Robert. *The Cold War on the Periphery: The United States, India, and Pakistan.* New York, 1994.

———. *Colonialism and Cold War: The United States and the Struggle for Indonesian Independence, 1945-49.* Ithaca, N.Y., 1981.

McNeill, William. *The Greek Dilemma.* Philadelphia, 1947.

Mackey, Sandra. *Lebanon: Death of a Nation.* New York, 1989.

Maier, Charles, ed. *The Cold War in Europe.* New York, 1991.

Malik, Charles. *The Problem of Coexistence.* Chicago, 1955.

Mammarella, Giuseppe. *Italy after Fascism: A Political History, 1943-1965.* Notre Dame, Ind., 1966.

Mark, Eduard. "Allied Relations in Iran: The Origins of a Cold War Crisis." *Wisconsin Magazine of History,* LIX (Autumn 1975), 51-64.

Marks, Frederick W. "The CIA and Castillo Armas in Guatemala, 1954: New Clues to an Old Puzzle." *Diplomatic History,* XIV (Winter 1990), 67-86.

Martin, Edwin. *Kennedy and Latin America.* New York, 1994.

Marton, Kati. *The Polk Conspiracy.* New York, 1990.

May, Ernest, and Richard Neustadt. *Thinking in Time: The Uses of History for Decision Makers.* New York, 1986.

Mazrâq, Mukhtâr. *Harakat adam al-inhiyâz fil alâqât al-dauliya [The Non-Aligned Movement in International Relations].* Cairo, 1990.

Meeker, Oden. *The Little World of Laos.* New York, 1959.

Meo, Leila. *Lebanon: Improbable Nation.* Westport, Conn., 1965.

Milani, Mohsen. *The Making of Iran's Islamic Revolution: From Monarchy to Islamic Republic.* Boulder, Colo., 1988.

Miller, James Edward. *The U.S. and Italy, 1940-1950.* Chapel Hill, 1986.

Mills, C. Wright. *Listen, Yankee: The Revolution in Cuba.* New York, 1960.

Miyata, Osamu. "The Tudeh Military Network during the Oil Nationalization Period." *Middle Eastern Studies,* XXIII (July 1987), 313-28.

Momen, Moojan. *An Introduction to Shi'i Islam.* New Haven, Conn., 1985.

Morgenthau, Hans. *Politics among Nations: The Struggle for Power and Peace.* New York, 1949.

Morley, Morris. *Imperial State and Revolution: The United States and Cuba, 1952-1986.* New York, 1987.

Mortimer, Robert. *The Third World Coalition in International Politics.* New York, 1980.

Mottahedeh, Roy. *The Mantle of the Prophet.* New York, 1985.

Murphy, Robert. *Diplomat among Warriors.* Garden City, N.Y., 1964.

Musaddiq, Muhammad. *Musaddiq's Memoirs.* Edited and translated by Homa Katouzian. London, 1988.

Nantet, Jacques. *Histoire du Liban.* Paris, 1963.

Nasser, Gamal Abdel. *The Philosophy of the Revolution.* Cairo, 1954.

Nehru, Jawaharlal. *Jawaharlal Nehru's Speeches, 1946-1949.* New Delhi, 1961.

———. *Jawaharlal Nehru's Speeches, 1949-1953.* New Delhi, 1961.

Neo Lao Haksat. *12 Anneés d'intervention et d'agression de impérialistes américains.* N.p., 1966.

O'Ballance, Edgar. *The Greek Civil War, 1944-1949.* New York, 1966.

Operation ZAPATA: The Ultrasensitive Report and Testimony of the Board of Inquiry on the Bay of Pigs. Frederick, Md., 1981.

Osgueda, Raul. *Operación Guatemala $$OK$$.* Mexico City, 1955.

Packenham, Robert. *Liberal America and the Third World.* Princeton, 1973.

Page, Joseph. *Perón: A Biography.* New York, 1983.

Pahlavi, Ashraf. *Faces in a Mirror: Memoirs from Exile.* Englewood Cliffs, N.J., 1980.

Pahlavi, Mohammad Reza. *Answer to History.* Briarcliff Manor, N.Y., 1980.

———. *Mission for My Country.* London, 1960.

Papandreou, George. *The Third War.* Athens, 1948.

Paterson, Thomas. *Contesting Castro.* New York, 1994.

———. *Meeting the Communist Threat.* New York, 1988.

Phillips, David Atlee. *The Night Watch.* New York, 1972.

Pérez, Louis. *Cuba.* New York, 1988.

Pérez-Stable, Marifeli. *The Cuban Revolution: Origins, Course, and Legacy.* New York, 1993.

Porter, Bernard. *The Lion's Share: A Short History of British Imperialism, 1850-1983.* London, 1984.

Powers, Thomas. *The Man Who Kept the Secrets: Richard Helms and the CIA.* New York, 1979.

Prados, John. *Keepers of the Keys: A History of the National Security Council from Truman to Bush.* New York, 1991.

————. *Presidents' Secret Wars: CIA and Pentagon Covert Operations since World War II.* New York, 1986.

Quandt, William. "Lebanon, 1958, and Jordan, 1970." In *Force without War,* edited by Barry Blechman and Stephan Kaplan. Washington, D.C., 1978.

Qubain, Fahim. *Crisis in Lebanon.* Washington, D.C., 1961.

Quirk, Robert E. *Fidel Castro.* New York, 1993.

Rabe, Stephen. *Eisenhower and Latin America: The Foreign Policy of Anticommunism.* Chapel Hill, 1988.

————. "The Clues Didn't Check Out: Commentary on 'The CIA and Castillo Armas.'" *Diplomatic History,* XIV (Winter 1990), 87-95.

Ramazani, Rouhollah. *Iran's Foreign Policy, 1941-1973.* Charlottesville, Va., 1975.

Ranelagh, John. *The Agency: The Rise and Decline of the CIA.* New York, 1986.

Reeves, Richard. *President Kennedy: Profile of Power.* New York, 1993.

Richter, Heinz. *British Intervention in Greece.* London, 1986.

Roca, Blas. *The Cuban Revolution.* New York, 1961.

Rodriguez, Felix, and John Weisman. *Shadow Warrior.* New York, 1989.

Romero, Federico. *The United States and the European Trade Union Movement, 1944-1951.* Chapel Hill, 1992.

Roosevelt, Kermit. *Countercoup: The Struggle for Control of Iran.* New York, 1979.

Rothstein, Richard. *The Weak in the World of the Strong.* New York, 1977.

Rubin, Barry. *The Great Powers in the Middle East, 1941-1947.* London, 1980.

————. *Paved with Good Intentions: The American Experience and Iran.* New York, 1980.

Ruehsen, Moyara de Moraes. "Operation Ajax Revisited: Iran, 1953." *Middle Eastern Studies,* XXIX (July 1993), 467-86.

Ruiz, Ramón Eduardo. *Cuba: The Making of a Revolution.* New York, 1968.

Sachar, Howard. *Europe Leaves the Middle East, 1936-1954.* New York, 1972.

Sadat, Anwar. *Revolt on the Nile.* Translated by Thomas Graham. London, 1957.

Said, Edward. *Culture and Imperialism.* New York, 1993.

Salibi, Kamal. *A House of Many Mansions: The History of Lebanon Reconsidered.* London, 1988.

————. *The Modern History of Jordan.* New York, 1993.

————. *The Modern History of Lebanon.* New York, 1965.

Samii, Kuross. *Involvement by Invitation: American Strategies of Containment in Iran.* University Park, Pa., 1987.

Sarafis, Marion, ed. *Greece: From Resistance to Civil War.* Nottingham, 1980.

Sartre, Jean-Paul. *Sartre on Cuba.* New York, 1961.

Sassoon, Donald. *The Strategy of the Italian Communist Party.* New York, 1981.

Schlesinger, Arthur M. Jr. *A Thousand Days: John F. Kennedy in the White House.* New York, 1965.

————. "Some Lessons from the Cold War." *Diplomatic History,* XVI (Winter 1992), 47-53.

Schlesinger, Stephen, and Stephen Kinzer. *Bitter Fruit: The Untold Story of the American Coup in Guatemala.* New York, 1982.

Seale, Patrick. *The Struggle for Syria.* London, 1986.

Selser, Gregorio. *El Guatemalazo.* Buenos Aires, 1961.

Serfaty, Simon, and Lawrence Gray. *The Italian Communist Party: Yesterday, Today, and Tomorrow.* Westport, Conn., 1980.

Sheahan, John. *Patterns of Development in Latin America.* Princeton, 1988.

Singer, Mark. *Weak States in a World of Powers: The Dynamics of International Relationships.* New York, 1972.

Sisouk Na Champassak, *Storm over Laos.* New York, 1961.

Smith, Earl. *The Fourth Floor.* New York, 1962.

Smith, Gaddis. *The Last Years of the Monroe Doctrine.* New York, 1995.

Smith, Robert. *The United States and Cuba.* New Haven, Conn., 1960.

Smith, Tony. *America's Mission: The United States and the Worldwide Struggle for Democracy in the Twentieth Century.* Princeton, 1994.

Snyder, Jack. *Myths of Empire: Domestic Politics and International Ambition.* Ithaca, N.Y., 1990.

Soraya, Princess. *The Autobiography of H.I.H. Princess Soraya.* London, 1963.

Soto, José Aybar de. *Dependency and Intervention: The Case of Guatemala in 1954.* Boulder, Colo., 1978.

Spiegel, Steven. *The Other Arab-Israeli Conflict.* Chicago, 1985.

Stavrakis, Peter. *Moscow and Greek Communism, 1944-49.* Ithaca, N.Y., 1989.

Stavrianos, L. S. *Greece: An American Dilemma and Opportunity.* Chicago, 1952.

Stephanson, Anders. *Kennan and the Art of Foreign Policy.* Cambridge, Mass., 1989.

Stevenson, Charles. *The End of Nowhere: American Policy toward Laos since 1954.* Boston, 1972.

Stewart, Desmond. *Turmoil in Beirut.* London, 1958.

Suárez, Andrés. *Cuba: Castroism and Communism.* Cambridge, Mass., 1967.

Suleiman, Michael. *Political Parties in Lebanon.* Ithaca, N.Y., 1967.

Sulh, Sami. *Mudhakarat [Memoirs].* Beirut, 1960.

Szulc, Tad. *Fidel: A Critical Portrait.* New York, 1986.

Tarchiani, Alberto. *Dieci anni tra Roma a Washington.* Milan, 1955.

Thayer, Charles. *Diplomat.* New York, 1959.

Thee, Marek. *Notes of a Witness: Laos and the Second Indochinese War.* New York, 1973.

Thomas, Evan. *The Very Best Men: Four Who Dared: The Early Years of the CIA.* New York, 1995.

Thomas, Hugh. *The Cuban Revolution.* New York, 1977.

Thorpe, James. "Truman's Ultimatum on the 1946 Azerbaijan Crisis: The Making of a Myth." *Journal of Politics,* IV (February 1978), 188-94.

Tillema, Herbert. *Appeal to Force.* New York, 1973.

Toriello, Guillermo. *La Batalla de Guatemala.* Mexico City, 1955.

Toye, Hugh. *Laos: Buffer State or Battleground.* New York, 1968.

Triska, Jan, ed. *Dominant Powers and Subordinate States.* Durham, N.C., 1986.

Truman, Harry S. *Memoirs of Harry S. Truman.* Vol. I, *Year of Decisions.* Garden City, N.Y., 1955.

————. *Memoirs of Harry S. Truman.* Vol. II, *Years of Trial and Hope.* Garden City, N.Y., 1956.

Vatikiotis, P. J. *Nasser.* London, 1978.

Vlavianos, Haris. *Greece, 1941-1949.* New York, 1992.

Vukmanovic, Svetozar. *How and Why the People's Liberation Struggle of Greece Met with Defeat.* London, 1950.

Walters, Vernon A. *Silent Missions.* New York, 1978.

Warner, Michael, ed. *The CIA under Harry Truman.* Washington, D.C., 1994.

Warner, Roger. *Backfire: The CIA's Secret War in Laos and Its Link to the War in Vietnam.* New York, 1995.

Weissman, Stephen. *American Foreign Policy in the Congo, 1960-1964.* Ithaca, N.Y., 1974.

Welch, Richard. *Response to Revolution: The United States and the Cuban Revolution, 1959-1961.* Chapel Hill, 1985.

West, Richard. *Tito.* New York, 1995.

Wilber, Donald N. *Adventures in the Middle East.* Princeton, 1986.

Williams, William Appleman. *The Tragedy of American Diplomacy.* New York, 1959.

Wise, David, and Thomas Ross. *The Invisible Government.* New York, 1964.

Wittner, Lawrence. *American Intervention in Greece, 1943-1949.* New York, 1982.

Woodhouse, Christopher M. *Modern Greece: A Short History.* Boston, 1977.

————. *Something Ventured.* New York, 1982.

————. *The Struggle for Greece, 1941-1949.* New York, 1976.

Woodward, Ralph Lee. *Central America: A Nation Divided.* New York, 1985.

Woolf, S. J., ed. *The Rebirth of Italy, 1943-50.* London, 1972.

Wyden, Peter. *The Bay of Pigs.* New York, 1979.

Yamak, Zuwiyya Labib. *The Syrian Socialist Nationalist Party.* Cambridge, Mass., 1966.

Ydígoras Fuentes, Miguel. *My War with Communism.* Englewood Cliffs, N.J., 1963.

Yergin, Daniel. *The Prize: The Epic Quest for Oil, Money, and Power.* New York, 1991.

————. *Shattered Peace: The Origins of the Cold War and the National Security State.* Boston, 1978.

al-Yusuf, Ismail Musa. *Thawrat al-ahrar fi Lubnan* [*Revolution of the Free in Lebanon*]. Beirut, 1965[?].

Zabih, Sepehr. *The Mossadegh Era.* Chicago, 1982.

Zamir, Meir. *The Formation of Modern Lebanon.* Ithaca, N.Y., 1985.

Zasloff, Joseph. *The Pathet Lao.* Lexington, Mass., 1973.

Zonis, Marvin. *Majestic Failure.* Chicago, 1991.

Index

America, 112-13; on U.S. policy in the
Middle East, 141-42; on U.S. policy in
Southeast Asia, 209. *See also* National
Security Council policy papers
National Security Council policy papers: NSC
1/1, pp. 39-40, 47; NSC 1/2, p. 47; NSC-
4, p. 41; NSC 4-A, p. 47; NSC 5412, p. 128
Nationalism, 15, 56, 58, 65, 71, 73, 78, 90,
111, 112, 139, 140, 141, 142, 145, 149,
152, 153, 171-72, 192
Nationalization: of oil in Iran, 56-61, 73, 76,
89, 90; of American assets in Cuba, 180
NATO. *See* North Atlantic Treaty Organization
Nehru, Jawaharlal, 65-67, 77, 109, 152, 155,
170, 213
Nenni, Pietro, 43-49
Neutralism, 15, 65, 73, 86, 109, 110, 112, 149,
159, 206, 207, 212-13, 218, 223
Neutralization, 226
"New Look." *See* Eisenhower administration
Nicaragua, 102, 103, 104, 107, 114, 122
NIEs. *See* National Intelligence Estimates (CIA)
Nixon, Richard, 180, 191
Nonaligned nations, 13-14
North Atlantic Treaty Organization (NATO), 49
Northern Tier, 54, 141
North Vietnam, 207, 208, 214, 223
NSC. See National Security Council

OAS. *See* Organization of American States
(OAS)
Office of Strategic Services (OSS), 38, 48, 128
Oil: 17, 137; and Iran, 3, 51, 52, 54-57, 59,
60-61, 62, 63, 64, 67-68, 69-71, 72-74, 77,
78, 80, 85, 90, 178, 180; in Lebanon, 143;
in Middle East in general, 17, 137, 153
Operation Ajax, 50, 61, 62, 85, 87, 88, 91
Operation Blue Bat, 166
Operation Mongoose, 187-88, 202
Operation PBSUCCESS, 91, 109, 125, 126-35,
138, 177
Operation Pluto, 174
Operation Torch, 35
Operation Trinidad, 174
Operation Zapata, 174, 182-83, 194-204
Oppenheimer, J. Robert, 83
Opus Dei, 120-21
Order of the Sons of Italy, 45
Organization of American States (OAS), 48,
128, 130
Osorio, Oscar, 122, 123
OSS. *See* Office of Strategic Services (OSS)
Oxford University, 61

Pahlavi, Ashraf, 79, 88
Pahlavi, Mohammed Reza (shah of Iran), 1, 2,
3, 4, 8, 13, 14, 50, 52, 54, 55, 61, 62, 64,
67, 68, 69, 70, 72, 74-79, 81, 82, 87-90, 226
Pahlavi, Reza (shah of Iran), 2, 4, 55, 63, 67
Pakistan, 6, 141, 149, 168, 169
Panama Canal Zone, 186, 187
Pan-Arabism, 143-45
Panchsheel, 110
Papagos, Alexander, 27, 31, 34-36
Papandreou, George, 20, 24-25, 27, 35
Partido de la Revolución Guatemalteca, 115
Parti Populaire Syrian (PPS). *See* Socialist
Nationalist Party (Syria)
Pathet Lao, 207-24 passim
Paul (king of Greece), 34
PCI. See Italian Communist Party (PCI)
Peace Corps, 216
People's Revolutionary Movement (MRP)
(Cuba), 185
Perón, Juan, 65-67, 112
Persian Gulf, 153
Peurifoy, John, 126, 129, 131, 134
Phalange (al-Kata'ib) Party, 146, 160, 165
Philby, Kim, 143
Philippines, 6, 212
Phillips, David Atlee, 132, 177-205
Phoumi Nousavan, 208, 212-14, 215,
216-17, 218, 219-20, 222-24
Pike, Otis, 187
Pishevari, Jafar, 52, 54
Plain of Jars (Laos), 216
Point IV aid mission, 82
Porter, Paul, 25
Present at the Creation, 17
Princeton University, 180
Propaganda, 41, 102, 121, 122, in Cuba, 197;
in Europe, 129; in Guatemala, 130-32; in
Lebanon, 166
Psychological warfare, 40-42, 83, 84, 92,
109-10, 129, 132, 134, 135
Psychological Strategy Board, 41; on Titoism,
41-42
Punic Wars, 227

Qashqai, 63
Qavam, Ahmed, 52, 54
Quevedo, Angel, 183

Rashidian brothers, 88
Ray, Manuel, 202
Razmara, General, 56